New Perspectives on English Word Stress

New Perspectives on English Word Stress

EDITED BY
EIJI YAMADA, ANNE PRZEWOZNY,
JEAN-MICHEL FOURNIER
AND NICOLAS BALLIER

EDINBURGH
University Press

Edinburgh University Press is one of the leading university presses in the UK. We publish academic books and journals in our selected subject areas across the humanities and social sciences, combining cutting-edge scholarship with high editorial and production values to produce academic works of lasting importance. For more information visit our website: edinburghuniversitypress.com

© editorial matter and organisation Eiji Yamada, Anne Przewozny, Jean-Michel Fournier and Nicolas Ballier, 2023, 2025
© the chapters their several authors, 2023, 2025

Edinburgh University Press Ltd
13 Infirmary Street,
Edinburgh, EH1 1LT

First published in hardback by Edinburgh University Press 2023

Typeset in 10/12 Times New Roman by
Cheshire Typesetting Ltd, Cuddington, Cheshire

A CIP record for this book is available from the British Library

ISBN 978 1 3995 1993 9 (hardback)
ISBN 978 1 3995 1994 6 (paperback)
ISBN 978 1 3995 1995 3 (webready PDF)
ISBN 978 1 3995 1996 0 (epub)

The right of Eiji Yamada, Anne Przewozny, Jean-Michel Fournier and Nicolas Ballier to be identified as the editors of this work has been asserted in accordance with the Copyright, Designs and Patents Act 1988, and the Copyright and Related Rights Regulations 2003 (SI No. 2498).

Contents

List of Figures vii
List of Tables ix
List of Appendixes xi
List of Contributors xii
List of Abbreviations xiv

   Introduction: Theories, Data and Variation in English Word Stress   1
   Eiji Yamada, Anne Przewozny, Jean-Michel Fournier and Nicolas Ballier

1 On the Treatment of English Word Stress within the Generative Tradition: History, Concepts and Debates   6
   Jacques Durand and Eiji Yamada

2 English Word Stress and the Guierrian School   53
   Quentin Dabouis, Jean-Michel Fournier, Pierre Fournier and Marjolaine Martin

3 Stress Placement in Etymologically Prefixed Disyllabic Noun–Verb Pairs Revisited: A Semantic and Diachronic Approach   83
   Jérémy Castanier

4 English Phonology and the Literate Speaker: Some Implications for Lexical Stress   117
   Quentin Dabouis

5 The Stress Patterns of English Verbs: Syllable Weight and Morphology   154
   Quentin Dabouis and Jean-Michel Fournier

6 Lexical Stress in Varieties of Australian English: A Corpus-Based Exploration   192
   Anne Przewozny and Marjolaine Martin

7 Melodic Complexity and Lexical Stress in Singapore English: An Experimental Study   240
   Gabor Turcsan and Oriana Reid-Collins

8 Input Optimization and Lexical Stress in English   264
   Michael Hammond

9 A Solution to Theoretical Shortcomings in the Stress Assignment of Words in English   288
   Eiji Yamada

Index   325

Figures

3.1	Moving average pronunciation (upper graph: average between 1 = forestressed and 2 = backstressed) and N+V frequency (lower graph) of *protest* in Sonderegger and Niyogi (2013)	86
3.2	Moving average pronunciation (upper graph) and N+V frequency (lower graph) of *progress* in Sonderegger and Niyogi (2013)	87
3.3	Frequency in Google Ngram Viewer of *progress* (inflected forms included) during the 1760–1880 period	87
3.4	Frequencies in Google Ngram Viewer of *relay* and *pretext* (inflected forms included) between 1700 and 2000	88
3.5	Frequency in Google Ngram Viewer of *progress* as a noun and as a verb (inflected forms included) from 1600 to 2000	90
3.6	*Progress* in Worcester 1860	90
3.7	Frequency in Google Ngram Viewer of *prefix*, *suffix* and *infix* (all categories and inflected forms included)	93
3.8	Frequency in Google Ngram Viewer of *convoy* as a noun and a verb (inflected forms included)	94
3.9	Frequency of *large convoy*, *small convoy(s)* and *whole convoy(s)* in Google Ngram Viewer	95
3.10	Frequency of *naval convoy(s)* and *troop convoy(s)* in Google Ngram Viewer	95
3.11	Frequency of *naval* and *troop(s)* in Google Ngram Viewer	96
3.12	Entry *refuse* in Worcester 1860	101
3.13	Frequency in Google Ngram Viewer of *exploit* (noun and verb, inflected forms included)	104
3.14	Frequency in Google Ngram Viewer of *defect* (noun and verb, inflected forms included)	105
3.15	Frequency in Google Ngram Viewer of *increase* (noun and verb, inflected forms included)	106
3.16	Frequency in Google Ngram Viewer of *decrease* (noun and verb, inflected forms included)	106

3.17	Frequency in Google Ngram Viewer of *research* (noun and verb, inflected forms included)	106
3.18	Frequency in Google Ngram Viewer of *refund* (noun, verb and total, inflected forms included)	107
3.19	Frequency in Google Ngram Viewer of *finance* (noun and verb, inflected forms included)	108
4.1	The system of spelling-to-sound rules for stressed vowels (after J.-M. Fournier 2010b: 141)	124
4.2	Vowel reduction in the initial pretonic position and right-hand context	136
5.1	Position of main stress in verbal compounds depending on the syntactic category of Constituent 1 and spelling	170
5.2	Stress distribution of disyllabic verbs depending on the weight of the final syllable (H = heavy and L = light) and of the presence or absence of an opaque prefix	178
6.1	Stress pattern /100/ Speaker 1-1172, WS1, *souvenir*	208
6.2	Stress pattern /201/ Speaker 1-2770, WS3, *souvenir*	208
6.3	Distribution of the 705 tokens studied, in %	209
6.4	Stress pattern /SUS/ Speaker 2-642, WS2, *tangerine*	210
6.5	'Flat' stress pattern Speaker 4-882, WS1, *silhouette*	210
6.6	Distribution of the 142 tokens studied for intraspeaker variation, in %	211
7.1	SgE (conversational) vowel system	242
7.2	RP and conversational SgE compared (adapted from Bao 1998)	243
7.3	PAC reading list, extract	244
7.4	SgE iambic pitch pattern (NAO_tupan_verb)	250

Tables

2.1	Intervarietal variation in Martin (2011)	70
3.1	Stress placement in four prefixed verbs in *-fix*, and date of first attestation of their grammatical meanings in the *OED*	92
3.2	Stress placement in *asphalt* and *chagrin* (nouns and verbs) in British dictionaries	109
4.1	Table of correspondence for stressed vowels (source: J.-M. Fournier 2010b: 98)	123
4.2	The behaviour of final silent <e>	138
4.3	The behaviour of orthographic geminates	140
5.1	Morphological distribution in the dataset	165
5.2	Binary logistic regression for the position of main stress in verbal compounds	170
5.3	Position of main stress in compounds which share a constituent	171
5.4	Weight coding adopted	177
5.5	Binary logistic regression with morphology (prefixed vs non-prefixed) and syllable weight (heavy vs light) as predictor variables and the position of primary stress (initial vs final) as the dependent variable	177
6.1	Initial stress hypothesis: results (source: Martin 2011b)	196
6.2	English stress pattern hypothesis (source: Martin 2011b)	196
6.3	Verb stress pattern variation /01/–/10/ in SAusE, SAmE and SBE (source: Martin 2011a)	198
6.4	Distribution of prefixed multicategorials by type (source: Martin 2011a)	199
6.5	Distribution of lexical items in terms of rule violation (source: Martin 2011a)	200
6.6	Distribution of loanwords from Aboriginal languages in terms of word length (source: Martin 2011a)	200
6.7	A quantitative synthesis of SAusE, SBE and SAmE stress patterns intervariation (source: Martin 2011a)	201
6.8	Complex syllable onsets and codas in basilectal AbE (source: Butcher 2008: 629)	202

6.9	Elision and stress shift to the initial syllable in AbE (source: Butcher 2008: 631)	203
6.10	Salient segmental and suprasegmental markers for five AusTalk speakers	214
7.1	Constraints on English stressed syllables, general pattern in bold, with systematic exceptions in italics	248
7.2	Non-existent final unstressed syllables (*)	248
7.3	Penult stress in disyllables	250
7.4	SgE trochees according to syllable weight	253
7.5	SgE and inner-circle (IC) trochees according to syllable weight	254
7.6	Number of trochees in SgE (bold) and inner-circle varieties (in parentheses) for CC final verbs	255
7.7	Number of trochees in SgE (bold) and inner-circle varieties (in parentheses) for VC noncoronals	255
7.8	Behaviour of prefixed-like words in SgE	256
7.9	Behaviour of prefixed-like words in inner-circle varieties (Turcsan and Herment 2015)	256

Appendixes

A2.1	Where does primary stress fall? (Source: J.-M. Fournier 2007: 221)	72
A6.1	Verbs displaying intervarietal stress pattern variation between SAusE, SAmE and SBE (source: Martin 2011a)	217
A6.2	Intervarietal variation for multicategorials – a detailed account (source: Martin 2011a)	219
A6.3.1	Exceptions to the rule Disyllabic word → /10/: 18 words	222
A6.3.2	Exceptions to the rule prefinal C_2 → /−10/: 5 words	222
A6.3.3	Exceptions to the Normal Stress Rule: 18 words (11+7)	223
A6.4	Loanwords from Aboriginal languages and intervarietal stability (source: Martin 2011a)	223
A6.5.1	Sociolinguistic descriptors per speaker	226
A6.5.2	Sociolinguistic descriptors per speaker's mother	227
A6.5.3	Sociolinguistic descriptors per speaker's father	228
A6.6.1	Results per speaker and item, AusTalk corpus: legend	229
A6.6.2	Results per speaker and item, AusTalk corpus	230
A6.7.1	Results per speaker and item, PAC-Australia [Ulladulla] corpus: legend	232
A6.7.2	Results per speaker and item, PAC-Australia [Ulladulla] corpus	232
A7.1	Results of a nonce experiment testing SgE native speakers' intuition about the stress of disyllables	258

Contributors

Nicolas Ballier is Professor of English linguistics at Université Paris Cité (CLILLAC-ARP, ERP 3967), France.

Jérémy Castanier is Senior Lecturer in English linguistics at the Department of English at Bordeaux Montaigne University (CLIMAS research unit: Cultures et Littératures des Mondes Anglophones – UR 4196), France.

Quentin Dabouis is Senior Lecturer in English linguistics at Clermont Auvergne University (Laboratoire de Recherche sur le Langage UR 999), France.

Jacques Durand is Emeritus Professor of English linguistics at Toulouse University and a member of the Cognition, Langues, Langage, Ergonomie research unit (CNRS UMR 5263), France.

Jean-Michel Fournier is Professor of English linguistics at the University of Tours (Laboratoire Ligérien de Linguistique, UMR 7270: Tours, Orléans, CNRS, BNF), France.

Pierre Fournier is Senior Lecturer in English linguistics at Sorbonne Paris Nord University (Pléiade Research Unit – UR 7338), France.

Michael Hammond is Professor of linguistics at the University of Arizona, Tucson, AZ, USA.

Marjolaine Martin is Senior Lecturer in English linguistics at the University of Tours and Laboratoire Ligérien de Linguistique (CNRS UMR 7270), France.

Anne Przewozny is Professor of English linguistics at Toulouse University, and Cognition, Langues, Langage, Ergonomie research unit (CNRS UMR 5263), France.

Oriana Reid-Collins is a researcher formerly affiliated with Aix-Marseille University (Laboratoire Parole et Langage, UMR 7309), France.

Gabor Turcsan is Senior Lecturer in English linguistics at Aix-Marseille University (Laboratoire Parole et Langage, UMR 7309, AMU and CNRS), France.

Eiji Yamada is Professor of English linguistics at the Department of English at Fukuoka University, Japan.

Abbreviations

AAE	Australian Aboriginal English (in Butcher 2008)
AbE	Australian Aboriginal English
AE	Adjective Extrametricality
ASR	Alternating Stress Rule
AusE	Australian English
C	consonant
CAS	Coordinate Axis Shift
CE	Consonant Extrametricality
CEPD	*Cambridge English Pronouncing Dictionary*
COCA	*Corpus of Contemporary American English*
DF	Deforestation
EDR	English Destressing Rule
EMS	English in Malaysia and Singapore
EPD	*English Pronouncing Dictionary*
ESR	English Stress Rule
F	foot
FCF	final combining form
GA	General American
G<small>EN</small>	candidate generator
GNV	Google Ngram Viewer
H	heavy
HH	heavy and heavy syllables
HL	heavy and light syllables
HV	Halle and Vergnaud (1987)
ICF	initial combining form
IPA	International Phonetic Alphabet; International Phonetic Association
L	light
LCPR	Lexical Category Prominence Rule
LH	light and heavy syllables
LiOn	*Literature Online*
LL	light and light syllables

LLL	Laboratoire Ligérien de Linguistique
LP	Liberman and Prince (1977); Lexical Phonology
LPD	*Longman Pronunciation Dictionary*
LVS	Long Vowel Stressing
MD	*Macquarie Dictionary*
MSA	main stress assignment
MSR	Main Stress Rule
NE	Noun Extrametricality
NSR	Nuclear Stress Rule; Normal Stress Rule
OED	*Oxford English Dictionary*
OO	output-to-output
OT	Optimality Theory
Outline	*An Outline of English Phonetics* (Jones [1918] 1964)
PAC	Phonologie de l'Anglais Contemporain – Phonology of Contemporary English
PFT	Positional Function Theory
RP	Received Pronunciation
RR	Rhythm Rule
SAbE	Standard Australian Aboriginal English
SAE	Standard Australian English (in Butcher 2008)
SAmE	Standard American English
SAusE	Standard Australian English
SBE	Standard British English
SgE	Singapore English
SOED	*Shorter Oxford English Dictionary*
SPE	*The Sound Pattern of English* (Chomsky and Halle 1968)
SR	Strong Retraction
SRR	Stress Retraction Rule
SSA	Stray Syllable Adjunction; subsidiary stress assignment
UG	universal grammar
V	vowel
VOT	voice onset time
WTC	Word Tree Construction

Introduction: Theories, Data and Variation in English Word Stress

Eiji Yamada, Anne Przewozny, Jean-Michel Fournier and Nicolas Ballier

The idea for this book emerged from conversations among participants at the 2015 conference in France entitled 'PAC 2015: Variation, Change and Spoken Corpora – Advances in the Phonology and Phonetics of Contemporary English'. Jacques Durand made the initial call for the book, devised the plan for its implementation, and set it in motion. Anne Przewozny and Eiji Yamada then took over the editing of the book but, due to the busy schedule of the editors, the pace of progress was slow. Later, Nicolas Ballier and Jean-Michel Fournier joined us as editors. In the end, it took six years after the original plan to publish the book, which is an incredibly long incubation period. However, the significance of publishing this book has never wavered in spite of all the difficulties, including the COVID pandemic that began at the end of 2019 and is not yet under control as of this writing.

The reason our plan did not vanish is that we believe stress is an important subject. It has been one of the central issues in research since the early days of linguistics. Its study became more active in the twentieth century, especially with the work of Daniel Jones and Leonard Bloomfield, and was taken over by the generative phonology of Chomsky and Halle (1968) (hereafter *SPE*). Since then, no study of word stress in English has been possible without reference to this work, whether one accepts the *SPE* view or not. Despite the importance of the subject, although a number of papers have been written, in more than fifty years there have been (to the editors' knowledge) only a few monographs in this tradition that have analysed word stress in English as a central issue. These include Fudge (1984), Burzio (1994), Hammond (1999), Wenszky (2004), Yamada (2010) and Zamma (2013).

Research on word stress in English since *SPE* can be roughly divided into 'pre-Optimality Theory (pre-OT)' and OT. Significant theories of 'pre-OT' include Segmental Phonology in *SPE*, Metrical Phonology in Liberman (1975), Liberman and Prince (1977), Hayes (1980, 1982), Prince (1983) and others, Lexical Phonology in Mohanan (1982) and Kiparsky (1982a, 1982b) and others, and later theory in Halle and Vergnaud (1987). These can be termed 'rule-based' theories because they attempt to account for stress assignment by means of stress rules, with the notion of the 'cycle' at their centre. Conversely, OT, initiated by Prince and Smolensky ([1993] 2004), abolishes rules and derivations, using ranked constraints to select the optimal candidate from a set of 'parallel'-generated candidates. This can be therefore called a 'non-rule-based' theory. Particularly in word stress in English, Hammond (1999) and Pater (1995, 2000) are representative of OT. The crucial difference between these two significant streams is that the former focuses on the notion of the cycle, in which rules are applied cyclically from smaller constituents to larger ones, resulting in a series of derivations, while the latter does not adopt the notion of the cycle since there are no 'rules' in the first place. However, in contrast to the idea of 'parallelism' in classic OT, Stratal OT (Kiparsky 1998, 2000, 2007, 2015; Bermúdez-Otero 1999, 2003, 2011, 2012, 2014; Collie 2007 and others) and Partially Ordered Grammar (Anttila 1997, 2006, 2007, 2012 and others) incorporating the so-called cyclic concept have also been proposed. In this context, this book presents fascinating discussions on word stress from various theoretical perspectives.

In terms of data, *SPE* used Kenyon and Knott (1944) as its source, but unfortunately the data were not quantitatively processed as normally the case today. The construction of the English pronunciation databases for varieties of English at PAC is probably due to the recognition of the need for quantitative empirical databases in the study of English phonetics and phonology. We need appropriate pronunciation databases, including morphological information and variation, to further develop research in this area. Analyses in this book are based on a number of such databases, which will be helpful for our readers.

This book is the result of the scholarship of twelve international researchers who have been working for many years on these subjects, which are central problems in phonology. The chapters range from an overview of the history and issues in the study of stress to the treatment of stress, the relationship between historical changes in stress and meaning, the relationship between spelling and stress, the theoretical treatment of exceptions, the stress mechanism in Australian English, and stress in Singapore English.

The first chapter outlines the history of research on English stress before *SPE* and identifies pathways leading to *SPE*. It then reviews the various studies stimulated by this research up to the present day and outlines their remaining issues. Chapter 2 is a presentation of the main characteristics of a French school of phonology – the Guierrian School, named after its founder, Lionel Guierre – which has focused on English stress and spelling-to-sound correspondences (Guierre 1979). Chapter 3 examines the trajectory and causes of historical changes in the stress position in prefixed disyllabic words from a semantic perspective. Chapter 4 discusses the relevance of orthography in English phonology and how integrating orthographic information might affect the analysis of the stress system of English. Chapter 5 provides a large empirical investigation of stress placement in English verbs, with a detailed analysis of each morphological category. It also compares two existing analyses of stress placement in monomorphemic or deradical verbs and argues that the 'mainstream' analysis, which uses syllable weight as its main explanatory factor, is not the only possible one, as clear effects of opaque morphological structure are found in the data. Chapters 6 and 7 focus on the diversity of Englishes, discussing word stress in Australian and Singaporean English. Chapter 8 develops a way to systematically explain exceptional word stress by optimising the input to the candidate generator GEN from the standpoint of OT.[1] Finally, Chapter 9 explores a unified solution to exceptional word stress treatment, which has been a constant problem in post-*SPE* discussions, and attempts to resolve further issues in the method.

Earlier, we mentioned that the project to publish this book began in 2015. Phillip Carr was one of the original contributors. He had already sent the editors a detailed outline of his chapter, entitled 'Word Stress, Mental Storage and Extraction of Generalisations: Neural Mechanisms and the Dual Mechanism Hypothesis'. Unfortunately, Phil passed away in 2020. Since the manuscript Phil sent us was only in outline, it was not possible to include it as a chapter in this book. In that outline, he states that 'both regular and irregular patterns are stored, but regularities are extracted from the stored forms'; he also examined 'the question of how best to regard the distinction between regular and irregular word stress patterns'. Phil's chapter would have added much depth to our book. We wish to dedicate this book to our colleague, Phillip Carr.

Acknowledgements

We are grateful to Jacques Durand for identifying the need for and initiating this project. Without his deep insight into English word stress, this publication would not have been possible. We appreciate his continual warm encouragement during our often-slow progress. Thanks also go to Stephen Howe, who assisted with the project's preparation. We are also thankful to Edinburgh University Press for recognising the importance of the project and agreeing to publish it. We would like to thank Laura Quinn, Helena Heald, Sam Johnson, Joannah Duncan and Eliza Wright for their assistance.

Note

1. The text of Chapter 8 is written in US English for theoretical reasons.

References

Anttila, A. (1997), 'Variation in Finnish phonology and morphology', PhD dissertation, Stanford University.

Anttila, A. (2006), 'Variation and opacity', *National Language & Linguistic Theory* 24(4), 893–944.

Anttila, A. (2007), 'Variation and optionality', in P. de Lacy (ed.), *The Cambridge Handbook of Phonology*, Cambridge: Cambridge University Press, pp. 519–36.

Anttila, A. (2012), 'Modeling phonological variation', in A. C. Cohn, C. Fougeron and M. Huffman (eds), *The Oxford Handbook of Laboratory Phonology*, Oxford: Oxford University Press, pp. 76–91.

Bermúdez-Otero, R. (1999), 'Constraint interaction in language change: Quantity in English and Germanic' [Opacity and globality in phonological change], PhD dissertation, University of Manchester and Universidad de Santiago de Compostela, <http://www.bermudez-otero.com/PhD.pdf>.

Bermúdez-Otero, R. (2003), 'The acquisition of phonological opacity', Manuscript, University of Manchester [ROA-593-0403, Rutgers Optimality Archive, <http://roa.rutgers.edu/>]. [In J. Spenader, A. Eriksson and Ö. Dahl (eds), *Variation within Optimality Theory: Proceedings of the Stockholm Workshop on 'Variation within Optimality Theory'*, Stockholm: Stockholm University, pp. 25–36.]

Bermúdez-Otero, R. (2011), 'Cyclicity', in M. van Oostendorp, C. Ewen, E. Hume and K. Rice (eds), *The Blackwell Companion to Phonology*, vol. 4, Malden, MA: Wiley-Blackwell, pp. 2019–48.

Bermúdez-Otero, R. (2012), 'The architecture of grammar and the division of labour in exponence', in J. Trommer (ed.), *The Morphology and Phonology of Exponence*, Oxford Studies in Theoretical Linguistics 41, Oxford: Oxford University Press, pp. 8–83.

Bermúdez-Otero, R. (2014), 'Amphichronic explanation and the life cycle of phonological processes', in P. Honeybone and J. C. Salmons (eds), *The Oxford Handbook of Historical Phonology*, Oxford: Oxford University Press, pp. 374–99.

Burzio, L. (1994), *Principles of English Stress*, Cambridge: Cambridge University Press.

Chomsky, N. and M. Halle (1968), *The Sound Pattern of English*, New York: Harper & Row.

Collie, S. (2007), 'English stress preservation and stratal optimality theory', PhD dissertation, University of Edinburgh.

Fudge, E. (1984), *English Word-Stress*, London: George Allen & Unwin.

Guierre, L. (1979), 'Essai sur l'accentuation en anglais contemporain: Éléments pour une synthèse', PhD dissertation, Université Paris, 7.

Halle, M. and J.-R. Vergnaud (1987), *An Essay on Stress*, Cambridge, MA: MIT Press.

Hammond, M. (1999), *The Phonology of English: A Prosodic Optimality-Theoretic Approach*, Oxford: Oxford University Press.

Hayes, B. (1980), 'A metrical theory of stress rules', PhD dissertation, MIT.

Hayes, B. (1982), 'Extrametricality and English stress', *Linguistic Inquiry* 13(2), 227–76.

Kenyon, J. S. and T. A. Knott [1944] (1953), *A Pronouncing Dictionary of American English*, 4th edn, Springfield, MA: G. & C. Merriam.

Kiparsky, P. (1982a), 'From cyclic phonology to lexical phonology', in H. van der Hulst and N. Smith (eds), *The Structure of Phonological Representations I*, Dordrecht: Foris, pp. 131–75.

Kiparsky, P. (1982b), 'Lexical morphology and phonology', in the Linguistic Society of Korea (ed.), *Linguistics in the Morning Calm*, Seoul: Hanshin, pp. 3–91.

Kiparsky, P. (1998), 'Paradigm effects and opacity', Manuscript, Stanford University.

Kiparsky, P. (2000), 'Opacity and cyclicity', *The Linguistic Review* 17, 351–65.

Kiparsky, P. (2007), 'Description and explanation: English revisited', in the Panel Meeting entitled 'Phonology: An Appraisal of the Field in 2007', a handout from the 81st Annual Meeting of the Linguistic Society of America, held on 5 January 2007, Anaheim, CA.

Kiparsky, P. (2015), 'Stratal OT: A synopsis and FAQs', in Y. E. Hsiao and L.-H. Wee (eds), *Capturing Phonological Shades Within and Across Languages*, Newcastle upon Tyne: Cambridge Scholars Publishing, pp. 2–44.

Liberman, M. (1975), 'The intonational system of English', PhD dissertation, MIT.

Liberman, M. and A. Prince (1977), 'On stress and linguistic rhythm', *Linguistic Inquiry* 8(2), 249–336.

Mohanan, K. P. (1982), 'Lexical phonology', PhD dissertation, MIT.

Pater, J. (1995), 'On the nonuniformity of weight-to-stress and stress preservation effects in English', Manuscript, McGill University.

Pater, J. (2000), 'Non-uniformity in English secondary stress: The role of ranked and lexically specific constraints', *Phonology* 17(2), 237–74.

Prince, A. (1983), 'Relating to the grid', *Linguistic Inquiry* 14(1), 19–100.

Prince, A. and P. Smolensky (1993), 'Optimality theory: Constraint interaction in generative grammar', Rutgers University and University of Colorado, Boulder. [(2004), *Optimality Theory: Constraint Interaction in Generative Grammar*, Oxford: Blackwell.]

Wenszky, N. (2004), *Secondary Stress in English Words*, Budapest: Akadémiai Kiadó.

Yamada, E. (2010), *Subsidiary Stresses in English*, Tokyo: Kaitakusha.

Zamma, H. (2013), *Patterns and Categories in English Suffixation and Stress Placement: A Theoretical and Quantitative Study*, Tokyo: Kaitakusha.

1 On the Treatment of English Word Stress within the Generative Tradition: History, Concepts and Debates

Jacques Durand and Eiji Yamada

0 Introduction

There is no doubt that with the publication of *The Sound Pattern of English* by Chomsky and Halle in 1968 a new era began for phonology. This was by no means the first important publication in generative phonology (see for example Chomsky 1964, 1967; Halle 1959, 1962), but it was the first extensive application to English, yielding basic principles for a novel approach to the nature of phonological representations and processes. The cornerstone of *The Sound Pattern of English* (hereafter *SPE*) is its treatment of word stress. Whether for or against, specialists now had to contend with an original way of envisaging English word stress that underlined its regularity if one was ready to delve under the surface. Within the generative tradition itself there emerged a rich tapestry of revisions and counter-positions leading eventually to a number of radical overhauls of phonological theory. Our aim here is to survey some of these main revisions and to provide a route through a complex technical literature.

Of course, *SPE* was by no means the first work to deal with English word stress: the topic had been discussed by a wealth of publications, descriptive, pedagogical and theoretical. Although we focus here solely on the generative tradition, we emphasise that the background to *SPE* cannot be neglected. We have chosen to cover some of this 'prehistory' by dividing it into a British and an American tradition, and by selecting a few major figures that paved the way for *SPE*. In the British camp, we focus on the contrasting views of Daniel Jones and Roger Kingdon. In the United States, we consider the work of Leonard Bloomfield and John Samuel Kenyon, as well as some of the conclusions reached by various post-Bloomfieldian phonologists. Of course, each tradition is not monolithic in its treatment of stress: these studies have influenced one another, and similar ideas were defended on both sides of the Atlantic. It is against this backdrop that *SPE* came into the world.

In *SPE*, sets of ordered rules are postulated for English stress, linking underlying phonological representations to phonetic representations. Rules are applied *cyclically* by means of a universal transformational cycle, from the innermost constituents to the outermost. One of *SPE*'s major contributions is the discovery of the Latin stress rule systematically embedded in English sound structure;[1] it is incorporated in *SPE* as the Main Stress Rule based on the novel concepts of 'strong and/or weak clusters'. Halle and Keyser (1971), Ross (1972) and others supported and modified the *SPE* account, although the concept of 'clusters' was challenged by Fudge (1969), Kahn (1976), Selkirk (1978, 1980, 1984a), Kiparsky (1979) and others.

The *SPE* model is termed 'linear' phonology. In contrast, Liberman (1975) and Liberman and Prince (1977) propose a 'non-linear' approach, introducing the concepts of 'prosodic constituency' and 'relative prominence', in tandem with Hayes's (1980, 1982) and Prince's (1983) analyses in favour of a 'tree' or 'grid' (Metrical Phonology).

Concurrently, Mohanan (1982) and Kiparsky (1982a, 1982b) integrated explorations of morphology by Siegel (1974), Aronoff (1976), Allen (1978) and others into Lexical Phonology. They introduced onto the scene the distinction between the lexical and post-lexical levels in morphology, showing their interactions with phonological rules.

Subsequent to Hayes's (1980, 1982, 1984) metrical analyses comes Halle and Vergnaud (1987a), where stress assignment is treated using sets of ordered stress rules, with parameters incorporated into each rule. By setting the parameters, we can obtain the entire finite system of rules by which the stress assignment of English is generated cyclically by recursion.

Burzio (1994), in contrast, develops his constraint-based stress theory without rules, which arguably led to the Optimality Theory (OT) treatment of stress. In OT, initiated by Prince and Smolensky ([1993] 2004), sets of rules and their cyclic application are abolished. Instead, a set of violable constraints and their rankings are employed in favour of 'parallelism'. In 'classic' OT, the recursive procedure has disappeared. One of the problems of classic OT may be that since it does away with rules and derivations, when dealing with opacity/cyclicity-related phenomena[2] it has to reintroduce such a device to relate one output to another as an 'output-to-output' (OO) Correspondence Theory of phonological faithfulness (McCarthy and Prince 1995, 1999; Benua 1997; Kager 1999; Hammond 1999; Pater 1995, 2000 and others). These kinds of approaches that adhere to parallelism are termed 'strict parallelism', in contrast to 'serialism' with intermediate stages or representations.

When it comes to stress assignment in English, however, we face a dilemma: whether to choose strict parallelism or serialism with regard to the opacity/cyclicity problem. In order to solve this issue with strict parallelism, new kinds of approaches are proposed within OT, including Sympathy Theory (McCarthy 1999), Stratal OT (Kiparsky 1998, 2000, 2007, 2015; Bermúdez-Otero 1999, 2003, 2011, 2012, 2014; Collie 2007 and others), Partially Ordered Grammar (Anttila 1997, 2006, 2007, 2012) and others. Of these, we will discuss Kiparsky (2007, 2015).

This chapter will review the historical development of the treatment of English word stress, showing how each theory deals with stress assignment. Our focus will be on the prehistory of the generative tradition and its passing on to the next tradition, *SPE*, Liberman and Prince (1977), Hayes (1980, 1982), Mohanan (1982), Halle and Vergnaud (1987a), Hammond (1999), Pater (1995, 2000) and Kiparsky (2007, 2015).

The organisation of the chapter is as follows: the prehistory of the research and various issues that led to *SPE* are examined in section 1, 'New dawn'. *SPE* is treated under 'Beginnings' in this tradition in section 2, followed by the Metrical Phonology of Liberman and Prince (1977) and Hayes (1980, 1982), and the Lexical Phonology of Mohanan (1982) and others under 'Development' in section 3. These two trends are integrated into Halle and Vergnaud (1987a) and are discussed under 'Unity' in section 4. OT is dealt with under 'A change of course' in section 5, followed by 'English stress, Plato's problem and the nature of language' in section 6. Some conclusions are drawn in the final section.

1 New dawn

1.1 Some twentieth-century antecedents

The generative tradition concerning word stress in English did not spring out of a vacuum. It stood in reaction against earlier proposals in the twentieth century which will not be studied extensively here but which deserve our attention. One important strand that we explore first was the British tradition; thereafter we consider the American descriptivists (or structuralists in another terminology). We start with the British tradition because some of its prominent members provide the greatest contrast with the approach initiated by Chomsky and Halle's *The Sound Pattern of English*.

1.2 The British tradition

The British tradition before *SPE* is best exemplified by the work of Daniel Jones. Jones is the author of two classics in the description of the RP (Received Pronunciation) variety of Southern British English: *An Outline of English Phonetics*[3] (hereafter *Outline*) and *English Pronouncing Dictionary*.[4] Jones's approach reflects two major commitments: he was heavily involved in the teaching of the pronunciation of English as a foreign language, and he was a prominent and influential member of the International Phonetic Association (IPA) (indeed, its president from 1950 to 1967). In the first editions of *Outline*, Jones articulated a view where many degrees of stress or prominence could be envisaged. Thus a five-syllable word such as *opportunity* could be described as bearing a stress contour 24153 (where 1 is the strongest stress, 2 the second strongest, and so on). However, Jones rejected such accuracy as 'not necessary for practical purposes'. From a practical point of view, he claimed that three degrees of stress were sufficient: primary, secondary and weakly stressed (= unstressed in another terminology). He gives as an example the word *examination*, which would have a secondary stress on the second syllable and a primary stress on the fourth (*e͵xami'nation*). This view remained essentially the same throughout his career.

On this basis, Jones proceeds to examine stress patterns within English words. There is no attempt in *Outline* to formulate a generalisation regarding monomorphemic words. On the other hand, complex and compound words do receive his attention. But the general claim is that English word stress cannot be learnt by rule. Despite this assumption, Jones identifies some interesting regularities. For instance, he notices that prefixes come in two groups. The first comprises what he calls 'separable' prefixes, as in the following examples: *ex-president, misrepresentation, pre-paid, unknown, vice-chancellor*. These prefixes are described as coming with a 'distinct meaning' of their own. They are those that receive a word-boundary (#) in the *SPE* tradition or are considered to be level 2 in Lexical Phonology. Jones attributes two main stresses to these words, as in for instance *'ex-'president*. On the other hand, there are many cases where the combination of prefix and base is not semantically transparent or where the base does not exist separately, as for instance in the verb *discourage* where *courage* is not used as a verb. For such words, no stress is assigned to the prefix (for example dis'kʌridʒ[5]).

The assumption that a word might carry two main stresses lexically may seem strange and in many accounts would be forbidden. But Jones completes the picture by a discussion of rhythmical variations which, in modern terms, would be said to operate at a post-lexical or utterance level and affect all polysyllabic words characterised by two primary stresses. Thus, a proper name like *Piccadilly* is transcribed as /'pikə'dili/ as a lexical entry but is stressed differently in *Piccadilly Circus* ['pikədili 'səːkəs] and in *close to Piccadilly* ['klous tə pikə'dili] (*Outline*: 253). There is no formulation of a generalisation where, other things being equal, the second of these primary stresses would be stronger; however, Jones does underline that in many such words the second primary stress may be the only one.

On the other hand, concerning suffixes, Jones offers no real discussion of the influence of morphology on stress assignment. To help the foreign learner, Jones makes some interesting observations. For instance, he compares a range of words such as *centralization, representation, aristocratic, mathematician*, with secondary stress on the first syllable, with words where the second syllable receives a secondary stress, such as *anticipation, examination, materialistic, academician*. There is no attempt beyond observation of this difference in stress to extract a possible generalisation. As a result, Jones fails to point out that, in the first set, the morphological make-up of the word could be invoked to explain why the first syllable bears a stress (for example ˈcentral → ˈcentralize → ˌcentraliˈzation) in contrast with the second set where the base exhibits primary stress on the second syllable, which is preserved as a secondary stress after suffixation (for example anˈticipate → anˌticiˈpation). The lack of reference to morphological structure does not derive in Jones's case from a theoretical point of view banning the mixing of levels (as in some later structural work in the United States), rather from a strong focus on phonetics. Throughout his career, Jones maintained the following assertion:

> Generally speaking there are no rules determining which syllable or syllables of polysyllabic English words bear the main stress. The foreign student is obliged to learn the stress of each word individually. He has to learn, for instance, that the main stress is on the first syllable of *photograph* ˈ**foutəgrɑːf** or ˈ**foutəgræf**, on the second in *photography* **fəˈtɔgrəfi**, on the third in *photographic* **foutəˈgræfik** and on the fourth in *photogravure* **foutəgrəˈvjuə**. When rules of word-stress can be formulated at all, they are generally subject to numerous exceptions.
>
> (*Outline*: 248–9)

It is interesting to note that the same type of alternations were to be at the core of the standard generative account of word stress in English which argues for the regularity of stress assignment – demonstrating that the theoretical lens through which we view the same data can lead to very different conclusions!

Jones's perspective was very much preserved in the work of his successor at University College London, A. C. Gimson. In his highly respected *Introduction to the Pronunciation of English* (1962), Gimson provides a clear account of accentual patterns with many examples of rhythmical shifts. However, he refrains entirely from attempting to formulate generalisations that would involve considering morphological structure. It is only in the re-editions of *Gimson's Pronunciation of English* prepared by Alan Cruttenden that we find a discussion of word stress in English that admits that many generalisations can be formulated, particularly if we pay a close attention to morphological structure (for example Cruttenden 2014).

There is, however, one major study which, in our eyes, deserves special attention: Roger Kingdon's *The Groundwork of English Stress* published in 1958. Like Jones, Kingdon's approach is primarily pedagogical and there is no attempt to draw theoretical conclusions from his practical survey of English word stress. However, Kingdon separates himself radically from Jones in arguing that, although it is frequently held that English word stress follows no rules, much regularity can be extracted from a close examination of English words and their make-up.

As far as degrees of stress are concerned, Kingdon is close to the British tradition which holds that full vowels in weak position do not necessarily carry a stress; and, by and large, he restricts himself to three levels of stress (primary, secondary, unstressed, or 1, 2, 0 in the symbolisation adopted here). However, on closer examination, some words are indeed given a stress contour involving a tertiary stress. Thus, for instance, the word *inaudibility* is given the following stress assignment, ˌin'audiˋbility, which is in effect a 320100 contour since the 'kinetic tone mark' or 'tonic', symbolised as (ˋ), indicates which syllable bears the main pitch change if the word is said in isolation. Kingdon would say that, within the word *inaudibility*, the second syllable and the fourth bear primary stresses. However, the singling out of the fourth syllable as bearer of the tonic does give it a privileged status within words. In other words, Kingdon anticipates the 'nuclear stress rule' which is central to the functioning of stress assignment in Chomsky and Halle's *The Sound Pattern of English* (see section 2).

The reason Kingdon rejects the assumption that lexical stress in English is random rests on the idea that the vocabulary of English contains layers which give rise to conflicting tendencies. The main cause of this superficial chaos, he argues,

> is an etymological one, arising from the fact that the vocabulary has been drawn from two principal sources, in one of which, the Teutonic, the tendency is towards early word stress, while in the other, the Romanic, late word stress prevails. In fact one may go still further and say that by Teutonic standards one should think of how close the stress is to the beginning of the word, while under the Romanic canon stresses are best visualised in relation to the final syllable.
>
> (Kingdon 1958b: 12)

Thus, if we look at what he calls the Teutonic stratum of the language (more usually termed 'Germanic'), we find many monosyllabic roots and a tendency to add weak suffixes that preserve the salience of the root (for example *hate* → *'hateful, king* → *'kingdom, town* → *'township, like* → *'likely, bold* → *'boldness*). Moreover, within the Germanic stratum, prefixes are also weak (for example *a'light, be'come, fore'tell*). However, Kingdon is not content with formulating vague generalisations: he explores in detail the functioning of prefixes and suffixes. Suffixes in particular, which were completely neglected by Jones, receive careful and extensive consideration. To take only one example, he considers *-ic* and *-ics* and formulates the generalisation that penultimate stress is the norm: *logic, metric, Homeric, laconic, episodic, photographic, telegraphic, ethics, acoustics*, and so on. Nor does he let the following set of exceptions – *'agaric, 'arsenic* (n.), *'catholic, 'chivalric, 'choleric, 'Dominic, 'lunatic, 'politic, 'rhetoric, 'turmeric, 'valeric, 'politics, a'rithmetic* (n.), ˌ*cli'macteric* (> *'climac'teric*), *phy'lacteric* (*'phylac'teric*) – prevent the formulation of a generalisation. He points out that *-ical, -ically, -icize, -icism* equally attract a penultimate stress and, crucially, notes that the above exceptions become regular when these more complex suffixes are involved: ˌar ˈsenical, doˈminical, heˈretical, poˈlitical, rheˈtorical, poˈlitically, rheˈtorically, caˈtholiˌcize, Caˈtholiˌcism, ˈarithˈmetical, ˈarithˈmetically (Kingdon 1958b: 87–8).

Besides the morphological structure of words, Kingdon pays close attention to rhythmical patterns.[6] He shows, for example, that as words grow in length the stress contour becomes more complex, as in ˈAntaˈnanaˈrivo or ˈPopoˈcateˈpetl (vs Mex. ˈPopocaˈtepetl). As his work on stress is linked to a detailed approach to intonation, he also takes into account larger contextual factors than the pronunciation of words in isolation. It is important to point out that, at the same time as he explored the groundwork of English stress, he also published *The Groundwork of English Intonation* (1958a). And like Jones, he argues that a number of words that can be considered double stressed lexically (for example ˈimmaˈture) lose one of these stresses when they shift between attributive and predicative position. Thus, a contrast can be observed between *He's an ˈimmature ˈyouth* and *He's ˈtoo immaˈture*, where the initial stress can be completely lost.

All in all, we can see that useful information was available concerning word stress within what we have called the British tradition, with positions ranging from quite extreme scepticism (Jones) to confidence in a high predictability of stress assignment (Kingdon). Pedagogically, Jones's position with a relative paucity of stresses beyond primary was to survive through his *English Pronouncing Dictionary*, which was edited after his death by Gimson and Ramsaran. It was taken over in 1997 by Cambridge University Press with Roach as editor (in collaboration with Setter and Esling) and began to include American English.[7] To this day, it operates with primary and secondary stresses, and does not consider in words such as *hesitate* that the full vowel of the third syllable should be assigned a stress mark. Even for compounds like *bearskin*, where the second element is monosyllabic, the suggested transcription merely indicates a primary stress on the first syllable. This is a major difference with what we will call the American tradition here, without any claim of offering a fully comprehensive account beyond the scope of our brief and selective historical sketch.[8]

1.3 The American tradition

Just before the publication of Jones's *English Pronouncing Dictionary* and *Outline of English Phonetics* (1918), Bloomfield published *An Introduction to the Study of Language* (1914). The second revised edition was to be the famous 1933 *Language*. Between the two editions there was a change of philosophical outlook. In 1914, Bloomfield defended a mentalistic view of language, whereas by 1933 he had become a militant advocate of behaviourism under the broader umbrella of what he terms the 'mechanistic theory'.

It seems, however, that Bloomfield did not tie linguistic analyses in a strong way to the psychological theory of the researcher, if we believe statements such as the following:

> Recall the difficulties and obscurities in the writings of Humboldt and Steinthal, and the psychological disputes of Paul, Wundt and Delbrueck. From our point of view, the last named was wrong in denying the value of descriptive data, but right in saying that *it is indifferent what system of psychology a linguist believes in*.
> (Bloomfield 1926: 20–1, our emphasis)[9]

It should also be noted that pedagogical considerations were very common in Bloomfield's overview of linguistics. In fact, the 1914 *Introduction* devotes a whole chapter (ch. 9) to the teaching of languages, and the same topic figures prominently in the last chapter of *Language*, entitled 'Applications and Outlook'.

The study of stress is one of the many topics addressed by Bloomfield in his 1914 *Introduction* and, although English is frequently cited, it is used only as part of a broader picture. Word stress is analysed as a component of group stress, which is itself a component of sentence stress. For English, each word is typically said to be a stress group 'containing one syllable with highest stress and, in longer words, one or more with intermediate stress' (1914: 49). The example Bloomfield gives is that of *procrastination*, which he represents as [ˈˈpɹʌ ˈkɹæs ti ˈˈˈnej ʃn̩], where the degrees of stress are indicated by the number of stress marks: the more stress marks, the more prominent the syllable. The word *procrastination* is therefore assumed to have 'four degrees of stress, highest on [ˈnej], least on [ti] and [ʃn̩] and intermediate degrees on [pɹʌ] and [kɹæs]' (1914: 49). If, for clarity of exposition we treat the completely weak syllables ([ti] and [ʃn̩]) as unstressed, the account can be said to defend three degrees of stress, and *procrastination* can be represented by a 23010 contour.

By the time *Language* was published in 1933, Bloomfield's account of phonology and phonetics had considerably advanced. At the core of his description, he places the notion of distinctiveness with greater clarity than before. He gives a wealth of examples from a variety of languages to show how certain features are not distinctive and not part of the phonology of the language (for example the 'puff of breath' produced with an initial stressed [p], [t], [k] in English *pin, tin, kin*). He therefore asserts that '[t]he phonemes of a language are not sounds, but merely features of sound which the speakers have been trained to produce and recognise in the current of actual speech sound' (1933: 80). The focus on distinctiveness leads him to base the phonology of a language such as English on what he terms 'primary phonemes' such as /p, t, k/ and 'secondary phonemes' such as stress. Primary phonemes are bundles of properties such as 'stop', 'unvoiced', and so on.

However, Bloomfield is at pains to argue that unless we complete this with statements concerning the distribution of these segments, our task is incomplete. At first sight, it looks as if the difference between 'primary' and 'secondary' phonemes in English matches the segmental/suprasegmental dichotomy. As we shall see directly, however, this is not entirely correct.

As far as stress is concerned, Bloomfield now uses the following symbols for English, ['',',,], which together give three degrees of stress if we leave aside the unstressed (or maximally weakly stressed) category. However, since the double vertical bar '' is reserved for 'emphatic stress', it seems that two degrees of stress are sufficient for the analysis of English words. Indeed, the example of *procrastination* is now transcribed as [pro͵kresti'nejšn̩]. The reason for the difference between the 1914 and 1933 analyses is not fully clear.

For word stress to be seen as distinctive by Bloomfield, we need evidence of stress oppositions between simplex forms. Russian is cited as an example since it includes monomorphemic words such as ['gorot] and [mo'ros], which are identical in terms of number of phonemes and syllabic structure but have different stress contours (1933: 111). In this case, Bloomfield states that stress belongs to the 'primary phonemes' of the language, in opposition to English where stress belongs to the 'secondary phonemes'. We can infer that, in English, stress is not seen as fully distinctive (despite the fact that Bloomfield cites pairs such as *protest* (noun) ['prowtest] and *protest* (verb) [prow'test], where presumably an alternation between verbs and nouns would be invoked).

Although the issue of the number of stress levels was not fully settled in subsequent work, quite a few influential specialists coming after Bloomfield argued that we need more than two degrees of stress at word level (leaving aside emphatic or expressive stresses and excluding unstressed syllables). For instance, Trager and Bloch (1941), Bloch and Trager (1942) and Trager and Smith ([1951] 1957) recognise three stress levels: primary, secondary and tertiary. A word like *elevator* is said to illustrate the pattern 1030 /élɨvèytŏr/. A secondary stress is mainly illustrated in compounds, for example *élĕvàtŏr ôpĕràtŏr* with the stress contour 1030 + 2030. Kenyon, in the various editions of his textbook between 1924 and 1951, posits three degrees of stress besides absence of stress. Secondary accents are frequent in compounds (for example 'mɪlk͵mæn) but also in simplex words like *ambush* ('æm͵bʊʃ). In addition, a light accent is assumed to occur in words such as ͵mis▲under'standing, with a 23010 stress contour.

The connection between stress and morphology was certainly noted. For instance, Kurath (1964) points out the importance of the native/non-native distinction since, in the native part of the English lexicon (namely Germanic), the base morpheme receives the main stress (for example *brótherly, fátherless, becóme, forgét*). Newman (1946) explores in a fair amount of detail the consequences of 'fused' vs 'unfused' suffixes for stress (for example *antecedent* vs *antifederalist*). He also examines a form of stress preservation in various classes of derived words (for example *sýstem* → *sỳstemátic*). However, we are not aware of a study of American English comparable in scope to Kingdon (1958b) as far as the link with morphology is concerned. Compounds, on the other hand, receive a great deal of attention from most specialists and lead them to assume that we need to go beyond primary and secondary stresses as in the *élĕvàtŏr ôpĕràtŏr* example already mentioned. One finds telling examples such as *light house keeper* (Smith 1954: 37–9) which has three meanings: (i) 'keeper of a lighthouse', (ii) 'person who does light housekeeping' and (iii) 'housekeeper who is light in weight'. These three meanings correspond to three different stress assignments: (i) *líght hòuse kêeper* (1320), (ii) *lìght hóuse kèeper* (3130) and (iii) *lîght hóuse kèeper* (2130). Such examples were to play an important role in the justification of the generative approach to stress assignment: on the basis of contrasting types of bracketing and simple grammatical labelling, a cyclical approach to stress assignment could predict the different stress contours in a fairly simple way.

If the connection between word stress assignment and morphological structure was not explored as much as merited, the post-Bloomfieldians did spend considerable energy on justifying contrasting stress levels in English words and utterances. For instance, the distinction between tertiary stress and lack of stress is illustrated by two possible pronunciations of the proper name *Plato*: some people realise the medial /t/ as a tap and concomitantly the following vowel is unstressed [pléyṱŏw], whereas other speakers use a longer [ey] diphthong, an aspirated [tʻ] and a final diphthong carrying a tertiary stress [pléytʻòw].

Most specialists underline that word stress must be examined within the context of utterance stresses. Newman (1946) is particularly clear in reminding the reader that (i) expressive accents can particularly affect syllables within utterances, and (ii) primary stresses can occur in nuclear and non-nuclear positions. Thus, in *It's an annual meeting*, of the two primary stresses on the first syllables of *annual* and *meeting*, the second would be likely to be a nuclear stress. Newman therefore emphasises that while words can be defined as containing one primary stress (which he calls a heavy stress), this is a potential feature only: it will occur if the word is uttered in its citation form, thereby constituting a minimal utterance. The ultimate number of stress levels one posits depends therefore on how far we integrate utterance levels into word phonology. For Newman, if we include the possibility of an expressive (or emphatic stress) and the nuclear stress, we can immediately see that the number of stress levels can increase by two in comparison with the potential stresses typically given in dictionary entries. These issues remain relevant up to the present day. They also show that while the generative tradition was to relaunch the question of word stress in English on an unprecedented scale, there had been a great deal of thinking providing an indispensable foundation for modern reflections.

From a descriptive and practical standpoint, we should note that the equivalent of Jones's *English Pronouncing Dictionary* in the United States was Kenyon and Knott's *A Pronouncing Dictionary of American English*, first published in 1944. It offers a broad or phonemic transcription in IPA notation solely based on primary and secondary accents, for example *clockwise* /ˈklɑkˌwaɪz/. Interestingly, unlike Kenyon ([1924] 1951), simplex words like *ambush* or *climax* are not assigned any stress mark on the second syllable. Moreover, like Jones in *Outline*, a considerable number of words such as *homemade* are assigned two primary stresses (/ˈhomˈmeɪd/). This assumes, of course, that rhythm rules at utterance level will regulate the eventual choice of a nuclear stress. This dictionary, which shows the strong connections between the British and American traditions, was to serve as a point of reference for Chomsky and Halle as they make the following remark:

> The dialect of English that we study is essentially that described by Kenyon and Knott (1944). We depart from their transcription occasionally, in ways that will be noted, and we also discuss some matters (e.g. stress contours beyond the word level) not included in their transcriptions. For the most part, however, we have used very familiar data of the sort presented in Kenyon and Knott.
>
> (*SPE*: ix)

The perspective, however, is now much more general since Chomsky and Halle suggest that the rules they propose apply to many other dialects of English. In fact, they hypothesise, subject to empirical confirmation, that 'the underlying lexical (or phonological) representations must be common to all English dialects, with rare exceptions, and that much of the basic framework of rules must be common as well' (*SPE*: x). This basic framework of rules is precisely the topic of our next section and will constitute the backbone of this chapter.

2 Beginnings: *SPE*

2.1 Predictability of stress

As pointed out by Shimizu (1978), Daniel Jones stated in 1950 that the placement of stress in English was not predictable (1).

(1)   Stresses are essentially subjective activities of the speaker ... [i]t is often difficult, and may be impossible, for the hearer to judge where strong stresses are.
            (Jones [1950] 2009: 134–5, cited in Shimizu 1978: 132)

History, Concepts and Debates

In contrast, Chomsky, Halle and Lukoff (1956) claimed that phrasal (and partially word-internal) stress placement (i.e. phrasal prominence) was predictable, depending on the accented/unaccented features of vowels organised into hierarchical syntactic constituents (2).[10]

(2)   a. [P]honetic differences in stress are predictable in terms of the representation[11]

(Chomsky et al. 1956: 77)

       b. [T]he distribution of stresses is accounted for automatically in terms of junctures,[12] ...

(Chomsky et al. 1956: 79)

Based on this insight, Chomsky and Halle wrote *SPE*. Before examining how stress placement becomes predictable, let us first consider some essential concepts that underlie their proposal.

2.2 Latin rule

One of *SPE*'s significant contributions is the discovery of the Latin (or Romance) stress rule incorporated in the sound structure of English, as expressed in (3a) below. Although English is, in origin, a Germanic language (i.e. stress is placed mainly on the left), the Latin or Romance rule is used to elaborate the Main Stress Rule based on a new concept of 'weak or strong cluster' (3).

(3)   a. Latin stress rule: Assign pitch accent to the antepenultimate vowel if the penultimate syllable ends with a lax or short vowel; otherwise, assign pitch accent to the penultimate vowel, that is, V́V̆V or V́V́V[13]
       b. Latin examples: *ad-ván-tus* 'arríval', *for-tū́-na* 'fórtune,' *Cí-ce-rō* 'Cícero'[14]
       c. Examples from Old English texts (loan words from Latin): *Hó-lo-fer-nus* 'Hòlofèrnus' (*Judith* 21) (Halle and Keyser 1971: 88), *Cón-stan-tī-nus* 'Cónstantìne' (*Elene* 79, 103, 1008), *Híe-ru-sa-lem* 'Jerúsalem' (*Elene* 273) (Fujiwara 1990: 15)

(Hale and Keyser 1971: 88; Fujiwara 1990: 15)

(3a) shows the Latin stress rule, stated as follows: 'assign pitch accent to the antepenultimate (i.e. third from right) vowel if the penultimate syllable ends with a lax or short vowel; otherwise, assign pitch accent to the penultimate vowel'. Latin examples (with stress on the right) are given in (3b), and examples of Latin *loanwords* in Old English (with stress on the left) are given in (3c). Note that the essence of the Latin stress rule is to count the vowel from the end of the word in contrast to counting from the beginning (or beginning of the root in the case of prefixed words) in Old English, where stress is placed on the first syllable of the Latin loans. In (3c), the Latin loans in Old English bear an initial Old English type stress. We can infer that in Latin they would have shown the Latin pitch stress pattern, if they followed the Latin stress rule in (3a), thus *Ho-lo-fér-nus*, *Con-stan-tí-nus* and *Hie-rú-sa-lem*. In Modern English, they are pronounced with the Latin stress accent as *Hòloférnus*, *Cónstantìne* and *Jerúsalem*.[15]

2.3 Weak and strong clusters

A weak cluster is defined below as (4a), a string consisting of a lax vowel (a nontense or [−tense] vowel) followed by not more than one consonant, that is, V̌(C). Any other clusters are strong, as in (4b). Note that for ease of exposition we use slightly different symbols and notations to those in *SPE*.

(4)   a. Weak cluster: a string consisting of a lax (nontense) vowel followed by not more than one consonant,[16] that is, V̌(C)
        b. Strong cluster: clusters other than (4a),[17] that is, V̄(C$_0$) or VC$_2$

2.4 Data analysed by cluster

Let us now consider actual examples from *SPE* and other works.

(5)   Nouns (by cluster; related parts only)[18]

I (V̌(C))	II (V̄(C$_0$))	III (VC$_2$)
Cán.ad.a	ar.óm.a	ag.énd.a
Amér.ic.a	mar.ín.a	ver.ánd.a
Calif.órn.i.a	hor.íz.on	cons.éns.us
alúm.in.um	cor.ón.a	syn.óps.is
sèrendíp.it.y	ònomàtop.óei.a	ut.éns.il
láb.yr.inth	Àpalàchic.ól.a	app.énd.ix

Here in (5) dots show the cluster division.[19] These are nouns. Above each column the *penultimate cluster* type is shown in parentheses. All the words in column I contain a weak cluster in the penultimate position, while those in columns II and III contain a strong cluster in the same position. Stress is assigned to the antepenultimate vowel in I, and the penultimate in II and III. Notice that if we disregard the final cluster of the words in (5), we can obtain the same generalisation in the case of verbs in (6) as well.

(6) Verbs (by cluster; related parts only)[20]

I (V̆(C))	II (V̄(C₀))	III (VC₂)
astón.*ish*	maint.*áin*	coll.*ápse*
imág.*ine*	er.*áse*	torm.*ént* (verb)
intérpr.*et*	car.*óuse*	conv.*ínce*
elíc.*it*	caj.*óle*	us.*úrp*
detérm.*ine*	ach.*íeve*	cav.*órt*

In column I stress is placed one position to the left of the final weak cluster, while in columns II and III it is placed on the vowel of the final strong cluster itself. Further, in the case of adjectives in (7), we find the same generalisation.

(7) Adjectives (by cluster; related parts only)

I (V̆(C))	II (V̄(C₀))	III (VC₂)
sól.*id*	supr.*éme*	abs.*úrd*
cért.*ain*	in.*áne*	rob.*úst*
vúlg.*ar*	discr.*éte*	dir.*éct*

It is interesting that in the next case (8), adjectives with certain types of derivational affixes, we find the same generalisation as in the *nouns* in (5).

(8) Certain Types of Derivational Affixes (by cluster; related parts only)[21]

I (V̆(C))	II (V̄(C₀))	III (VC₂)
pérs.*on*.al	anecd.*ót*.al	dial.*éct*.al
magnán.*im*.ous	des.*ír*.ous	mom.*ént*.ous
víg.*il*.ant	compl.*ác*.ent	rep.*úgn*.ant

Further, in (9), nouns with a final *tense* vowel behave like Type II verbs (6) or Type II adjectives (7).

(9) Nouns (= Type II Nouns) (by cluster; related parts only)[22]
II (V̄(C₀))
reg.*íme* bar.*óque* toup.*ée* pol.*íce* baz.*áar* broc.*áde* attach.*é* kangar.*óo*

2.5 Main Stress Rule

Considering all these generalisations, Chomsky and Halle put forward the Main Stress Rule in (10).

(10) Main Stress Rule (relevant parts only; simplified version)
 a. V → [1 stress] / [X___C₀W(At)+affix]$_{\text{NSPVA}}$
 b. V → [1 stress] / [X___C₀(At)+affix]$_{\text{NSPVA}}$

c. $V \rightarrow [1 \text{ stress}] / [X\_\_\_C_0W\check{V}C_0]_{NSP}$
d. $V \rightarrow [1 \text{ stress}] / [X\_\_\_C_0\check{V}C_0]_{NSP}$
e. $V \rightarrow [1 \text{ stress}] / [X\_\_\_C_0W(At)\acute{\Sigma}]_{NSPVA}$
f. $V \rightarrow [1 \text{ stress}] / [X\_\_\_C_0(At)\acute{\Sigma}]_{NSPVA}$
g. $V \rightarrow [1 \text{ stress}] / [X\_\_\_C_0W]$
h. $V \rightarrow [1 \text{ stress}] / [X\_\_\_C_0]$

where W = weak cluster, '+' = formative boundary, 'affix' = certain types of affix, that is, $+C_0$ [−stress, −tense, V] C_0 such as *-al*, *-ant*, *-ent*, *-ous* listed in (8), $\check{V}$ = lax vowel, $_N$ = noun, $_S$ = stem, $_P$ = prefix, $_V$ = verb, $_A$ = adjective. X does not contain a # boundary internally, and Σ́ is a stressed syllable.[23]

(10) is a simplified version with only relevant parts displayed. The weak cluster is shown by W. Let us examine how these rules apply to the word in (11).

(11)   Cán.ad.a

                C   a   n   ad   a
                | | | |
    V → [1 stress] / [X ___ C_0 W $\check{V}C_0]_{NSP}$ (10c)
                     |
                     V → [1 stress], i.e. á

For this word, rule (10c) applies because the condition for application is first met in the linear sequence of rules (10a–h). The final vowel 'a' of the word is lax, represented as 'V̌' in the rule, and the cluster to its left is weak, that is, 'W'. Thus, the main stress is placed on the antepenultimate vowel, the third from right. In (12), on the other hand, stress is assigned by rule (10d) to the penultimate strong cluster, corresponding in this case to part '___ C_0' of the rule.

(12)   ag.énd.a

                a g   e   nd   a
                       | | |
    V → [1 stress] / [X ___ C_0 $\check{V}C_0]_{NSP}$ (10d)
                        |
                        V → [1 stress], i.e. é

To summarise, the list in (13) shows how all the canonical data shown previously are accounted for by the Main Stress Rule.

(13) Word Types and Application of the MSR

Word Types	Categories	Rules
(8I)	Certain Types of Derivational Affixes I	(10a)
(8II, III)	Certain Types of Derivational Affixes II, III	(10b)
(5I)	Nouns I	(10c)
(5II, III)	Nouns II, III	(10d)
(6I)	Verbs I	(10g)
(6II, III)	Verbs II, III	(10h)
(7I)	Adjectives I	(10g)
(7II, III)	Adjectives II, III	(10h)
(9)	Type II Nouns	(10h)

For example, nouns I in (5I) are all accounted for by (10c), while verbs I in (6I) are accounted for by (10g).

2.6 Cyclic application of rules

Notice that the rules in (10) are linearly ordered and applied cyclically from the innermost constituents to the outermost in cyclic domains. This is shown later in the case of derivation of a noun in (14). Further, some parts of the cyclic block of rules such as those in (10a–d) and (10g–h) are disjunctively ordered, meaning that if one of the rules of the block applies in a cyclic domain, the remaining rules are not applicable in that cycle. Rules not subject to this restriction are conjunctively ordered, meaning that they can apply to the output of rules in the same domain again if the condition for the rule is satisfied. The so-called Stressed Syllable Rule in (10e, f) is conjunctively ordered in relation to those in (10a–d) and (10g–h), since by definition this rule is applied *after* the application of one of the disjunctively ordered rules in the same cycle.[24]

Let us now examine a case of the cyclic application of rules in (14).

(14) còndênsátion (< condénse) (see *SPE*: 116)[25]

$$[_N \# [_V \# k\text{ɔ}N = deNs \#]_V At + i\check{V}n \#]_N$$

1st cycle		1			(10h)
		2	1		(10c)
		3	1		[108] (*SPE*: 116)[26]
	2	3	1		[107b] (*SPE*: 114)
2nd cycle	3	4	1		[63] (*SPE*: 90)

(14) shows an analysis of the word *còndênsátion*, derived from the verb *condénse*. In the first cycle, rule (10h) is applied to the innermost constituent, that is, the verb *condénse*, giving stress on the vowel of the ultimate string *dénse*. We then go on to the second cycle, where rule (10c) is applied, giving stress to the penultimate cluster, as in *còndênsátion*, followed by other rules that are not relevant here.[27]

Note that in *SPE* stress is assigned by means of stress rules based on underlying phonological representations with syntactic structures marked, which are given in the syntactic component of the grammar. In other words, underlying phonological representations are mapped onto phonetic representations by way of stress rules in a transformational cycle of the grammar. For example, in *còndênsátion* (14) the underlying phonological representation is shown at the top of the derivation, that is, [$_N$ # [$_V$ # kɔN = deNs #]$_V$ At + iV̆n #]$_N$, including a structural description along with boundaries such as #, =, +. Stress rules in the phonological component change these underlying phonological representations to phonetic representations with the help of information on categorical structures along with boundaries. In addition, their application crucially depends on the information regarding distinctive features of segments, such as lax or tense vowels, which leads to the distinction between weak and strong clusters of segments (see Durand 1990: 110–33 for a discussion of the relationship between stress structure and underlying representations as part of the abstractness/concreteness debate in phonology).

To summarise, *SPE* claims that it is possible to predict the placement of English stress by stress rules based on the Latin stress rule using structural information (i.e. word-internal structure) given from the syntax. One of the features of *SPE* is the cyclic application of rules; another is the concept of weak/strong clusters that are dependent on the underlying distinction of [±tense] vowels.

3 Development: Metrical Phonology and Lexical Phonology

3.1 Metrical Phonology

3.1.1 Liberman and Prince (1977)
Halle and Keyser (1971), Ross (1972) and Halle (1973b) supported and modified the *SPE* account, while the *SPE* concept of 'clusters' was challenged by Fudge (1969), Kahn (1976), Selkirk (1978, 1980, 1984a), Kiparsky (1979) and others. Note, however, that in Halle (1973a) the concept is retained, as it is in Liberman and Prince's (1977) Metrical Phonology; note further that in their account Liberman and Prince admit to using 'syllable' indulgently unless it causes any inconvenience. What is important about Liberman and Prince's (1977) analysis is that they propose a new account of English stress, utilising the relative prominence of phonological constituents in contrast to the segmental treatment of *SPE*.

In Liberman and Prince (1977), the feature [+stress] is assigned to the vowel by the English Stress Rule (ESR) in (15a) below, whose function is similar to the Main Stress Rule of *SPE*: 'If the penultimate vowel is short,

History, Concepts and Debates

and followed by (at most) one consonant, stress falls on the preceding vowel. If the penultimate vowel is long or followed by two (or more) consonants, then it must bear stress itself' (Liberman and Prince 1977: 271) (see Chapter 4 of this volume). Along with the feature [+stress] given by the iterative (and cyclic) ESR and the Stress Retraction Rule (SRR) (15b), the underlyingly long ([+long]) vowels also receive the feature [+stress], while the underlyingly short ([−long]) vowels are assigned the feature [−stress]. Based on the [±stress] features of vowels, a 'metrical tree' is constructed leftward from the end of the word in accordance with the Lexical Category Prominence Rule (LCPR) in (15c).

(15) a. ESR:[28] $V \rightarrow [+stress] / \_\_\_ C_0 (\breve{V}(C))(\breve{V}C_0) \left\{ \begin{array}{c} \# \\ V \\ [+stress] \end{array} \right\}$

   b. SRR:[29] $V \rightarrow [+stress] / \_\_\_ C_0 (\breve{V}(C))(VC_0) \quad \begin{array}{c} V \\ [+stress] \end{array}$

   c. Lexical Category Prominence Rule (LCPR) (simplified preliminary version) In the configuration $[N_1\ N_2]$, N_2 is strong iff it branches; otherwise N_2 is weak.[30]

   d. Deforestation (DF): Before applying any rules on a cycle, erase all prosodic structure in the domain of that cycle.[31]

Consider, for example, the following analysis with a tree and grid representation in (16).

(16) a.
```
              *                                    
         *    *    *                               
       [ or   ig   in_N]                           
        −    −    −                                
ESR1    +    −    −                                
LCPR1   s    w    w                                
         \__/                                      
           s                                       
```

b.
```
                    *                              level 2
              *     *     *     *                  level 1
           [[ or    ig    in_N]  al_A]
DF2         +     −     −     −
ESR2        +     +     −     −
LCPR2  w    s     w           w
            \__/
              s
```
→

c.

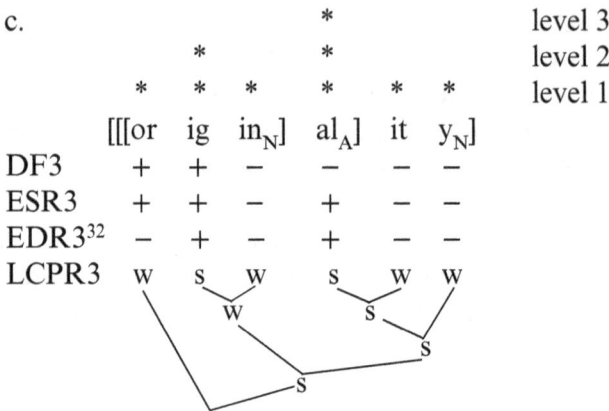

Here we show the derivation of *originálity* from *órigin* by way of *original*. The numeral after the rule abbreviation indicates the phonological cycle in which each rule is applied. For example, 'ESR1' in (16a) means that the ESR is applied in the first cycle.

In the first cycle in (16a), ESR1 applies, giving [+stress] antepenultimately. Based on the [+stress] given by ESR1, the tree structure is constructed in accordance with the LCPR1 of (15c).[33] In the second cycle (16b), after DF2, the ESR2 gives [+stress] on the second vowel as well as on the first vowel given in the first cycle.[34] In the third cycle (16c), DF3, ESR3 and EDR3 apply, followed by the tree construction in accordance with LCPR3, which can be taken as 'well-formedness conditions' on the tree shape.

Liberman and Prince (1977) uses two ways of representation: the tree and the grid. The relative prominence, that is, *s* (strong) vs *w* (weak), of constituents with their hierarchical structure is well represented in the tree, in contrast to the numerical representation of *SPE* based on segmental concatenation. Additionally, the grid can be appropriately used to account for the so-called stress clash (*thirtéen mén* → *thìrteen mén*) since in the grid representation the level distinction can be clearly shown.[35]

One might think that proposing two similar devices in one system would be redundant, and this question has naturally been raised. Kiparsky (1979) and Hayes (1980, 1982) argue for the tree, while Prince (1983) insists on a grid-only treatment. Halle (1984) and Halle and Vergnaud (1987a) eventually show that both the grid and the information from the tree are necessary.[36]

3.1.2 Hayes (1980, 1982)

Liberman and Prince (1977) brought significant improvement in the representation and account of stress in English, but one point remained unsolved: in some cases, the placement of [+stress] is crucially dependent on the underlying [±long] distinction of vowels,[37] except for [+stress] given by the ESR. Is there any way to predict the placement of stress without recourse to the underlying information? Hayes (1980, 1982) shows that it is quite possible to predict the placement of stress in a principled way with the help of

History, Concepts and Debates

a theoretical device: 'extrametricality' in tandem with a 'foot' construction, based on *'syllable* weight' (see Chapter 5 of this volume for syllable weight and extrametricality).

Hayes postulates three extrametrical rules: Consonant Extrametricality (CE), Noun Extrametricality (NE) and Adjective Extrametricality (AE). These render a single phonological constituent – such as consonant (in the case of CE), rhyme (in the case of NE), or suffix (in the case of AE) – invisible to the stress rules at the end of the word. Interacting with the three extrametrical rules, the English Stress Rule (ESR)[38] after Long Vowel Stressing (LVS)[39] constructs a maximally binary foot on the rhyme projection.[40] In other words, the foot is constructed on the basis of information from the *syllable* structure.

Take the characteristic 'Latin stress' type words, for instance, where 'stress is generally assigned to a heavy penult, while the antepenult receives stress if the penult is light' (Hayes 1982: 239). Their rhyme projection at the end of nouns becomes 'extrametrical' as shown by the delete mark: *lábyrinth* (a i in̶θ̶), *Àrizóna* (a i ow a̶) and *agénda* (a en a̶), as in (17) below for example (see Hayes 1982: 240).[41] Then, a unary *foot* (F) is constructed from the end of the word on the *branching* rhyme in *Àrizóna* and *agénda*, while a binary *foot* (F) is constructed on the two nonbranching rhymes in *lábyrinth*:[42]

(17)
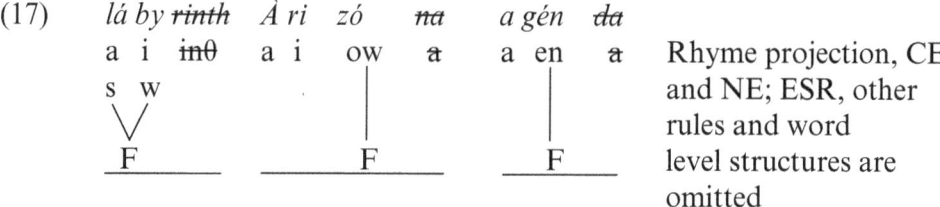

where a horizontal line represents the division between the foot and the word trees.

Let us next consider other cases relating to the phonological cycle in (18) and (19) below, showing the derivations from verbs to nouns (see Hayes 1982: 250). In the first cycle in (18a), LVS applies to the final long vowel [eɪ] of -s[eɪ]te, creating a unary *foot*.[43] The ESR vacuously applies to the final vowel, since the unary foot is already constructed on the vowel [eɪ], followed by Strong Retraction (SR); this gives a binary foot labelled *s w* to *compen-*, *without* regard to *syllable quantity* (i.e. *syllable weight*) across the word. Word Tree Construction (WTC) will give the tree of *cómpensàte* (18a).[44] The main stress of the word falls on the head of the binary foot. In the second cycle of (18b), NE, ESR, Stray Syllable Adjunction (SSA) and WTC give the final foot -*sation*, which is *s w*.[45]

(18) a. [[compensate]_V ion]_N → b. [còmpen sátion]_N

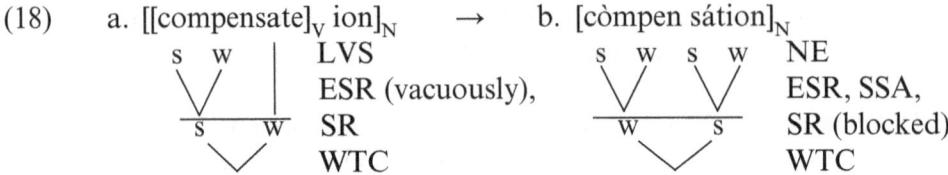

Notice here that the application of SR is blocked in (18b) because the binary foot structure on *compen-* is already given in the first cycle.[46] Note, however, that the cyclic application of ESR deletes structure that was assigned earlier in the derivation: in this case, the right boundary and unary foot on the final syllable *-sate* in (18a) are deleted.[47] The foot *sa-* in (18b) is constructed by ESR in the second cycle again, followed by SSA for *-tion*.

By way of contrast, in (19) we show the derivation from the verb *condénse* to the noun *còndènsátion*.

(19) a. [[condense]_V ation]_N → b. [còndèn sá tion]_N

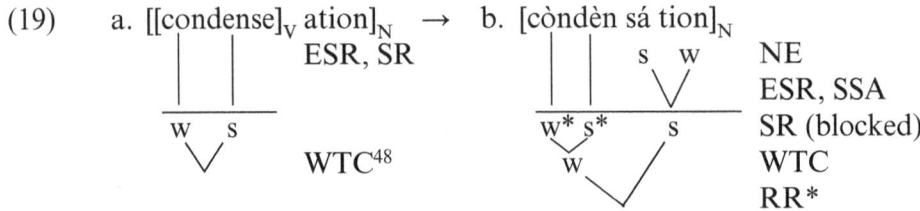

In (19a) ESR applies to the final branching rhyme of the heavy syllable *dense*, creating a unary foot, followed by other rules such as SR[49] and WTC, giving *condénse*. In (19b), the application of the rules is almost identical[50] to that of (18b), except for the Rhythm Rule (RR), which reverses the relationship of *w-s* to *s-w* at the so-called stress clash. The reversal will occur between the nodes with asterisks *w* s** immediately followed by another *s*.[51]

Note here that in Metrical Theory (Hayes 1980, 1982), the so-called preservation of stress (or stress inheritance) can be explained by the status of the relevant vowel of the base word in the earlier cycle. In the case of *còndènsátion* in (19b) with subsidiary (actually tertiary, in this case) stress on the second syllable *den*, the second syllable is the head of the unary foot in the first cycle, while in *còmpensátion* in (18b) without subsidiary stress on the second syllable *pen*, it is not the head of foot in the first cycle, rather a weak member of the foot. This is how the phonological cycle is handled in Hayes (1980, 1982).

To summarise, Hayes (1980, 1982) succeeded in excluding the feature [+stress] from phonological representations by adopting the foot construction, making a single word-final phonological constituent extrametrical in a principled way. However, the division of English vowels into 'long' versus 'short' remains.

3.2 Lexical Phonology

Based on studies by Kingdon (1958a, 1958b) and others, *SPE* points out that there are two types of suffixes in English: stress-shifting and stress-neutral. Stress-shifting suffixes include *-al, -ic, -ify, -ion, -ity* and *-ous*, while stress-neutral suffixes include *-able, -hood, -ish, -ing, -like, -ly, -ness* and *-wise*, for example.[52] To illustrate we can take a contrastive pair of words: *originálity* and *géntlemanliness*. In the case of *originálity*, the main stress of the base word *órigin* shifts rightward in *orígin-al* and *originál-ity* with the addition of each suffix. In contrast, in the case of *géntlemanliness*, the main stress position of the base word, on the first syllable *gén-*, does not shift when suffixes such as *-ly(-li)* and *-ness* are added. *SPE* accounts for this by using boundaries interspaced in the word structure of the words as in (20).

(20)   a. $[[[origin]_N + ál]_A + ity]_N$
          b. $[[[géntleman]_N \#li]_A \#ness]_N$

In *originality* (20a), the MSR in (10a) applies,[53] giving the required stress. In (20b), no MSR (10) applies to the outermost domain of *gentlemanliness*, nor the next outermost stress domain of *gentlemanly*, since it is blocked by one of its conditions for application: 'X does not contain a # boundary internally'.[54]

Note here that boundary marks are present at the phonological surface structure, which will be input to the phonological rules. The phonological surface structure consists of the underlying lexical and phonological representations, all of which are the output from the syntactic component of the grammar. In *SPE*, the word-formation component is considered to be included in the syntax. Phonology merely changes the output from the syntax into phonetic representations by means of the phonological rules. The phonological operation has no way of 'knowing' the mechanism of the word-formation itself, the result of which is simply given to phonology from a kind of black box in the syntactic component.[55]

After publication of Chomsky (1970), which suggested the importance of the lexicon in the grammar, the situation changed. Halle (1973a), Siegel (1974), Aronoff (1976), Allen (1978), Selkirk (1981) and Williams (1981) began arguing for the independence of the lexicon and morphology from the syntax in the grammar. Siegel (1974) initiated the argument with the observation that there are two types of affixes in the lexicon, Classes I and II, with Class I including *in-, -ion, -ity* and *-al*, and Class II *un-, -ness, -less* and *-ful*, for example. Class I affixes are associated with the + boundary in *SPE*, while Class II affixes are associated with the # boundary (see Siegel 1974: 102).[56]

Then, if phonological rules are allowed 'to have direct access to morphological information' (Mohanan 1982: 2), boundary symbols will be unnecessary for phonology. With this idea, Mohanan assumes that 'the lexicon consists of ordered lexical strata which function as the domains of application of phonological and morphological rules'.[57] The strata are ordered as in (21).

(21) Stratum ordering in English (Mohanan 1982: 73)[58]
  Stratum 1: Class I affixation (-al, -ic, in-, -ion, -ity, ...)
  Stratum 2: Class II affixation (-dom, -ly, -ness, re-, -ship, un-, ...)[59]
  Stratum 3: Compounding
  Stratum 4: Inflection

Using this organisation of the lexicon and the morphology with strata included, Lexical Phonology in Mohanan (1982) 'accounts for the stress neutrality of class II affixes by assuming that *the domain of foot construction is stratum 1*' (1982: 77, our emphasis), as in (22).[60]

(22) a. [[[o   ri   gin] +ál]$_I$ +ity]$_I$ b. [[[géntleman] #ly]$_{II}$ #ness]$_{II}$
             | | | |
         Foot-1*[61] Foot-2   Foot-3   Foot-1

In accordance with the assumption about foot construction (i.e. stress assignment or placement), the foot construction by ESR and SR in Hayes (1980, 1982) is operative in (22a) on +*al* suffixation (i.e. on the second cycle) and +*ity* suffixation (on the third cycle) because these suffixations are handled at stratum 1 (shown by a subscript 'I' in (22a)). After each suffixation (i.e. morphological process) the result is sent to phonology, the phonological rules apply, and the output is sent back to morphology.[62] This process is repeated until the end of the suffixation at stratum 1. Eventually (in 22a), primary stress is assigned to the vowel of the antepenultimate syllable of a foot as Foot-3, and secondary stress to the second syllable as Foot-2. In (22b), on the other hand, no further foot construction can apply since both the #*ly* and the #*ness* suffix are grouped into stratum 2 (shown by a subscript 'II' in (22b)).

Here a brief note on cyclicity is in order. In Pesetsky (1979), Mohanan (1982) and Kiparsky (1982a, 1982b), 'the rules of *lexical phonology*' are 'intrinsically cyclic because they reapply after each step of word-formation at their morphological level' (Kiparsky 1982a: 3). Conversely, the rules of *postlexical phonology* are intrinsically noncyclic. Note, however, that Halle and Mohanan (1985) show stratum 1 in English as a cyclic stratum, and stratum 2 as a noncyclic stratum.

Now we will highlight one of the drawbacks of Mohanan's treatment, the so-called ordering paradox. This problem is seen in words like *ungrammaticality* in (23) below. Mohanan himself admits that 'assuming that *un-* is attached to adjectives and not to nouns (*unfortunate*, but **unfortune*), the bracketing has to be *[[un[grammatical]$_I$]$_{II}$ity]$_I$, which involves the attachment of a class I affix to a stem containing a class II affix' (1982: 80–1).[63]

History, Concepts and Debates 29

(23)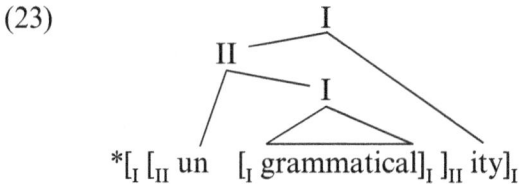

To summarise, in Lexical Phonology the relationship between phonology and morphology is investigated. The rules of phonology and morphology can interact with one another, sending information back and forth between them. Thus, phonology is now able to view the morphological process information directly. This enables us to eliminate the boundary symbols proposed by *SPE*.

4 Unity: Halle and Vergnaud's Metrical Theory of Stress

4.1 Unity

Since *SPE*, there have been significant developments in the phonological study of English word stress. Clusters have been replaced by syllables (Hayes 1980, 1982). The importance of representing notationally the relative prominence of the phonological constituents is assumed (Liberman and Prince 1977). The concept of extrametrical elements helps to simplify generalisations about the stress assignment mechanism (Hayes 1980, 1982). The status of the lexicon in the grammar is established (Siegel 1974; Allen 1978), and the relationship between phonology and the lexicon is explored in detail, producing the concept of ordered strata relating to the lexicon and phonological rules (Mohanan 1982; Kiparsky 1982a, 1982b; Giegerich 1999). And the problem of cyclicity is again highlighted (Mascaró 1976; Pesetsky 1979; Kiparsky 1979, 1982a, 1982b; Mohanan 1982; Halle and Mohanan 1985; Mohanan 1985). Based on the generative traditions, Halle and Vergnaud (1987a, hereafter *HV*) attempt to integrate all the concepts, findings and developments into a single theory (see also Halle and Vergnaud 1987b).[64]

4.2 Generalisation and Extrametricality

Consider the following generalisation concerning the stress system of English words in (24) (see also Chapter 8 of this volume). Words are analysed in terms of syllables rather than clusters, with dots showing the syllable division. All are drawn from the first row of examples (5), (6), (7), (8) and (9) in section 2.4, where analysis was by cluster. Extrametrical elements are enclosed in angle brackets.[65]

(24)   a. Nouns   I   II   III
                           Cá.na.<da>   a.ró.<ma>   a.gén.<da>   (5)
        b. Affixed Adj.   I   II   III
                           pér.so.<nal>   anec.dó.<tal>   dia.léc.<tal> (8)
        c. Verbs   I   II   III
                           as.tó.nish   main.táin   co.llápse   (6)
        d. Adjectives   I   II   III
                           só.lid   sup.réme   ab.súrd   (7)
        -
        e. Nouns (Type II[66])   re.gíme   ba.róque   tou.pée   po.líce   (9)

Both nouns (24a) and adjectives with certain types of affixes (24b) match the so-called Latin stress rule pattern. And if the final syllables with a rime containing a short vowel are enclosed by angle brackets, that is, if they are extrametrical, their remaining strings show an identical pattern to those of verbs (24c) and adjectives (24d). Further, nouns ending in a tense vowel (24e) are identical in stress assignment to the verbs and adjectives of columns II (24cII, 24dII). Therefore, in order to exclude from consideration the final syllables in angle brackets in (24), Halle and Vergnaud put forward 'Extrametricality' (25) (*HV*: 234), based on Hayes (1980, 1982).

(25)   Extrametricality (*HV*'s version)
        * → . / ___] line 0   in nouns and in certain suffixes, provided
                                * dominates a rime with a short vowel
                                (nonbranching nucleus)

4.3 English Stress Rules: rules and parameters

With the help of Extrametricality (25), which makes a specific final syllable invisible to stress rules, Halle and Vergnaud propose the system in (26) to account for stress assignment in English.

(26)   English Stress Rules in *HV*[67]
        a. c   Extrametricality [19]
        b. c   Accent Rule [11]
        c. n   Stress Copy [46]
        d. c/n   Line 0 parameter settings are [+HT, +BND, left, right to left] [5a]
        e. c/n   Construct constituent boundaries on line 0 [5b]
        f. c/n   Locate the heads of line 0 constituents on line 1 [5c]
        g. c   Line 1 parameter settings are [+HT, −BND, right] [5d]
        h. c   Construct constituent boundaries on line 1 [5e]
        i. c   Locate the head of the line 1 constituent on line 2 [5f]
        j. c   Stress Conflation: Conflate lines 1 and 2 [5g]

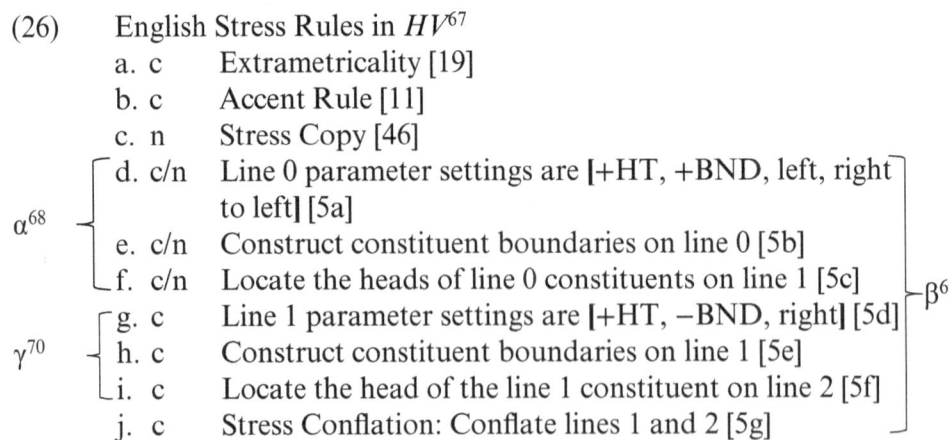

History, Concepts and Debates   31

    k. c   Shortening [57]
    l. n   Line 2 parameter settings are [+HT, −BND, right] [39a]
    m. n   On line 2 construct constituent boundaries [39b]
    n. n   Locate the line 2 constituent head on line 3 [39c]
    o. n   Rhythm Rule [21]
    p. n   Stress Enhancement [38]

δ^{71}

Rules are ordered linearly from (26a) to (26p) and cyclically applied. We find that each rule is assigned to a cyclic block of rules indicated by the letter 'c', or to a noncyclic block shown by the letter 'n', or to both. (26a) and (26b) are cyclic rules, while (26c) is noncyclic. Rules (26d–f) are allotted to both a cyclic block and a noncyclic block. We can note that the organisation of rules in (26) inherits the concept of strata from Lexical Phonology, with a slightly different interpretation.[72]

The concept of 'syllable weight' is also adopted in the Accent Rule in (26b), the original definition of which in *HV* is: 'Assign a line 1 asterisk to a syllable with a branching rime with the proviso that the word-final consonant is not counted in the determination of rime branchingness in the case of the final syllable of underived verbs and adjectives' (*HV*: 231).[73]

Some letters and symbols are enclosed by *boldface* square brackets [ ] in (26). These are parameters, whose value (i.e. parameter settings) will be set by the linguistic experience of the child, acquiring a particular language. These are (26d), (26g) and (26l). By setting the parameters, we can obtain the entire finite system of rules.

4.4 Application

Then, let us examine how the 'rules-and-parameters' method in (26) can account for the placement of stress in English words, using a canonical example in (27).

(27)   Cá.na.da

	a.	b.	c.	d.	
			*	*	line 2
			(*)	(*)	line 1
	* * *	* * .	(* *) .	(* *) *	line 0
	Canada	(26α) Cana<da>	(26β) Cana<da>	⇨ Canada[74]	

The word *Cánada* is accounted for by Extrametricality (25) (= 26a) and the ESR (26β) through the Binary Constituent Construction (26α) with the left-headed parameter value of the 'line 0 parameter settings' and the Unbounded Constituent Construction (26γ) with the right-headed value of the 'line 1 parameter settings'.

In contrast, *agénda* in (28) is explained by (26a) and the Accent Rule (26b), followed by the cyclic ESR (26β) ((26α, γ) and (26j)). The crucial point is whether the Accent Rule (26b) is activated on the heavy penult 'gen' in (28c). If it is not activated here, the result will be the same as the *Cánada* type stress pattern of (27), whose stress pattern is not acceptable for the *agénda* word-type.

(28)   a.gén.da

	a.	b.	c.	d.	
			*	*	line 2
				(* *)	line 1
	* * * (26a)	* * . (26b)	* * . (26α, γ)	(*)(*) .	line 0
	agenda →	agen<da> →	agen<da> →	agen<da>	

	e.	f.	g.	
	*	*	*	line 2
	(. *)	(* *)	(. *)	line 1
(26j)	*(*) .	(*)(* *)	*(* *)	line 0
→	agen<da> ⇒	agenda →	agenda	

Notice also that in *HV*, the relative prominence and hierarchical structure proposed by Liberman and Prince (1977) are expressed by means of the level (i.e. row) of dots (*) and parentheses, that is, the *foot* is constructed on *line 0* in parentheses at the end of the derivation.

Consider now the derivation in suffixation. In the case of *còndênsátion*, derived from the verb *condénse* by suffixation, we can properly account for its stress assignment as in (29).

(29)   còn dên sá tion (2310) (< *condénse*)[75]

Stress Enhancement (26p)[76]
Stress Copy (26c)

[[condens]$_V$ a tion]$_N$
2   3   1   0

(*HV*: 250)

Here only the final result in the noncyclic stratum is shown – most of the long derivation has been omitted for the sake of brevity. The point is that the result is crucially dependent on the activation of Stress Copy (26c),[77] followed by subsequent Stress Enhancement (26p) in the noncyclic domain.

Finally, let us return to the 'ordering paradox' shown in (23). Halle and Vergnaud 'adopt from Lexical Phonology the organisation of phonological rules into a number of blocks called *strata* and allow a given rule to be assigned to more than one stratum' (*HV*: 77). Further, 'strata are stipulated as being *cyclic* or *noncyclic*' (*HV*: 77). They also 'postulate that the prefix *un-* is noncyclic, whereas the suffixes *-ic*, *-al*, and *-ity* are cyclic' (*HV*: 81).

Thus, the problem is solved since the rules of the *noncyclic* stratum 'only apply when the outermost constituent of the word has been reached' (*HV*: 81; see also Kenstowicz 1995).

To summarise, Halle and Vergnaud successfully integrate a number of findings of previous generative accounts: syllable weight with extrametricality in Metrical Phonology and strata in Lexical Phonology are neatly interwoven into one system with the Latin stress rule as a core.

5 A change of course: Optimality Theory

5.1 A change of course

Concurrently with Burzio (1994), who puts forward a stress-checking analysis of English words based on well-formedness conditions, a new trend in phonology appears in Prince and Smolensky (1993) and McCarthy and Prince (1993a, 1993b): Optimality Theory (OT). In OT, sets of rules and their cyclic application are abolished. Instead, a set of *violable* constraints and their rankings are employed in favour of 'parallelism'. To see how OT treats word stress in English, let us take up Pater's (1995, 2000) account, examining canonical words such as *Cánada*, *horízon* and *còndènsátion* (see Chapter 8 of this volume).

5.2 Pater (2000)

To account for the noun *horízon*,[78] we need to introduce two constraints: ALIGN-HEAD and NON-FIN.[79] In short, ALIGN-HEAD requires that 'the main stressed "syllable" be at the rightmost syllable'; NON-FIN requires that 'the main stressed "foot" must *not* be at the rightmost syllable'. NON-FIN is ranked higher than ALIGN-HEAD. Thus, the optimal candidate is selected in (30a).

(30)　　*ho.rí.zon*　　NON-FIN >> ALIGN-HEAD

horizon	NON-FIN	ALIGN-HEAD
☞ a. ho[rí]zon		*
b. [hóri]zon		**!
c. [hòri][zón]	*!	

To account for the word *Cánada*, it is necessary to introduce two further constraints: FTBIN and TROCH.[80] As shown below (31), the three constraints, FTBIN, TROCH and NON-FIN, are equally ranked and ranked higher than ALIGN-HEAD. FTBIN is used to rule out candidate (31c), while TROCH is used to rule out (31d). Then, in the competition between (31a) and (31b), (31b) is ruled out because of the violation of NON-FIN. Thus, (31a) is selected as the optimal candidate.

(31)   Cá.na.da   FTBIN, TROCH, NON-FIN >> ALIGN-HEAD

Canada	FTBIN	TROCH	NON-FIN	ALIGN-HEAD
☞ a. [Cána]da				**
b. Ca[náda]			*!	*
c. Ca[ná]da	*!			*
d. [Caná]da		*!		*

Notice here that the concept of 'extrametricality' in Hayes (1980, 1982) and *HV* is embodied by NON-FIN. The final non-footed syllable 'da' of '[Cána]da' in (31a) is left unfooted, that is, extrametrical. One portion of the Latin stress rule (i.e. if the penult is light, stress is placed on the antepenult) is expressed by a combination of FTBIN and TROCH, along with NON-FIN. In (31a), the candidate '[Cána]da' shows a light penult; thus stress is placed on the antepenult by the left-headed binary foot.

Another portion of the Latin stress rule (i.e. if the penult is heavy, stress is placed on the penult itself) is expressed by a relationship between NON-FIN and ALIGN-HEAD. This is shown in (32), repeating (30) with two more columns, FTBIN and TROCH, to the left of NON-FIN. Although these do not change the outcome, they play an essential role.

(32)   ho.rí.zon   FTBIN, TROCH, NON-FIN >> ALIGN-HEAD

horizon	FTBIN	TROCH	NON-FIN	ALIGN-HEAD
☞ a. ho[rí]zon				*
b. [hóri]zon				**!
c. [hòri][zón]			*!	

In (32a), the penult vowel [rí] (i.e. [raɪ]) is long, satisfying FTBIN, which requires a bimoraic foot. Thus, the preference for (32a) or (32b) is not determined by FTBIN, TROCH and NON-FIN alone. Therefore, ALIGN-HEAD works. ALIGN-HEAD requires the main stressed 'syllable' to be rightmost; this is violated by one syllable *zon* in (32a) and two syllables *ri-zon* in (32b). This is an effect of another portion of the Latin stress rule: namely, if the penult is heavy, stress falls on the penult. To summarise briefly, the effect of the Latin stress rule is expressed by NON-FIN, functioning as 'extrametricality', and its combination with other constraints such as FTBIN, TROCH and ALIGN-HEAD.

Up to this point, the account is smooth. However, as shown below in (33), a problem arises in the case of derived words. The *còndênsátion* (2310) word type in (33c) has to be treated *exceptionally* or *lexically*, in distinct contrast with *SPE* and *HV* treatments.[81]

History, Concepts and Debates 35

(33)　*ín.for.má.tion* (2010) vs *còn.dên.sá.tion* (2310)

a. ID-STRESS-S₁ >> *CLASH-HEAD >> ID-STRESS

b.

infórmation (input)	ID-STRESS-S₁	*CLASH-HEAD	ID-STRESS
☞ i. [ìnfor][má]tion			*
ii. [ìn][fòr][má]tion		*!	

c.

condénsation (input) (i.e. *condénsation* in S₁)			
i. [cònden][sá]tion	*!		*
☞ ii. [còn][dèn][sá]tion		*	

Only the relevant constraint ranking is given in (33a). What is crucial here is the highest-ranked 'ID-STRESS-S₁'. Thus, before directly considering the analysis of (33), let us look at the definition of ID-STRESS in Pater (2000: 252): 'If α is stressed, then *f(α)* must be stressed. In this constraint, *f* is the correspondence relation between input (lexical) and output (surface) strings of segments'; briefly, ID-STRESS requires that the 'stress of input (lexical) and output (surface) should be on the same position'. Then, what function does ID-STRESS-S₁ serve, in contrast to the similar ID-STRESS? The difference is that a suffix '-S₁' is added to the former. The meaning of the suffix S₁ is as follows: S₁ is a *lexically* specified set of words, including examples such as *còndênsátion* and *àdvântágeous*. The higher ranked ID-STRESS-S₁ is triggered *only for* these *lexically* specified words grouped as S₁, while the lower-ranked ID-STRESS is used for 'regular' words, as shown in (34).

(34)　Hierarchy of Constraint Ranking

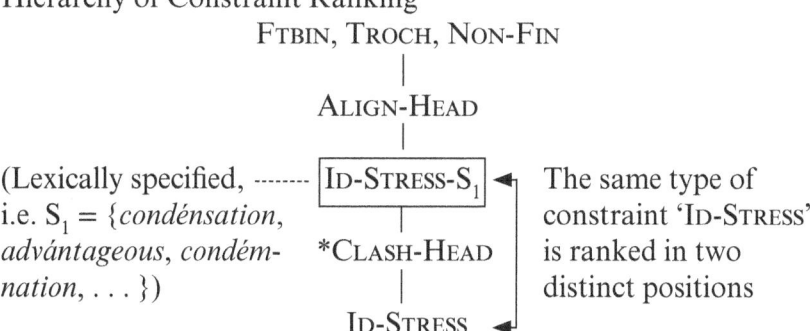

The problem is that the same type of constraint is ranked in two distinct positions: one for *lexically* specified words, and the other for the rest.

To return to the tableau in (33),⁸² (33cii) is selected because the input *còndênsátion* (33c) is a lexically specified word in S₁, showing lexical stress on the second syllable (*condénsation*), which rules out (33ci) by the constraint ID-STRESS-S₁. Thus, (33cii) is the optimal selection, while in the case of *informátion* the candidate without stress on the second syllable is selected.

5.3 Hammond (1999)

Next, let us briefly review the treatment of the word in question in Hammond (1999). Based on his statement on the *condensation* word type (1999: 328), the following tableau (35) will be created:[83]

(35)   còn.dên.sá.tion (2310)

/kandɛ̊nseʃən/	USC	F(v̊)	BE	FB	P-σ
a. [kànden][séʃən]		*!	*		
☞ b. [kàn][dèn][séʃən]			*	**	
c. kan[dèn][séʃən]	*!			*	*

where a lexical accent (v̊), that is, a diacritic accent in Hammond's scheme, is expected for the *condensation* word type. This marks the second syllable with an accent, as *condènsation*, leading to the desired result. Without the lexical accent on the second syllable, the square of (35a) under the constraint FAITH(v̊)[84] would be blank, meaning that the candidate (35a) would be incorrectly selected. We can state that Hammond's employment of a lexical accent weakens his otherwise persuasive account of English word stress.

However, it is important to note that this kind of lexical treatment is found in every phonological theory. As mentioned in note 81, *SPE* resorts to an exceptional account to explain the *informátion* word type, assuming that it has no internal structure [information]$_N$, in contrast to the *còndênsátion* word type with an internal embedded structure, [[condens]$_V$ ation]$_N$. *HV* inherits this idea. By contrast, Pater (2000) treats the *còndênsátion* word type *exceptionally*, while the *informátion* word type is accounted for *regularly*.

5.4 Kiparsky (2007, 2015)

The OT treatments discussed so far are termed 'strict parallelism', as mentioned in the introduction to this chapter. In order to solve some of the problems of strict parallelism, new kinds of approaches have been proposed within OT, including Stratal OT (Kiparsky 1998, 2000, 2007, 2015; Bermúdez-Otero 1999, 2003, 2011, 2012, 2014; Collie 2007) and Partially Ordered Grammar (Anttila 1997, 2006, 2007, 2012) and others. Of these, we will discuss Kiparsky (2007, 2015).

Recall that the starting point of OT is the elimination of rules from the grammar, meaning that their ordered application is also put aside, resulting in no derivations in the analysis. The parallelism in classical OT implies that all computation and evaluation is performed in parallel, once for each word, that is, there is no 'relay' of information from one word to another by means of 'derivation'. The information in the lexicon is put into the candidate generator GEN as its input, that is, the underlying representation. Then, GEN produces a number of candidates, which are evaluated by ranked constraints, and the candidate with the least constraint violation is selected as the optimal output. This process occurs once only and has no relation to any other parallel processes.

Let us now take the generation processes of the words *imágine* and *imàginátion* as examples. There will be no relation between one process, from *imagine* in the lexicon to its final optimal output *imágine*, and the other, from *imagination* in the lexicon to its output *imàginátion*. Thus, the two items will be independently stored in the mental lexicon as [*imagine*]$_V$ and [*imagination*]$_N$.

Now, if we suppose that the information for *imagination* in the lexicon is written as [[*imágin*]$_V$ *ation*]$_N$, with its word structure labelled by categorical brackets and stress specification on the word *imágine* (i.e. [*imágine*]$_V$ as the base and [*imagination*]$_N$ as its derivative), we can obtain the relationship between the two items: the output from one evaluation process becomes an input to the other, as in (36).

(36)

Lexicon	
Base (*imagine*)	[[Base]+Derived Form] ([*imágin*] *ation*])
↓	↓
Input (*imagine*)	Input ([*imágin*] *ation*])
↓	↓
GEN	GEN
↓	↓
Output (base) (*imágine*)	Output (derived form) (*imàginátion*)
------ Tableau A ------	------ Tableau B ------

With this 'relay' of information, the stress pattern of *imàginátion* will be accounted for. This is the method adopted in Stratal OT, as shown in the input of tableau (37) from Kiparsky (2007).

(37) Cyclic Inheritance: *imàginátion*

Input: [[imágin] ation]	IDENT-STRESS	ALIGN-LEFT
a. (ìma)gi(ná)tion	*	
☞ b. i(màgi)(ná)tion		*

Although the Stratal OT in serialism seems to have deviated from one of the initial tenets of classical OT, this might be an appropriate way to handle 'derivation' or 'cycle'-related phenomena in phonology, since 'it deals with phonology/phonology and phonology/morphology interactions by organising the grammar into strata (levels) analogous to those posited in Lexical Phonology and Morphology' (Kiparsky 2015: 1).

To summarise, OT initially attempted to solve problems of the theories preceding it by removing rules and derivations, introducing a new concept of violable constraints and ranking by which candidates are evaluated and the optimal output selected. As this process is performed in parallel, classical OT was termed 'Parallelism'. Later, a new kind of OT called 'Serialism' appeared to solve problems caused by strict parallelism. Stratal OT is one of these, admitting the serial 'relay' of phonological information from the base as output to the derived form as input.

6 English stress, Plato's problem and the nature of language

Let us now look briefly at how studies of English word stress can be placed within the generative phonological tradition (see Yamada 2018). The aim of generative grammar research can be largely summarised by the following questions: (i) How are people able to acquire a language in such a short time? And (ii) what is the nature of human language and how is this reflected in the structure of the particular languages we come to acquire? The first question is termed 'Plato's problem' (or the 'poverty of stimulus' problem), that is, how is it possible for a child to acquire a language (in a language community) so rapidly, and so uniformly, even though the stimulus to the child from the outside world (the language input and experience) is limited (see Chomsky 1986: xxv)? The second question investigates what it is that makes human languages so different from the communication systems of other animal species.

Regarding the first question, it is assumed that we are born with an a priori, innate endowment as human beings, namely a 'universal grammar' (UG) (see 'innateness hypothesis', Chomsky 1959, 1965; *SPE*: 4). This view is radically different from the inductive and empiricist view of American structural linguistics, such as Bloomfield's. It places generative grammar firmly in the rationalist camp with the assumption that people are endowed with a natural gift for language acquisition. An early version of this idea was presented by Chomsky already in 1955:

> A speaker of a language has observed a certain limited set of utterances in his language. *On the basis of this finite linguistic experience he can produce an indefinite number of new utterances which are immediately acceptable to other members of his speech community.* He can also distinguish a certain set of 'grammatical' utterances, among utterances that he has never heard and might never produce. He thus projects his past linguistic experience to include certain new strings while excluding others.
> (Chomsky [1955] 1975: 61, our emphasis)

The second question, 'the nature of human language', is also described in the above literature in similar terms: 'the process of transformational generation

History, Concepts and Debates 39

is *recursive* – infinitely many sentences can be generated' (Chomsky [1955] 1975: 74, our emphasis) (see Chomsky 2012: 17, 23; Hauser et al. 2002).

We are now in a position to ask how, in the theories of stress assignment we have examined, these two significant perspectives are expressed. In the case of *SPE*, the first issue, 'Plato's problem', seems to be partly expressed by 'universal phonetics' in relation to 'underlying phonological representations'. Universal phonetics provides us with a set of innately available 'distinctive features' from which each language draws a subset. Experience of a particular language will obviously underlie this selection, but the whole process will also be guided by universal constraints that set limits on what is a possible language phonologically. Indeed, markedness considerations which are the topic of *SPE*'s ch. 9, and have been extensively developed thereafter, have provided a fertile ground of experimentation for ideas concerning universality (see Durand 1990: 72–109). In addition, it is also assumed that there is a principle of the 'transformational cycle' in UG. The transformational cycle (or the 'recursiveness' of language) (see *SPE*: 6) seems to be very much associated with the second question, the nature of human language. Within *SPE*, similar rules are repeatedly applied, beginning with the smallest constituents and proceeding to larger ones; in other words, computations in language operations are 'recursive'.[85]

However, with regard to 'Plato's problem', *SPE* has its limitations since the stress rules it assumed were not themselves evaluated in terms of naturalness or universality; rather, they constituted very powerful transformational devices which could arrange and rearrange underlying structures at will. We had to wait for the publication of *HV* for an explicit answer to this problem in phonology (i.e. in the form of 'principles and parameters'). In subsequent studies in OT, this aspect has been expressed by the 'parametric' ranking of constraints; further, the formulation of the constraints themselves has often attempted to be as natural and universal as possible. It should, however, be noted that this has often led researchers away from the type of innateness assumed in early generative phonology towards models defending general cognitive capacities at the core of language acquisition. As far as (ii) 'recursiveness' (in the form of the 'cycle') is concerned, there have been various proposals, from *SPE* to *HV*, but the argument for its existence has generally been maintained as a premise. When it came to OT, this idea was initially rejected; subsequently, however, proposals have been made to incorporate recursiveness once more.

7 Conclusions

In this chapter, we have reviewed a significant portion of the study of English word stress in its historical context. We first outlined research prior to *SPE* in the British tradition and the American tradition and saw that the work of this period provided a valuable foundation and motivation for generative phonology. One of *SPE*'s contributions was the discovery of the Latin stress rule interwoven in the word stress system of English. Chomsky and Halle argue that stress assignment in English is predictable by means of the cyclic application of stress rules to segmental sequences of clusters in words, which are structured categorically and hierarchically. Boundaries such as '+', '#' and '=' are used to represent the phonological structure, with the feature [±tense] of vowels the basic building block of the theory.

In the Metrical Theory of Liberman and Prince (1977), the relative prominence of constituents is shown in the form of trees and grids. These representations enabled a more conceptually acceptable account of the stress system. The concept of *extrametricality* in tandem with *foot* construction based on *syllable weight* prompted Hayes (1980, 1982) to advance Metrical Theory further, leading to the removal from the theory of the [±stress] specification of vowels.

Concurrently with Metrical Theory, Kiparsky (1982a, 1982b) and Mohanan (1982) put forward Lexical Phonology (LP) based on Siegel (1974), Aronoff (1976) and Allen (1978). In LP, the concept of levels or strata is introduced in the lexicon, where word-formation (morphological) rules and phonological rules interact. The levels or strata serve as domains of phonological rules, thus eliminating the need for boundary symbols within underlying phonological representations. Further, the cyclic application of rules is much simplified once we operate with levels or strata.

In Halle and Vergnaud (1987a) all of the previous ideas and concepts are integrated: *syllable weight* and *extrametricality*, and the *cyclic* or *noncyclic* application of rules on the *cyclic* stratum or *noncyclic* stratum. Suffixes are also grouped as cyclic or noncyclic, or both. The relative prominence relation between constituents is represented by grids and their parentheses grouped into a hierarchical structure.

Next, we have Optimality Theory (OT), marking a change of course. OT rejects rules and derivations, instead introducing violable ranked constraints. Candidates are evaluated in parallel by the violable constraints, termed *parallelism*. The effect of the Latin stress rule is expressed by a combination of constraints such as FTBIN, TROCH and ALIGN-HEAD, along with NON-FIN functioning as 'extrametricality'. However, strict parallelism poses some problems. In order to solve these, *serialism* is introduced. One type of serial OT is Stratal OT by Kiparsky (2007, 2015) and others.

Generative phonology began by utilising the *cyclic* application of rules, yielding *derivations*. OT started by denying derivation as a result of cyclic rule application. Now, Stratal OT seems to admit derivation once again. History, too, is a cycle.

Notes

We would like to thank Stephen Howe for helpful suggestions for improving the manuscript and style. Thanks also go to the anonymous reviewers for valuable comments and suggestions, which were of great help in improving this chapter. Needless to say, all remaining inadequacies are ours. This work was supported by JSPS KAKENHI Grant Numbers 15K02622 and 19K00675.

1. Prior to *SPE*, a number of studies, for instance Cooper (1687; see Sundby 1953), Elphinston (1765) and Marchand (1969), noted the effect of Latin stress, though their treatments are less comprehensive. Newman (1946) also attempted to find the underlying principles determining the stress phenomena of English.
2. The term 'opacity' is related to *rule ordering*, while 'cyclicity' is connected with *recursion*, that is, cyclic inheritance.
3. First edition, 1918; last edition, 1964.
4. First edition, 1917; last edition published in Jones's lifetime, 1967.
5. In our transcriptions in this section, we follow in each case the system adopted by the respective author.
6. Also explored by Arnold (1956–7).
7. The publication of the well-known *Longman Pronunciation Dictionary* by J. C. Wells (first edition, 1990; third edition, 2008) no doubt acted as a stimulus for the new format and scope of the *English Pronouncing Dictionary*.
8. The assumptions made about degrees of stress by the *English Pronouncing Dictionary* have been adopted by the Guierre tradition in France; see Chapter 2 of this volume.
9. For a more detailed discussion, see Durand and Laks (2002: 18–23).
10. According to one anonymous reviewer, the importance of Chomsky, Halle and Lukoff's (1956) contribution to generative grammar is also noted in Dresher and Hall (2022). We believe this supports our point here.
11. The term 'representation' here means a transcription system with 'accented/unaccented' vowels.
12. Note also that 'their [that is, the junctures'] distribution and hierarchical arrangement are reasonably in accord with independently known syntactic and morphological properties' (Chomsky et al. 1956: 77).
13. A lax vowel is represented in this chapter by V̆. A stressed or pitch-accented vowel is shown as V́.
14. A long vowel is shown by a diacritic (¯) over the vowel.
15. The concept of the so-called foot does not appear in *SPE*. However, if we assume that two consecutive weak syllables are a 'foot' (enclosed

by brackets below) and one heavy syllable a 'foot' by itself, the loan *Holofernus* from Latin becomes (*Hó lo*) (*fèr*) <*nus*> (< > indicating an extrametrical element to be discussed in section 3.1.2). Main stress is assigned to the leftmost foot, showing the so-called Countertonic Principle (Danielsson 1948, based on Walker 1791), according to an anonymous reviewer. We believe this strengthens our contention. See Dresher and Lahiri (2022) for details.

16. (C) = an optional single consonant.
17. $\bar{V}$ = a tense [+tense] vowel; (C_0) = optional zero or more consonants; V = any vowel; C_2 = two or more consonants.
18. The words are grouped into Types I, II and III based on the *penultimate cluster* type.
19. The cluster divisions by dots are shown only for the portions relating to the current discussion.
20. The words are grouped into Types I, II and III based on the *final cluster* type.
21. The words are grouped into Types I, II and III based on the *penultimate cluster* type.
22. The *final cluster* behaves like Type II of the verbs (6II) and adjectives (7II).
23. Notice that no categorical restriction is specified for (10g, h); the parentheses in '(*At*)' in (10a, b, e, f) show that *At* is used when it occurs in words such as *còndênsátion*, *dèvastátion*, although the cycle where it is used is different (for [[*condens*]*ation*] the second cycle, for [[*devastat*]*ion*] the first) (see *SPE*: 38, 39, 106). For more on the application of (10e, f), see the discussion in section 2.6 and note 24. Tertiary stress is represented as (ˆ) in this note and below when necessary for later reference and discussion. See also notes 25 and 75 on boundaries and tertiary stress respectively.
24. For example, (10e) is applied to the *dýnamìte* word type, while (10f) is applied to the *confiscatòry* word type. Since *dýnamìte* is a noun with no affixes, and its last vowel is tense, the first rule matching the condition is (10h). Therefore, primary stress is assigned to the last vowel. Next, a conjunctively ordered rule (10e) is applied, and primary stress is assigned to the first syllable, making it *dýnamìte* (102). On the other hand, in *confiscatòry*, after primary stress is assigned to *confiscate* in the first cycle, yielding *cónfiscàte* (102), the rule (10b) is applied to the adjective *confiscatory* in the second cycle, giving *cònfiscâtóry* (2031). Then a conjunctively ordered rule (10f) is applied, with *At* appearing before *o+ry*, giving *cônfiscatòry* (3142) (see *SPE*: 42). Note that stress subordination has been applied after each stress assignment. A final rule to be applied to both is not shown since it is not relevant to the discussion here.
25. (#) = word boundary, (=) = equal boundary, (+) = formative boundary. See *SPE* for detailed discussions.

26. The numbers in square brackets refer to the original reference numbers in *SPE*.
27. Since '+affix' is defined as '+C_0[−stress, −tense, V]C_0' in (10), the final part of the word in (14), '+iV̌n', cannot be treated by (10b). The affix *-ion* '+iV̌n' is analysed as disyllabic from a phonological point of view in *SPE*, contrasting with its monosyllabic phonetic realisation. Note also that if the boundary '+' is presented in a rule, it has to be used; if it is not presented, its presence in a word has no effect on the rule's application.
28. When immediately followed by #, '(V̌C_0)' is used only for nominals and certain affixes; otherwise (that is, when followed by [+stress]) it is used for all categories.
29. SRR: Stress Retraction Rule. This rule is irrelevant to the discussion here, but related to a rule in section 3.1.2.
30. 'N' indicates 'node' here.
31. The [+stress] mark itself will not be erased by Deforestation.
32. The 'EDR' is the English Destressing Rule, by which [+stress] on the first vowel, 'o' in this case, is eventually destressed to [−stress, −long] in the final stage of derivation. Thus, in the case of *original* in (16b), the EDR applies to the first syllable 'o' if the derivation is stopped at the adjective *original*.
33. 'Because of the condition limiting [−stress] to weak positions, and because of the bivalent (binary-branching) character of metrical trees, the structure and labeling of the sequences is uniquely determined. We have, necessarily, left-branching trees' (Liberman and Prince 1977: 266) here in (16a).
34. The affix *-al* is considered to belong to 'certain affixes'. That is, the word *original* is treated as a 'nominal' in stress assignment.
35. The grid is expressed by the asterisks over the underlying representation with its categorical structure marked in (16). The stress value of each column is represented by the height of the grid columns. The LCPR in (15c) is not applied to *thirteen men* since it is a noun phrase rather than a constituent in a 'lexical category', that is, a word.
36. In Halle and Vergnaud (1987a), 'the information from the tree' is expressed by the brackets incorporated into the grid.
37. '[T]ense vowels and true diphthongs' are underlyingly long (Liberman and Prince 1977: 271).
38. ESR: 'At the right edge of a word, form a maximally binary foot on the rhyme projection using the template X (x) [i.e. incorporated into a branching foot (our note)] – that is the right node [i.e. '(x)' (our note)] of a branching foot must dominate a nonbranching rhyme. Label feet *s w*' (Hayes 1982: 238). Notice that the ESR here differs from that of *SPE* or Liberman and Prince (1977).
39. LVS: 'the stressing of final syllables containing long vowels' (Hayes 1982: 239).

40. According to Hayes (1980: 26), the idea of 'rime projection' was shown by Morris Halle around 1978. The term 'rime' in Hayes (1980) is changed to 'rhyme' in Hayes (1982), and back to 'rime' again in Halle and Vergnaud (1987a). The seminal idea of 'extrametricality' was first shown by Liberman and Prince (1977).
41. Rhyme projection is shown in parentheses. Here, all the rhymes of the syllable are projected. Then, CE applies to the '/θ/' of *labyrin/θ/*, followed by application of NE to the 'in' of *labyrin/θ/*, and to the final 'a' of *Arizona* and *agenda*.
42. Clusters in *SPE* consist of vowels followed by optional consonants, and so do rhymes. In this respect, they share a similar view.
43. The existence of any type of foot indicates 'stress'.
44. WTC creates 'a word tree which is right-branching, with sister nodes labelled *w s*' (Hayes 1982: 230) along with its default pattern *w s*, on the *word tree* level, as supported by the following description: 'the word tree labeling rule for English is simply "make right nodes strong"' (Hayes 1982: 271). In (18a), however, note that the *s w* tree, rather than the *w s* tree, is constructed since the word tree in (18a) is left-branching (see Hayes 1980: 233). Note also that at the word tree level the default stress pattern is *w s*, while at the syllable level it is *s w*.
45. In (18, 19) below, rhyme projection and CE are omitted for ease of description. During the cyclic transition from (18a) (first cycle) to (18b) (second cycle), the innermost brackets are deleted and *-sate* /seɪt/ is resyllabified to *sa-tion* /seɪ.ʃən/. The final extrametrical syllable *-tion*, first omitted from consideration by NE in (18b), is reincorporated into the structure by SSA, by which a stray syllable is adjoined 'as a weak member of an adjacent foot' (Hayes 1982: 239).
46. '[Strong Retraction] is blocked whenever its application would obliterate previously created metrical structure' (Hayes 1982: 250).
47. 'Only the English Stress Rule is allowed to obliterate previously created structure' (Hayes 1982: 251).
48. The default *w s* tree is constructed here since the first node *con-* is not branching at the *foot* level.
49. SR also creates a unary foot if a binary foot *s w* cannot be constructed (see Hayes 1982: 243).
50. The feet on *con-* and *-den-* are not deleted since ESR and SSR create a *s w* foot on *-sation*, rather than on *-den-*.
51. The ordering of the relevant rules is as follows, with notes in parentheses: Rhyme Projection → LVS (final syllables) → CE, NE, AE → ESR (can delete previously created structure; *s w* stress pattern) → SSA → SR (cannot delete previously created structure; *s w* default stress pattern) → WTC (*w s* default stress pattern) → RR.
52. For example orígin<u>al</u>, heró<u>ic</u>, persón<u>ify</u>, communicát<u>ion</u>, majór<u>ity</u>, cerremón<u>ious</u>; cónquer<u>able</u>, néighbor<u>hood</u>, péacock<u>ish</u>, néighbor<u>ing</u>, búsiness<u>like</u>, géntleman<u>ly</u>, géntleman<u>liness</u>, cóntrari<u>wise</u>.

53. In *SPE*, +*ity* is analysed as +*i*+*ty*.
54. Note that '#, as opposed to +, must be mentioned in a rule if that rule is to apply to a string containing #' (*SPE*: 85).
55. The unsettled state of the problem is shown in *SPE*: 370.
56. The difference between *in-* (Class I) and *un-* (Class II) can be illustrated by *immoral* (*in+moral*) vs *unmoral* (*un#moral*), with and without nasal assimilation. Further, examples of *-less* (Class II) and *-ful* (Class II) are *párentless* and *béautiful*, respectively.
57. See Pesetsky (1979), Kiparsky (1982a, 1982b) and others for similar arguments, where relevant parts of phonological rules are in the lexicon and the term 'level' is used instead of 'stratum'.
58. Some examples of affixes are added here for ease of exposition.
59. For example, *officialdom*, *proféssorship*, *redetérmine*.
60. Recall here that *foot construction* means *stress placement* on the head in Hayes (1980, 1982).
61. The numerals after 'Foot-', that is, '1', '2', '3', designate the cycle. Foot-1, for example, means that the head of a foot is constructed on that position in the 'first' cycle. The foot with the asterisk (Foot-1) here will be destressed after the suffixation of *-al* by Prestress Destressing in Hayes (1982).
62. In Kiparsky's (1982a, 1982b) Lexical Phonology and others, the relevant phonological rules termed 'cyclic rules' are placed in the lexicon as lexical rules.
63. By contrast, we can show examples without the ordering paradox: $[[[logic]+al]_I \#ly]_{II}$, $[[[mysteri]+ous]_I \#ly]_{II}$.
64. Halle and Kenstowicz (1991) and Idsardi (1992) follow *HV*. Hammond (1984) also independently develops his own account of English stress. See Durand (1990) for analyses of 'non-linear' approaches after *SPE*, including Underspecification Theory and Lexical Theory, Metrical Theory, CV Theory, Autosegmental and Multidimensional Phonology, Dependency Phonology, and others.
65. The definition of Extrametricality here is somewhat different to that of Hayes (1980, 1982).
66. Type II here corresponds to Type II of the verbs (24cII) and adjectives (24dII).
67. The numerals in square brackets in (26) refer to the original reference numbers in *HV*. Some rules are omitted here for ease of exposition. For detailed definitions and the application of each rule, see *HV*.
68. (26a) = Binary Constituent Construction: when these apply in the non-cyclic stratum, they are the counterpart to Hayes's (1980, 1982) Strong Retraction, termed 'Alternator' in *HV*.
69. The rules in (26d–j) are the Main Stress Rule (MSR).
70. Unbounded Constituent Construction on line 1.
71. Unbounded Constituent Construction on line 2.

72. Pesetsky (1979), Mohanan (1982) and Kiparsky (1982a, 1982b) assume that all lexical strata are cyclic, but in *HV* lexical strata may be either cyclic or noncyclic, following Halle and Mohanan (1985).
73. The concept of Consonant Extrametricality in Hayes (1980, 1982) is expressed as part of the Accent Rule. Further, Hayes's English Stress Rule is expressed by (26a, b, β) when applied cyclically.
74. Hereafter, the final result of the application of noncyclic (26d–f) rules or other rules in the noncyclic stratum is shown after a special arrow (⇨), while a normal transition in the derivation is indicated by an arrow (→). Note also that in (27d) in the noncyclic stratum, the last syllable is given an asterisk on line 0 since Extrametricality in (26) is no longer applied in the noncyclic stratum.
75. The stress pattern is also shown numerically in parentheses: 2 = secondary stress, 3 = tertiary stress, 1 = primary stress, 0 = zero stress.
76. Stress Enhancement: [enhance] stress on the first or second syllable of a word (*HV*: 242).
77. Stress Copy: place a line 1 asterisk over an element that has stress on any metrical plane (*HV*: 247). Note also that in the noncyclic stratum, Stress Copy and the Alternator 'supply line 1 asterisks to both syllables preceding main stress' (*HV*: 250).
78. The word *horízon* is an '*aróma*' type word in *SPE* and is categorised into column II of (5). This '*aróma*' word type is treated in the same way as the '*agénda*' word type, which has appeared frequently in our discussion.
79. ALIGN-HEAD: align the right edge of the Prosodic Word with the right edge of the *syllable that is the head of the foot that bears main stress*. The part in italics has been modified slightly by the present authors to make clear Pater's (2000) original meaning. NON-FIN: the foot that bears main stress must not be final (Pater 2000). In the tableau used in OT, each candidate that violates the constraint is marked with (*). If the violation is crucial, an exclamation mark (!) is added to the right of the asterisk. The winning candidate is the one that does not violate the higher-ranked constraint.
80. FTBIN: Feet must be minimally bimoraic (= binarity). TROCH: Feet are trochaic (= left-headedness).
81. Curiously, in fact, the *informátion* word type in (33b) is treated *exceptionally* in *SPE* and *HV*, while the *còndênsátion* word type is *not* exceptional. Note also that the tableau (33b, c) is cited from Pater (2000: 259) with slight modification.
82. The slashed line in the square under ID-STRESS-S_1 for (33bi, ii) in this chapter indicates that ID-STRESS-S_1 is *not* activated because *information* is *not* included in S_1.
83. USC = Upbeat-Secondary Constraint. F($\mathring{v}$) = FAITH($\mathring{v}$). BE = BASE-IDENTITY. FB = FOOT BINARITY. P-σ = PARSE-σ. For definitions of the

constraints in this tableau, see Hammond (1999). For the drawing of the tableau and detailed discussion of this topic, see Yamada (2010). A more recent discussion by Hammond can be found in Chapter 8 of this volume.
84. FAITH ($\acute{v}$): accented elements are stressed.
85. There have been many debates on whether this 'recursiveness' also exists in phonology, or whether in phonology the operations are performed based only on information from syntax or morphology.

References

Allen, M. (1978), 'Morphological investigations', PhD dissertation, University of Connecticut.
Anttila, A. (1997), 'Variation in Finnish phonology and morphology', PhD dissertation, Stanford University.
Anttila, A. (2006), 'Variation and opacity', *Natural Language and Linguistic Theory* 24(4), 893–944.
Anttila, A. (2007), 'Variation and optionality', in P. de Lacy (ed.), *The Cambridge Handbook of Phonology*, Cambridge: Cambridge University Press, pp. 519–36.
Anttila, A. (2012), 'Modeling phonological variation', in A. C. Cohn, C. Fougeron and M. Huffman (eds), *The Oxford Handbook of Laboratory Phonology*, Oxford: Oxford University Press, pp. 76–91.
Arnold, G. F. (1956–7), 'Stress in English words', *Lingua* 6(3–4), 221–441.
Aronoff, M. (1976), *Word Formation in Generative Grammar*, Cambridge, MA: MIT Press.
Benua, L. (1997), 'Transderivational identity: Phonological relations between words', PhD dissertation, University of Massachusetts, Amherst [ROA-259-0498, Rutgers Optimality Archive, <http://roa.rutgers.edu/>].
Bermúdez-Otero, R. (1999), 'Constraint interaction in language change: Quantity in English and Germanic' [Opacity and globality in phonological change], PhD dissertation, University of Manchester and Universidad de Santiago de Compostela, <http://www.bermudez-otero.com/PhD.pdf>.
Bermúdez-Otero, R. (2003), 'The acquisition of phonological opacity', Manuscript, University of Manchester [ROA-593-0403, Rutgers Optimality Archive, <http://roa.rutgers.edu/>]. [In J. Spenader, A. Eriksson and Ö. Dahl (eds), *Variation within Optimality Theory: Proceedings of the Stockholm Workshop on 'Variation within Optimality Theory'*, Stockholm: Stockholm University, pp. 25–36.]
Bermúdez-Otero, R. (2011), 'Cyclicity', in M. van Oostendorp, C. Ewen, E. Hume and K. Rice (eds), *The Blackwell Companion to Phonology*, vol. 4, Malden, MA: Wiley-Blackwell, pp. 2019–48.
Bermúdez-Otero, R. (2012), 'The architecture of grammar and the division of labour in exponence', in J. Trommer (ed.), *The Morphology and Phonology of Exponence*, Oxford Studies in Theoretical Linguistics 41, Oxford: Oxford University Press, pp. 8–83.
Bermúdez-Otero, R. (2014), 'Amphichronic explanation and the life cycle of phonological processes', in P. Honeybone and J. C. Salmons (eds), *The Oxford Handbook of Historical Phonology*, Oxford: Oxford University Press, pp. 374–99.

Bloch, B. and G. L. Trager (1942), *Outline of Linguistic Analysis*, Baltimore, MD: Linguistic Society of America.

Bloomfield, L. (1914), *An Introduction to the Study of Language*, New York: Henry Holt.

Bloomfield, L. (1926), 'A set of postulates for the science of language', *Language* 2, 153–64.

Bloomfield, L. (1933), *Language*, New York: Henry Holt.

Burzio, L. (1994), *Principles of English Stress*, Cambridge: Cambridge University Press.

Chomsky, N. (1959), Review of *Verbal Behavior* by B. F. Skinner (1957), New York: Appleton-Century-Crofts, *Language* 35(1), 26–58.

Chomsky, N. (1964), *Currents Issues in Linguistic Theory*, The Hague: Mouton.

Chomsky, N. (1965), *Aspects of the Theory of Syntax*, Cambridge, MA: MIT Press.

Chomsky, N. (1967), 'Some general properties of phonological rules', *Language* 43(1), 102–28.

Chomsky, N. (1970), 'Remarks on nominalization', in R. A. Jacobs and P. S. Rosenbaum (eds), *Readings in English Transformational Grammar*, Waltham, MA: Ginn, pp. 184–221.

Chomsky, N. [1955] (1975), *The Logical Structure of Linguistic Theory*, New York: Plenum.

Chomsky, N. (1986), *Knowledge of Language: Its Nature, Origin, and Use*, New York: Praeger.

Chomsky, N. (2012), *Foundations of Biolinguistics: Selected Writings*, ed. by N. Fukui, Tokyo: Iwanami Shoten.

Chomsky, N. and M. Halle (1968), *The Sound Pattern of English*, New York: Harper & Row.

Chomsky, N., M. Halle and F. Lukoff (1956), 'On accent and juncture in English', in M. Halle (ed.), *For Roman Jakobson: Essays on the Occasion of His Sixtieth Birthday, 11 October 1956*, The Hague: Mouton, pp. 65–80.

Collie, S. (2007), 'English stress preservation and stratal optimality theory', PhD dissertation, University of Edinburgh.

Cruttenden, A. (2014), *Gimson's Pronunciation of English*, 8th edn, London: Routledge.

Danielsson, B. (1948), *Studies on the Accentuation of Polysyllabic Latin, Greek, and Romance Loan-Words in English, with Special References to Those Ending in -able, -ate, -ator, -ible, -ic, -ical, and -ize*, Stockholm: Almqvist & Wiksell.

Dresher, B. E. and D. C. Hall (2022), 'Developments leading toward generative phonology', in B. E. Dresher and H. van der Hulst (eds.), *The Oxford History of Phonology*, Oxford: Oxford University Press, pp. 372–95.

Dresher, B. E. and A. Lahiri (2022), 'The foot in the history of English: Challenges to metrical coherence', in L. Bettelou, C. Cowie, P. Honeybone and G. Trousdale (eds), *English Historical Linguistics: Change in Structure and Meaning*, Current Issues in Linguistic Theory 358, Amsterdam: John Benjamins, pp. 42–59.

Durand, J. (1990), *Generative and Non-Linear Phonology*, London: Longman.

Durand, J. and B. Laks (eds) (2002), *Phonetics, Phonology, and Cognition*, Oxford Studies in Theoretical Linguistics, Oxford: Oxford University Press.

Elphinston, J. (1765), *The Principles of the English Language Digested; or, English Grammar Reduced to Analogy*, London: James Bettenham.

Fudge, E. C. (1969), 'Syllables', *Journal of Linguistics* 5(2), 253–86.
Fujiwara, Y. (1990), *Koeishi Inritsu Kenkyuu*, Hiroshima: Keisuisha.
Giegerich, H. J. (1999), *Lexical Strata in English: Morphological Causes, Phonological Effects*, Cambridge: Cambridge University Press.
Gimson, A. C. (1962), *An Introduction to the Pronunciation of English*, London: Edward Arnold.
Halle, M. (1959), *The Sound Pattern of Russian*, The Hague: Mouton.
Halle, M. (1962), 'Phonology in generative grammar', *Word* 18(1–3), 54–72.
Halle, M. (1973a), 'Prolegomena to a theory of word formation', *Linguistic Inquiry* 4(1), 3–16.
Halle, M. (1973b), 'Stress rules in English: A new version', *Linguistic Inquiry* 4(4), 451–64.
Halle, M. (1984), 'Grids and trees in metrical phonology', in W. U. Dressler, H. C. Luschützky, O. E. Pfeiffer and J. R. Rennison (eds), *Phonologica 1984*, Cambridge: Cambridge University Press, pp. 79–93.
Halle, M. and M. Kenstowicz (1991), 'Free element condition and cyclic versus non-cyclic stress', *Linguistic Inquiry* 22(3), 457–501.
Halle, M. and S. J. Keyser (1971), *English Stress: Its Form, Its Growth, and Its Role in Verse*, New York: Harper & Row.
Halle, M. and K. P. Mohanan (1985), 'Segmental phonology of modern English', *Linguistic Inquiry* 16(1), 57–116.
Halle, M. and J.-R. Vergnaud (1987a), *An Essay on Stress*, Cambridge, MA: MIT Press.
Halle, M. and J.-R. Vergnaud (1987b), 'Stress and the cycle', *Linguistic Inquiry* 18(1), 45–84.
Hammond, M. (1984), 'Constraining metrical theory: A modular theory of rhythm and destressing', PhD dissertation, University of California.
Hammond, M. (1999), *The Phonology of English: A Prosodic Optimality-Theoretic Approach*, Oxford: Oxford University Press.
Hauser, M. D., N. Chomsky and W. T. Fitch (2002), 'The faculty of language: What is it, who has it, and how did it evolve?', *Science* 298(5598), 1569–79.
Hayes, B. (1980), 'A metrical theory of stress rules', PhD dissertation, MIT.
Hayes, B. (1982), 'Extrametricality and English stress', *Linguistic Inquiry* 13(2), 227–76.
Hayes, B. (1984), 'The phonology of rhythm in English', *Linguistic Inquiry* 15(1), 33–74.
Idsardi, W. J. (1992), 'The computation of prosody', PhD dissertation, MIT.
Jones, D. [1918] (1964), *An Outline of English Phonetics*, Cambridge: Heffer.
Jones, D. [1950] (2009), *The Phoneme: Its Nature and Use*, Cambridge: W. Heffer & Son. Reprint, New York: Cambridge University Press.
Jones, D. [1917] (2011), *Cambridge English Pronouncing Dictionary*, Cambridge: Cambridge University Press, ed. by A. C. Gimson (until 14th edn), S. Ramsaran (14th edn), P. Roach (15th–18th edn), J. Hartman (15th–17th edn), J. Setter (17th–18th edn) and J. Esling (18th edn).
Kager, R. (1999), *Optimality Theory*, Cambridge: Cambridge University Press.
Kahn, D. (1976), 'Syllable-based generalizations in English phonology', PhD dissertation, MIT.

Kenstowicz, M. (1995), 'Cyclic vs. non-cyclic constraint evaluation', *Phonology* 12(3), 397–436.
Kenyon, J. S. [1924] (1951), *American Pronunciation*, Ann Arbor, MI: George Wahr.
Kenyon, J. S. and T. A. Knott [1944] (1953), *A Pronouncing Dictionary of American English*, Springfield, MA: Merriam-Webster.
Kingdon, R. (1958a), *The Groundwork of English Intonation*, London: Longmans Green.
Kingdon, R. (1958b), *The Groundwork of English Stress*, London: Longmans Green.
Kiparsky, P. (1979), 'Metrical structure assignment is cyclic', *Linguistic Inquiry* 10(3), 421–41.
Kiparsky, P. (1982a), 'From cyclic phonology to lexical phonology', in H. van der Hulst and N. Smith (eds), *The Structure of Phonological Representations I*, Dordrecht: Foris, pp. 131–75.
Kiparsky, P. (1982b), 'Lexical Morphology and Phonology', in the Linguistic Society of Korea (ed.), *Linguistics in the Morning Calm*, Seoul: Hanshin, pp. 3–91.
Kiparsky, P. (1998), 'Paradigm effects and opacity', Manuscript, Stanford University.
Kiparsky, P. (2000), 'Opacity and cyclicity', *The Linguistic Review* 17, 351–65.
Kiparsky, P. (2007), 'Description and explanation: English revisited', in the Panel Meeting entitled 'Phonology: An Appraisal of the Field in 2007', Handout from the 81st Annual Meeting of the Linguistic Society of America, held at Anaheim, CA, on 5 January 2007.
Kiparsky, P. (2015), 'Stratal OT: A synopsis and FAQs', in Y. E. Hsiao and L.-H. Wee (eds), *Capturing Phonological Shades Within and Across Languages*, Newcastle upon Tyne: Cambridge Scholars Publishing, pp. 2–44.
Kurath, H. (1964), *A Phonology and Prosody of Modern English*, Ann Arbor: University of Michigan Press.
Liberman, M. (1975), 'The intonational system of English', PhD dissertation, MIT.
Liberman, M. and A. Prince (1977), 'On stress and linguistic rhythm', *Linguistic Inquiry* 8(2), 249–336.
McCarthy, J. J. (1999), 'Sympathy and phonological opacity', *Phonology* 16(3), 331–99.
McCarthy, J. J. and A. Prince (1993a), 'Generalized alignment', in G. Booij and J. van Marle (eds), *Yearbook of Morphology 1993*, Dordrecht: Kluwer, pp. 79–153.
McCarthy, J. J. and A. Prince (1993b), 'Prosodic morphology I: Constraint interaction and satisfaction', Manuscript, University of Massachusetts, Amherst and Rutgers University.
McCarthy, J. J. and A. Prince (1995), 'Faithfulness and reduplicative identity', Manuscript, University of Massachusetts, Amherst and Rutgers University [ROA-60-0000, Rutgers Optimality Archive, <http://roa.rutgers.edu/>].
McCarthy, J. J. and A. Prince (1999), 'Faithfulness and identity in prosodic morphology', Manuscript, University of Massachusetts, Amherst and Rutgers University [ROA-216-0997, Rutgers Optimality Archive, <http://roa.rutgers.edu/>].
Marchand, H. (1969), *The Categories and Types of Present-Day English Word-Formation: A Synchronic-Diachronic Approach*, Munich: C. H. Beck.
Mascaró, J. (1976), 'Catalan phonology and the phonological cycle', PhD dissertation, MIT.
Mohanan, K. P. (1982), 'Lexical phonology', PhD dissertation, MIT.

Mohanan, K. P. (1985), 'Syllable structure and lexical strata in English', *Phonology Yearbook* 2, 139–55.
Newman, S. S. (1946), 'On the stress system of English', *Word* 2, 171–87.
Pater, J. (1995), 'On the nonuniformity of weight-to-stress and stress preservation effects in English', Manuscript, McGill University.
Pater, J. (2000), 'Non-uniformity in English secondary stress: The role of ranked and lexically specific constraints', *Phonology* 17(2), 237–74.
Pesetsky, D. (1979), 'Russian morphology and lexical phonology', Manuscript, MIT.
Prince, A. (1983), 'Relating to the grid', *Linguistic Inquiry* 14(1), 19–100.
Prince, A. and P. Smolensky (1993), 'Optimality Theory: Constraint interaction in generative grammar', Manuscript, Rutgers University and University of Colorado, Boulder. [(2004), *Optimality Theory: Constraint Interaction in Generative Grammar*, Oxford: Blackwell.]
Ross, J. R. (1972), 'A reanalysis of English word stress', in M. Brame (ed.), *Contributions to Generative Phonology*, Austin: University of Texas Press, pp. 229–323.
Selkirk, E. O. (1978), 'The syllable', Manuscript. [Published in H. van der Hulst and N. Smith (eds) (1982), *The Structure of Phonological Representations*, Part II, Dordrecht: Foris, pp. 337–83, and also partly in J. A. Goldsmith (ed.) (1999), *Phonological Theory: The Essential Readings*, Malden, MA: Blackwell Publishers, pp. 328–50.]
Selkirk, E. O. (1980), 'The role of prosodic categories in English word stress', *Linguistic Inquiry* 11(3), 563–605.
Selkirk, E. O. (1981), 'English compounding and the theory of word structure' in M. Moortgat, H. van der Hulst and T. Hoekstra (eds), *The Scope of Lexical Rules*, Dordrecht: Foris, pp. 229–78. [Also in Selkirk (1984b).]
Selkirk, E. O. (1984a), 'On the major class features and syllable theory', in M. Aronoff and R. T. Oehrle (eds), *Language Sound Structure*, Cambridge, MA: MIT Press, pp. 107–36.
Selkirk, E. O. (1984b), *Phonology and Syntax: The Relation between Sound and Structure*, Cambridge, MA: MIT Press.
Shimizu, K. (1978), *Seisei Oninron Gaisetu*, Tokyo: Shinozakishorin.
Siegel, D. (1974), 'Topics in English morphology', PhD dissertation, MIT.
Smith, H. L., Jr. (1954), *Linguistic Science and the Teaching of English*, The Ingris Lecture 1954, Cambridge, MA: Harvard University Press.
Sundby, B. (1953), *Chistopher Cooper's English Teacher (1687)*, Copenhagen: Ejnar Munksgaard.
Trager, G. L. and B. Bloch (1941), 'The syllabic phonemes of English', *Language* 17(3), 223–46.
Trager, G. L. and H. L. Smith, Jr. [1951] (1957), *An Outline of English Structure*, Studies in Linguistics: Occasional Papers 3, Washington DC: American Council of Learned Societies.
Walker, J. (1791), *A Critical Pronouncing Dictionary and Expositor of the English Language*, London: Robinson.
Wells, J. C. (1990), *Longman Pronunciation Dictionary*, London: Longman.
Wells, J. C. (2008), *Longman Pronunciation Dictionary*, 3rd edn, Harlow: Pearson Education.

Williams, E. (1981), 'On the notions "lexically related" and "head of a word"', *Linguistic Inquiry* 12(2), 245–74.

Yamada, E. (2010), *Subsidiary Stresses in English*, Tokyo: Kaitakusha.

Yamada, E. (2018), 'Plato's problem and recursiveness in English word stress theory: The case of *SPE*', in N. Nishioka, M. Fukuda, K. Matsuse, N. Nagatani, T. Ogata and M. Hashimoto (eds), *Kotoba wo Amu*, Tokyo: Kaitakusha, pp. 156–67.

2 English Word Stress and the Guierrian School

Quentin Dabouis, Jean-Michel Fournier,
Pierre Fournier and Marjolaine Martin

0 Introduction

At the end of the sixties, Lionel Guierre had been studying English stress for a number of years in view of a French doctoral dissertation when Chomsky and Halle published *The Sound Pattern of English* (1968, hereafter *SPE*), a truly revolutionary view of the workings of English stress, though its actual concern was more likely to have been linguistics and phonological theory than English stress *per se*. In view of what he considered a momentous scientific event, Guierre took the rare decision to re-start his analysis from scratch by resorting to computer analysis, which was becoming more easily available to scientists at the time. Let us recall that at the time, the challenge was daunting: each entry of Jones's *English Pronouncing Dictionary* (12th edition) had to be transferred on to a punched card, with an appropriate and efficient coding transfer, even before attempting any kind of systematic analysis. Guierre finally succeeded in completing his analysis of the very first computerised corpus of English pronunciation by the end of the seventies, when he presented his doctoral dissertation which allowed him to become the first Professor of English pronunciation in the history of French university.

Except for a few specialists around the world, his dissertation remained mostly unknown, however, as it was never published as such: unlike Chomsky and Halle's book, its scope was strictly limited to English stress and pronunciation, with no linguistic theoretical ambitions. Guierre's work is best known through his *Drills in English Stress-Patterns* (1984a), a book aimed at students of English as a foreign language, but with a foreword by A. C. Gimson himself:

> L. Guierre has carried out a computer analysis of the stress-patterns of the majority of words in the Jones *English Pronouncing Dictionary* and has been able to derive from this analysis sufficient rules of general validity to be of great practical help for the foreign learner. [...]

> The tendencies of word-stress which have emerged are likely to reflect the underlying rules which the native English speaker has as part of his linguistic generative capability [. . .]
>
> (Guierre 1984a: 7)

Because of the very nature of his corpus, Guierre integrated the written form into his analysis, arguing that a 'grammar of the reader' was as relevant as a 'grammar of the speaker' (purely oral rules) in the case of most English speakers, and should be taken into account when endeavouring to understand the stress system of English. A key illustration of this is the behaviour of consonant geminates, which share certain features with 'actual' consonant clusters.[1] Generally speaking, the written form adds clues to a purely oral grammar: thus penultimate stress in words such as *vanilla* can be accounted for within a grammar of the reader but is exceptional from an oral point of view.

Similarly, Guierre adopted the dictionary view of stress as a rhythm (and intonation) marker, and thus worked with three levels of stress, namely primary, secondary and unstressed,[2] even though the latter might contain a full vowel. Contrary to Chomsky and Halle's work, his large-scale empirical study led him to seriously question the relationship between syllable weight and stress placement and to look for other parameters as viable explanations.[3]

Though he never actually founded any kind of 'school', his students, including Jean-Michel Fournier and his own students in turn, have endeavoured to refine and expand Guierre's analysis: the aim of the present chapter is to summarise the views on English stress we have developed over the years. This approach can be defined through five main characteristics, which will be detailed in the course of this chapter:

- It is an empirical approach which favours the use of large datasets, often from computerised pronouncing dictionaries.
- Orthographic information is taken into consideration, unlike most phonological theories which tend to ignore it.
- The morphological approach which is adopted is distinct from mainstream practice in analyses of English phonology in that we assume that semantically opaque constituents play a role in stress assignment (and other phonological processes).
- The role of syllable structure in stress assignment is assumed to be more restricted than assumed in generative analyses.
- We assume that English phonology includes a number of different subsystems which correspond to different lexical strata of borrowings (or words perceived as such).

We will start by discussing the first characteristic of this approach, the use of large corpora (section 1), before we turn to the analysis of English stress developed within this framework (section 2). We will then turn to another characteristic of the Guierrian approach: the assumption that English phonology is not monolithic but rather a dynamic system of interactive subsystems (section 3). Another expansion of Guierre's analysis was to compare Standard British English, on which Guierre based his work, with other varieties of English around the world. This will be discussed in section 4.

1 An empirical approach

At the dawn of generative phonology, Chomsky and Halle defined English phonology in a way that has dominated most phonologists' approaches to the field ever since:

> Given the goals of the research reported on here [universal grammar], exceptions to rules are of interest only if they suggest a different general framework or the formulation of deeper rules. In themselves they are of no interest.
>
> (Chomsky and Halle 1968: ix)

Therefore, they seemed to justify the absence of a systematic empirical enquiry, which would be the only way to obtain full lists of exceptions, on the grounds of their interest in universal grammar. We would certainly agree with their view on exceptions, as they can indeed provide useful evidence of areas of conflicts within the phonology as well as useful data in which other researchers might perceive a regularity where the original authors did not. However, we can hardly see how an interest in more 'general principles' could justify the absence of an endeavour to empirically confirm those principles.

In recent years, however, this issue has been drawing increasing attention. Collie (2007: 3) remarks in the introduction of her dissertation on stress preservation that 'up until now, stress preservation has simply been assumed to occur in English, with no support from any serious and extensive empirical investigation'; Wenszky (2004: 12) notes in the introduction of her book on secondary stress, 'My last general remark about some of the stress theories that I reviewed is that it seemed that the stress rules in them were developed on the basis of the analysis of some typical words, but not whole classes of words.' This criticism has also been extended to one of the last general books on English phonology, Hammond (1999); McMahon's review reads as follows:

> At no point [. . .] does the author tell us which databases [he used], and how they were and can be accessed. This seems unacceptable. For one thing, courtesy in scientific enquiry involves ensuring that your results can be repeated by other investigators, and without knowing where the

sample comes from, that isn't possible; it is true that linguistics has not always lived up to that high aim, with its concentration on intuition and introspection.

(McMahon 2001: 424)

This seems to be a major issue in English phonology: the same example words are used over and over again without any discussion about the representativeness of these examples. One striking case is the use of Amerindian names in the literature on English stress,[4] as these words clearly are borrowings, which implies that there is no guarantee that they can be used to illustrate general principles of native English phonology, on top of being proper nouns, which often behave distinctly from regular words (see section 3 and Guierre 1979: §1.4.5; Raffelsiefen 1993: 90–3). However, the Guierrian School has a rather different approach.

In his 1979 dissertation, Guierre adopted an empirical approach; this was because he felt that a true description of English was still lacking, which was making it extremely difficult to conduct a rigorous evaluation of phonological theories (Guierre 1979: §1.4.1). He argued that exceptions should be extensively listed, enabling researchers to evaluate the efficiency of the postulated rules and to see whether these irregularities could be attributed to the fact that certain words belong to two or more classes governed by contradictory rules (Guierre 1979: §1.4.3). Other authors have carried on this mostly descriptive work, looking for the most efficient system to account for stress placement and the pronunciation of vowels, without claiming that such a system should be regarded as a model of the competence of an average or ideal speaker. Guierre's initial study consisted of a description of the 34,000-word corpus he had constituted using the 12th edition of Jones's *English Pronouncing Dictionary*, and virtually all subsequent works in the Guierrian approach have used pronouncing dictionaries as their main data source. Dictionaries have qualities, and they have flaws. The criticisms addressed to Guierrian works often point out the limitations of pronunciation dictionaries but often fail in providing a viable alternative. We see the study of pronunciation dictionaries as one way to approach the issue of English stress, with its advantages and disadvantages, but we do not claim that this is the only way this issue should be studied. Indeed, nonce-word reading tasks (Domahs et al. 2014; Turcsan and Herment 2015), or grammaticality judgement tasks (Steriade and Stanton 2020), or the study of spontaneous speech (Hanote et al. 2010) are other valid ways to approach the issue.

The obvious advantage of studying pronunciation dictionaries is their size: they give us access to large numbers of words and allow us to assess the validity of rules in quantitative terms and not simply postulate their existence on the grounds of intuition, introspection or someone else's lists of examples. Aronoff (1976: 116) even argued that consulting a dictionary is 'the closest we can come to the lexicon of a speaker's language'. Therefore, the study of a dictionary could be argued to be the study of a form of an 'ideal' speaker's lexicon. If we are to use these dictionaries as our main data source, however, it is essential to also acknowledge their limitations. As Dahak (2006) points out, the transcriptions, although closer to a phonemic representation, are neither truly phonological nor phonetic: the use they make of [ŋ], [i], [u], for instance, clearly points towards a hybrid representation. Obviously, dictionaries contain mistakes (typing errors, missing symbols, and so on). Dictionaries often describe 'standard' varieties of English, which should probably be described as a form of model towards which regional accents converge when they neutralise rather than as an English accent in itself.[5] Dictionaries can also be reliable for certain things and not for others. For example, they are generally reliable for the position of stresses, but different dictionaries have been shown to employ different syllabification choices (Ballier and Martin 2010). This means that any use of the syllabifications in a given dictionary has to acknowledge that choice in the first place, as they will necessarily be biased by that choice. Finally, pronunciation dictionaries are often regarded as 'one person's works' as they are mostly based on the authors' speech and intuition. However, the most recent editions tend to display 'preference polls', and some recent works have endeavoured to verify certain dictionary transcriptions with native speakers (Martin 2011) or in spontaneous speech (Videau 2013) and have generally confirmed the dictionary data.

2 Main stress rules and the role of morphology

In this section, we present the system of stress placement, based mostly on J.-M. Fournier (2007, 2010b). We start by presenting the general principles governing stress placement (section 2.1), then discuss the importance of morphological factors (section 2.2) and segmental factors (section 2.3). Finally, we briefly discuss secondary stress (section 2.4).

2.1 General principles

There are four general principles governing stress placement in English, which we adapt from J.-M. Fournier (2010b: 12) in (1).

(1)   General stress principles
        1. Every lexical unit has one and only one major stress.[6]
        2. There can be no sequence of two stresses within a lexical unit.
        3. No lexical unit can begin with two unstressed syllables.
        4. Syllables which receive neither stress /1/ nor stress /2/ are unstressed.

These principles can be found in other theoretical frameworks expressed in different ways, for example constraints on feet well-formedness in frameworks using feet, like Prosodic Phonology (Hammond 1999; Nespor and Vogel 1986; Pater 1995, 2000; Selkirk 1980) or Burzio (1994). In Optimality Theory, this is done through the use of constraints like PARSE-σ, FTBIN and *CLASH.

Guierrian authors also make use of the notion of functional consonant clusters (hereafter C_2), which play an important role in English phonology and are defined in (2).

(2)   Functional consonant cluster
- <x>;
- Every cluster of at least two consonants, except <Ch>, <Cr> and <C + syllabic C>, including orthographic consonant geminates or pseudo-geminates (for example <tt>, <rr>, <gg> or <sc>).

(J.-M. Fournier 2010b: 28)

These clusters are defined by their behaviour (see Guierre 1979: §§3.4.1–3.5.11):

- They tend to 'attract' stress when found in pre-final position (for example *colóssus, advántage, elíxir*).
- The vowels that precede them are short[7] (for example *acc[ó]mplice, [æ]mber, spagh[é]tti*).
- They forbid reduction when they follow an initial pre-tonic vowel[8] (for example *[ɔː]rchéstral, [æ]ctívity, c[e]nsórial*).

The phonological behaviours here associated with the right-hand context of a vowel (the number of following consonants) are more widely described using syllable structure. However, syllable-based analyses oppose open syllables to closed syllables, a distinction which cannot capture the distinctions observed between C^0 (absence of any following consonant, i.e. prevocalic or word-final positions), C (one following consonant, or non-functional clusters) and C_2. Crucially, C^0 and C quite generally correspond to open syllables, but the behaviour of preceding vowels distinguishes these two structures: stressed vowels followed by C^0 are always long while those followed by C may be long or short. Moreover, the definition in (2) includes /Cl/ clusters among functional consonant clusters but excludes /Cr/ clusters. This is based on the analysis of words in (-)V́C_1V#, in which the stressed vowel is expected to be long unless it is followed by a C_2. Words with /Cl/ usually have short vowels (for example *ígloo, úgly, kíbla, tábla*) while those with /Cr/ usually have long vowels (for example *cóbra, mícra, négro, zébra*), which suggests that /Cl/ clusters should be analysed as functional consonant clusters. However, these two types of C + liquid clusters are traditionally expected to behave in similar ways in most frameworks as they may both form branching onsets. It remains to be seen whether these distinctions can be captured by other theoretical devices such as feet, or in frameworks which do not use the notion of syllables such as CV Phonology (Scheer 2004) or theories using intervals (Hirsch 2014; Steriade 2012).

Let us now present the importance of morphological factors in stress assignment in English.

2.2 Morphological factors

In this section, we discuss the three main morphological elements which influence stress placement in English. We start by discussing the different types of prefixation (section 2.2.1), then discuss suffixation and the role of strong endings (section 2.2.2) and conclude with compounding, which includes neoclassical compounding (section 2.2.3).

2.2.1 Prefixation

In the Guierrian tradition, two types of prefixes are distinguished: separable prefixes and inseparable prefixes. Separable prefixes have a transparent meaning and are attached to a free base in such a way that the meaning of the prefixed construction can be directly deduced from the meaning of the prefix and that of the base (for example *re-do*, *unlike*, *ex-boyfriend*). Inseparable prefixes can be attached to either a free or a bound base, but the meaning of the prefixed construction cannot be deduced from the meaning of its parts even when they have an independent meaning (for example *below*, *recover*, *restrain*, *collect*). The classification of a prefix into one of these two categories must therefore be done in a given construction, so a prefix may be separable in certain constructions and inseparable in others. Both of these types of prefixes have an impact on stress, which is discussed below.

Separable prefixes have a stress behaviour comparable to that of independent words: they often receive (generally secondary) stress, even if it contradicts principle 2 (see (1) above), for example *rè-dó, impóssible, cò-wórker*.[9] This observation leads J.-M. Fournier (2010b: 12) to define stress in English as an identifier of lexical units, lexical units being defined as semantically inseparable units. In English, he identifies two types of lexical units:

- autonomous lexical units: words, which receive primary stress
- non-autonomous lexical units: separable prefixes, which receive secondary stress.

This means that principle 2 applies only within the domain of a lexical unit, as sequences of stresses are commonly attested for adjacent lexical units.

In fact, this stress behaviour can also be found in antonymic pairs[10] such as *include* ~ *exclude* or *inflate* ~ *deflate* in which the prefixes have semantic and phonological properties comparable to separable prefixes (Raffelsiefen 1993, 2007, 2015) and for which J.-M. Fournier (1996) notes that 'the semantic opposition between prefixed constructions can virtually be brought down to that between prefixes'. Such a behaviour is occasionally found in words with transparent prefixes outside such pairs (for example àcéphalous, dècápitate, dèsálinate), which suggests that the semantic motivation of the prefix can be sufficient to open the possibility of stressing the prefix, even when the base is bound (Dabouis 2016b).

Inseparable prefixes include what are traditionally known as Class I prefixes as well as historical prefixed constructions such as *preclude, obtain, insist* or *select*, which are a well-known problem in morphology (Anderson 1992: 55; Aronoff 1976: 12–15; Bauer et al. 2013: 15–16; Katamba and Stonham 2006: 23; Mudgan 2015; Plag 2003: 30–3), for the constituents of these constructions share a number of properties with morphemes but do not have any clearly identifiable meaning. Early generative phonology did make reference to these prefixes (Chomsky and Halle 1968: 94; Halle and Keyser 1971: 37; Liberman and Prince 1977), but they were abandoned on the grounds of their supposed unlearnability. However, there is ample evidence from psycholinguistics that speakers do access such opaque structures, as seen in lexical decision tasks (Forster and Azuma 2000; Pastizzo and Feldman 2004), reading studies (Ktori et al. 2016, 2018; Rastle and Coltheart 2000) and event-related potential (ERP) studies (McKinnon et al. 2003). These structures are also associated with different phonological behaviours. Stress is one of them, as inseparable prefixed constructions other than nouns (and without strong suffixes or endings, see the following section) always receive primary stress on their root, never on their prefixes (for example recéive, seléct, alóud, amóng, devélop, còntradíct, intervéne), unlike non-prefixed words which follow the general rules detailed in section 2.3 (for more details, see Chapter 5 of this volume). Inseparable prefixes also display a distinct vowel reduction behaviour in the initial pretonic position, as vowels in closed syllables usually do not reduce, unless they are part of such a prefix. This observation appears throughout the literature on English phonology (Chomsky and Halle 1968: 118; Halle and Keyser 1971: 37; Liberman and Prince 1977: 284–5; Guierre 1979: 253; Selkirk 1980; Hayes 1982; Halle and Vergnaud 1987: 239; Pater 2000; Hammond 2003; Collie 2007: 129, 215, 318–19) and has recently been empirically confirmed (by Dabouis and J.-M. Fournier 2019). However, the issue of how speakers access such semantically opaque structures is still an open question.[11]

2.2.2 Suffixation and endings

In the Guierrian approach, two categories of suffixes are generally acknowledged: strong suffixes and neutral suffixes.[12] The expression 'strong endings' is generally preferred to 'strong suffixes' within the Guierrian School because endings, not just suffixes, may influence the location of primary stress.[13]

For example, *-ion* is a suffix in *location* because the morphological and semantic links between the verb *locate* and the noun *location* through a derivational process are obvious. On the contrary, in *Napoleon*, *-eon* actually belongs to the root and cannot be considered as a suffix. Nonetheless, the location of primary stress in both words (*location* and *Napoleon*) can be accounted for by the stress rule corresponding to the *-eon/-ion* ending.[14]

The category to which a given ending belongs is determined through a systematic comparison between the stress patterns of bases and their derivatives. If stress (or vowel) shifts are observed, they demonstrate the influence of the ending which is then classified as 'strong' since it can modify the original stress or vocalic pattern of the base. But if no stress shifts between bases and derivatives are attested, then the ending is considered as 'neutral'.

The derivational link between bases and derivatives is local and semantically constrained.[15] The local nature of the process is illustrated by the words *hístory*, *históric* and *histórìcism*. The base of *histórìcism* is *históric* and the base of *históric* is *hístory*: *histórìcism* should not be derived from *hístory* because of the very existence of *históric*, as the morpho-semantic reference for the reproduction/imitation process of the Neutral Derivation Law (J.-M. Fournier 2007).[16] Of course, the base must be attested to play such a role: consider the word *theátrical* whose base is necessarily *théatre* because *theátric* is not attested in contemporary English.[17]

In the base–derivative pairs in (3), no stress shifts are observed.

(3)   *abórtion → abórtionist, emótion → emótionless, cólour → cólourful, fáte → fátal, intérpret → intérpreting, jóurnal → jóurnalism, relígious → relígiously, éscalate → éscalator, achíeve → achíevable*

The adjunction of these suffixes does not modify the original stress patterns of the bases. Consequently, they are classified as neutral. These examples are representative of the Neutral Derivation Law.

On the contrary, in the pairs in (4), stress shifts are attested.

(4)   *púlse → pulsáte*,[18] *réfuge → rèfugée, Chína → Chinése, thém → themsélves, fóur → fourtéen, héro → heróic, ínstinct → instínctive, sphéroid → spheróidal, sýllable → syllábify, módern → modérnity, vólume → volúminous, spéctacle → spectácular, túmult → tumúltuous, cóurage → courágeous, consíder → consìderátion, céremony → cèremónial*

The stress shifts that can be observed between the stress patterns of the bases and their derivatives are the direct result of the influence of the endings. If an ending is associated with a set position of stress and can therefore entail stress shifts, then it is classified as a strong ending. In other words, strong endings compel us to ignore the relationship between base and derivative that is otherwise phonologically actualised through the Neutral Derivation Law. In the examples in (4), strong endings are classified according to the stress patterns of the derived forms[19] (stress is either on the final syllable, the penultimate syllable or the antepenultimate syllable). Strong endings are often called 'stress-imposing' endings in the literature, or described as such. This point will not be dealt with here in detail, but it has been demonstrated that the term 'stress-imposing' is not coherent with their role in the derivational process. They do not in fact 'impose' a specific and systematic stress pattern, but actually prevent any reference to the phonological properties of bases as concerns primary stress (J.-M. Fournier 1998).

Stress shifts are not systematic when dealing with the base/derivative stress comparison (for example *vanílla* → *vaníllic*). Such cases are called non-relevant pairs and can be accounted for by the convergence of two different stress rules with the same resulting stressed syllable. The prefinal stress of *vanilla* is enough to justify the stress of *vanillic* through the Neutral Derivation Law. But the word *vanillic* would also be stressed on the penultimate syllable because of the *-ic* suffix. This suffix is a strong one, but its influence cannot be demonstrated in this pair. However, considering that the adjunction of *-ic* in *hístory* → *históric* and thousands of other base–derivative pairs triggers a stress shift whenever the Neutral Derivation Law contradicts the penultimate stress associated with *-ic*, *-ic* is classified as a strong ending and analysed as the cause of penultimate stress, even in the particular case of non-pertinent pairs; the analysis is identical for all strong endings.

The neutral/strong distinction is determined through a systematic analysis of the stress patterns of corresponding bases and derivatives. But it is also extended to suffixed words which do not have any attested base in English, as long as the semantic properties of the suffix are preserved. For example, *acóustic*, *ánxious*, *idéntity*, *sapónify* are suffixed words with bound bases. However, the influence of the suffix is obvious, and the resulting stress patterns are identical to those of derived words which are built with the same suffixes. Therefore, the strong nature is first determined through a stress comparison between bases and derivatives and then extended to suffixed words with bound bases (for example *acoustic*), as well as to words exhibiting the same ending which does not correspond to a morphological boundary (for example *Napoleon*), on account of the associated stress pattern.

The category of neutral suffixes also has to be refined because one might think that the presence of a neutral suffix necessarily implies the principle of the Neutral Derivation Law and a stress analysis directly based on the base. In some rare cases, words whose suffixes are neutral are attached to bound bases (for example *grateful*, *gormless*). In these specific cases, these items are not interpreted as derivatives as far as stress assignment is concerned. Morphological parameters are neutralised, and stress rules are based on segmental considerations such as the number of syllables.

Moreover, the segmental environment preceding a suffix may affect its behaviour. For example, *-ive* is neutral in *accúmulative*, where no stress shift is to be observed relative to its base *accúmulate*, even if it generates preantepenultimate stress just as all other words whose base ends with a single consonant. But when this suffix is used to create adjective derivatives and preceded by a consonant cluster, it appears that it becomes strong (for example *ínstinct → instínctive*).[20]

As in other frameworks, an intermediate category of 'mixed' suffixes can be used. Indeed, certain suffixes show contradictory behaviours by being sometimes stress-affecting and sometimes not (for example *-able*, *-ist*, *-ory*, *-ly*). Such intermediate cases are discussed by Trevian (2007) and are often caused by ongoing change in the stress behaviour of the suffix, as shown by Castanier (2016).

2.2.3 Compounding

Compounds in English form another morphological class which obeys specific stress rules.[21] If compounds are considered to be semantically inseparable units (i.e. if they are lexical units), this implies that there is only one primary stress which is assigned to the whole, whether the two elements that constitute the compound be orthographically attached, hyphenated or separated by a space. According to Guierre (1979), compounds are usually stressed on their first element. However, this principle does not determine the location of the stressed syllable but rather indicates on which element stress assignment rules should apply. The first element is then subject to the same exact morphophonological rules that govern the rest of the lexicon. Here are some examples in (5) of compounds that are stressed on their first element.[22]

(5)   *bláckbird, létterbox, bláckmail, sérvice station, róad-test, Báker Street, machínegun*

The few exceptions are neither numerous nor coherent enough to allow for sub-rules accounting for the stressing of the second element.[23]

Neoclassical compounds constitute a specific sub-group of compounds in English because they are composed of elements of (mostly) Greek and Latin origin, often referred to in the literature as 'combining forms' (for example *hetero-*, *hydro-*, *philo-*, *ortho-*, *-vor(ous)*, *-gene*). This specific vocabulary, which is either borrowed from Greek and Latin or directly created through English lexicographic rules, is in constant expansion especially because of scientific innovation. The English lexicological tradition is unclear concerning the status of these elements because no clear distinction is made between compounding and affixation (Bauer 1983, 2005, 2006; Katamba and Stonham 2006: 336; Plag 2003: 74). The frontier between these two notions is also quite unclear in lexicographic sources, and the *Oxford English Dictionary* may categorise as prefixes what seem to be representatives of the category of 'initial combining forms' (ICFs).[24] Concerning the stressing of neoclassical compounds, syllable weight is still considered to be the main factor in the literature.

The Guierrian approach uses an alphabetical representation of neoclassical compounds (Guierre 1984a: 117), A+B(+C), which stands for both existing types: bound root + bound root + suffix (for example *carni+vor+ous*) or prefix + bound root + suffix (for example *ana+log+ous*). It highlights the importance of morphological boundaries and in particular the one existing between the second element and a potential suffix. First, stress shifts are more frequently observed through a base/derivative stress analysis than for words with other morphological structures. Indeed, suffixes such as *-al* or *-ous* always behave as strong endings within neoclassical compounds (for example *cárnivore → carnívorous, ísocline → isoclínal*). Second, some B roots, when suffixed, seem to have a certain degree of 'attractiveness' relative to the location of primary stress. Thus, neoclassical compounds with suffixed attractive roots are stressed in /(-)10/, whereas compounds with suffixed non-attractive roots are stressed in /(-)100/.[25]

Finally, Guierre (1979: 740) claims that neoclassical roots are accentually invariant. This means that whenever they are not constrained by the stress patterns associated with strong suffixes or by clash avoidance, they tend to retain the same stress pattern. In non-suffixed neoclassical compounds, primary stress is normally assigned as it is assigned in 'normal' compounds: the first element receives primary stress and is stressed following the general segmental factors detailed in the following section.[26] This pattern of stress assignment can lead to extended stress lapses (for example *rádiograph, cínemascope, láparoscope, stéreoscope*). Stress invariance, Guierre claims, also manifests in secondary stress placement, as the preferred stress pattern of a given root would be adopted, even if that contradicts stress preservation from its closest base. For example, the root *laryngo-* usually has penultimate stress (for example *larýngograph, larýngoscope*) and keeps its pen-initial stress in *laryngológical*, regardless of the fact that *làryngólogy* has initial stress. However, no systematic investigation of secondary stress placement in neoclassical compounds has yet been conducted to test this claim.

2.3 Segmental factors

When morphological factors are neutralised and can no longer account for the location of stress, segmental criteria come into play with two distinct sub-parameters. The first sub-parameter is the number of syllables. Disyllables are stressed on their first syllable (for example *cóllege, súburb, párent, públish, fóllow*) and words of more than two syllables are stressed on the antepenultimate according to the Normal Stress Rule (NSR), which accounts for the stress pattern of a large majority of long words in English, as illustrated in (6).

(6)   álphabet, áttitude, spécimen, páradise, tólerance, ambássador, aspáragus

The NSR applies except for a (relatively) limited number of words where the second sub-parameter, the segmental characteristics of the end of the word, are regularly associated with penultimate stress. First, when a word contains a prefinal consonant cluster (i.e. a cluster found between the last two syllables) (7).

(7)   appréntice, Novémber, intéstine, seméster, repúgnance

However, as argued by J.-M. Fournier (2010a), this rules works best in recent Latinate borrowings from modern Latin (for example pròpagánda, enígma, memento) or languages such as Italian, Spanish or Portuguese (for example anacónda, extràvagánza, dìlettánte). Its efficiency is far more limited in words which do not fall into that category (for example sácristan, cálendar, lávender, mínister, índustry).

Second, when a word has the segmental characteristics of what Guierre dubbed the 'Italian rule' (words which ends with a <VCV#> structure, where the pre-final consonant is an alveolar (except <l> and <r>) followed by a non-mute monographic vowel (except <y>)) (8).

(8)   banána, bikíni, potáto, armáda, mosquíto, kimóno, angína

The rule is named 'Italian' after the high number of Italian loanwords that it applies to, but it also concerns a number of Spanish, Portuguese, Japanese and Latin loanwords. Since the stressed vowel is usually long in this latter case, one could think that this part of the Guierrian analysis is quite close to the *SPE* conception of the role of syllable weight. In Guierre's view, however, if consonant clusters do indeed seem to play some role in stress placement, the nature of the vowel in 'Italian' cases is actually *due* to the stress pattern, and therefore in no way a factor of stress location as *SPE* proposed (see Chapter 4 of this volume).

2.4 Secondary stress

The position of secondary stress is mostly constrained by the general principles in (1) and stress preservation from the base in suffixed words. We have already discussed the secondary stress of separable prefixes in section 2.2.1, which is of a different nature, and will not comment any further here.

In non-derived words, secondary stress tends to be on the first syllable (for example èlecampáne, càtamarán, àbracadábra, còriánder, ànacónda), which is the only possible pattern for words with only two pre-tonic syllables, as principle 2 forbids adjacent stresses. There are a few non-derived words which may have secondary stress on their second syllable, for example *amòntilládo, Epìmanóndas, Monòngahéla*), which Dabouis et al. (2017) have found to be attributable to the closedness of the first two syllables and the presence or absence of an initial onset. Pen-initial stress was found to be more likely if:

- the word has no initial onset
- the first syllable is open
- the second syllable is closed.

In suffixed derivatives, the position of secondary stress is determined by the position of stresses in the base, which is almost systematically preserved[27] (for example *nátionalist → nàtionalístic, spíritual → spìrituálity, official → officialése, imágine → imàginátion, instruméntal → instrumentálity*) unless the resulting pattern would violate principle 2 (*morphólogy → mòrphológical* (*morphòlógical*), *objective → òbjectívity* (*objèctívity), *deríve → dèrivátion* (*derìvátion)).[28]

When a derivative has several embedded bases and primary stress shifts several times rightward in the course of derivation, it is usually the stresses of the immediately embedded base which are preserved (for example *canál → cánalize → cànalizátion* (*canàlizátion), *person → persónify → persònificátion* (*pèrsonificátion)), except in rare cases where the two patterns of secondary stress are associated with different meanings, as in the example in (9).[29]

(9) *cértify* ⟨ *certíficate — certìficátion* 'providing with a certificate'
  cèrtificátion 'act of certifying'
(Guierre 1979: 325)

For an overview of recent empirical studies regarding secondary stress, see Dabouis (2020).

3 Several phonologies in English?

English is a 'hybrid' language because its phonological system is the result of a fusion process between Romance and Germanic principles (J.-M. Fournier 2007; Minkova 2006), which follow different logics when it comes to stress assignment. In Romance languages, stress is assigned from the right edge, whereas in Germanic languages, it is assigned from the left edge and is normally root-initial (which often translates into word-initial stress; also note that prefixes are not relevant, as far as primary stress assignment is concerned). Such a situation leads to the idea of several co-existing phonologies in contemporary English and, more generally, of several subsystems associated with different parts of the lexicon, each with phonological, graphophonological, morphological and semantic specificities.

The English lexicon proper, mainly of French and Germanic origins whose stress rules are governed by Romance and Germanic principles, is the first category. As we have seen previously, morphological considerations play a crucial role in the stress system of contemporary English, which stands in stark contrast to Romance and Germanic phonologies; indeed, while attested bases play no role in Romance phonology, since its rules are indifferent to their morphology, the exact reverse holds true for Germanic phonology where suffixation has no impact on stress patterns established relative to the beginning. For opposite reasons, derivation is thus a parameter in neither of the two systems: once combined, however, suffixes acquired a role they did not have before, where Romance suffixes ('strong endings') signal independent stress rules as opposed to Germanic suffixes ('neutral suffixes') that are stress preserving (the Neutral Derivation Law).[30] Although these two subsystems can still be distinguished, they are strongly intricated and overall follow the same generalisations.

The second lexical category that must be distinguished from the rest of the English lexicon is loanwords that constitute at least two subsystems within the English stress system. French loanwords constitute a distinct subsystem because their behaviour is distinct from that of other loanwords. The reproduction of the French final demarcative stress has led the way to the creation of a final stress pattern which is clearly associated with words of French origin today in English (for example *noblésse, gazétte, chandelíer, balláde, liquéur, uníque*). As for other subsystems, this stress specificity is correlated to non-phonological properties (for example 'prestige' semantics, specific graphophonological correspondences such as silent final consonants).

Other loanwords in English mainly come from Italian, Spanish, Portuguese, Arabic or Japanese. They generally share semantic characteristics and are restricted to specific semantic areas such as food, arts, leisure, clothing, law or scientific glossaries. But they also often exhibit one of two common segmental structures: either <-VCV#>, with final <a,e (non-mute),i,o,u> (for example *martíni, peséta, karáte, Medína, Iráqi, màcchiáto*), or <-VC$_2$V(C$_0$(e))#> (for example *anténna, aráchnid, referéndum, andánti, piménto, vanílla*) with a distinctive preferential stress pattern for primary stress on the penultimate syllable.[31] This specific stress pattern seems to be a strong indicator of the foreign origin of these loanwords.

Finally, another subsystem which can be identified is that concerning learned words, many of which are neoclassical compounds. The latter are best identified through their stress behaviour, as argued by Guierre (1979: 740), and they have several specificities when it comes to stress (compound-like stress assignment, penultimate stress in words with a prefinal consonant cluster, stress invariance), but also non-phonological properties (specific morphological constituents, specialised semantics, certain graphophonological correspondences).

Therefore, we argue that English phonology should not be viewed as a monolithic system, but rather as a dynamic system composed of several interacting subsystems, each with its own phonological, graphophonological, morphological, segmental and semantic specificities. This idea is developed at length in Dabouis and P. Fournier (2022).

4 Variation between English varieties

4.1 Lexical stress intervarietal variation in the literature

The topic of lexical stress variation between standard varieties of English was studied by Martin (2011) based on extensive data-supported research in line with the Guierrian approach. She specifically worked on Standard British English (SBE), Standard American English (SAmE) and Standard Australian English (SAusE). Other works of note include Collins and Mees (2008), Cruttenden (2014), Duchet (1994), Mitchell and Delbridge (1965) and Peters (2007) regarding this issue, bearing in mind that they do not always agree.

For Collins and Mees the variations are significant:

> There are some significant differences between British and American in (1) allocation of stress, (2) the pronunciation of unstressed syllables.
> (Collins and Mees 2008: 154)

Whereas Duchet states:

> There are few systematic differences between the British stressing system and the American one.
> (Duchet 1994: 118)

For most of these authors the differences mainly occur in dissyllabic verbs ending in *-ate* which tend to be stressed on their final syllable in SBE rather than on their initial syllable, and in nouns and adjectives ending in *-ative*, *-ary*, *-ery* and *-ory* for which a penultimate secondary stress can be observed in SAmE (for example *military, arbitrary, mandatory* being stressed /1020/ in SAmE and /10(0)0/ in SBE according to Collins and Mees 2008).

Using all the 148 items given in the references cited above regarding SBE, SAmE and SAusE, Martin showed that all had at least one variant with a stress pattern present in at least one of the other two varieties (see Martin 2011: 111–14). This result shows a greater stress stability than what is usually assumed, and it led Martin to conduct a larger investigation of intervarietal stress variation.

4.2 An extended study on a specific corpus

Since no extended corpus dedicated to intervarietal lexical stress variety was available in any of the studies mentioned above, Martin specifically put together such a corpus (approximately 3700 words) divided into four subsets:

- 2550 dissyllabic verbs (complete class): *alter, bury, follow, injure, lament, scavenge*...
- 370 prefixed multicategorial words: *access, account, believe, offer, record, transport*...
- 542 exceptions to the rules of word-stress assignment as described in J.-M. Fournier (2010b), for example exceptions to the rule according to which disyllables are stressed /10/: *cigár, canál, degrée, diséase, hotél, políce, routíne*...
- and 280 borrowings from Aboriginal languages:[32] *billabong, boomerang, didgeridoo, dingo, koala, paddymelon, wombat*...

It is crucial to emphasise that these 3742 items were chosen on purpose: indeed, they are words which specifically tend to show word-stress variation in contemporary English. Exceptions to stress rules and variation are often the manifestations of unresolved conflicts in the phonology (J.-M. Fournier 1990; Guierre 1982). Therefore, we could expect such conflicts to evolve in different ways in different varieties. The different sets which were selected were retained precisely for this reason:[33]

- **Disyllabic verbs:** According to the pronunciation dictionaries used for Martin's study, 50% of dissyllabic verbs are initially stressed, while the other 50% bear stress on their final syllable.
- **Prefixed multicategorial words:** They undergo a tension between the verbal logic in which the prefix is ignored to determine the position of stress (/01/) and the substantive logic in which it is taken into account (/10/) (see section 2.2.1).
- **Exceptions:** They constitute obvious areas of conflict between the preservation of their exceptional stress patterns and regularisation.
- **Aboriginal loanwords:** They could also be problematic in terms of stress because of their inherent foreign status.

Martin's approach follows Guierre's and offers a dictionary treatment in which the elements of the corpus are studied using the data of the *Longman Pronounciation Dictionary* (2008, hereafter *LPD3*), the *Cambridge English Pronouncing Dictionary* (Jones 2006, hereafter *CEPD17*) and the *Macquarie Dictionary* (Delbridge et al. 2009, hereafter *MD Online*), all reference books on English pronunciation.

In order to consolidate the dictionary data, Martin led a number of oral tests on specifically chosen elements of the corpus (following a protocol similar to that which is applied in the first part of the Phonologie de l'Anglais Contemporain – Phonology of Contemporary English project).[34] She also used frequency data extracted from the *Corpus of Contemporary American English*.[35] The figures given in the present chapter are not the ones consolidated by the oral test which Martin undertook in her study. Indeed, this will allow the reader to falsify her work using *LPD3*, *CEPD17* and *MD Online*. For more details on the oral data, see Martin (2011).

Overall, Martin showed that SAusE, SBE and SAmE contain a high level of accentual intervarietal stability. Table 2.1 gives a detailed quantitative account for each subset and for the corpus as a whole (for a more detailed account, see Chapter 6 of this volume).

The results in Table 2.1 confirm Martin's initial result that intervarietal variation is indeed much more restricted than is commonly assumed. 90% of all the words in the study have exactly the same stress pattern in all three varieties, that is to say that both the main pronunciation and the variants (if any) are strictly identical. If only the main pronunciation is considered, then that proportion rises to 94%. These results confirm Cling's hypothesis that 'the prosodic traits (and mainly the stress system) must be retained as fundamental invariants of any English accent variety' (1984: 200, our translation).[36] This study has limitations, of course, notably the fact that the subset dealing with exceptions to stress rules is based on previous work dealing with SBE only. This implies that there could be words which are exceptional in SAmE and in SAusE but not in SBE but which are not included in this study.

Martin's study has provided us with an initial valuable insight on the subject of intervarietal stress variation, even though much work remains to be done to reach a greater understanding of the issue.

Table 2.1 Intervarietal variation in Martin (2011)

	Disyllabic verbs	Multicategorial prefixed words	Exceptions to stress rules	Aboriginal loanwords	Total
No attested difference	2397 (94%)	264 (71%)	467 (86%)	44 (94%)	**3172 (90%)**
Variant in one or two varieties	Not studied	76 (20%)	36 (7%)	2 (4%)	**114 (12%)**
Identical main pronunciation	2397 (94%)	340 (92%)	503 (93%)	46/47 (98%)	**3286 (94%)**
Total	2549	370	542	47	3508

5 Conclusions

The Guierrian School shares a number of assumptions with contemporary theories, such as the importance of morphology in stress assignment or the importance of stress preservation, but it also diverges in key issues such as the role of endings, the marginal role we attribute to syllable weight, the recognition of semantically empty or obscure morphological units or the relationship between orthography and phonology. Guierre (1979: §1.4.6) saw generative formalisms in *SPE* and the works that followed it as being mostly premature as a lot of empirical work was yet to be done and more caution should have been applied. A lot is still to be done, but empirical work in the Guierrian tradition has allowed us to show that some commonplace assumptions about English phonology, such as the neglect of opaque prefixation (see Chapter 5 of this volume), the extent of intervarietal variation (see Chapter 6 of this volume) or phonologists' lack of consideration of orthographic information (see Chapter 4 of this volume), were (at least partly) incorrect. A criticism which has been addressed to the Guierrian School is that, while it proposes accurate descriptions of accentual and vocalic patterns, its scope is too restricted. Indeed, it does not offer any account of allophonic processes such as aspiration and flapping or of phonotactics and, therefore, there is still a lot of work to be conducted to widen the scope of Guierrian analyses. In recent years, Guierrian researchers have turned to new topics and methods, such as the diachronic evolution of stress patterns (Castanier 2016), the systematic study of vowel reduction (Dabouis and J.-M. Fournier 2019),[37] the comparison of dictionary data and speech data (Arndt-Lappe and Dabouis submitted), the formalisation of certain regularities using Government Phonology (Dabouis et al. 2020) or the study of loanwords (P. Fournier 2016, 2018, 2021). Our knowledge of English phonology can still be advanced in a number of ways, and an extensive dialogue between different approaches, both empirical and theoretical, can only eventually lead to a better comprehension of English phonology.

Appendix

The diagram in A2.1 is a simplified version of the stress system of English as it is analysed by J.-M. Fournier (2007, 2010b). The explanation on how it is to be read and what it represents is to be found below.

First, we have to make clear the fact that this representation is not meant to represent the stress assignment system of an average or ideal English speaker. This diagram represents a form of optimal organisation of the different rules, but we should expect it to differ from speaker to speaker depending on the vocabulary they know.

A2.1 Where does primary stress fall? (Source: J.-M. Fournier 2007: 221)

Where does primary stress fall?

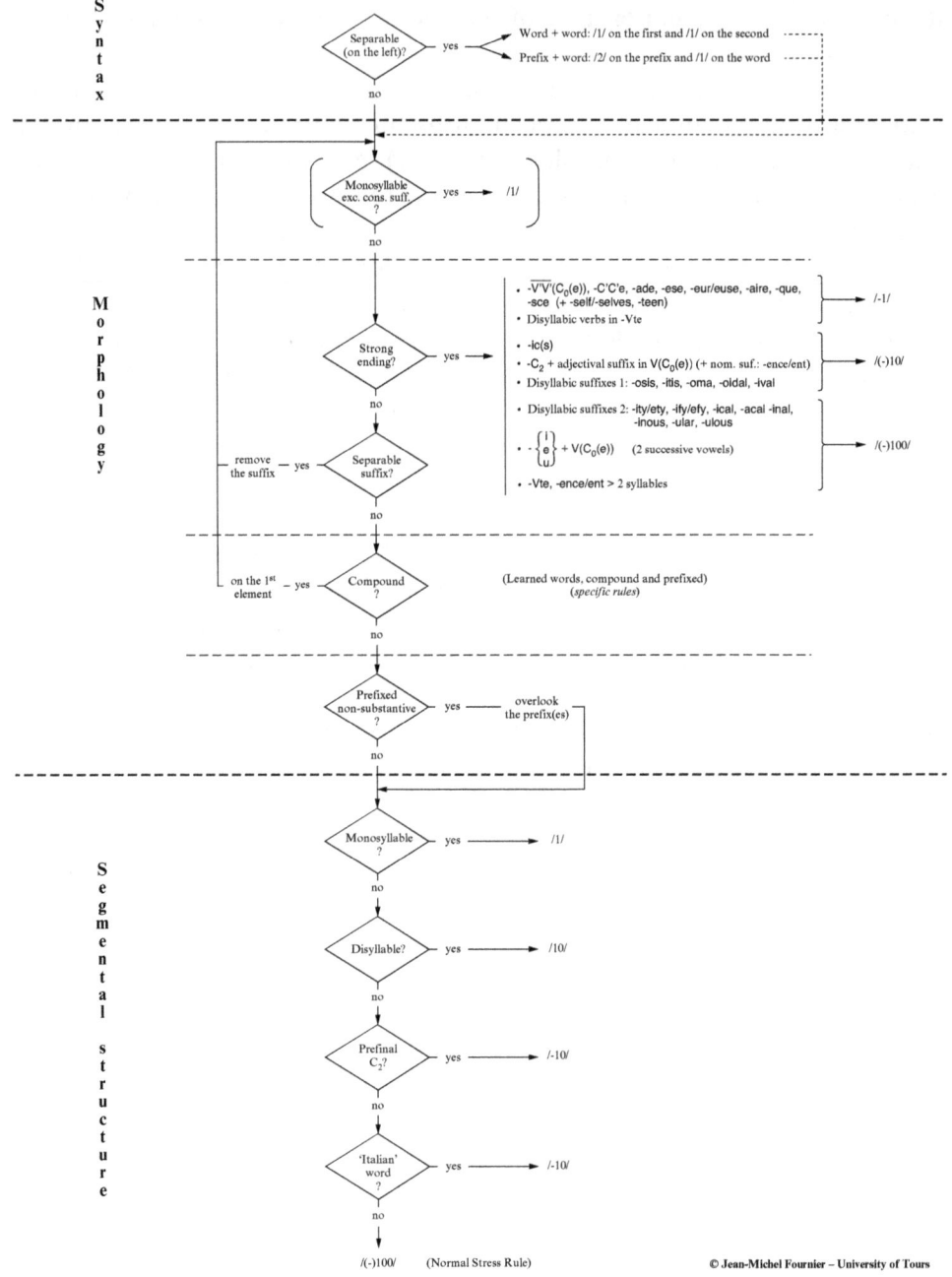

Second, the hierarchy in this diagram represents the relative domination of certain parameters over others. This hierarchy is represented in the form of questions for didactic purposes: at every step, one should ask whether the conditions for the application of that rule are met and, if they are, then the rule applies. If these conditions are not met, then one should proceed to the next rule and so on until all rules have been considered. What this means is that the different parameters for stress placement are hierarchically ordered and that, at every step, one of these parameters becomes neutralised. For example, at the step of the rule of the 'prefinal C_2,' we have, on the one hand, words with a prefinal C_2 which all behave in the same way with regards to the phenomenon we are trying to predict (stress), and in that case they all have penultimate stress (for example *mèmorándum, utensil, vanílla*); and, on the other hand, we have words with only one prefinal consonant which do not behave uniformly: they may have penultimate or antepenultimate stress (for example *tomáto, tornádo ~ álcohol, élephant*). What this means is that the parameter associated with a variable behaviour (here, one prefinal consonant) becomes neutral in the sense that it no longer determines the position of stress and that additional parameters are required to explain the remaining words. Therefore, at every step a part of the corpus is accounted for and the parameter under consideration is neutralised for the rest of the corpus.

The relative ordering of rules is based on the analysis of relevant cases, which are cases in which two contradictory rules may apply. If these relevant cases always behave in the same way, then it is their behaviour which will indicate which of the two contradictory rules dominates the other. For example, a word that has three syllables or more and a prefinal C_2 may follow the 'prefinal C_2' rule or the NSR. As the vast majority of these words have penultimate stress, we know that the rule of the prefinal C_2 dominates the NSR. In the case where two rules are not contradictory, that is, when they produce the same results, the principle of transitivity may allow us to establish the whole ordering.[38]

The diagram is divided into three main parts: syntax, morphology and segmental structure. They correspond to the three main conditioning factors which are hierarchically ordered according to the principles discussed above; we followed that ordering in our detailed presentation of the rules in this chapter.

The part on syntax deals with determining the number of lexical units under consideration. As was pointed out in the chapter, stress can be argued to be an identifier of lexical units, hence the first question to solve is obviously that of identifying the lexical units under consideration, as each should be considered separately.

The second part on morphology details the influence of morphological structure on stress, mainly (stress-affecting and stress-neutral) affixation and compounding.

Finally, the third part deals with the remaining items which are all, at this stage, morphologically simple (or behave as such). The rules in this part are of two kinds: length rules (number of syllables) and rules that refer to specific segmental structures.

Such a system can account for the vast majority of English words, and all exceptions to these rules are listed extensively in J.-M. Fournier (2010b). However, as J.-M. Fournier (2007) underlines, the stress system of English should be seen as a dynamic system in which contradictory forces are in conflict, and that dynamism cannot be represented in such a diagram. To our knowledge, a formalism that would account for that dynamism has not yet been proposed.

Notes

1. See section 2.1 below. See also Chapter 4 of this volume.
2. In this chapter, we will use the following notation: /1/ for primary stressed syllables, /2/ for secondary stressed syllables, /0/ for stressless syllables, and /(-)/ for optional syllables.
3. See Chapter 5 of this volume for an analysis of stress placement in English verbs. For a general discussion on the nature of stress see Dabouis (2020).
4. For example, either one or both of the two words *Ticonderoga* and *Monongahela* can be found in Burzio (1994); Chomsky and Halle (1968); Collie (2007); Hayes (1982, 1984); Kiparsky (1982); Liberman and Prince (1977); Pater (1995, 2000); Schane (1979); Selkirk (1980).
5. Collie (2007: 118) speaks of 'artificial idiolects'.
6. Primary stress for words, secondary for prefixes. See section 2.2.1 below for a definition of these two types of lexical units.
7. Except if they are orthographic digraphs, for example *áuction* [ɔ́ː], *acóustic* [úː], *recéipt* [íː].
8. That last property knows two exceptions:
    - When the first syllable is a prefix, it reduces regardless of the following consonantal structure.
    - When the cluster is made of orthographic geminates, they do not block reduction as systematically as 'true' consonant clusters (for example *t*[ɒ]*rréntial*, *t*[ə]*rrífic*).
9. Overall, separable prefixes correspond to so-called Class II prefixes (Siegel 1974) although they are defined mostly by their semantic and stress behaviour and therefore include prefixes like *iN-*, which can have a transparent meaning and receive stress (for example *impróper*, *ináccurate*, *incúrable*). This is despite the fact that *iN-* undergoes nasal assimilation, a property generally restricted to Class I affixes (see Raffelsiefen 1999, for

whom the difference between *un-*, which does not undergo nasal assimilation, and *iN-* is a segmental one).
10. That behaviour can also be observed in groups of more than two words, as long as they are still opposed only by their prefixes, for example *import ~ export ~ deport* (Videau 2013: 21).
11. For a general discussion of the issue of semantically opaque prefixes in English phonology, see Dabouis (2017).
12. This distinction is close to the distinctions put forward in other frameworks, for example Class I vs Class II (Siegel 1974), Level I vs Level II in Lexical Phonology (Giegerich 1999; Kiparsky 1982) or stem-level vs word-level in Stratal Phonology (Bermúdez-Otero 2018).
13. This distinction between suffixes and endings appears to be relevant in a few cases, however, such as the words in *-ee*, which normally receive final stress. J.-M. Fournier (2010b: 24) points out that there are more exceptions to the rule when *-ee* represents an ending (for example *cóffee, tróchee, yánkee*) than when it represents a suffix (for example *règugée, trainée, trustée*).
14. Actually the -{i,e,u}+V(C_0(e)) family of endings, characterised by two successive vowels. See the Appendix.
15. For example, *ration vs rational, cult vs culture* where the semantic relationship is demotivated.
16. This is what Burzio (1994) calls 'Strong Preservation'.
17. However, Guierre (1979) posits 'potential bases' (noted preceded by °) to account for the stress pattern of some suffixed words (for example °*prócurate* (and not *procúre*) → *prócurator*).
18. This particular instance of stress shift is only found in Standard British English because disyllabic verbs ending in *-ate* are generally stressed on their first syllable in Standard American English.
19. The whole list of strong endings can be found in the diagram in the Appendix.
20. See also Dabouis (2016a), who argues that the adjectival suffix *-al* is strong only in combination with other elements such as a preceding consonant cluster, certain suffixes or neoclassical roots.
21. The definition of compounding is indeed controversial because the boundary between syntax and the lexicon is not easy to identify. This issue has been widely discussed in the literature (see for example Bauer et al. 2013: 431ff.; Giegerich 2004; Plag 2003: 132ff.).
22. Compounding is the only case for which the Guierrian School accepts the possibility for a secondary stress to appear to the right of primary stress, much as dictionaries do.
23. Nevertheless, research was carried out (Arndt-Lappe 2011; Bell and Plag 2013; Moore-Mauroux 2002; Plag 2006) to try to account for these cases.
24. As opposed to the 'final combining forms' (FCFs) category (see Marchand 1969).

25. See P. Fournier (2011) on neoclassical compounds ending in -*ous* for further detail and in particular stress variation which is particularly common in that part of the lexicon. See also Dabouis (2016a) for a similar discussion of neoclassical compounds ending in -*al*.
26. However, neoclassical roots, like recent Latinate borrowings, show a clear sensitivity to the presence of a prefinal C_2.
27. Cases of (sometimes variable) non-preservation have been found to occur (for example *antícipate* → *ànticipátion* ~ *antìcipátion*); see Collie (2007, 2008).
28. Violations of principle 2 actually do occasionally occur (for example *collèctívity, elèctóral, encrùstátion*) and are discussed by Dabouis (2019).
29. Dabouis (2016b) also reports two cases of possible stress preservation from a non-local base where no such semantic distinctions are found:

    acádemy → *àcadémic* → *academician* /020100/ ~ /200100/
    aróma → *àromátic* → *aromaticity* /200100/ ~ /020100/

30. However, these differences in stress behaviour need not necessarily be attributed to the Germanic/Romance distinction and may have to do with the segmental make-up of Germanic suffixes (which tend to be consonant-initial) and Romance suffixes (which tend to be vowel-initial), as argued by Raffelsiefen (2015).
31. For a complete analysis of the sensitivity of the English language to the phonological properties of source languages and its interaction with the penultimate stress pattern as an indicator of 'foreignness', see P. Fournier (2016).
32. Martin's study first aimed at focusing on SAusE. P. Fournier (2013) also conducted a study on the stress pattern of French loanwords in SBE and in SAmE and found that the proportion of French loanwords stressed on the final syllable was higher in the latter than in the former (73% compared with 58%).
33. It is, of course, also important to note that the three varieties at stake in the study are all stressed-timed and can therefore undergo the same tests in terms of stress assignment: 'While BrE, AmE, AusE and NZE are stress-timed, the Caribbean Creoles, most West African varieties, most dialects of SAfE, StHE, and all Asian Englishes and Pacific contact varieties (including Maori English and AbE) display a strong tendency towards a syllable-timed rhythm' (Schneider 2004: 1126).
34. This decision also follows Guierre's wish to extend the study of English stress beyond pronouncing dictionaries and to work on oral data (Guierre 1984b).
35. <https://www.english-corpora.org/coca/>.
36. 'les traits prosodiques (et principalement le système accentuel) doivent être retenus comme invariants fondamentaux de toute variété d'accent anglophone'.

37. There were earlier exploratory works conducted within the Guierrian framework (Dahak 2011; Guierre 1979; Trocmé 1975) but none sought to clearly delineate the role of each factor influencing vowel reduction.
38. This principle can be expressed as follows: if A > B and B > C, then A > C.

References

Anderson, S. R. (1992), *A-Morphous Morphology*, Cambridge: Cambridge University Press.
Arndt-Lappe, S. (2011), 'Towards an exemplar-based model of stress in English noun–noun compounds', *Journal of Linguistics* 47(3), 549–85.
Arndt-Lappe, S. and Q. Dabouis (submitted), 'Secondary stress and morphological structure: New evidence from dictionary and speech data', Manuscript, Université Clermont Auvergne; Universität Trier.
Aronoff, M. (1976), *Word Formation in Generative Grammar*, Cambridge, MA: MIT Press.
Ballier, N. and P. Martin (2010), 'Corrélats prosodiques et acoustiques de la syllabification: Le cas du français et de l'anglais', Paper presented at the 8th meeting of the French Phonology Network, held at the Université d'Orléans, Orléans, France, on 1–3 July 2010.
Bauer, L. (1983), *English Word-Formation*, Cambridge: Cambridge University Press.
Bauer, L. (2005), 'The borderline between derivation and compounding', *Amsterdam Studies in the Theory and History of Linguistic Science Series 4* 264, 97–108.
Bauer, L. (2006), 'Compounds and minor word-formation types', in B. Aarts, A. McMahon and L. Hinrichs (eds), *The Handbook of English Linguistics*, 2nd edn, Malden, MA: Blackwell, pp. 483–506.
Bauer, L., R. Lieber and I. Plag (2013), *The Oxford Reference Guide to English Morphology*, Oxford: Oxford University Press.
Bell, M. and I. Plag (2013), 'Informativity and analogy in English compound stress', *Word Structure* 6(2), 129–55.
Bermúdez-Otero, R. (2018), 'Stratal phonology', in S. J. Hannahs and A. R. K. Bosch (eds), *The Routledge Handbook of Phonological Theory*, Abingdon: Routledge, pp. 100–34.
Burzio, L. (1994), *Principles of English Stress*, New York: Cambridge University Press.
Castanier, J. (2016), 'L'évolution accentuelle du lexique anglais contemporain appréhendée à travers les dictionnaires de prononciation (XVIIIe–XXIe siècles)', PhD dissertation, Université de Poitiers.
Chomsky, N. and M. Halle (1968), *The Sound Pattern of English*, New York: Harper & Row.
Cling, M. (1984), 'Vers l'archisystème phonologique de l'anglais', in M. Cling and J. Humbley (eds), *2ème colloque d'avril sur l'anglais oral*, Villetaneuse: Université Paris Nord: CELDA, diffusion APLV, pp. 193–204.
Collie, S. (2007), 'English stress preservation and stratal optimality theory', PhD dissertation, University of Edinburgh.

Collie, S. (2008), 'English stress preservation: The case for "fake cyclicity"', *English Language and Linguistics* 12(3), 505–32.

Collins, B. S. and I. M. Mees (2008), *Practical Phonetics and Phonology: A Resource Book for Students*, London: Routledge.

Cruttenden, A. (2014), *Gimson's Pronunciation of English*, 8th edn, London: Routledge.

Dabouis, Q. (2016a), 'Is the adjectival suffix -al a strong suffix?', *Anglophonia* 21, <https://doi.org/10.4000/anglophonia.754>.

Dabouis, Q. (2016b), 'L'accent secondaire en anglais britannique contemporain', PhD dissertation, Université de Tours.

Dabouis, Q. (2017), 'Semantically opaque prefixes and English phonology', Paper presented at the 14th Old World Conference in Phonology, held at Universität Düsseldorf, Düsseldorf, Germany, on 20–22 February 2017.

Dabouis, Q. (2019), 'When accent preservation leads to clash', *English Language and Linguistics* 23(2), 363–404.

Dabouis, Q. (2020), 'Secondary stress in contemporary British English: An overview', *Anglophonia* 30, <https://doi.org/10.4000/anglophonia.3476>.

Dabouis, Q., G. Enguehard, J.-M. Fournier and N. Lampitelli (2020), 'The English "Arab Rule" without feet', *Acta Linguistica Academica* 1(67), 121–34.

Dabouis, Q. and J.-M. Fournier (2019), 'On the role of morphology, syllable structure, frequency and spelling in English vowel reduction', Poster presented at the 27th MFM Conference, held at the University of Manchester, Manchester, UK, on 23–25 June 2019.

Dabouis, Q., J.-M. Fournier and I. Girard (2017), 'Ternarity is not an issue: Secondary stress is left edge marking', Paper presented at the MFM25 Fringe Meeting – PTA Dataset Workshop, held at the University of Manchester, Manchester, UK, on 24 May 2017.

Dabouis, Q. and P. Fournier (2022), 'English PhonologieS', in V. Arigne and C. Rocq-Migette (eds), *Modèles et modélisation en linguistique / Models and Modelisation in Linguistics*, Brussels: Peter Lang, pp. 215–58.

Dahak, A. (2006), 'Quel statut pour un corpus "oral" écrit ? Le dictionnaire de prononciation comme corpus (quasi-)exhaustif de la langue', in *Actes des IXèmes rencontres Jeunes Chercheurs de l'École Doctorale 268 'Langage et Langues'*, Paris: Université de la Sorbonne Nouvelle, pp. 1–5.

Dahak, A. (2011), 'Etude diachronique, phonologique et morphologique des syllabes inaccentuées en anglais contemporain', PhD dissertation, Université de Paris Diderot.

Delbridge, A. et al. (eds) (2009), *The Macquarie Dictionary, Australia's National Dictionary Online*, Sydney: Macquarie Library, <http://www.macquariedictionary.com.au>.

Domahs, U., I. Plag and R. Carroll (2014), 'Word stress assignment in German, English and Dutch: Quantity-sensitivity and extrametricality revisited', *The Journal of Comparative Germanic Linguistics* 17(1), 59–96.

Duchet, J.-L. (1994), *Code de l'anglais oral*, 2nd edn, Paris: Ophrys.

Forster, K. I. and T. Azuma (2000), 'Masked priming for prefixed words with bound stems: Does submit prime permit?', *Language and Cognitive Processes*, 15(4–5), 539–61.

Fournier, J.-M. (1990), 'Analogie et isomorphisme, conflits et conspirations', in *5ème Colloque d'Avril sur l'anglais oral*, Villetaneuse: Université Paris Nord: CELDA, diffusion APLV, pp. 74–87.

Fournier, J.-M. (1996), 'La reconnaissance morphologique', in *8ème Colloque d'Avril sur l'anglais oral*, Villetaneuse: Université Paris Nord, CELDA, diffusion APLV, pp. 45–75.

Fournier, J.-M. (1998), 'Que contraignent les terminaisons contraignantes?', in *Topiques, Nouvelles recherches en linguistique anglaise, Travaux XCIII du CIEREC*, Université de Saint-Etienne, pp. 44–75.

Fournier, J.-M. (2007), 'From a Latin syllable-driven stress system to a Romance versus Germanic morphology-driven dynamics: In honour of Lionel Guierre', *Language Sciences* 29, 218–36.

Fournier, J.-M. (2010a), 'Accentuation lexicale et poids syllabique en anglais: L'analyse erronée de Chomsky et Halle', Paper presented at the 8th meeting of the French Phonology Network, held at the Université d'Orléans, Orléans, France, on 1–3 July 2010.

Fournier, J.-M. (2010b), *Manuel d'Anglais Oral*, Paris: Ophrys.

Fournier, P. (2011), 'Accentuation et prononciation des suffixés en -ous en anglais contemporain', PhD dissertation, Université de Tours.

Fournier, P. (2013), 'L'accentuation des emprunts français en anglais britannique et américain', in *Annales de l'Université de Craïova – Série Langues et Littératures Romanes*, Craïova: Universitaria, pp. 102–26.

Fournier, P. (2016), 'Nouvelles perspectives sur l'accentuation des emprunts en anglais contemporain', *Itinéraires* 2015-2, <https://doi.org/10.4000/itineraires.2827>.

Fournier, P. (2018), 'Stress assignment in Italian loanwords in English and its impact on the stressing of foreign words by native English speakers', *Corela*, HS-24 *Multicultural Spoken English*, <https://doi.org/10.4000/corela.5113>.

Fournier, P. (2021), 'Les emprunts au gaélique écossais en anglais', in S. Juillet-Garzon, P. Fournier and A. Fiasson (eds), *L'Écosse, la différence*, Presses Universitaires de Franche-Comté, pp. 215–29.

Giegerich, H. J. (1999), *Lexical Strata in English: Morphological Causes, Phonological Effects*, Cambridge: Cambridge University Press.

Giegerich, H. J. (2004), 'Compound or phrase? English noun-plus-noun constructions and the stress criterion', *English Language and Linguistics* 8(1), 1–24.

Guierre, L. (1979), 'Essai sur l'accentuation en anglais contemporain: Éléments pour une synthèse', PhD dissertation, Université Paris 7.

Guierre, L. (1982), 'L'isomorphisme vocalique en phonologie de l'anglais', *Recherches en Linguistique Etrangères* 8, 84–98.

Guierre, L. (1984a), *Drills in English Stress-Patterns: Ear and Speech Training Drills and Tests for Students of English as a Foreign Language*, 4th edn, Paris: Armand Colin-Longman.

Guierre, L. (1984b), 'Remarques sur les conflits en morphophonologie', in CELDA, diffusion APLV (ed.), *2ème Colloque d'Avril sur l'Anglais Oral*, Villetaneuse: Université Paris Nord, pp. 139–52.

Halle, M. and S. Keyser (1971), *English Stress: Its Form, Its Growth, and Its Role in Verse*, New York: Harper & Row.

Halle, M. and J.-R. Vergnaud (1987), *An Essay on Stress*, Cambridge, MA: MIT.

Hammond, M. (1999), *The Phonology of English: A Prosodic Optimality-Theoretic Approach*, Oxford: Oxford University Press.

Hammond, M. (2003), 'Frequency, cyclicity, and optimality', University of Arizona, <http://www.u.arizona.edu/~hammond/kslides.pdf>.

Hanote, S., N. Videau, F. Zumstein and P. Carré (2010), 'Les préfixes anglais *un-* et *de-*: Étude phonétique et acoustique', *Corela* HS-9, <https://doi.org/10.4000/corela.1081>.

Hayes, B. (1982), 'Extrametricality and English stress', *Linguistic Inquiry* 13(2), 227–76.

Hayes, B. (1984), 'The phonology of rhythm in English', *Linguistic Inquiry* 15(1), 33–74.

Hirsch, A. (2014), 'What is the domain for weight computation: The syllable or the interval?', *Proceedings of the 2013 Annual Meeting on Phonology*, 1–12.

Jones, D. (2006), *Cambridge English Pronouncing Dictionary*, 17th edn, Cambridge: Cambridge University Press.

Katamba, F. and J. Stonham (2006), *Morphology*, Basingstoke: Palgrave Macmillan.

Kiparsky, P. (1982), 'From cyclic phonology to lexical phonology', in H. van der Hulst and N. Smith (eds), *The Structure of Phonological Representations I*, Dordrecht: Foris, pp. 131–75.

Ktori, M., P. Mousikou and K. Rastle (2018), 'Cues to stress assignment in reading aloud', *Journal of Experimental Psychology* 147(1), 36–61.

Ktori, M., J. J. Tree, P. Mousikou, M. Coltheart and K. Rastle (2016), 'Prefixes repel stress in reading aloud: Evidence from surface dyslexia', *Cortex* 74, 191–205.

Liberman, M. and A. Prince (1977), 'On stress and linguistic rhythm', *Linguistic Inquiry* 8(2), 249–336.

McKinnon, R., M. Allen and L. Osterhout (2003), 'Morphological decomposition involving non-productive morphemes: ERP evidence', *NeuroReport* 14(6), 883–6.

McMahon, A. (2001), Review of *The Phonology of English: A Prosodic Optimality-Theoretic Approach* by M. Hammond (1999), Oxford: Oxford University Press, *Phonology* 18, 421–6.

Marchand, H. (1969), *The Categories and Types of Present-Day English Word-Formation*, Munich: C.H. Beck.

Martin, M. (2011), 'De l'accentuation lexicale en anglais australien standard contemporain', PhD dissertation, Université de Tours.

Minkova, D. (2006), 'Old and Middle English prosody', in A. van Kemenade and B. Los (eds), *The Handbook of the History of English*, Oxford: Blackwell, pp. 95–125.

Mitchell, A. G. and A. Delbridge (1965), *The Pronunciation of English in Australia*, rev. edn, Sydney: Angus and Robertson.

Moore-Mauroux, S. (2002), 'Les mots composés: Analyse de schémas accentuels de l'anglais britannique standard', PhD dissertation, Université de Poitiers.

Mudgan, J. (2015), 'Units of word-formation', in P. O. Müller, I. Ohnheiser, S. Olsen and F. Rainer (eds), *Word-Formation: An International Handbook of the Languages of Europe*, vol. 1, Berlin: Mouton de Gruyter, pp. 235–301.

Nespor, M. and I. Vogel (1986), *Prosodic Phonology*, Foris: Dordrecht.

Pastizzo, M. J. and L. B. Feldman (2004), 'Morphological processing: A comparison between free and bound stem facilitation', *Brain and Language* 90(1–3), 31–9.

Pater, J. (1995), 'On the nonuniformity of Weight-to-Stress and stress preservation effects in English', Manuscript, McGill University.

Pater, J. (2000), 'Non-uniformity in English secondary stress: The role of ranked and lexically specific constraints', *Phonology* 17(2), 237–74.

Peters, P. (2007), *The Cambridge Guide to Australian English Usage*, 2nd edn, Melbourne: Cambridge University Press.

Plag, I. (2003), *Word-Formation in English*, Cambridge: Cambridge University Press.

Plag, I. (2006), 'The variability of compound stress in English: Structural, semantic and analogical factors', *English Language and Linguistics* 1(10), 143–72.

Raffelsiefen, R. (1993), 'Relating words: A model of base recognition. Part I', *Linguistic Analysis* 23, 3–161.

Raffelsiefen, R. (1999), 'Diagnostics for prosodic words revisited: The vase of historically prefixed words in English', in T. A. Hall and U. Kleinhenz (eds), *Studies on the Phonological Word*, Current Issues in Linguistic Theory 174, Amsterdam: John Benjamins, pp. 133–201.

Raffelsiefen, R. (2007), 'Morphological word structure in English and Swedish: The evidence from prosody', in G. Booij, L. Ducceschi, B. Fradin, E. Guevara, A. Ralli and S. Scalise (eds), *Online Proceedings of the Fifth Mediterranean Morphology Meeting (MMM5)*, Fréjus, 15–18 September 2005, pp. 209–68.

Raffelsiefen, R. (2015), 'Phonological restrictions on English word-formation', in P. O. Müller, I. Ohnheiser, S. Olsen and F. Rainer (eds), *Word-Formation: An International Handbook of the Languages of Europe*, vol. 2, Berlin: Mouton de Gruyter, pp. 894–917.

Rastle, K. and M. Coltheart (2000), 'Lexical and nonlexical print-to-sound translation of disyllabic words and nonwords', *Journal of Memory and Language* 42, 342–64.

Schane, S. A. (1979), 'Rhythm, accent, and stress in English words', *Linguistic Inquiry* 10(3), 483–502.

Scheer, T. (2004), *A Lateral Theory of Phonology, Vol 1: What Is CVCV, and Why Should It Be?*, Berlin: Mouton de Gruyter.

Schneider, E. W. (2004), 'Global synopsis: Phonetic and phonological variation in English world-wide', in B. Kortmann, E. W. Schneider, K. Burridge, R. Mesthrie and C. Upton (eds), *A Handbook of Varieties of English: A Multimedia Reference Tool*, vol. 4, Berlin: Mouton de Gruyter, pp. 1111–37.

Selkirk, E. O. (1980), 'The role of prosodic categories in English word stress', *Linguistic Inquiry* 11(3), 563–605.

Siegel, D. C. (1974), 'Topics in English morphology', PhD dissertation, MIT.

Steriade, D. (2012), 'Intervals vs. syllables as units of linguistic rhythm', handout at EALing in Paris on 11–15 September 2012.

Steriade, D. and J. Stanton (2020), 'Productive pseudo-cyclicity and its significance', talk given at LabPhon 17 on 6–8 July 2020.

Trevian, I. (2007), 'Stress-neutral endings in contemporary British English: An updated overview', *Language Sciences* 29(2–3), 426–50.

Trocmé, H. (1975), 'Aspects de la réduction des voyelles prétoniques en anglais moderne', PhD dissertation, Université Paris 7.

Turcsan, G. and S. Herment (2015), 'Making sense of nonce word stress in English', in J. A. Mompean and J. Fouz (eds), *Investigating English Pronunciation: Current Trends and Directions*, Basingstoke: Palgrave Macmillan, pp. 23–46.

Videau, N. (2013), 'Préfixation et phonologie de l'anglais: Analyse lexicographique, phonétique et acoustique', PhD dissertation, Université de Poitiers.
Wells, J. C. (2008), *Longman Pronunciation Dictionary*, 3rd edn, London: Longman.
Wenszky, N. (2004), *Secondary Stress in English Words*, Budapest: Akadémiai Kiadó.

Stress Placement in Etymologically Prefixed Disyllabic Noun–Verb Pairs Revisited: A Semantic and Diachronic Approach

Jérémy Castanier

0 Introduction

It is well known that in some cases English stress performs a grammatical function in encoding the syntactic categories of the words concerned. For instance, this phenomenon can be observed with disyllabic words in *-ate*, with *create* and *negate* being backstressed ([01]) because they are verbs,[1] while *climate* and *senate* are forestressed ([10]) because they are nouns. The difference holds for those which belong to several syntactic categories, as with *fil'trate* and *dic'tate* (verbs) vs *'filtrate* and *'dictate* (nouns). The same phenomenon affects words with separable prefixes, like ˌup'date and ˌover'dose (verbs) vs *'update* and *'overdose* (nouns).[2]

One class of words is especially affected by this type of stress alternation, namely disyllabic noun–verb pairs starting with an etymological, inseparable Latin prefix, such as *ob'ject* and *re'cord* (verbs) vs *'object* and *'record* (nouns). Interestingly, this alternation is far from being a general rule, since two other tendencies exist: pairs where both members are backstressed (*con'cern*, *de'feat*) and pairs where both members are forestressed (*'comment*, *'convoy*). Using their own corpus, Abasq et al. (2014) indicate that the isotonic CON'CERN type represents 59% of all pairs, the isotonic 'COMMENT type 13%, while the alternating OBJECT type fits in-between with 28%.[3]

This broad description obviously raises the problem of understanding why this threefold distribution exists, specifically the alternating type. Yet it conceals at least two even more intricate problems. The first – and more immediate – is the existence of synchronic stress variation, as can be seen with *dispute* (noun) and *increase* (noun or verb), which may be stressed on either syllable. The second problem is diachronic variation. For instance, *perfect* (verb), now backstressed, used to be forestressed. Conversely, *convoy* (verb) changed from [01] to [10]. Of course, both problems are linked. For example, while *discount* (verb), *alloy* (noun) and *research* (noun and verb) used to be only backstressed, they may now be stressed on either syllable.

1 Description in the literature

This change in stress placement, which dates back to at least the sixteenth century (Minkova 2014: 311), has often been described, but most studies refer to Sherman (1975) as being the first to examine the phenomenon in detail. In fact, earlier studies also addressed the question, such as Bradley (1922) and Hill (1931), although they lacked quantitative data. In his 1975 study, Sherman used over 30 dictionaries from 1570 (Peter Levin's *Manipulus Vocabulorum*) to 1800 (the 28th edition of Bailey's *Universal Etymological English Dictionary*), as well as the *Shorter Oxford English Dictionary* (1934, hereafter *SOED*). Using the *SOED*, Sherman found 1757 polysyllabic N–V homographs, 1315 of which were disyllabic. Among these, only 150 pairs were diatonic (using his own terminology) (11%), while 950 were oxytonic and 215 paroxytonic. In addition to 8 diatonic pairs that he noticed already existed by the sixteenth century, he found 25 new disyllabic diatones by the seventeenth century, 35 new pairs by the eighteenth century, then an estimated 60 new pairs by the nineteenth century, and an interpolated 90 new pairs by the twentieth century. As a result of his study, he concluded that diatonic stress placement was to become more and more frequent:

> [It] is [. . .] possible to make an informed guess as to which of the current isotonic English N-V homographs will become diatonic at some time in the future. These future diatones will probably be drawn largely from the current oxytonic N-V inventory, and may ultimately include all those pairs as well as future pairs formed on currently oxytonic nouns or verbs. In the interest of verifying this hypothesis, Appendix II contains a list of 215 current oxytonic N-V homographs which will, according to this view, someday become diatonic.[4]
>
> (Sherman 1975: 55)

Comparing *EPD12* with *CEPD15* and/or *LPD1*, Trevian notices the change, which he does not consider significant enough (although we think that leaving variants aside introduces a strong methodological bias):

> If we consider main stress patterns only, variants aside, the number of *abstract* type pairs has risen from 27% of relevant items to 46% in *LPD* and/or *EPD15*, which is not negligible but does not look significant enough to conclude that all disyllabic prefixed N–V pairs as a class are inexorably drifting to diatonic stress.
>
> (Trevian 2003: 167–8, our translation)

Although many studies have addressed the specific subject of stress placement change in such pairs (those cited above but also Abasq et al. 2014;

Svensson and Hering 2013 and others), most have simply documented this change without really seeking to explain it. Exceptions include Phillips (2014) and Sonderegger and Niyogi (2013). Concerning stress change from oxytonic to diatonic, Betty Phillips mainly concluded that the least frequent N–V pairs were first affected:

> For the diatonic stress shift, this paper [. . .] found that less frequent words, as measured by their noun + verb frequency, are first affected in a change motivated by the overwhelming type frequency in English of forestressed two-syllable nouns and backstressed two-syllable verbs.
> (Phillips 2014: 92–3)

Using 46 dictionaries from 1800 to 2003 (on top of the 33 dictionaries used by Sherman), as well as diachronic frequency trajectories built from the *Literature Online* (*LiOn*) database for six N–V pairs, Morgan Sonderegger and Partha Niyogi made an apparently similar observation:

> All [six] words show negative correlations between year and N+V frequency, four out of six of which are significant [. . .]. Although any conclusion must be tentative in view of the small number of frequency trajectories considered, [. . .] we thus adopt the working hypothesis that change occurs in a N/V pair when its frequency drops below a critical level.
> (Sonderegger and Niyogi 2013: 274–5)

Sonderegger and Niyogi also found that 'N/V pairs sharing a prefix tend to have more similar trajectories' and that 'larger classes show stronger analogical effects' (2013: 276, 277). For instance, 'many *re*- pairs were historically {2,2} [i.e. both noun and verb backstressed], then began to change some time between 1875 and 1950' (2013: 275).

It is true indeed that the set of diachronic trajectories which Sonderegger and Niyogi were able to build is very small, counting only six pairs. Unfortunately, we do not think they may be considered as representative, for three main reasons.

The first is heterogeneity, as five pairs are prefixed (*combat*, *decrease*, *perfume*, *progress*, *protest*) while the sixth (*dictate*) is not and complies with the general rule of its -*ate* ending. In particular, it is well known that it is the whole class of disyllabic verbs in -*ate* that changed from paroxytonic to oxytonic in the last centuries (see notably Gąsiorowski 1997). In Duchet et al. (2012) and Castanier (2016: 423–5), we suggest that this change was due to the analogical model represented by the then oxytonic nouns in -*ator* borrowed directly from Latin, even without any deriving verb in English (for example *gladi'ator*, *spec'tator*). Additionally, *combat* has remained an essentially oxytonic pair in British English.

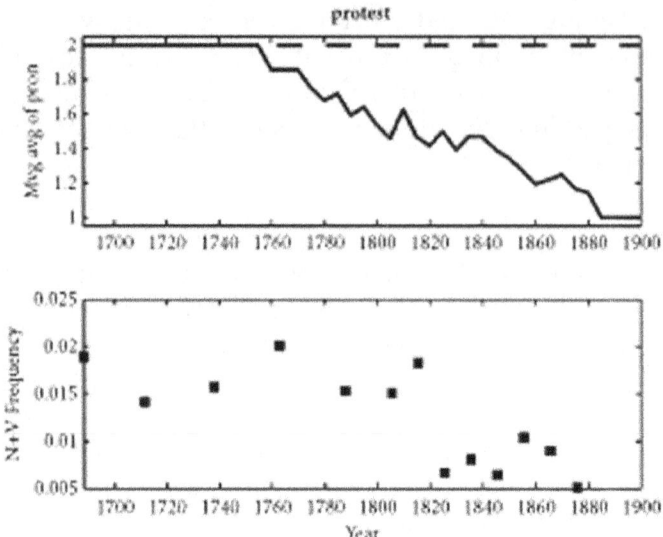

Figure 3.1 Moving average pronunciation (upper graph: average between 1 = forestressed and 2 = backstressed) and N+V frequency (lower graph) of *protest* in Sonderegger and Niyogi (2013). In the upper graph, the solid line corresponds to the noun and the dotted line to the verb

The second reason is that some of the frequency trajectories do not seem perfectly unequivocal. Consider, for example, the trajectory obtained for *protest* in Figure 3.1. The upper trajectory shows that *protest* (n.) started to be forestressed as early as 1760. Meanwhile, the frequency of *protest* became lower from 1820 but nothing clearly indicates that it had started to decrease from 1760. On the contrary, frequency in 1760 seemed to be at its highest, and it is doubtful that data in 1790 and 1805 show any decline, since frequency in 1815 remains higher than before 1760. On average, the 1690–1815 frequency of *protest* should be considered as somewhat level, especially as the fluctuations visible take place within too short intervals. Should a frequency slump be considered responsible for a change in pronunciation, it would need to come first, which the graphs do not show. The trajectories of other pairs given by Sonderegger and Niyogi seem somewhat unclear to us, because some sequential periods seem too long for the dotted lines to prove relevant and/or because some proposed graphs apparently include outliers that may create misleading trends.[5]

The third reason is that some frequency trajectories are fully contradicted by Google Ngram Viewer (GNV).[6] For example, the frequency trajectory provided by the authors for *progress* suggests a gradual decline during the nineteenth century, or at least from 1815 onwards, as shown in Figure 3.2.

On the contrary, GNV displays a totally opposite trend for the same period, as shown in Figure 3.3. Relatively similar contradictions can be observed at least with *decrease*. It is true that some researchers do not

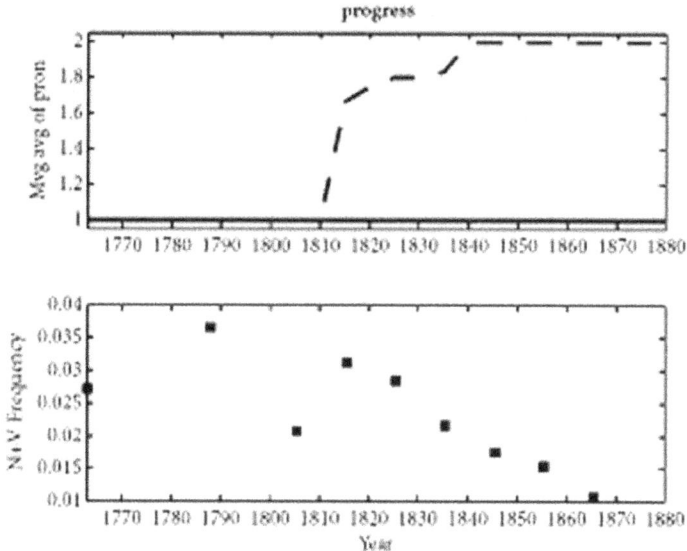

Figure 3.2 Moving average pronunciation (upper graph) and N+V frequency (lower graph) of *progress* in Sonderegger and Niyogi (2013)

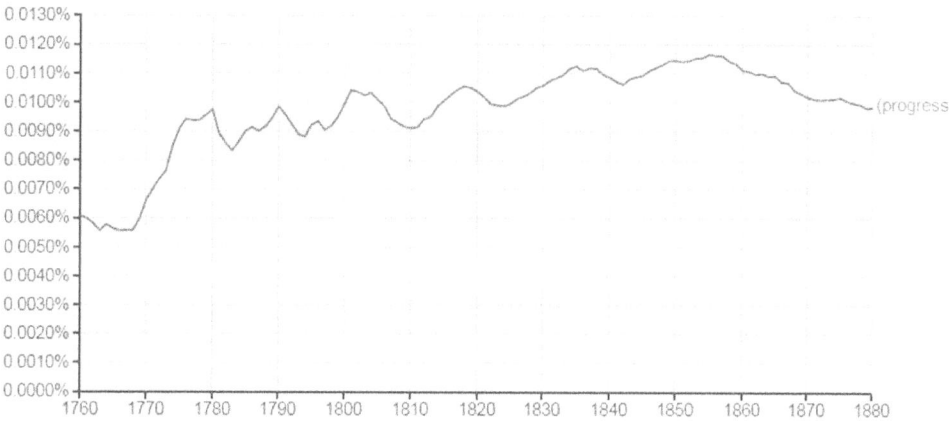

Figure 3.3 Frequency in Google Ngram Viewer of *progress* (inflected forms included) during the 1760–1880 period. Overall, the frequency of *progress* rose slightly during the period, which contradicts Sonderegger and Niyogi's (2013) downward frequency trajectory for the nineteenth century

consider GNV as a perfectly reliable tool (see note 6). However, the *LiOn* database is probably even more unrepresentative of spoken English through time, being a database too – not a corpus – and including literary writings only. In any case, the frontal contradictions between data inferred from the *LiOn* database and from the Google Ngram database should call for caution when using the *LiOn* database to analyse such a restricted set of words. Overall, for one reason or other (choice of words, too small set of words, interpretation of frequency trajectories, reliability of these graphs), we do not think that Sonderegger and Niyogi's six frequency trajectories can be considered as sufficiently representative and reliable.

The fact that Phillips came to apparently similar conclusions as Sonderegger and Niyogi does not really constitute any sort of confirmation to us. Indeed, she used a different type of statistical approach, resorting not to diachronic frequency trajectories but to synchronic sources. In her 1984 study she used the *American Heritage Word Frequency List*. In her 2014 study she used the *Corpus of Contemporary American English* (COCA). In this respect, Phillips's *static* statement that '**less frequent** words [. . .] are first affected' (2014: 93, our emphasis) is fundamentally different from Sonderegger and Niyogi's *dynamic* conclusion that 'change occurs in a N/V pair when its frequency **drops** below a critical level' (2013: 275, our emphasis). As a consequence, we think that using such synchronic sources to state that the N+V frequency of a disyllable is low does not allow Phillips to specify whether its frequency was indeed low at the time when this disyllable became diatonic. Additionally, a currently low frequency can result from a decreasing frequency over time, but may also result from the word at stake's having been borrowed recently, and it does not give us any information as to whether the current frequency trend is up, down or level. For example, if the frequencies of *relay* and *pretext* can be said to be rather similar at some points during the twentieth century, the situation was clearly different before that period, as shown in Figure 3.4.

Finally, it can be objected that many very high-frequency disyllabic pairs such as *object* and *present* do have diatonic stress, which fully contradicts the idea that those pairs whose frequency is lower are first affected by stress change.

Incidentally, in his well-documented and thoroughly justified study which analyses an unabridged corpus of 252 prefixed N–V pairs, C.-Y. Chen (2017) point out a whole series of methodological and interpretational anomalies within Phillips's study, similar to the ones we pointed out in both Phillips's and Sonderegger and Niyogi's studies. Such anomalies include the use of

Figure 3.4 Frequencies in Google Ngram Viewer of *relay* and *pretext* (inflected forms included) between 1700 and 2000

frequencies based on 'straightforward numbers [instead of] lemma frequency' (2017: 233), frequency averages despite 'extensive internal disparities' or within 'groups too small in size' / 'inadequate sampling' (2017: 235), the exclusion from the corpus of some highly relevant words whose exclusion completely reverses conclusions or allows false statements (2017: 242), and so on. Chen demonstrates that Phillips's analysis is 'proven to be implausible' and explains about her methodology, 'This selective sampling and extensive counter-evidence lead to serious questions about Phillips' methodology and, hence, the validity of her strong claim' (2017: 240, 235).

For all the reasons we mentioned earlier, supplemented by Chen's accurate demonstration, we consider that frequency alone cannot be held responsible for all shifts and we wish, as a complement, to explore another path, namely that of semantics.

2 Presentation of our corpus

We used a total of 55 dictionaries ranging from 1727 (*Nathan Bailey's Universal Etymological English Dictionary*) to 2011 (Peter Roach et al.'s *CEPD18*) to study the phenomenon of stress change in prefixed two-syllable N–V pairs. As for the twentieth century, these include the three editions of John C. Wells's *Longman Pronunciation Dictionary* (1990–2008), but also all eighteen editions of Daniel Jones's (then Alfred C. Gimson's, and finally Peter Roach et al.'s) *English Pronouncing Dictionary* (1917–2011).

Our lexical corpus consists of a selection of 99 Latin-type etymologically prefixed 2-syllable N–V pairs whose stress placement (in the noun and/or the verb) appears to have changed or varied, at least at some point in our dictionaries. For each word, the stress pattern found in each dictionary was noted. The wordlist excludes disyllables which start with a separable prefix, such as *reprint*. The selected words are listed in Appendix 3.1. When analysing the corpus, particular attention was paid to the meaning(s) of words in relation to their stress pattern(s), and to the semantic relation possibly existing between the members of each pair.

3 Stress placement in verbs

Original stress placement in verbs unsurprisingly conforms to Latin-type pronunciation, since all verbs but three in our corpus were originally stressed on the root. Only two verbs show real historical change from [10] to [01], namely *perfect* and *progress*, but both seem to have involved conversion. The verb *perfect* has oxytonic stress in all dictionaries of our corpus prior to the twentieth century, the only exception being JAMESON 1827, where it also optionally stressed [01]. On the contrary, it is mainly stressed [01] from

EPD1 (1917) to *EPD14R* (1988), then losing completely the paroxytonic variant in subsequent *EPD* editions and in *LPD*. Yet *perfect* as a verb (first attested in 1398 according to the *OED*) was originally a conversion from the adjective (first attested in 1300 and itself forestressed in all our dictionaries), hence its original forestressing. However, because of 'the overwhelming type frequency in English of [. . .] backstressed two syllable verbs' (Phillips 2014: 93), the stressing 'perfect must have looked unjustifiable to English speakers, hence its subsequent relatinisation, leading it to be integrated into the common verbal pattern. *Progress* was paroxytonic only in the eighteenth century in our corpus, before it shifted to oxytonic. This time the verb (1579) is explicitly considered by the *OED* as a conversion from the paroxytonic noun (1443). Stress change in dictionaries from [01] in the eighteenth century to [10] since the beginning of the nineteenth century was concomitant with a rise in verbal frequency, as shown by GNV in Figure 3.5.

This frequency rise as well as stress change are supported by a differentiation in verbal meaning, as is evidenced in WORCESTER 1860 in Figure 3.6.

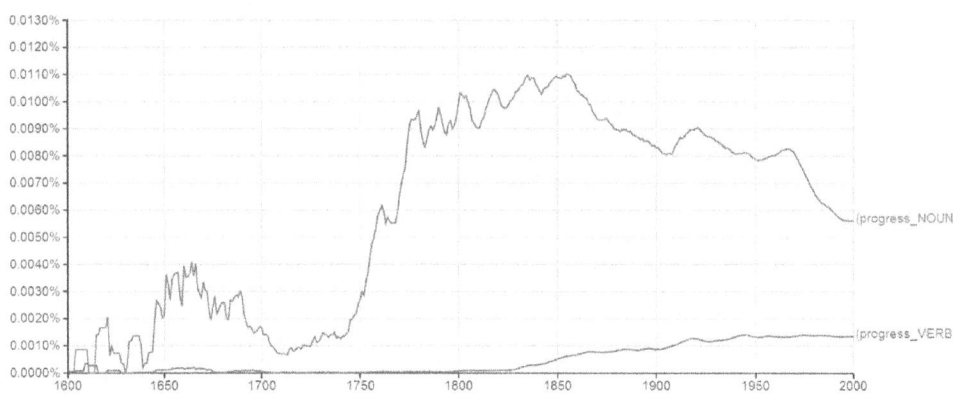

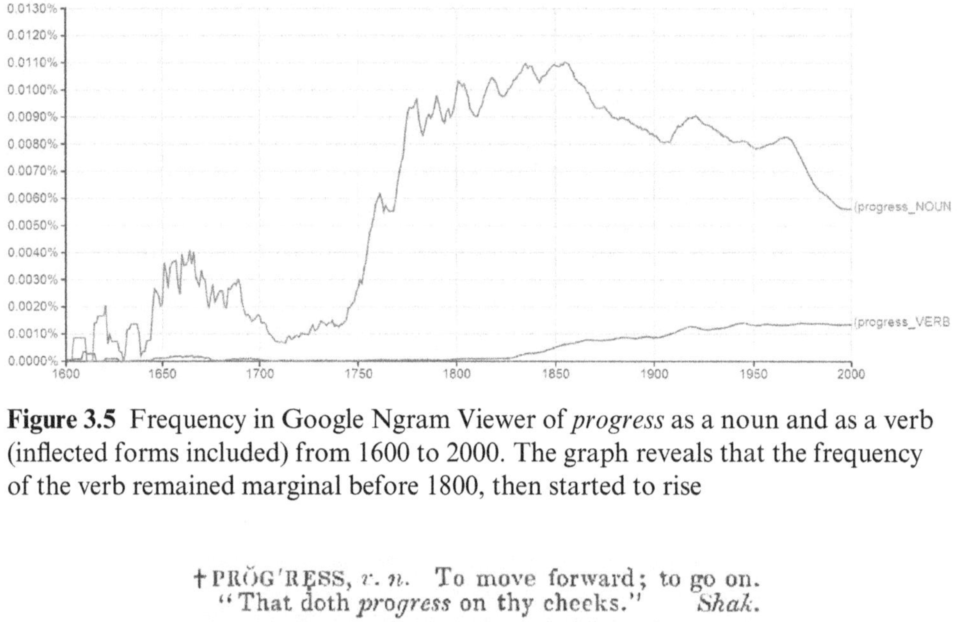

Figure 3.5 Frequency in Google Ngram Viewer of *progress* as a noun and as a verb (inflected forms included) from 1600 to 2000. The graph reveals that the frequency of the verb remained marginal before 1800, then started to rise

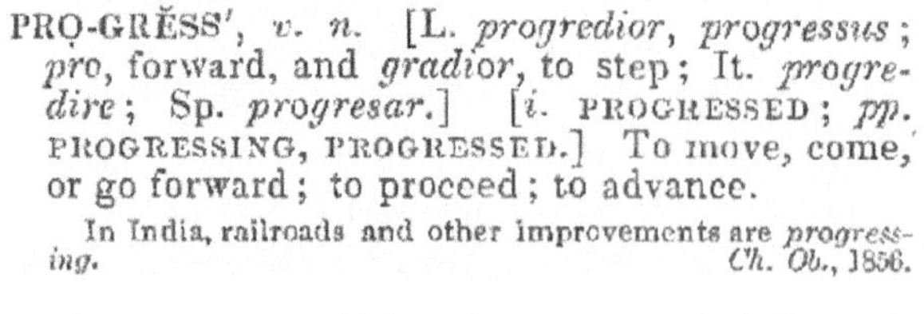

    † PRŎG'RĔSS, *v. n.* To move forward; to go on.
    "That doth *progress* on thy cheeks."   *Shak.*
    † PRŎG'RĔSS, *v. a.* To go forward in.
      In supereminence of beatifie vision, *progressing* the dateless and irrevoluble circle of eternity.   *Milton.*
    PRO-GRĔSS', *v. n.* [L. *progredior, progressus*; *pro*, forward, and *gradior*, to step; It. *progredire*; Sp. *progresar.*] [*i.* PROGRESSED; *pp.* PROGRESSING, PROGRESSED.] To move, come, or go forward; to proceed; to advance.
      In India, railroads and other improvements are *progressing.*   *Ch. Ob.*, 1856.

Figure 3.6 *Progress* in WORCESTER 1860. The stress-mark follows the stressed syllable

It thus seems safe to assume that the emergence of the figurative meaning, correlated to a frequency rise, led the verb to be no longer stressed as a converted noun form but as a verb in its own right. Finally, the verb *comment* is a conversion from the noun, as explicitly stated in the *OED*, hence its [10] pattern. Yet it also has a backstressed variant in *EPD11–18* and *LPD1–3* (although *EPD11–14R* consider it *rare*, and *LPD* indicates that it is *non-RP*) as well as in a minority of dictionaries in the eighteenth century, which shows here again the full attractiveness of the general pattern of prefixed disyllabic verbs.[7]

On the contrary, stress change in verbs from oxytonic to paroxytonic is frequently observed more recently in our corpus, here again involving conversion. And indeed, as explicitly stated by Balteiro (2007: 82), 'when verbs are formed from nouns by conversion, this conversion is neutral, that is, stress does not shift from the first syllable to the second, as the following pair evidences: 'pattern (n) → 'pattern (*pat'tern) (v)'.

Thus, in our corpus, after *perfume* (n.) became mainly paroxytonic in the nineteenth century, *perfume* (v.) also became stressed [01/10] in *EPD1–18*, or [10/01] in *LPD1–3*. These two stressings presumably match the two meanings of the verb, namely either 'To fill or impregnate with the smoke or vapour of incense or another substance emitting a pleasant odour' or 'to apply perfume to' (*OED*), the latter showing a closer relationship with the noun. In the case of *concrete*, only the sense meaning 'cover with concrete' is forestressed, while it is backstressed when meaning 'solidify'. Similarly, *retail* is backstressed when it means 'to tell' but mainly forestressed when it means 'to sell', that is, when it is related to the noun 'retail, which appeared in the language more than two centuries earlier. Other examples include *detail*, *impact*, *contract*, and so on. In the latter case, *LPD3* indicates that the forestressed variant pronunciation of the verb is related to the noun: 'in the meaning "agree under contract, make a contract" sometimes 'kɒntrækt'.

In a few cases, conversion concerns very specialised meanings of the verbs. For example, *discount* (v.) showed first signs of forestressing in WEBSTER 1836 and this stressing was generalised in the twentieth century.[8] This seems to correspond to meaning Id in the *OED* (first attested in 1828): 'Originally: to make a reduction of (a specified percentage) from a selling price or sum due. **Later: to reduce (a selling price) by means of a discount**; (hence) to sell (a product) at a discount' (*OED*, our emphasis).

In the case of *relay*, *EPD4–13* implicitly show the relationship between the noun in the sense 'electrical apparatus' (as opposed to 'relief gang') and the verb in its 'broadcasting sense', while *LPD* explicitly states that *relay* [10/01] means 'send by relay'.

Four pairs sharing the same root show interesting semantic and diachronic coherence despite apparent disparities: *prefix*, *suffix*, *infix* and *affix*. All four nouns have always been backstressed in our corpus, while stress placement in verbs is shown in Table 3.1.

Table 3.1 Stress placement in four prefixed verbs in -*fix*, and date of first attestation of their grammatical meanings in the *OED*

	19th century	EPD1–3 1917–26	EPD4–10 1937–49	EPD11–14R 1960–88	CEPD15–18 1997–2011	LPD3 2008	First attestation in grammatical sense (*OED*)
prefix (v.)	[01]	[01/10]	[01/10]	[01/10]	[01/10]	[10/01]	1646
suffix (v.)	[01]	[01]	[01/10]	[10/01]	[10/01]	[10/01]	1778
infix (v.)	[01]	[01]	[01]	[01]	[10/01]	[10/01]	1881
affix (v.)	[01]	[01]	[01]	[01]	[01/10]	[01]	1600

As to the first three words, the *OED* indicates that *prefix* appeared first, followed by *suffix* a century later, and then by *infix* another century later. Combining all categories, GNV shows a similar hierarchy in terms of frequencies.

The graph in Figure 3.7 shows that *prefix* had always been historically dominant in terms of frequency, while the frequency of *suffix* rose significantly from the mid-nineteenth century on. *Infix* has always had a marginal frequency. Even though the grammatical verbs *prefix*, *suffix* and *infix* can all be seen as conversions of the corresponding nouns, the non-simultaneous retraction of stress to their first syllables as shown in Table 3.1 thus certainly results from their unequal progression in terms of frequencies. In the specific case of *infix*, whose frequency is marginal and which started to be backstressed very recently (first found in *CEPD15*), it is assumed that *prefix* and *suffix* had to constitute firmly established models first for *infix* to subsequently imitate them. That *affix* did not follow this trend (it has the [10] variant in *CEPD15–18* only and not even in *LPD*) may be surprising considering that it is the most frequent disyllable of the four,[9] having a frequency similar to that of *prefix* up to 1800, and even superior to it afterwards. However, contrary to *prefix*, *suffix* and *infix*, whose meaning is mainly grammatical, the verb *affix* has many different senses, among which the grammatical one is marginal (see *OED*), which explains the marginality of its [10] stress pattern itself.

In two pairs (*convoy* and *ally*), the retraction of the stress in the verbs results from late conversions triggered by extra-linguistic events. The pair *convoy* used to be diatonic in our corpus from the eighteenth century[10] until *EPD6* (1944), then the verb suddenly became forestressed in *EPD7* (1945), and still is now. The *OED* does not consider the verb (1405) as a

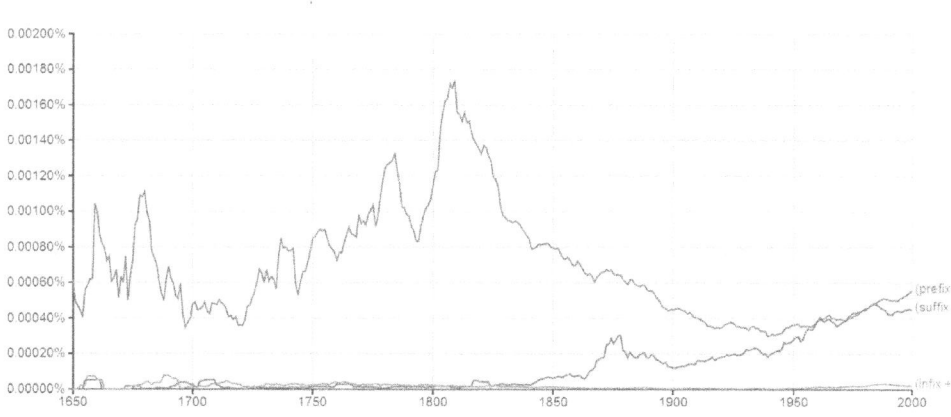

Figure 3.7 Frequency in Google Ngram Viewer of *prefix*, *suffix* and *infix* (all categories and inflected forms included)

conversion from the noun (1513) but signals a late association between the two:

> Etymology: < Middle French *convoyer* (French *convoyer*), variant of *conveier* convey v.1. **In later use reinforced by association with *convoy* n.** N.E.D. (1893) gives the pronunciation as (kǫnvoi·) /kən'vɔɪ/. **The shift of the main stress to the first syllable results from association with *convoy* n.**
>
> (verb *convoy*, *OED*, our emphasis)

Nothing in the *OED* yet clearly gives any evidence in favour of this hypothesis.

Meanwhile, GNV provides interesting frequencies shown in Figure 3.8, as we can clearly see two frequency peaks for the noun which are concomitant with the two world wars. This seems relevant, as stress change for the verb *convoy* suddenly takes place in *EPD7*, published in 1945. A semantic drift can be noticed for the verb *convoy* in the *OED*, from 'to accompany or escort (a person or group of people)' (1405), to 'to accompany as a guide; to conduct, lead; to show the way to, direct' (1480), to 'to accompany as a guard or armed escort; to provide with a protective escort' (1488) but also 'of a military vessel or aircraft: to accompany (another vessel or aircraft, esp. a merchant or passenger vessel) for protection from hostile forces' (1598). In short, *convoy* changed from the simple notion of accompanying somebody to a military escort involving vessels. However, the latter meaning – the most recent one in the *OED* – dates back to 1598 and no early twentieth-century new meaning is to be found in the *OED*. The BNC confirms the military contemporary meaning of *convoy* (n.), since the most frequent collocations involve modifiers such as the nouns *aid*, *relief*, *army*, *vehicle* or *police*, and the adjectives *military*, *nuclear* or *armed*, on top of neutral adjectives such as *small*, *whole* or *large*. Yet neutral collocations with *convoy* were neither new nor increasing in frequency in the early twentieth century, as is indicated by the control queries in GNV in Figure 3.9.

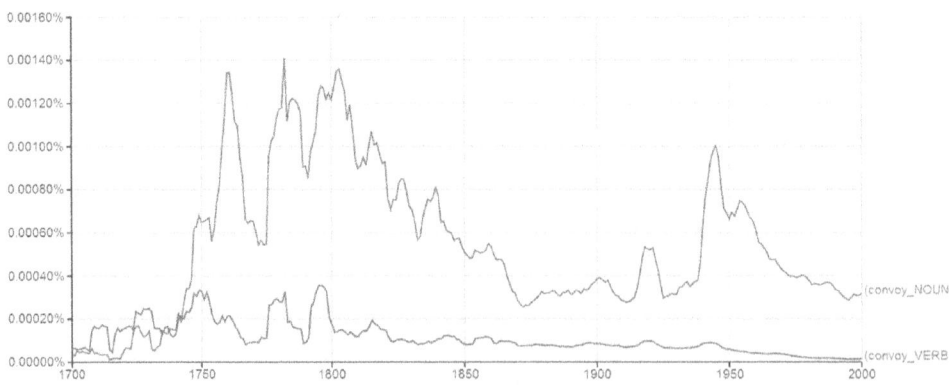

Figure 3.8 Frequency in Google Ngram Viewer of *convoy* as a noun and a verb (inflected forms included)

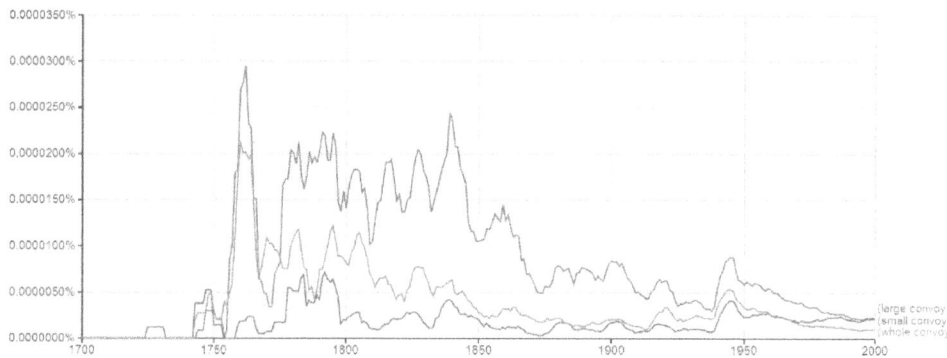

Figure 3.9 Frequency of *large convoy*, *small convoy(s)* and *whole convoy(s)* in Google Ngram Viewer

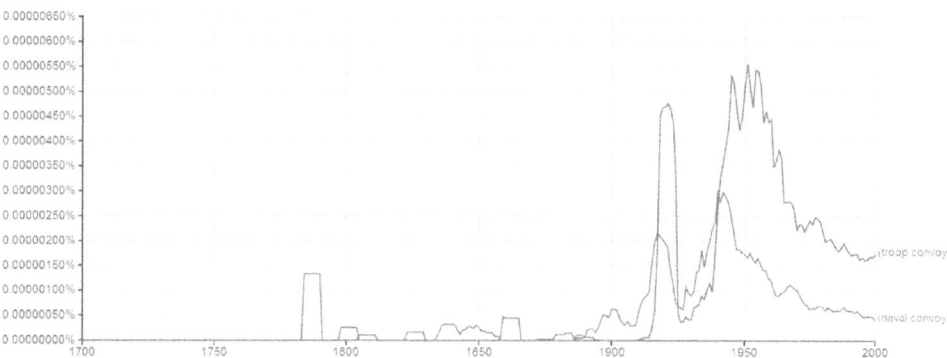

Figure 3.10 Frequency of *naval convoy(s)* and *troop convoy(s)* in Google Ngram Viewer

However, in line with Figure 3.8, military-related collocations show particularly salient peaks which are concomitant with the world wars. The most striking collocations are *naval convoy(s)* and *troop convoy(s)*, as shown in Figure 3.10.

In the meantime, the terms *naval* and *troop(s)* themselves were not new, as shown in Figure 3.11. It thus seems that *convoy* (n.) experienced a particular frequency rise because of the world wars, and that this was related to its use in a strictly war-related sense. As a consequence, it can be assumed that the frequency rise of the noun at these very moments led the verb, which was much less frequent (see Figure 3.8), to appear as a conversion from the noun. This supports the *OED*'s statement of a 'later [. . .] association' with the noun.

A similar demonstration could be made using GNV for *ally* (v.), with obvious reference to the *Allies* during World War I. If the verb itself only started to be optionally forestressed in *EPD13*, the inflected form *allied* received initial stress 'when attributive' from *EPD4* (1937) onwards. In the meantime, *ally* (n.) had started to be forestressed as early as in *EPD1* (1917), in obvious reference to World War I. It can therefore be concluded that *ally* (v.) has started to be forestressed not only because of its semantic development

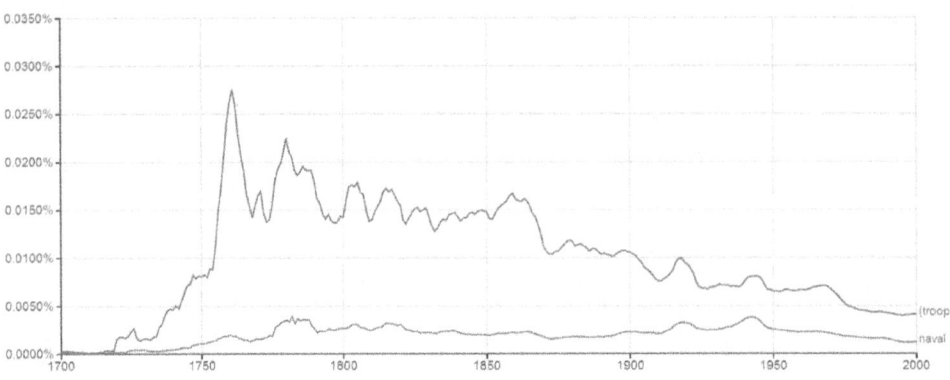

Figure 3.11 Frequency of *naval* and *troop(s)* in Google Ngram Viewer

during World War I in relation to the Allies, but also more importantly because of the phenomenon of stress-shift in *the allied forces*. This is supported by Gower's second edition of *Fowler's Modern English Usage*:

> *Ally*, n. and v. These words and their inflected forms used all to be pronounced with the accent on the second syllable [. . .]. But the noun, both singular and plural, is now commonly accented on the first syllable, and so is the p.p. of the verb when used attributively (*the allied forces*).
>
> (*Ally*, Gowers 1965)

More generally, and apart from obvious cases of conversion, many verbs seem to have acquired a marginal forestressed variant pronunciation at the very end of the twentieth century. For example, the verbs *abstract, accent, alloy, conflict, contest, contrast, discharge, imprint, progress, protest*,[11] *transfer* and *transform* are only backstressed in all *EPD* editions but may also be forestressed in *LPD*. A few others may be optionally forestressed both in *LPD* and in the latest editions of *EPD* only (*compound, decrease, export, impact, increase, reflex, refund, research*, etc.) For all such cases the corresponding noun has always been forestressed (at least optionally) for a longer time, which, in the light of all the cases we have already treated, leads us to consider that, be it overt or not, the process of late N>V conversion is nowadays increasingly frequent within such pairs. Some verbs may even be converted from nouns, themselves originally converted from verbs, as with *protest*. Balteiro thus explains:

> [This] also leads to the prediction that there are zero-derived triples of the type V → N → V as in pro'test (v) → 'protest (n) → 'protest (v) ('stage a protest'), di'gest (v) → 'digest (n) → 'digest (v) ('make a digest').
>
> (Balteiro 2007: 82)

F. Zumstein goes as far as considering that

> the nouns set the pace and the verbs enter the dance. [. . .] [T]he verb *protest*, which may have been a model for the noun, as Walker's comment suggested, takes the shape of the noun by adopting the /10/ stress variant. Verbo-nominal pairs should therefore rather be called nomino-verbal pairs, in which the noun, being the dominant semantic element, is the attraction pole in the variational relation, which always goes from /01/ to /10/.
>
> (Zumstein 2007: 366–7, our translation)

4 Stress placement in nouns: semantic differentiation

As explained in the introduction to this chapter, many N–V pairs are diatonic in contemporary English, nouns such as *object, contest, dispute, increase, present*, and so on being optionally, mainly or compulsorily forestressed. Yet, as Sherman (1975) points out, few diatonic pairs existed a few centuries ago (see section 1). And indeed, our corpus reveals that nearly all nouns old enough to be present in eighteenth-century dictionaries were originally back-stressed, at least in one dictionary. This applies, for example, to the nouns *affix, compress, confine, contest, convoy, extract, insult, premise, protest*, and so on. In seven cases for which our corpus does not show any sign of final stress, the *OED* confirms that they were indeed oxytonic at an earlier stage too: *compact, compound, converse, exile, process, produce, present*. For example:

> Originally accented on the second syllable (so 6 times out of 7 in Shakespeare), but noted in Phillips 1696 as accented on the first.
>
> (noun *compact*, *OED*)

> In verse in Middle English, early modern English, and Older Scots with variable stress. Stress on the final syllable is particularly common in rhyming position; thus still in Milton and other poets of the 17th and even 18th cent.
>
> (noun *process*, *OED*)

> In Middle English apparently usually stressed on the second syllable.
>
> (noun *present*, *OED*)

Eventually the only nouns (found in dictionaries as early as in the eighteenth century) for which we could not find any direct or indirect sign of oxytonic stress are *collect, comment, contact, discord, (object[12]), project, prospect* and *subject*. Yet this does not necessarily mean that they cannot have been backstressed at earlier periods to which we do not have access, as Chen (2014: 407–8) explains: 'Certainly prior changes could have taken place before the earliest coding. In other words, O → P had already been completed before the first coding.'

However this in itself does not explain why most of the nouns in our corpus changed from oxytonic to paroxytonic. More importantly, it does not explain why numerous nouns outside our corpus have remained oxytonic. The CONCERN type (oxytonic, isotonic) thus opposes the CONTEST type (diatonic).

Although she does not give any examples precisely involving homographic prefixed disyllabic pairs, Donka Minkova makes a point:

> In addition to differentiating word-class, stress-shifting can involve semantic differentiation, with or without word-class change. There is nothing surprising about variant pronunciations of polysemous words resulting in the split of the original base into two separate lexical entries. A famous case in point is the semantic bifurcation in the pair *palace-palate* < Lat. *Palātum*. [. . .] '*human-hu*'*mane*, [etc.].
>
> (Minkova 2014: 311–12)

And indeed, upon detailed examination of the synchronic and diachronic meaning(s) of the verbs and nouns in our corpus, we suggest that stress alternation works as a marker of semantic differentiation, serving to signal **semantic symmetry** or **semantic asymmetry** between the two members of the pair.

By **semantic symmetry** we mean that the meaning of the noun is equivalent to the meaning of the verb, being a **verbal noun** which can be paraphrased as *the act of V-ing* or *the state of being V-en*. In such cases, semantic symmetry is signalled by stress isomorphy, hence the [01] pattern for both members of the pair. For example, *attack, concern, defeat, desire, embrace, reproach, revolt, support*, and so on are verbal nouns: an *attack* is the act of attacking; a *defeat* is the act of defeating or of being defeated; *support* is the act of supporting, and so on.

On the other hand, when the noun is not a verbal noun corresponding to the exact meaning of the verb, **semantic asymmetry** is marked by stress alternation, hence the [10] nominal stress pattern. Such cases may correspond to several broad types of N–V relations:

- There is **no obvious semantic link between the noun and the verb** in contemporary English.
- The noun corresponds to a later **semantic specialisation of the verb**, not to its proper meaning.
- The noun refers to **a physical object or person** (this includes N–V relations such as resultative and locative), and so on.

In many cases N–V semantic asymmetry is easily detectable, for example: *abstract* (a summary, not the act of abstracting), *compact* (a contract, not the act of compacting), *compress* (a thing, not the act of compressing), *discount* (commercial deduction in modern sense, not the proper meaning of the verb), *discourse* (linguistic discourse as an object: spoken or written unit for analysis), *extract* (result of the extraction process, not the act of extracting), *object* (a thing, not the act of objecting), *perfume* (substance usually contained in a bottle, not the act of perfuming), *present* (moment or gift, not the act of presenting), *record* (thing recorded, not the act of recording), and so on.

In other trickier cases it is necessary to explore semantic changes through time. For example:

- The noun *dispute* has been recorded with initial stress as a variant pronunciation since *EPD13* (1967), preferred by 38% of British speakers (*LPD*). *Dispute* originally referred to 'the act of disputing or arguing against' (early seventeenth century) but the *OED* reports a more recent use dating back to 1892: 'attrib., as *dispute benefit*, *dispute pay*, pay to members of a trade union while on strike or locked out', which is a semantic specialisation compared with the original verbal meaning. This is supported by Burchfield's third edition of *Fowler's Modern English Usage*: '*Dispute*. Both the verb and the noun are stressed on the second syllable. In the 1970s and 1980s, first-syllable stressing of the noun came into prominence in the language of northern trade union leaders [. . .]' (Burchfield 1996).
- The noun *protest* originally meant 'A solemn, formal, or emphatic declaration or affirmation; an avowal' (1460) but rapidly referred to something written, 'a formal declaration in writing' (1479, 1644), and more specifically 'A written statement of dissent from any motion carried in the House of Lords, recorded and signed by any peer of the minority' (1712). However a more modern meaning of the noun has now departed from the proper meaning of the verb: 'The expression of social, political, or cultural dissent from a policy or course of action, typically by means of a public demonstration; (also) an instance of this, a protest march, a public demonstration' (1852). *Protest* referring to an object (a written statement) or to a specialised meaning (street demonstrations) both justify stressing the noun on the first syllable. And indeed, the noun *protest* started to take initial stress in our corpus as early as 1804 in S. JONES.
- The noun *control* is a verbal noun expressing the act of controlling or the state of being controlled, hence its [01] pattern. However, *LPD15–18* also mention a [10] variant accompanied by the comment 'in machinery'. This corresponds to meaning 3d in the *OED* (first attested in 1908), where *control* is an object: 'The apparatus by means of which a machine, as an aeroplane or motor vehicle, is controlled during operation; also, any of the mechanisms of a control apparatus [. . .]'.

Interestingly, this phenomenon explains why apparently similar nouns are stressed differently. For example, *decline* (n.), which refers to 'The process of declining or sinking to a weaker or inferior condition' (*OED*), is backstressed accordingly. Meanwhile, *incline* (n.) does not refer to the act of inclining but to 'An inclined plane or surface; a slope, declivity (esp. on a road or railway)' (*OED*) and is forestressed. A similar explanation may be given concerning *export* and *import*. If both are stressed [10] today, their stress patterns were different in JOHNSON 1756 and DYCHE 1759, where *import* (n.) was stressed [01] because it meant 'the act of importing' ('imported goods' was first attested later) while *export* (n.) was stressed [10] because it meant 'exported goods' ('the act of exporting' was first attested later).

Some pairs saw the meaning of the noun change forever, which triggered stress change as well. As a result the original [01] stress pattern of nouns usually corresponds to now obsolete verbal nouns. For instance, *permit* (n.) originally meant 'Permission or liberty [. . .] to do a particular thing' (*OED*) and was stressed [01] accordingly in the eighteenth and early nineteenth centuries. Then it changed to [10] when it started referring to an object: 'A document giving permission to do something' (*OED*). The same applies to *suspect* (n.): from [01] before the twentieth century (even as a variant pronunciation in *EPD1–3*) when meaning 'suspicion' (verbal noun, 'act of suspecting') to [10] during the twentieth century when referring to 'a suspected person'. Similarly, WALKER 1842 is the only dictionary in our corpus that mentions oxytonic stress in the noun *record* (as a variant pronunciation), but it is explicitly associated to courts of justice. And indeed, a *court of record* (namely a court of justice, first attested in 1387 according to the *OED*) is to be understood as a place where the act of recording testimonies is performed. The same goes for *refuse*, as can be seen in WORCESTER 1860 in Figure 3.12, where the obsolete noun meaning 'refusal, denial' (verbal noun) is backstressed.

On the contrary, the modern meaning of *refuse* (namely 'Anything that is rejected, discarded, or thrown away; rubbish, waste, residue; (now esp.) household waste', *OED*) is forestressed.

In many contemporary cases it seems that the coexistence of both [01] and [10] stress patterns for a single noun results from incomplete change, which may become complete in the future. It is also very likely that polysemy within some nouns helps maintain the two stress patterns, at least for some time. For example, *alloy* (n.) used to be backstressed before the twentieth century and recorded as such down to *EPD3*. It was stressed [10/01] in *EPD4–14R* (and *LPD1–3*) and finally only [10] in *CEPD15–18*. *EPD4–11* gave an interesting detail to help readers make a distinction: *alloy* was stressed [10/01] when referring to a 'mixture of metals', but only [01] in its 'figurative sense'. The figurative meaning being much closer to a verbal noun (for example, 'the account was an alloy of truth and fiction' means that the account was the act of alloying truth and fiction) than the proper meaning of *alloy* ('a metal

> † RE-FŪṢE' (rẹ-fūz'), *n.* Refusal; denial. *Fairfax.*
>
> RE-FŪṢE' (rẹ-fūz'), *v. a.* [It. *rifiutare*; Sp. *rehusar*; Fr. *refuser.* — From L. *refuto*, to repress, to refute. *Menage.*] [*i.* REFUSED; *pp.* REFUSING, REFUSED.]
>
> 1. To deny, as something solicited or required; to decline. " To make them give or *refuse* credit." *Locke.*
>
> 2. To reject; to repudiate; to exclude. "The stone which the builders *refused.*" *Ps.* cxviii. 22.
>
>   *Refuse* profane and old wives' fables.   1 *Tim.* iv. 7.
>
> Syn. — A person *refuses* what is asked of him for want of inclination to comply, *declines* what is proposed from motives of discretion, and *rejects* what is offered because it does not fall within his views. To *repel* is to *reject* with violence; to *rebuff*, to *refuse* with contempt. *Refuse* assent or a request; *deny* a claim; *decline* an offer; *reject* a proposal; *repel* a foe; *rebuff* an intruder.
>
> RE-FŪṢE', *v. n.* 1. To decline to accept; not to comply.
>
>   Too proud to ask, too humble to *refuse*.   *Garth.*
>
> 2. (*Mil.*) To keep out of that regular alignement which is formed when troops are upon the point of engaging an enemy.   *Stocqueler.*
>
> RĚF'ŪSE [rĕf'ūs, *W. J. F. Ja. K. Sm. Wr. Wb.*; rĕf'fūz, *S. P. E.*], *n.* [Fr. *refus.*]
>
> 1. † A refusal.   *Fairfax.*
>
> 2. That which is left or rejected as worthless after the rest is taken; waste or worthless matter; dregs; lees; dross; scum.   *Bacon.*
>
>   The scum and *refuse* of the people.   *Gov. of the Tongue.*
>
> Syn. — See DREGS.

Figure 3.12 Entry *refuse* in WORCESTER 1860

made by intimately combining two or more metals' (*OED*), hence a physical substance), stress distinction was applicable. However, because the proper meaning was probably the more usual, forestressing became the only possibility according to the subsequent *EPD* editions. This probably does not hold for *control*, where the [10] stress pattern 'in machinery' represents a marginal meaning of the noun *control*, which suggests that [10] will certainly not prevail.

It would be untrue to say that no studies had already pointed out this phenomenon of semantic distinction, but it was never established as a general rule. Contrary to recent studies, which mainly focused on quantitative analysis especially involving frequency, older studies made reference, however limited, to semantics. For example:

> After nearly three centuries of comparative stability, these desertions, acknowledged or unacknowledged, have suddenly become surprisingly numerous. In fact this dwindling remnant of nouns, **often more or less dissociated in meaning from their verbs**, seems ready at any moment to give way to the powerful attraction of the great mass of English dissyllabic [*sic*] verbs with initial stress, or even to that of some much smaller group, if only it seem [*sic*] to be nearer of kin.
>
>   (Bradley 1922: 15, our emphasis)

If Bradley did not seem to realise that this parenthetical precision might have been a key to the problem, Hill did explicitly relate stressing to semantics:

> Dictionaries still give *'address* (n.) and *ad'dress* (vb.), for all the various meanings of this word. My own usage, however, and so far as observation and questioning of students and friends can tell me, the usage of many if not most Americans is thus – I *'address* a letter, and I put the *'address* on the letter, but I *ad'dress* the meeting and I deliver an *ad'dress*. Here if my observations are correct, the differences in the meaning of the word have brought about a tendency to sort out the stress forms to correspond to differences in meaning.
>
> (Hill 1931: 447)

And indeed, the noun *address* in 'deliver an address' is a verbal noun, which it is not in 'put the address on the letter'. But this distinction only holds for American English, while British English only has *ad'dress*. Hill then gives a few more examples such as:

> *tra'verse* (vb.), and *'traverse* (n.), but to *'traverse* a gun. [...] *di'gest* (vb.), and *'digest* (n.), but to *'digest* a long argument. [...] *'accent* (n.), *ac'cent* (vb.) in 'I would *ac'cent* the structure not the style,' but 'I *'accent* the first syllable.' This distinction is disappearing, however, since the distinction in meaning is slight. Present usage seems to prefer *'accent* throughout.[13]
>
> On the basis of these examples I feel safe in saying that should the noun *collect* through some revival of religious enthusiasm give us a new verb meaning to pray briefly, that it would preserve fore-stress, and that should the verb *col'lect* subsequently give us a new noun, it would preserve end-stress.
>
> (Hill 1931: 447)

Although he relied more on conversion than on semantic differentiation, Hill probably made a point. Only considering this phenomenon as a 'limitation to the force of [the] tendency to distinguish noun from verb' (1931: 447), Hill did draw a very accurate conclusion which curiously diverged from that of Sherman in 1975 (see section 1):

> Bearing in mind these limitations to the tendency to differentiate noun from verb by stress – namely that only new nouns can be distinguished from old verbs, and not vice-versa, that the tendency is often interfered with by considerations of analogy, rhythm, etc. that foreign suffixes and prefixes tend to fall in with similar invariable native ones, and finally that distinctions in meaning tend to produce a redistribution of the

variant forms, not only is the comparatively small number of noun-verb pairs in which the differentiation occurs sufficiently understandable, but also one can safely prophesy that the tendency will not ever become fruitful of general grammatical distinction in English.

(Hill 1931: 447–8)

To find an explicit description of prefixed disyllabic N–V pairs truly similar to ours, we need to go back even further in time: 'The same word, when it signifies an action, is accented upon the last syllable, as to *con 'tract*, to *re 'bel*: when it signifies a thing, the accent is sometimes transferred to the first, as a *'contract*, a *'rebel'* (Watts 1721: 34–5). In fact, this statement is not part of a study on disyllables but is found in I. Watts's 1721 treatise entitled *The Art of Reading and Writing English*. By not using the terms *noun*, *verb* or *adjective*, but resorting to meaning ('it signifies') rather than to syntactic labels, Watts referred to the problem more accurately. And indeed, if a verb can be described in most cases as referring to 'an action' (verbal noun), a noun cannot be so reduced as to refer to 'a thing' (not a verbal noun). For example, *attack* refers to an 'action' both as a verb and as a noun, hence oxytonic stress in both cases.

Much more recently, after having analysed stress variation in many N–V pairs, Zumstein concluded:

> The nouns, emancipated from the verbs, build their own meanings – figurative, specialized or learned [...]. *[D]ispute* supports Trevian's conclusions by becoming a 'real' noun with its own senses and departs from the verb through its /10/ variant stress pattern [...].
>
> (Zumstein 2007: 366, our translation)

His conclusion is very similar to ours and his study in fact only lacked the conversion of these observations into a more general and explicit semantic rule so as to explain not only stress variation but also all those pairs such as *con 'cern* that seem to have always been isotonic.

5 Stress placement in nouns: a structural phenomenon

Many cases of stress shifts in nouns were found to exhibit an unexpected corollary in terms of frequencies. Contrary to Phillips (2014) and Sonderegger and Niyogi (2013), who found N+V frequency only to be relevant, we found that it was verb frequency rather than noun frequency that turned out to be significant from a diachronic perspective.

Using GNV allowed us to highlight a frequent pattern, as is evidenced in Figures 3.13 and 3.14 by *exploit* and *defect*, both being pairs where the noun is semantically unrelated to the verb.

Figure 3.13 Frequency in Google Ngram Viewer of *exploit* (noun and verb, inflected forms included)

Before the twentieth century, the noun *exploit* was backstressed while there existed a semantically related and now obsolete verb *exploit* ('accomplish, achieve, perform', first attested in 1400 – *OED*), also backstressed. Figure 3.13 shows that the noun was more frequent before 1900. However, the frequency of the verb significantly rose from the late twentieth century onwards, which presumably corresponds to the use of the contemporary verb *exploit* ('to utilize for one's own ends, treat selfishly as mere workable material', first attested in 1838 – *OED*), which this time is semantically unrelated to the noun. In the meantime, the noun shifted to [10/01] in *EPD1–10* then [10] in subsequent editions. This resulted in the contemporary diatonic pair, which according to our semantic (a)symmetry hypothesis is justified, since the noun *exploit* does not refer to the act of exploiting or the state of being exploited.

A similar description can be made for *defect*. Although there existed a verb semantically related to the noun ('To fail, fall short, become deficient or wanting', first attested in 1587 – *OED*), it is now obsolete and Figure 3.14 suggests that it had in fact never gained ground. The contemporary meaning of the verb ('To fall away from (a person, party, or cause); to become a rebel or deserter' – *OED*) is not new (first attested in 1596) but Figure 3.14 suggests that it only started to gain ground in the mid-twentieth century. This is confirmed by the fact that the verb *defect* only entered *EPD* with the publication of the fourteenth edition (1977). However, whereas the noun had always been backstressed before the twentieth century, it is precisely from *EPD14* on that it became stressed [10/01].[14] Here again, forestressing is justified by semantic asymmetry, as a *defect* does not refer to the act of defecting.

In both cases and in many others, it thus seems that the moment when the nouns changed from [01] to [10] corresponds to the moment when semantically related – but asymmetrical – verbs actually started to gain ground in the language in terms of frequency. On the contrary, as long as the nouns did not face any 'competing' verbs, they were able to retain final stress. This implies the existence of a structural system in which, when a prefixed noun belongs

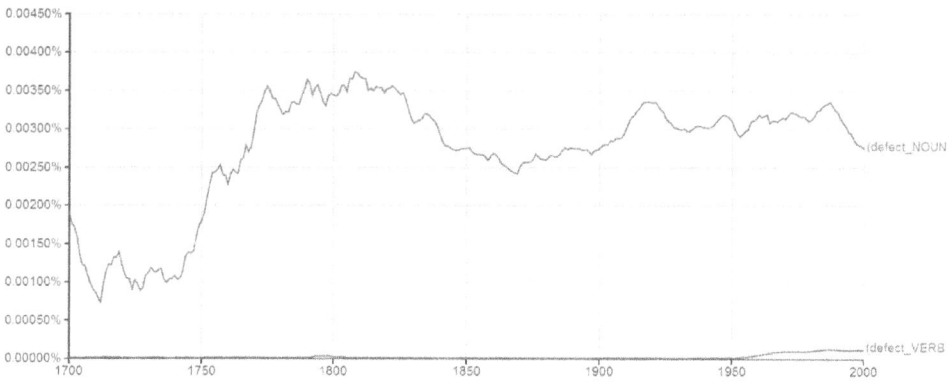

Figure 3.14 Frequency in Google Ngram Viewer of *defect* (noun and verb, inflected forms included)

to a N–V pair, it does not have a stress pattern of its own but is stressed in contrast with the verb. Ultimately, in many such cases, this allows semantic differentiation to go along with syntactic opposition. Very importantly, it should be noted that this phenomenon is to be observed only in the twentieth century.

6 Stress placement in nouns: from semantic differentiation to syntactic marking?

The structural phenomenon exposed in section 5 – namely, that the emergence of an asymmetrical backstressed verb triggers forestressing in the noun in the twentieth century – seems to find an echo in some semantically symmetrical N–V pairs such as *increase, decrease, research, refund*, and so on. According to our semantic (a)symmetry hypothesis, such pairs should not show any signs of diatonic stress, since *an increase* refers to the act of increasing, *research* refers to the act of researching, and so on. And yet the nouns have surprisingly become optionally forestressed too. However, interestingly, these nouns only did so in the late twentieth century. The frequency patterns for such pairs evidenced in Figures 3.15–3.18 show interesting phenomena.

The common point between all patterns is a significant frequency rise. In the case of *decrease, research* and *refund*, the rise clearly takes place in the twentieth century. In the case of *increase*, frequency had already been rising since the eighteenth century but this rise became much sharper in the twentieth century. In some cases (*increase, decrease*), the frequency of both members of the pair rises in a similar way. The same goes for *research*, although the noun is far more frequent in itself than the verb; yet the frequency pattern of the verb is the same as that of the verb *defect* in section 5. The case of *refund* is in fact similar to those of *increase* and *decrease*, although both noun and verb frequencies eventually slumped in the late twentieth century.

Figure 3.15 Frequency in Google Ngram Viewer of *increase* (noun and verb, inflected forms included)

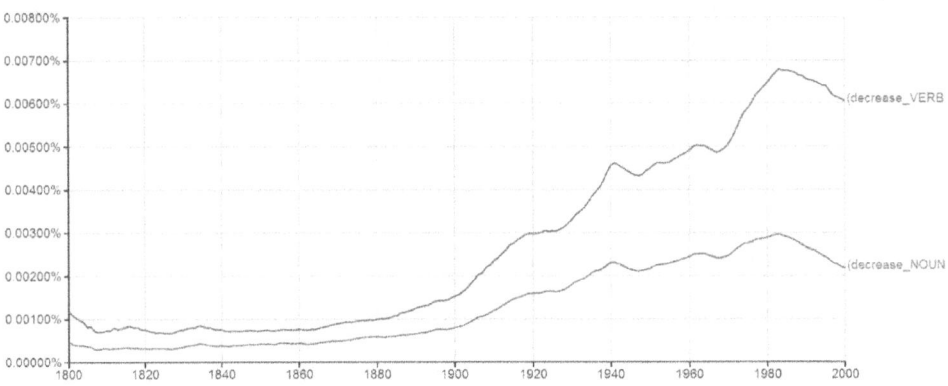

Figure 3.16 Frequency in Google Ngram Viewer of *decrease* (noun and verb, inflected forms included)

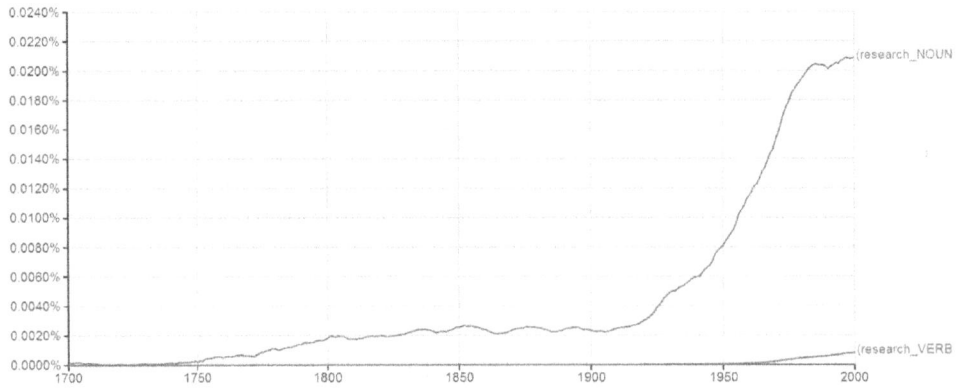

Figure 3.17 Frequency in Google Ngram Viewer of *research* (noun and verb, inflected forms included)

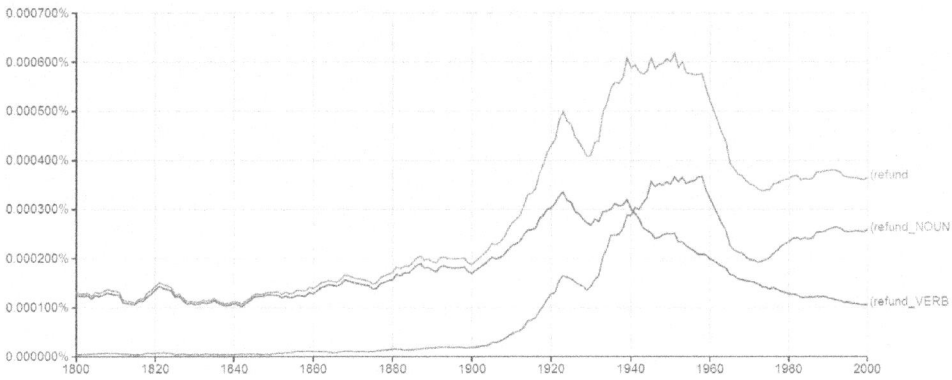

Figure 3.18 Frequency in Google Ngram Viewer of *refund* (noun, verb and total, inflected forms included)

Overall the total N+V frequency of *refund* still remains much higher than before the twentieth century.

On the whole it thus seems that a boom in frequency taking place in the twentieth century and usually affecting both the noun and the verb can be related to optional forestressing in the nouns in the late twentieth century, even without any signs of N–V semantic asymmetry.

Additionally, because of the conversion-like effect mentioned at the end of section 3, whereby many verbs have very recently optionally acquired the [10] stressing of the corresponding nouns, some pairs now exhibit stress variations in both the noun and the verb. This often takes the shape of [01/10] for the verb, and [10/01] for the noun, or possibly [01/10] for both, providing the noun acquired the [01] variant first. The latter case notably applies to *research*, stressed [01/10] for both the noun and the verb in *LPD* and *CEPD18* in British English, but only for the noun in *EPD1–17*, while the verb was only backstressed before the eighteenth edition. *LPD3* and *CEPD18* provide interesting comments:

> The pronunciation with initial stress is relatively new to British English and is disliked by many people.
>
> (noun *research*, CEPD18)

> The -'sɜːtʃ ‖ -'sɜ˞ːtʃ form appears still to predominate in universities, although 'riːsɜːtʃ ‖ 'riːsɜ˞ːtʃ has increasingly displaced it in general usage both in Britain and in America. Some speakers may distinguish between the verb •'• and the noun '••. – preference polls, British English •'• 80% (university teachers 95%), '•• 20%; American English, noun: '•• 78%, •'• 22%.
>
> (*research*, LPD3)

In several other cases, *LPD* confirms that 'some speakers may distinguish the verb •'• from the noun '••', as with *recess*, stressed [01/10] both as a noun and a verb. Under the entry *increase*, where the verb is stressed [01/10] and the noun [10/01], *LPD3* states:

> The stress distinction between verb •'• and noun '•• is not always made consistently. Nevertheless, in a British English preference poll 85% preferred to make this distinction (as against 7% preferring '•• for both verb and noun, 5% •'• for both, and 3% '•• for the verb, •'• for the noun).
> (*increase*, *LPD3*)

Overall, it seems that the semantic differentiation process marked by stress alternation as shown in sections 4 and 5 may have finally started to turn into a purely syntactic opposition process, stress alternation serving – at least for some speakers – to mark the syntactic category of each member of the pair. In other words, because it has existed for several centuries and because it triggers stress opposition, it is likely that the semantic marking system is now the object of a purely syntactic reinterpretation. We do not know for sure why it affects only certain symmetrical N–V pairs (*research* type) and not others (*concern* type), but rising frequency in the twentieth century is found to be a frequent correlation. In any case, this strongly contradicts both Phillips's (2014) and Sonderegger and Niyogi's (2013) frequency hypotheses (see section 2), since the nouns treated above are in no way infrequent and show strong rising frequencies concomitant with stress change.

Interestingly, this phenomenon was also found to affect some non-prefixed disyllabic N–V pairs in the twentieth century, namely pairs borrowed from French, as with *finance* in Figure 3.19. This figure also suggests that the frequency of both members of the pair boomed in the twentieth century. More specifically, as with some verbs in sections 4 and 5, the verb started to gain ground only during that period. In the meantime, both noun and verb remained backstressed until *EPD11* (1960) but, according to *LPD3*, the verb is still backstressed now while the noun is stressed [10/01].[15]

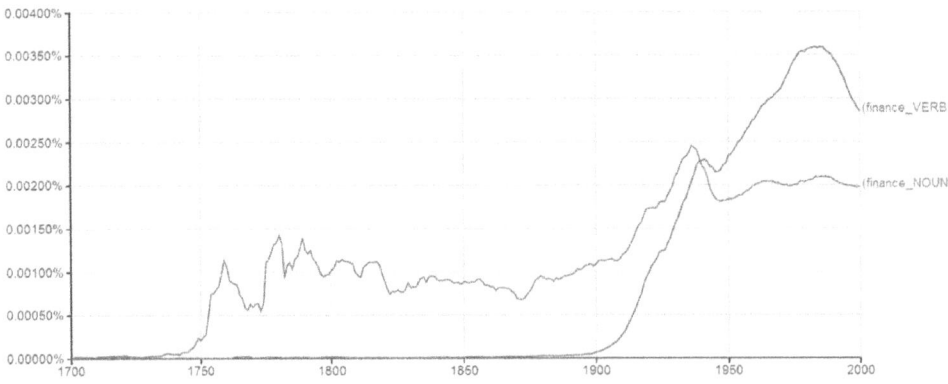

Figure 3.19 Frequency in Google Ngram Viewer of *finance* (noun and verb, inflected forms included)

Table 3.2 Stress placement in *asphalt* and *chagrin* (nouns and verbs) in British dictionaries

		(18th–)19th century	EPD1–3	EPD4–18
asphalt	noun	[01]	[10]	[10]
	verb	not found	[10/01]	[10/01]
chagrin	noun	[01/10]	[01]	[10]
	verb	[01/10]	[01]	[10/01]

In some other N–V pairs borrowed from French, although stress has retracted to the first syllable for both categories (which is usual for French loanwords), the verb retains a marginal backstressed pronunciation, as can be seen with *asphalt* and *chagrin* in Table 3.2.

Even though final stress is only optional in these verbs, it shows that stress alternation may still affect these converted pairs parasitically as a mere way to encode syntactic categories.

7 Discussion

With our corpus of etymologically prefixed disyllabic N–V pairs we have shown that stress placement and change in such pairs can be explained. Backstressing is the historical stressing in verbs, and the rare items in our corpus (*perfect*) that used to be forestressed confirm the default attractivity of verbal roots. However, numerous cases of late N>V conversion (*relay*), sometimes taking the shape of semantic specialisation, explain the more recent tendency for many verbs to become forestressed. In that respect, we agree with Chen's (2017) observation, already demonstrated in Chen (2014), that contrary to what Sherman thought, diatone is not an end point coming from both oxytone and paroxytone sources. Chen states that his study 'clearly delineate[s] an O → D → P migration path' (2017: 232), and therefore that 'Diatone is a transient phase from historical point of view' (2014: 430), as he shows that 48% of Sherman's diatones have progressed toward P (2014: 406). Yet, it is not sure whether all verbs will become paroxytones, depending on their semantic relationship with the corresponding nouns.

In most cases, diatonic stress in N–V pairs results from the emergence of new nominal meanings, which are forestressed as a result when they are not verbal nouns (i.e. the *act of V-ing* or *the fact of being V-en*) as a way to signal semantic asymmetry (*suspect*). On the contrary, verbal nouns retain verb stress to signal semantic symmetry (*concern*). In many cases the coexistence of symmetrical and asymmetrical nominal meanings results in the possibility of stressing the nouns on either syllable, at least for some time (*alloy*). Here again, our analysis confirms and completes Chen's study, where he found a correlation between stress placement in prefixed N–V pairs and the fact that either the noun or the verb entered the language first historically (2017: 252–60), then paving the way for semantic differentiation.

Because this semantic marking system has existed for a long time and triggers stress alternation, we suspect it may have started to be reinterpreted as a syntactic marking system in the twentieth century, hence new possible diatones even with semantic symmetry. This, combined with a possible extension of the principle of conversion, explains cases of pairs where both members may be stressed on either syllable (*increase*). The reinterpretation of a semantic to a syntactic marking system might also explain stress alternation in some non-prefixed pairs (*finance, asphalt*).

As regards pairs that have become diatonic in the twentieth century, we have confirmed that frequency plays a role. Yet contrary to earlier studies suggesting that low or falling frequencies were responsible for diatonic stress, we suggest that, for the twentieth century, the emergence of diatonic stress is often correlated to a rise in verbal frequency whereby nouns may stop being backstressed (this rise may be linked to the emergence of new meanings), or to a rise in N+V frequency. However, more refined observations on frequency need to be made in relation to diachronic semantics, especially before the twentieth century.

Isolated as they might be, a few N–V pairs seem to challenge our semantic (a)symmetry hypothesis. The morphological differences in semantically asymmetrical pairs such as *expand/se, expend/se, intend/t* or *extend/t* (an *extent* is not the act of extending or of being extended, etc.) may suffice to explain why they are not diatonic. However, a few semantically asymmetrical pairs such as *disguise, preserve, reserve*, but also *address* (British English only), are not diatonic either. More work therefore needs to be – and will be – done to assess the efficiency of our hypothesis by examining the set of etymologically prefixed disyllabic N–V pairs in its entirety in contemporary English.

Appendix 3.1

abstract, accent, access, affect, affix, alloy, ally, annex, assay, comment, compound, compress, concrete, confab, confine, conflict, conserve, consult, contact, content, contest, contract, contrast, control, converse, convoy, decline, decrease, default, defect, desert, despatch, despond, detail, digest, discard, discharge, discord, discount, discourse, dispatch, dispute, excerpt, excess, excise, exhaust, exile, exploit, export, extract, impact, import, imprint, incline, increase, indent, index, infarct, infix, insult, intern, inverse, object, perfect, perfume, permit, prefix, premise, present, pretense, pretext, process, produce, progress, project, prolapse, prospect, protest, recess, reclaim, record, recount, recourse, redress, reflex, refund, regress, relapse, relay, remit, remount, research, retail, subject, suffix, suspect, transfer, transform, transverse

Notes

1. This holds for British English. In American English, prefixed verbs are backstressed (*ablate, relate*, etc.) while non-prefixed verbs are usually forestressed (*mutate, locate*, etc. except *create*).
2. See also Chapters 2, 5 and 6 of this volume for more details about stress placement in disyllables and prefixed words.
3. Basing themselves on *LPD2*, Svensson and Hering (2013: 134) provide surprisingly different tendencies: the *con'cern* type would represent 48.5% of all pairs, the *'comment* type 31% and the alternating *object* type 20.5%.
4. Unfortunately, we consider Sherman's corpus too heterogeneous to be representative of diatonic stress in N–V pairs as a unified phenomenon. It contains not only etymologically prefixed pairs (*abuse, delay*, etc.) and synchronically prefixed pairs (*retouch, disquiet*, etc.), but also numerous pairs having notorious auto-stressed endings such as -*ade* (*cascade, parade*, etc.), -*ese* (*siamese*), double vowels (*career, dragoon, pontoon, salaam, shampoo*, etc.) and double consonants (*bastille, finesse, garotte*, etc.). It seems doubtful that such pairs might eventually become diatonic. His list also contains notorious French loanwords (*garage, massage, guitar*, etc.), for which we know that stress retraction – if any – affects both the noun and the verb. Finally, it must be said that, having based his inventory of N–V pairs on the *SOED* without restraining himself to pairs having a minimal frequency, Sherman included doubtful pairs involving conversion, such as *rebus, vandyke, guitar, bespeak*, and so on.
5. We use the term 'outlier' after Hilpert and Gries (2016: 49), which they define as follows: 'data points that deviate considerably from the overall trend in the data and/or from other temporally close data points, and that may therefore reflect "anomalies" in the data (which in turn may result from sampling problems, author idiosyncrasies, etc.)'.
6. <https://books.google.com/ngrams>. The use of Google Ngram Viewer, based on the Google Books database, as a tool is controversial in linguistics as well as in many other social sciences, notably because it is not a corpus but a database. It includes books, journals, and so on which are possibly unrepresentative of the English language, especially of spoken English. Other problems include mistakes resulting from OCR processing. For lack of space, we cannot provide the reader of this chapter with detailed arguments in favour of the relative reliability of GNV. However we demonstrate in Castanier (2016: 178–92) that its

use does have linguistic relevance and that its potential deficiencies can be avoided. Although this tool is imperfect, it proved consistent when analysing data within the 1700–2000 time period (frequencies prior to 1700 are usually inconsistent and should be discarded), providing one focuses on significant frequency trends and makes sure that other tools and sources of reasoning (the BNC, dictionaries, etc.) corroborate what GNV may lead us to infer. This is in line with the conclusion of a historical paper by Gibbs and Cohen entitled 'A Conversation with Data: Prospecting Victorian Words and Ideas': 'Far from replacing existing intellectual foundations and research tactics, text mining is yet another tool for understanding the history of culture – without pretending to measure it quantitatively – and one that complements how we already sift historical evidence. [. . .] In this context, isolated textual elements such as n-grams aren't universally unhelpful; examining them can be quite informative if used appropriately and with their limitations in mind, especially as preliminary explorations combined with other forms of historical knowledge. Neither the Ngram Viewer nor Google searches are offensive to history, but rather making overblown historical claims drawn from either of them alone. [. . .] Historical trends – or anomalies – might be revealed by data, but they need to be investigated in detail in order to avoid conclusions that rest on superficial evidence. This is also true for more traditional research processes that rely too heavily on just a few anecdotal examples' (2011: 76).
7. Additionally, the first sense of the verb *comment*, now obsolete ('To devise, contrive, invent') was not a conversion from the noun but represented the Latin *commentāre*, hence its possible historical backstressed pronunciation.
8. The [01] stress pattern found in *EPD13–18* may be a mistake, as the verb is stressed [10/01] in *EPD1–12* but also *LPD1–3*, and [10] in *ODP*.
9. We did not include *affix* in Figure 3.7 for the sake of readability in black and white print. GNV shows that *affix* is as frequent as *prefix* in British English today, but more frequent in American English. The frequency hierarchy established thanks to GNV is strongly confirmed by the COCA: *prefix* 304 total occurrences, *suffix* 260, *infix* 10, *affix* 1074 (inflected forms included). The BNC is less definite: *prefix* 191, *suffix* 228, *infix* 1, *affix* 166.
10. Despite occasional [10] noun stress patterns, *namely* in FENNING 1771 and JAMESON 1827.
11. The verb *protest* did have the new [10] stress variant in *EPD14–14R* only, but it disappeared with the publication of *CEPD15*.
12. SPIERS 1877 stresses *ob'ject* but it may be a mistake.
13. In fact the distinction has not disappeared, since dictionaries stress the verb *accent* [10/01] in American English. *CEPD15–18* seem deficient, as they only stress it [01].

14. After being stressed [01/10] in *EPD1–13*, which suggests that the verb might have started to be actually used earlier although it is not present in *EPD* before *EPD14*.
15. However *EPD* disagrees with *LPD*, stressing the noun and the verb alike, viz. [01/10] in *EPD12–14R* and [10/01] in *CEPD15–18*.

References

Abasq, V. et al. (2014), 'Les préfixés pluricatégoriels dissyllabiques: Réflexions méthodologiques sur l'analyse de corpus', paper presented at the ALOES 2014 Conference, held at the University of Paris 13 Villetaneuse, Paris, France, on 4–5 April 2014.

Balteiro, I. (2007), *The Directionality of Conversion in English: A Dia-Synchronic Study*, Bern: Peter Lang.

Bradley, C. B. (1922), 'The accentuation of the research-group of words', in C. M. Gayley, H. K. Schilling and R. Schevill (eds), *Modern Philology XI, The Charles Mills Gayley Anniversary Papers*, Berkeley: University of California Press, pp. 1–19.

Burchfield, R. W. (1996), *The New Fowler's Modern English Usage*, 3rd edn, Oxford: Clarendon Press.

Castanier, J. (2016), 'L'évolution accentuelle du lexique anglais britannique contemporain appréhendée à travers les dictionnaires de prononciation (XVIIIe–XXIe siècles)', PhD dissertation, University of Poitiers.

Chen, C.-Y. (2014), 'Direction of stress-shift in noun-verb pairs and progressions in American and British English', *English Linguistics* 31(2), 401–38.

Chen, C.-Y. (2017), 'Word frequency, entry date and entry status in relation to stress-shifts in English noun-verb pairs', *English Linguistics* 33(2), 231–77.

Duchet, J.-L., N. Trapateau and J. Castanier (2012), 'Stress placement in pronouncing dictionaries (1727–2010): Latin etymology *vs* English derivation', *Language and History* 55(1), 34–46.

Gąsiorowski, P. (1997), 'Words in *-ate* and the history of English stress', in J. Fisiak (ed.), *Studies in Middle English Linguistics*, Berlin: Mouton de Gruyter, pp. 157–80.

Gibbs, F. W and D. J. Cohen (2011), 'A conversation with data: Prospecting Victorian words and ideas', *Victorian Studies* 54(1), 69–77.

Gowers, E. (1965), *Fowler's Modern English Usage*, 2nd edn, Oxford: Oxford University Press.

Hill, A. A. (1931), 'Stress in recent English as a distinguishing mark between dissyllables used as noun or verb', *American Speech* 6(6), 443–8.

Hilpert, M. and S. T. Gries (2016), 'Quantitative approaches to diachronic corpus linguistics', in M. Kytö and P. Pahta (eds), *The Cambridge Handbook of English Historical Linguistics*, Cambridge: Cambridge University Press, pp. 36–53.

Minkova, D. (2014), *A Historical Phonology of English*, Edinburgh: Edinburgh University Press.

Phillips, B. S. (1984), 'Word frequency and the actuation of sound change', *Language* 60(2), 320–42.

Phillips, B. S. (2014), 'Gradience in an abrupt change. Stress shift in English disyllabic noun-verb pairs', in S. E. Pfenninger, O. Timofeeva, A.-C. Gardner,

A. Honkapohja, M. Hundt and D. Schreier (eds), *Contact, Variation, and Change in the History of English*, Amsterdam: John Benjamins, pp. 83–94.

Sherman, D. (1975), 'Noun-verb stress alternation: An example of the lexical diffusion of sound change in English', *Linguistics* 159, 43–71.

Sonderegger, M. and P. Niyogi (2013), 'Variation and change in English noun/verb pair stress: Data and dynamical systems models', in A. C. L. Yu (ed.), *Origins of Sound Change: Approaches to Phonologization*, Oxford: Oxford University Press, pp. 262–84.

Svensson, A.-M. and J. Hering (2013), 'Stress distinction in prefixed disyllabic noun/verb pairs in English: One of the most settled analogies of our language?', *Interdisciplinary Journal for Germanic Linguistics and Semiotic Analysis* 18(2), 129–41.

Trevian, I. (2003), *Morphoaccentologie et processus d'affixation de l'anglais*, Bern: Peter Lang.

Watts, I. (1722), *The Art of Reading and Writing English*, 2nd edn, London: for J. Clark, Em. Matthews & R. Ford.

Zumstein, F. (2007), 'Variation accentuelle, variation phonétique: Étude systématique fondée sur des corpus lexico-phonétiques informatisés anglais', PhD dissertation, University of Poitiers.

Primary sources

[AHDEL1–5] Morris, W. (A. H. Soukhanov for *AHDEL3*; J. P. Pickett for *AHDEL4–5*) (1969–2011), *American Heritage Dictionary of the English Language*, 5 edns, Boston: Houghton Mifflin.

[BAILEY] Bailey, N. (1727), *An Orthographical Dictionary, Shewing both the Orthography and the Orthoepia of the English Tongue*, London: for T. Cox.

[BARCLAY] Barclay, J. [1774] (1824), *A Complete and Universal English Dictionary*, 4th edn, London: for William Baynes and Son.

[BOYER 1829] Boyer, A. et al. [1702] (1829), *Dictionnaire anglais–français et français–anglais*, nouvelle édition, Paris: chez Ledentu.

[BOYER 1837] Boyer, A. et al. (1837), *Dictionnaire anglais-français et français-anglais, Abrégé de Boyer*, Paris: Charles Hingrey.

[BUCHANAN] Buchanan, J. (1766), *An Essay towards Establishing a Standard for an Elegant and Uniform Pronunciation of the English Language*, London: for Edward and Charles Dilly.

[CEPD15–18] Roach, P. et al. (1997–2011), *Cambridge English Pronouncing Dictionary*, 15th–18th edns, Cambridge: Cambridge University Press.

[CHAMBERS] Donald, J. [1867] (1872), *Chambers's Etymological Dictionary of the English Language*, 2nd edn, London, Edinburgh: Chambers.

[CPDBAE] Lewis, J. W. (1972), *A Concise Pronouncing Dictionary of British and American English*, Oxford: Oxford University Press.

[DYCHE] Dyche, T. [1735] (1759), *A New General English Dictionary*, 10th edn, London: for C. Ware.

[ENTICK] Entick, J. [1764] (1798), *New Spelling Dictionary teaching to Write and Pronounce the English Tongue*, London: for C. Dilly.

[*EPD1–12*] Jones, D. (1917–63), *English Pronouncing Dictionary*, 1st–12th edns, London: Dent & Sons.

[*EPD13–14*] Jones, D and A. C. Gimson (1967; 1977), *English Pronouncing Dictionary*, 13th and 14th edns, London: Dent & Sons.

[*EPD14R*] Jones, D., A. C. Gimson and S. Ramsaran (1988), *English Pronouncing Dictionary*, 14th edn with revisions and supplement, London: Dent & Sons.

[FENNING] Fenning, D. [1761] (1771), *The Royal English Dictionary*, 4th edn, London: for L. Hawes et al.

[FULTON & KNIGHT] Fulton, G. and G. Knight [1802] (1833), *A General and Explanatory Dictionary of the English Language*, London: Whittaker, Treacher & Arnot.

[JAMESON] Jameson, R. S. (1827), *A Dictionary of the English Language*, London: William Pickering.

[JOHNSON] Johnson, S. (1756), *A Dictionary of the English Language*, London: for J. Knapton et al.

[KENYON & KNOTT] Kenyon, J. S. and T. A. Knott (1944), *Pronouncing Dictionary of American English*, Springfield: Merriam.

[*LPD1–3*] Wells, J. C. (1990–2008), *Longman Pronunciation Dictionary*, 1st, 2nd and 3rd edns, Harlow: Longman.

[*ODP*] Upton, C., W. A. Kretzschmar Jr and R. Konopka (2001), *Oxford Dictionary of Pronunciation for Current English*, New York: Oxford University Press.

[PERRY] Perry, W. [1775] (1800), *The Royal Standard English Dictionary*, 5th edn, Boston: Isaiah Thomas and Ebenezer T. Andrews.

[RANDOM HOUSE] Flexner, A. B. et al. [1966] (1997), *Random House Webster's Unabridged Dictionary*, 2nd edn, New York: Random House.

[SHERIDAN] Sheridan, T. (1780; 1797), *A Complete Dictionary of the English Language, Both with Regard to Sound and Meaning*, 1st and 4th edns, London: for C. Dilly.

[S. JONES] Jones, S. [1798] (1804), *A General Pronouncing and Explanatory of the English Language*, 9th edn, London: for Vernor and Mood.

[SPIERS] Spiers, A. [1846] (1877), *Dictionnaire général anglais–français*, 26th edn, Paris: Librairie européenne de Baudry.

[SPIERS & SURENNE 1886] Spiers, A. and G. Surenne [1840] (1886), *Standard Pronouncing Dictionary of the French and English Languages in two parts*, School edn, New York: D. Appleton.

[SPIERS & SURENNE 1891] Spiers, A. and G. P. Quackenbos [1852] (1891), *Spiers and Surenne's French and English Pronouncing Dictionary*, New York: D. Appleton.

[WALKER] Walker, J. [1791] (1842), *A Critical Pronouncing Dictionary and Expositor of the English Language*, London: Robinson, Cadell & Davies.

[WEBSTER 1836] Webster, N. [1828] (1836), *An American Dictionary of the English Language, abridged version*, New York: N. and J. White.

[WEBSTER 1898] Porter, N. [1890] (1898), *Webster's International Dictionary of the English Language*, Springfield: Merriam.

[WEBSTER 2000] Gove, P. B. [1961] (2000), *Webster's Third New International Dictionary of the English Language*, Springfield: Merriam.

[WEBSTER 2003] Mish, F. C. et al. [1898] (2003), *Merriam Webster's Collegiate Dictionary*, 11th collegiate edn, Springfield: Merriam Webster.

[WEBSTER-MORRIS] Webster, N. and C. Morris (1908), *The Universal Self-Pronouncing Dictionary of the English Language*, Philadelphia, Chicago: John C. Winston.

[WORCESTER 1860] Worcester, J. E. (1860), *Dictionary of the English Language*, Boston: Hickling, Swan and Brewer.

[WORCESTER 1874] Worcester, J. E. (1874), *A Comprehensive Dictionary of the English Language*, Boston: Brewer & Tileston.

[WRIGHT] Wright, T. (1852–6), *The Universal Pronouncing Dictionary and the General Expositor of the English Language*, London: London Printing and Publishing Company.

4 English Phonology and the Literate Speaker: Some Implications for Lexical Stress

Quentin Dabouis

0 Introduction

Reference to orthographic information is almost absent from phonological research, and one might ask why this should be. Is the question of the relationship between orthography and phonology considered as being 'solved' or is it simply ignored? Can phonology completely do away with orthographic information? This chapter argues that it should not and brings forward arguments which I hope will arouse interest for the links between these two representations of the *signifiant*.

Interest in the relationship between orthography and phonology has come mainly from psycholinguistics and reading acquisition. Several experiments have shown that orthographic information can influence tasks which do not involve any visual stimuli, such as rhyme judgement, lexical decision or auditory word recognition (Chéreau et al. 2007; Peereman et al. 2009; Perre and Ziegler 2008; Perre et al. 2009; Seidenberg and Tanenhaus 1979; Taft 2006; Taft and Hambly 1985). Brewer (2008) also found that the number of letters representing word-final voiceless obstruents had a positive influence of on the phonetic duration of these segments in both experimental conditions and spontaneous speech.[1] Zamuner and Ohala (1999) found orthographic effects on syllable segmentation in preliterate children, for example *cabin* [kæ] – [bɪn] vs *cabbage* [kæb] – [bɪdʒ], although their experiment was replicated by Treiman et al. (2002), who did not confirm the results and only found orthographic effects in literate speakers. Significantly, an experiment on French speakers (Bürki et al. 2012) showed that a single orthographic presentation of a nonce-word is sufficient to induce a significant change in the phonological representation of that same nonce-word, which was constructed through 25 oral presentations of that word over several days. These results have been interpreted as signs that phonological knowledge is restructured when orthography is learned (Bürki et al. 2012; Ehri and Wilce 1980; Jaeger 1986; Perre and Ziegler 2008; Taft and Hambly 1985; Wang and Derwing 1986) and that this modification of the cognitive system is permanent. It might seem trivial to mention it but, as underlined by Jaeger (1986) and Laks (2005), learning how to read and how to write is a very long and tedious process and constitutes a powerful force to restructure phonological knowledge.

Recently, a number of studies in second language acquisition have looked at the relationship between orthography and phonology (see Bassetti et al. 2015 for an overview). Let us focus on a recent study to illustrate the sort of evidence that has been put forward. Mairano et al. (2018) studied a group of Italian learners of English, who have to learn not to geminate consonants spelled with orthographic geminates (which I will represent as <C'C'>; for example *oppose, attacking, accuse*) and to increase their voice onset time (VOT) for voiceless plosives. They report that the participants had a harder time avoiding gemination than adjusting their VOT. They see this difference as determined by orthography: gemination is represented in the spelling but not VOT. This shows that orthography can be a determining factor in the acquisition of the phonological properties of the target language. In a related field, a number of recent studies on loanword adaptation have shown how spelling can determine the pronunciation of borrowings (see Hamann and Colombo 2017; Neuman 2009: §5 and references therein).

Although there has been accumulating evidence that orthography can strongly influence the phonology, the relationship between the two has been largely ignored in phonological research on English[2] (and in phonological research in general), maybe except in the case of orthographic consonant geminates – which are discussed in various works and to which I will come back in section 4.3 – and the tentative proposal by Chomsky and Halle (1968: 49, hereafter *SPE*) that 'English orthography, despite its often cited inconsistencies, comes remarkably close to being an optimal orthographic system for English' when they note that the underlying representations which they propose often come to be very close to spelling. A few works in the generative literature have also dealt with this issue but it clearly remains marginal (Giegerich 1992, 1999; Hamann and Colombo 2017; Montgomery 2001, 2005).

According to Derwing (1992) and Giegerich (1992; 1999: 155), the reason for this scarcity of research integrating orthography is that early linguists such as Saussure and Bloomfield considered that 'spoken forms alone constitute the object [of linguistic study]', and that subsequent theorists have argued that all languages have a spoken form but not all have a written form.[3] However, as Giegerich (1999: 155) points out, this 'tells us nothing about the relationship between spoken and written form in languages that have both'. Guierre (2000) also suggested that this disinterest in orthography is due to the 'trend' of the quest for linguistic universals. He suggested that, as orthography is not a universal feature of natural languages, some may have deduced that it should not have any influence on phonology.

To my knowledge, the only strand of the literature in phonology which has always explicitly[4] taken orthography into consideration is the framework developed by the French linguist Lionel Guierre (1975, 1979), which can be described as a corpus-driven approach to English accentual and graphophonological patterns (see Chapter 2 of this volume). In his thesis (1979), Guierre argued that out of four possible grammars (reader, writer, listener, speaker), the grammar of the reader is the most efficient to formulate generalisations on stress placement and on the realisation of vowels. Additionally, he argued that there are few orthographic differences which are not exploited or exploitable for distinctive purposes in the domain of derivation (1979: 179). This view has been pursued in subsequent works such as Deschamps (1994), Deschamps et al. (2004) and J.-M. Fournier (2007, 2010b). Large data-driven studies based on pronunciation dictionary data have led to the establishment of very efficient generalisations to derive the pronunciation of words from their spelling, against the assumption shared by many according to which, 'given that English orthography is opaque and allows for certain pronunciation variants, it is almost impossible to predict the actual pronunciation' (Domahs et al. 2014: 68).[5] Although the different topics reviewed in the rest of this chapter are mostly based on research conducted within the Guierrian approach, several arguments will be taken from the generative literature.

In sum, there is accumulating evidence from a variety of strands of the literature that the relationship between orthography and phonology should be studied more closely than it has been so far. In the next section, I will lay out the research questions which I will seek to answer. I will then discuss aspects of the relationship between orthography and phonology, namely vowels (section 2), consonants (section 3) and orthographic diacritics (section 4). Then, I will discuss some of the consequences that the views developed in this chapter have on the analysis of English stress (section 5) before concluding on the place of orthography in a theory of grammar (section 6).

1 Aims of the chapter

Generative linguistics postulates the abstract concept of an 'ideal speaker-hearer' (Chomsky 1986: 20). In the generative phonological literature, a great deal of attention has been paid to phenomena such as vowel alternations or stress shifts, which mostly occur in parts of the vocabulary which are probably known almost exclusively by literate speakers. Let us consider one such phenomenon, the Vowel Shift Rule, which accounts for the vowel alternations in (1).

(1)   *div*[aɪ]*ne* ~ *div*[ɪ]*nity*
        m[əʊ]*de* ~ *m*[ɒ]*dify*
        prof[eɪ]*ne* ~ *prof*[æ]*nity*
        ser[iː]*ne* ~ *ser*[e]*nity*[6]

Chomsky and Halle (*SPE*: 187) argued that this rule, which has been widely discussed in the literature (for example Bermúdez-Otero and McMahon 2006; McMahon 2007; J. Myers 1999; S. Myers 1987), is 'without doubt the pivotal process of Modern English phonology'. However, it has been shown to be only marginally productive and to be the most productive for literate speakers, and only for alternations which are encoded in spelling with the same grapheme (Jaeger 1986; Wang and Derwing 1986).[7] In recent stratal models of phonology, this rule is usually placed on the first stratum, also called the 'stem-level' in Stratal Phonology (Bermúdez-Otero and McMahon 2006), even though classical Lexical Phonology placed it on the second stratum (see Halle and Mohanan 1985). Bermúdez-Otero (2012: 76) claims that some aspects of the stem-level phonology may be acquired by some speakers 'late, or not at all'. We could add that rules like the Vowel Shift Rule are even less likely ever to be acquired by illiterate speakers. Therefore, it seems necessary to define which phenomena can be accounted for (partially or completely) by orthography. Some phonologists may want to disregard such an enterprise because it does not have to do with 'pure' or 'real' phonology. A rather obvious answer to such an objection is precisely that the phenomena which I am going to discuss most likely have little to do with 'pure' or 'real' phonology.

Therefore, the main aim of this chapter is to provide a survey of those phenomena in English which require a reference to orthography to be accounted for. I will not seek to propose a formal model of phonology which integrates orthography, but I will seek to lay down the different empirical facts that such a theory would have to account for. I will then evaluate how integrating orthography might affect the analysis of stress placement in English. Finally, I will suggest some of the theoretical options which could be adopted in such a model in order to account for these phenomena.

2 Vowels: series and alternations

In this section, I discuss how orthography may be relevant in the analysis of the distribution of English vowels and the generalisations that govern this distribution. As will be discussed in section 5, this will be particularly relevant for the analysis of the stress system.

2.1 The limits of phonology: reduced–full alternations

Certain alternations 'breach the limits of what can be predicted on phonological grounds alone' (Giegerich 1999: 5), especially those between reduced vowels and full vowels, as in (2).

(2) <atom> → <atomic> ; <symbol> → <symbolic>
     ['ætəm]   [ə'tɒmɪk]   ['sɪmbəl]   [sɪm'bɒlɪk]

Such alternations were not problematic for *SPE*, as surface schwas could be derived from underlying vowels, which means that surface full vowels could too. However, if we are to avoid free rides and useless reduction rules, we have to posit that *atom* only has schwa in its second syllable. Therefore, if the alternation is to be predicted at all, the [ɒ] in these words has to come from somewhere. Giegerich (1992, 1999), Guierre (1979) and Montgomery (2001, 2005) argue that these alternations can only be driven by orthographic information. Indeed, in both these examples, the second vowel is reduced in the base and cannot provide any information as to what full vowel should appear in the corresponding derivative, in which that vowel is stressed. The vowel quality has to be retrieved from somewhere else than the (phonological) base and the most likely source of this information is orthography.

Giegerich (1992) notes that the link between [ə] and [ɒ] is completely arbitrary for an illiterate speaker but not for a literate speaker, who will establish a link between the base and the derivative through <o>, which is shared by both. Giegerich also rejects the alternative hypothesis of 're-structuring' proposed by Anderson (1981), which consists in saying that *atom* has a melodically blank second vowel which is restructured at the underlying level when *atomic* is learned. The reason for rejecting this hypothesis, Giegerich argues, is that it cannot predict the generation of novel forms. A similar argument can be found in Guierre (1979), who proposes that spelling can restrict what full vowel is to be chosen in this type of derivation. For example, if a speaker wanted to form the *-ic* adjective of *cymbal* and has only access to phonological information, then they could derive [sɪmˈbuːlɪk], [sɪmˈbelɪk] or [sɪmˈbælɪk], because the schwa in the second syllable of *cymbal* can alternate with almost any vowel (for example *brutal* [ˈbruːtəl] → *brutality* [bruˈtæləti], *totem* [ˈtəʊtəm] → *totemic* [təʊˈtemɪk], *autumn* [ˈɔːtəm] → *autumnal* [ɔːˈtʌmnəl], *atom* [ˈætəm] → *atomic* [əˈtɒmɪk] and, in American English, *hostile* [ˈhɑːstəl] → *hostility* [hɑːsˈtɪləti]; see Giegerich 1999: §5.1).[8] However, the knowledge of spelling would only predict [sɪmˈbælɪk].

Therefore, derivations such as these breach the limits of what can be achieved on phonological grounds alone and spelling simply cannot be ignored.[9] I believe, along with Bauer et al. (2013: 170), that an account that 'makes crucial reference to the orthographic form' seems to be 'the most adequate'. However, there is one problem which I have not yet addressed with regards to these derivations. Following some of the authors which I have cited, I presented these cases as if the full vowel to be chosen was necessarily [ɒ]. However, this is only one of the possible realisations of <o>. What parameters determine which realisation of a given orthographic vowel is to be chosen? Why can *atomic* not be [əˈtəʊmɪk]?

2.2 Vowel series

As shown by the Vowel Shift alternations presented in (1), or the additional examples in (3), a given orthographic vowel can have several realisations, which can occur in pairs of cognate words. Thereafter, we will call these different realisations 'values', following J.-M. Fournier (2010b).

(3)   a.   <divine> [dɪˈvaɪn] ~ <divinity> [dɪˈvɪnəti]
           <profane> [prəˈfeɪn] ~ <profanity> [prəˈfænəti]
           <serene> [səˈriːn] ~ <serenity> [səˈrenəti]

       b.   <isobar> [ˈaɪsəʊbɑː] ~ <isobaric> [ˌaɪsəʊˈbærɪk]
           <fluor> [ˈfluːɔː] ~ <fluoric> [fluˈɒrɪk]
           <scar> [ˈskɑː] ~ <scarify> [ˈskærɪfaɪ]

       c.   <barbarian> [bɑːˈbeəriən] ~ <barbaric> [bɑːˈbærɪk]
           <satire> [ˈsætaɪə] ~ <satiric> [səˈtɪrɪk]
           <compare> [kəmˈpeə] ~ <comparative> [kəmˈpærətɪv]

Alternations between different values have been the source of much debate on questions such as abstraction, learnability or free rides. Various formalisations of such alternations have been proposed. The three main ones are:

- Both vowels in a morphophonologically related pair are related to an abstract underlying vowel, and the context determines which surface vowel should appear (for example /I/ → [ɪ] or [aɪ]).[10]
- One vowel is derived from the other in a given context (for example [aɪ] → [ɪ] / X__Y).
- No derivation occurs; they are simply related on the surface (for example '[aɪ] alternates with [ɪ]').

However, with orthography, a fourth option (which could be related to the third option above) may be proposed. Indeed, if we follow Deschamps (1994), Deschamps et al. (2004) and J.-M. Fournier (2010b), vowels can be described as having a 'quality' and a 'value'. The 'quality' represents a series of surface vowels (for example {[æ], [eɪ], [ɑː], [eə]} or {[e], [iː], [ɜː], [aɪə]})[11] which may alternate with each other in given contexts, taking different 'values' in different contexts.[12] Values represent series of vowels which appear in the same environments but also which, to an extent, form natural classes: in Received Pronunciation, r vowels are long monophthongs, checked vowels are short vowels, free vowels are closing diphthongs[13] and r-coloured free vowels are mostly centring diphthongs or triphthongs. The different qualities and values for Received Pronunciation are shown in Table 4.1.

English Phonology and the Literate Speaker

Table 4.1 Table of correspondence for stressed vowels (source: J.-M. Fournier 2010b: 98)[14]

V̊ r vowel	V̆ checked vowel	Monographs <V>	V̄ free vowel	V̄ʳ r-coloured free vowel	Digraphs <V̄V̄>
[ɑː]	[æ]	<a>	[eɪ]	[eə]	<ai, ay / ei, ey>
[ɜː]	[e]	<e>	[iː]	[ɪə]	<ea, ee / ie**>
[ɜː]	[ɪ]	<i>	[aɪ]	[aɪə]	<ie*, ye>
[ɔː]	[ɒ]	<o>	[əʊ]	[ɔː]	<oa**, oe*>
[ɜː]	[ʌ (ʊ)]	<u>	[(j)uː]	[(j)ʊə]	<e(a)u, ew / ue*>
			[ɔː]	[ɔː]	<au, aw>
			[uː]	[ɔː]	<oo>
			[ɔɪ]		<oi, oy>
			[aʊ]	[ɔː (aʊə)]	<ou, ow>

*: final   **: non-final

One of the issues with the relationship between orthography and phonology concerns what restructuring of phonological knowledge could occur when spelling is learned. I propose that what learning how to spell does to the phonology is to link vowels into these series of values, which can alternate with each other in certain contexts. To answer the question at the end of the previous section, I will present the rules which determine which value is to be chosen in a given context in the following section.

2.3 The rules to determine vowel values

The value which a given orthographic vowel, if stressed, is most likely to have in a given context is regulated by a series of ordered generalisations, which have all been established using large empirical investigations based on pronouncing dictionaries. The main rules[15] found in J.-M. Fournier (2010b) are set out below. They are hierarchically ordered, in the sense that if a given vowel meets the description of the first rule, that rule applies, but if it does not, the next rule is considered and so on until the last rule. The hierarchical organisation of the rules reflects the neutralisation of certain parameters at each step, along with the relative domination of certain parameters over others. For example, the first rule deals with all vowel digraphs, which means that the following rules deal only with vowel monographs. This means that the value 'monograph' for the variable 'spelling of the vowel' is neutral in the sense that it does not determine vowel values and that additional parameters (such as the right-hand context or the nature of the vowel) are required to determine those values. The whole system of rules is shown in Figure 4.1 and the individual rules are detailed in (4)–(15).

124 New Perspectives on English Word Stress

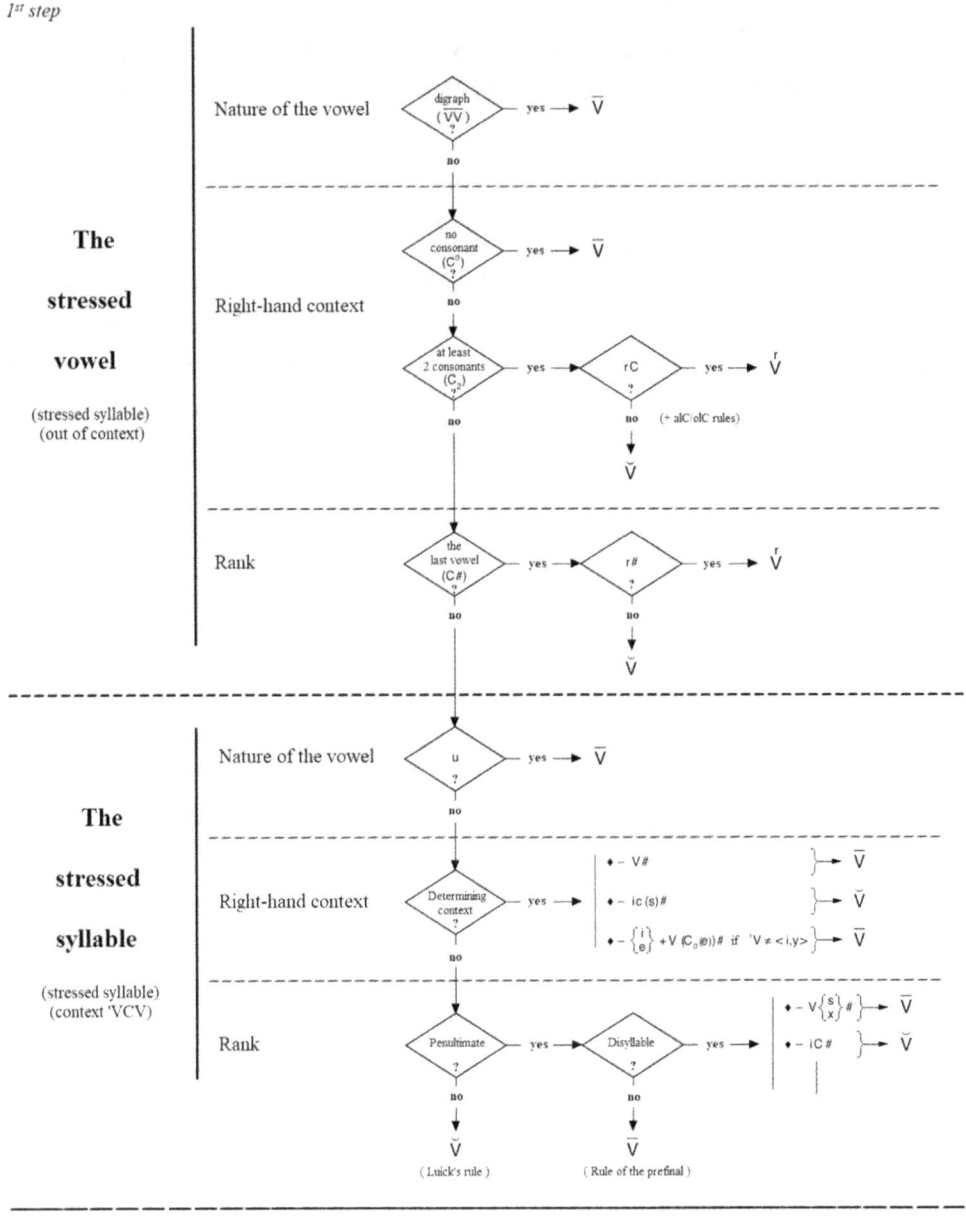

Figure 4.1 The system of spelling-to-sound rules for stressed vowels (after J.-M. Fournier 2010b: 141)

English Phonology and the Literate Speaker

(4) $\overline{VV} \to \bar{V}$
Vowels spelled with a digraph (for example <ow>, <ai>) are $\bar{V}$ (for example *hydraulic*, *augment*, *sea*)

(5) $C^0 \to \bar{V}$
If a vowel is followed by zero consonant (if it is followed by another vowel or is at the end of the word), it is a $\bar{V}$ (for example *lion*, *chaos*, *me*)

(6) If a vowel is followed by C_2 (= a functional consonant cluster):[16]
  a. $rC \to \overset{r}{\check{V}}$
  It is a $\overset{r}{\check{V}}$ when the first consonant of that cluster is <r> (for example *person*, *fortunate*, *curtain*)
  b. $C_2 \to \check{V}$
  It is a $\check{V}$ for all other clusters (for example *nest*, *mystery*, *vanilla*)

(7) If a vowel is followed by the final consonant of the word:
  a. $r\# \to \overset{r}{\bar{V}}$
  It is an $\overset{r}{\bar{V}}$ when that consonant is <r> (for example *car*, *sir*, *nor*)
  b. $C\# \to \check{V}$
  It is a $\check{V}$ for all other consonants (for example *cat*, *pet*, *permit*)

(8) $u \to \bar{V}$
If the vowel is <u>, it is a $\bar{V}$ (for example *acute*, *constitution*, *crucify*)

(9) $-V\# \to \bar{V}$
In the context <-CV#>,[17] the vowel is a $\bar{V}$ (for example *aroma*, *baby*, *cave*)

(10) $-ic(s)\# \to \check{V}$
If a vowel is in the syllable preceding *-ic(s)#*, it is a $\check{V}$ (for example *tonic*, *angelic*, *oceanic*)[18]

(11) $-C\{^i_e\} + VC_0(e)\#$ if $'V \neq$ <i, y> $\to \bar{V}$
If a vowel is followed by $-C\{^i_e\} + VC_0(e)\#$, and if it is not <i> or <y>, then it is a $\bar{V}$ (for example *zodiac*, *appreciate*, *spontaneous*)

(12) Luick[19] $\to \check{V}$
If the vowel is in the antepenultimate syllable (or further from the end), it is a $\check{V}$ (for example *cylinder*, *austerity*, *ritual*)[20]

(13) Prefinal → V̄
If the vowel is in the penultimate syllable in a word longer than two syllables, it is a V̄ (for example *neurosis, hiatus, horizon*)

(14) The remaining dissyllables are mostly unregulated, apart from the two following subclasses (but see Deschamps 1994 for more details):
a. Those ending in <s> or <x> have a V̄ (for example *crisis, motus, matrix*)
b. Those ending in <-iC#> have a V̆ (for example *credit, solid, zenith*)

Additionally, V̄s which are followed by <r> become V̄^{r}s:

(15) Digraphs: *their, beer, Europe,* ...
<u>: *curious, fury, obscurity,* ...
-VCV#: *aurora, era, vary,* ...
-C$\{^i_e\}$ + VC$_0$(e)#: *auditorium, cafeteria, variance,* ...
Penultimate: *decorum, oxymoron, papyrus,* ...

The ordering of rules is based on the study of relevant cases, which are words for which two contradictory rules could apply (for example in *áugment* (n.), the rules $\overline{VV} \rightarrow \bar{V}$ and $C_2 \rightarrow \breve{V}$ could both apply). If all the words for which two contradictory rules are in conflict behave uniformly, then we can determine which rule dominates the other (for example, virtually all digraphs followed by a consonant cluster are realised as free vowels, therefore the rule $\overline{VV} \rightarrow \bar{V}$ dominates the rule $C_2 \rightarrow \breve{V}$). If rules are not contradictory, transitivity can be used. For example, the rule $C_2 \rightarrow \breve{V}$ can be shown to dominate the rule u → V̄, as all vowels spelled <u> followed by a consonant cluster are checked vowels (for example *butter, function, mustard*) and rule u → V̄ can be shown to dominate the rule -ic(s)# → V̆, as all vowels spelled <u> followed by -ic(s)# are free vowels (for example *cubic, mercuric, music*). Therefore, by transitivity, the rule $C_2 \rightarrow \breve{V}$ can be argued to dominate the rule -ic(s)# → V̆.

However, the application of these generalisations in suffixed words depends on the type of suffixation which is involved, and vowel shifts typically occur in words with Level I or Class I suffixes, usually called 'strong suffixes' in the Guierrian approach.

2.4 Level I alternations and stress shifts

Most descriptions of English morphophonology agree on the fact that there are two types of suffixes, often called Class I and Class II (since Siegel 1974). Different theories have proposed different accounts of these two classes: +/# boundaries in *SPE*, strata in Lexical Phonology (Giegerich 1999; Kaisse and Shaw 1985; Kiparsky 1982, 1985), or Stratal Phonology (Bermúdez-Otero and McMahon 2006; Bermúdez-Otero 2012, 2018; Kiparsky 2000), or, more generally, what Scheer (2011) calls 'no look-back devices' which, in his model, is the Phase Impenetrability Condition. Fundamentally, the difference between the two classes can be boiled down to what J.-M. Fournier (1998) calls 'modes of computation'. Class I suffixes trigger a 'direct computation' of the position of stress and of vowel values, whereas Class II suffixes trigger a 'computation by reference', that is to say that the derivatives that they form preserve these properties from their bases. In other words, Class I suffixes inhibit any reference to the base for the positioning of primary stress and the pronunciation of the primary stressed vowel[21] and trigger the direct application of normal rules (or suffix-specific rules in the case of suffixes such as *-ee*, *-ette* or *-ic*). Consequently, this 'direct computation' is the mechanism which is at the source of both vowel alternations and stress shifts, as in the examples in (16).

(16)   ˈorigin → oˈriginal
       ˈrite [aɪ] → ˈritual [ɪ]

In Giegerich's (1992) view, there are no derivations from one vowel to another but rather spelling-to-sound generalisations which apply at Level I. I believe this view to be essentially correct. In the view presented in section 2.2, the different values in a given series are not derived from one another but are selected according to the environment in which the vowel appears. If this environment is modified by suffixation, rules will apply again if it is Class I suffixation, but they will not apply again in the case of Class II suffixation. In the former case, the rules apply transparently, but they are opaque in the latter (for example Luick's rule is opaque in *evasiveness*).

Interestingly, the spelling of words can be used to solve some apparent problems such as those in (17).

(17)   *ocean* [ˈəʊʃən] → *oceanic* [ˌəʊʃiˈænɪk]
       partial [ˈpɑːʃəl] → *partiality* [ˌpɑːʃiˈæləti]

In these examples, the number of syllables in the derivative exceeds that of its base added to that of the suffix by one: *ocean* has two syllables, *-ic* has one and *oceanic* has four, as opposed to the expected three. In both of these cases, the mismatch is the result of a historical process of syneresis, a reduction process which leads sequences of two unstressed vowels to merge into a single vowel. One way to solve this kind of problem is to assume that the bases underlyingly have more syllables than what is actually pronounced. This is also reflected in the spelling of these words, which clearly shows these underlying syllables. Therefore, directly using the spelling can account for cases like (17) but could also be used to predict what would happen in neologisms or nonce-words with a similar structure. For example, there are no common derivatives in *-ic* formed from words in *-ion*. We could expect most speakers to pronounce such words as [-i'ɒnɪk].[22]

2.5 Foreign vowels

Many words such as those in (18) have irregular spelling-to-sound correspondences.

(18)   *armada, angina, banana, bikini, martini, mosquito, sake, tomato, ...*

Tournier (1993: 149) notes that these correspondences can be attributed to the principle of articulatory proximity, according to which the source phoneme is reproduced in English by the closest English phoneme, articulatorily speaking. This is to be opposed to the principle of graphic analogy according to which regular spelling-to-sound correspondences are used to pronounce foreign words. The most common 'odd' correspondences can be summarised as in (19), in which $\bar{V}^f$ represents foreign free vowels.[23]

(19) $\bar{V}^f$ $\bar{V}$
        [ɑ:]   <a>   [eɪ]
        [eɪ]   <e>   [i:]
        [i:]   <i>   [aɪ]

These irregular correspondences can help us identify this 'foreign' vocabulary. This is one of a series of characteristics which define foreign vocabulary, along with other characteristics such as morphology, segmental structure, semantics and stress (see Dabouis and P. Fournier 2022 for an extended discussion of these characteristics).[24]

Additionally, Guierre (1979: 831) points out that only spelling could predict interdialectal variation such as that found in the examples in (20).

(20)   <albino>   [æl'bi:n əʊ] (GB) ~ [æl'baɪnoʊ] (US)
        <tomato>   [tə'mɑ:təʊ] (GB) ~ [tə'meɪtoʊ] (US)

He argues that the solution which consists in deriving one vowel from the other (as proposed by *SPE* and Halle and Keyser 1971) was a phonetic solution, not a phonological one, and that it missed the predictability of the anglicisation of these words. Guierre discusses mainly vowels, but the analysis could extend to consonantal alternations such as [ʒ] ~ [dʒ] (for example *barrage, genre*).[25]

3 Consonantal phenomena

In this section, I discuss four phenomena related to consonants, and which could be better analysed using orthographic information. There is a direct relationship with stress placement only in the case of syllabic consonants, as they raise the question of syllable count, which is essential in stress assignment. The other two processes, Velar Softening and alternations involving nasal clusters, only have an indirect relationship to stress, as they are related to the Level I/Level II distinction, which itself is related to stress.

3.1 Velar Softening

Velar Softening refers to a consonantal alternation between velar stops and coronal fricatives or affricates, as in the examples in (21).

(21) $criti$[k]   → $criti$[s]ise
       $electri$[k]   → $electri$[s]ity
       $alle$[g]$ation$ ← $alle$[dʒ]e
       $analo$[g]   → $analo$[dʒ]y

Standard descriptions of Velar Softening read as in (22), taken from Kiparsky (1982) for the alternation between [k] and [s], but the alternation between [g] and [dʒ] occurs in the same environment.[26]

(22)   k → s / __ $\begin{bmatrix} \text{-back} \\ \text{-low} \end{bmatrix}$

This formulation of the generalisation can capture the facts only if all vowels which trigger Velar Softening are indeed $\begin{bmatrix} \text{-back} \\ \text{-low} \end{bmatrix}$. However, if we consider simply the first and the third examples in (21), the first alternation is triggered by [aɪ], which is not $\begin{bmatrix} \text{-back} \\ \text{-low} \end{bmatrix}$, and the second alternation occurs before nothing as, in *allege*, [dʒ] is word-final. In order to account for that, one needs to postulate both that the alternations are triggered by underlyingly $\begin{bmatrix} \text{-back} \\ \text{-low} \end{bmatrix}$ vowels (for example [i] and [e]) and that these vowels may be deleted (as for final [e]). This is one of the reasons which led some to call Velar Softening alternations 'unnatural' (J. Myers 1999; Pierrehumbert 2006). Moreover, Velar Softening generally involves a restricted set of suffixes (*-ity*, *-ism*, *-ify*, *-ize*) and has a number of exceptions. These elements have led some scholars to reject it as a phonological rule (Hyman 1975; Kaye 1995).

So how should Velar Softening be accounted for? Once again, the answer seems to lie with orthography. As Montgomery (2001: 226) argues, it 'can only be accounted for synchronically through assuming either orthographic reference or more controversially through assuming an orthographic underlyer [sic]'. This is also the position adopted by Raffelsiefen (2010: 197), who argues that 'synchronically, Velar Softening concerns the relation between spelling and sound, in particular, it expresses a rule for how to pronounce the graphemes <c> or <g> before the graphemes <i>, <e> or <y>'. She formulates this rule as in (23).

(23) $\left. \begin{array}{l} \text{<c>} \rightarrow \text{[s]} \\ \text{<g>} \rightarrow \text{[dʒ]} \end{array} \right\} \left| \begin{array}{l} \text{-<i>} \\ \text{-<e>} \\ \text{-<y>} \end{array} \right.$

Building upon what was developed for vowels in the previous sections, we could propose that orthographic consonants such as <c> and <g> are the nodes that link the series {[k], [s]} and {[g], [dʒ]}, just as <a> does for {[æ], [eɪ], [ɑː], [eə]}, and that the specific realisation is determined contextually.

3.2 Stem-final clusters involving a nasal

There is a number of widely discussed alternations involving a nasal consonant, where a consonant absent from the base 'reappears' in a related Class I/Level I derivative. As pointed out by Scheer (2011: §167), there are three types of alternations: [mn] ~ [m] (24a), [mb/ŋg] ~ [m/ŋ] (24b) and [gn/gm] ~ [n/m] (24c).

(24) a. *damn* [ˈdæm]   →   *damnation* [dæmˈneɪʃən]
          autumn [ˈɔːtəm]   →   *autumnal* [ɔːˈtʌmnəl]
          solemn [ˈsɒləm]   →   *solemnity* [səˈlemnɪti]
       b. *bomb* [ˈbɒm]   →   *bombard* [bɒmˈbɑːd]
          long [ˈlɒŋ]   →   *longer* [ˈlɒŋgə]
       c. *sign* [ˈsaɪn]   →   *signature* [ˈsɪgnətʃə]
          paradigm [ˈpærədaɪm] →   *paradigmatic* [ˌpærədɪgˈmætɪk]

Giegerich argues that

> [mn] sequences only occur in a small number of stratum-1 derivatives, and that such occurrence is reliably reflected by (and arguably predicted by) the orthographic representation. [. . .] [t]he derivation of phonological properties from orthographic ones is not unreasonable in cases such as the present one, and downright unavoidable [. . .] in others.
> (Giegerich 1999: 130)

Similarly to reduced–full vowel alternations, we are faced with a phenomenon which the phonological information contained alone in the base cannot predict. Therefore, once again we can propose an orthographically guided generalisation to account for this phenomenon. This is what Giegerich (1999: 130) proposes with the rule in (25), and similar rules could be put forward to account for cases such as (24b) and (24c).

(25)   *n-insertion* (Stratum 1)

$$\emptyset \rightarrow [n] / [m] \underline{\quad\overset{<mn>}{|}\quad} V$$

Bermúdez-Otero and McMahon (2006: 398) propose an alternative analysis within the framework of Stratal Phonology. They assume that the English lexicon contains three items: a root [dæmn], a free noun stem [dæm] and a derived noun stem [dæmneɪʃn]. The consonantal alternation between the root and the free noun stem is captured using a lexical redundancy constraint of nasal cluster simplification. The *-ation* suffixation is assumed to apply to the root and not the free noun stem, and the derivation from the stem is avoided using morphological blocking, 'in the same way that *went* blocks **goed*' (Bermúdez-Otero and McMahon 2006: 398).

The problem with that analysis has to do with the source of the root [dæmn]. One can assume that it is learned once the speaker encounters *damnation*, but this would create the same problem as the hypothesis of restructuring proposed by Anderson (1981) for reduced–full vowel alternations discussed in section 2.1. Once again, the issue is that such an analysis cannot predict the generation of novel forms. Note that generating [dæm] from [dæmneɪʃn] is fairly unproblematic and does not require any reference to orthography. One only needs to assume that there is a productive rule or constraint of nasal cluster simplification. This has been shown to be the case using nonce words like [lɪmneɪʃən] and asking speakers to produce the verbal base by back formation and its *-ing* form (Mohanan 1986: 23). Speakers produced [lɪm] and [lɪmɪŋ] rather than *[lɪmn] and *[lɪmnɪŋ]. It appears that the reference to orthography is necessary to predict novel forms with a nasal cluster. We could imagine an experiment in which participants would be asked to form the *-ation* derivative from a base ending in [m], with one group being shown the spelling of the word with <mn> and another group in which the word is only presented orally. I would expect participants to produce [mn] in the first group, but not in the second.

3.3 Syllabic consonants

There is disagreement in the literature on what the phonological representation of the syllabic consonants should be. Some authors defend that they should be represented uniformly as /əC/ (Bonilla 2003; Wells 1965), while others argue that they can sometimes be represented as a single underlying consonant with no /ə/, and some have argued that this depends on the nature of the consonant (for example [n̩] would be /ən/ while [l̩] would be /l/; see Toft 2002) or on other factors, which I will discuss now (J.-M. Fournier 2010b; Giegerich 1999).

According to J.-M. Fournier, syllabic consonants can be the result of the elision of a schwa before a coda /m/, /n/ or /l/ (or /r/ in American English) or the syllabic realisation of a sonorant when it is found in the coda of an unstressed syllable. Consider the examples in (26), taken from J.-M. Fournier (2010b: 191–2).[27]

(26)   a. *balsam* [ˈbɔːlsm̩]   →   *balsamic* [bɔːlˈsæmɪk]
            angel [ˈeɪndʒl̩]   →   *angelic* [ænˈdʒelɪk]
            ether [ˈiːθə]   →   *etheric* [iːˈθeɹɪk]
    b. *cycle* [ˈsaɪkl̩]   →   *cyclic* [ˈsaɪklɪk]
            plasm [ˈpl̥æzm̩]   →   *plasmic* [ˈpl̥æzmɪk]
            nitre [ˈnaɪtə]   →   *nitric* [ˈnaɪtɹɪk]

The *-ic* suffix systematically places stress on the preceding syllable and therefore the difference between the words in (26a) and (26b) can be interpreted as a difference in the phonological representations of the bases of the *-ic* derivatives. If the syllable containing the syllabic consonant in the base can receive stress when suffixed with *-ic*, it can be argued to be underlyingly /VC/, which is what is found for the words in (26a). When that syllable does not receive stress when *-ic* is added, then it must be underlyingly /C/, that is to say that it is not a 'stressable' syllable because it has no vowel, as in (26b).

It could be argued that alternations such as those in (26) are rare and could not cause a difference in underlying representations. However, it could be argued that spelling can make such a difference. Indeed, all the words in (26a) end in <VC> while those in (26b) end in <C(e)>. If we assume this difference to be transferred into the phonological representations of these words, then the alternations in (26) can be accounted for. Evidence supporting this claim comes from a small survey reported by Giegerich (1992; 1999: 163). He asked ten native speakers of English to form de-nominal adjectives with *-ian* from proper names, on the model of *Newton* → *Newtonian*. The tested words included four names with a potential syllabic consonant: *Lendl*, *Penzl*, *Mendel* and *Handel*. As predicted by the spelling, the first two were never derived with a vowel appearing between the /l/ and the preceding consonant but the last two always were.

However, the picture is not as clear as these first facts would lead us to believe. First, there are issues with syllabic /r/ because it varies between the two spellings (<Cre#> and <Cer#>) and because there are cases such as *calendar* [ˈkæləndə] → *calendrical* [kəˈlendɹɪkəl] which contradict what spelling would predict. Moreover, there are whole classes of words for which there is no relevant vowel in the spelling of the base and one 'appears' anyway in the derivative, as in (27).

(27) **-Cle → -ular/-ulous**   **-ble → -bility**
      circle → circular   accountable → accountability
      spectacle → spectacular   falsifiable → falsifiabiliy
      miracle → miraculous   credible → credibility
      fable → fabulous   noble → nobility

This could suggest that the final syllabic /l/ in the bases actually represents a syllable, contrary to what spelling seems to indicate. An alternative analysis would be to treat these cases as allomorphies.

There are two additional phonological cues which can inform us on the phonological status of these consonants. The first is Luick's rule (see (12)), more commonly known as Trisyllabic Shortening. If words with phonetic antepenultimate stress which meet the conditions of Luick's rule all have checked vowels, then it could be argued that the last syllable is in fact a true phonological syllable, contrary to what spelling suggests.[28] A manual search in Wells (2008) for words ending in <-Cle> yields the results in (28).[29]

(28) a. V̆: amícable, carúncle, cénacle, chrónicle, clávicle, compátible, crédible, despícable, dirígible, dissóluble, divísible, édible, équable, explícable, extrícable, indélible, légible, mánacle, mániple, míracle, mónocle, óracle, pánicle, párable, pédicle, plácable, próbable, rádicle, sánicle, sóluble, ténable, vísible, vóluble (33/40 – 82%)
     b. V̆ ~ V̄: aménable, rísible, spíracle, vésicle (4/40 – 10%)
     c. V̄: cápable, pótable, véhicle (3/40 – 8%)

Clearly, checked vowels represent the majority of cases, as 92% of words can be realised with that value and 82% can only have that value.[30]

The second phenomenon has to do with primary stress placement. Monomorphemic words or suffixed words derived from bound roots of three syllables or more generally have antepenultimate stress. If words with a final syllabic consonant can have pre-antepenultimate stress, then that could suggest that the final syllable is not phonological. This is systematically the case in -able adjectives derived from -ate words by affix truncation (29a) (taken from Trevian 2007), in -able adjectives derived from bound roots (29b) (taken from Bermúdez-Otero 2018) or in -ism nouns derived from bound roots (29c).

(29) a. cálculable, commúnicable, dissóciable, éducable, pénetrable . . .
      b. indómitable, indúbitable, inéxorable, irréfragable, équitable . . .
      c. áctinism, álbinism, dýnamism, éxorcism, féminism, sýllogism . . .

It seems that most (if not all) words with pre-antepenultimate stress are suffixed. Therefore, it could be argued that the suffixes -able and -ism are extrametrical (Hayes 1982) and that the stress pattern of words in (29) does not substantially diverge from those observed in other words in which the suffix or the final syllable is extrametrical.

Overall, it appears that different phenomena provide contradictory evidence on the phonological status of final syllabic consonants. More research is required to distinguish what has to do with morphology or with extrametricality and to establish whether or not orthography can really be of any help in determining the underlying status of syllabic consonants.

3.4 /r/-related phenomena

The issue of /r/ is a highly debated topic in English phonology (for a review, see Navarro 2017), and it would be impossible to do justice to all the arguments which have been put forward by various authors in a small section such as this one. Therefore, I will focus on three issues and relate them to the question of orthography.

3.4.1 R-sandhi
One of the main issues is related to /r/ is r-sandhi phenomena, which are usually divided between:

- 'linking-r', where an [ɹ] can be found between a word ending in an orthographic (or etymological) r and a vowel-initial word (see (30a)),[31] and
- 'intrusive-r', where an [ɹ] can be found between a word ending in [ə, ɑː, ɔː] (and, more rarely, [ɪə] as in *idea*), which is not present in the spelling or etymologically, and a vowel-initial word (see (30b)).

(30)   a. *ca*[ɹ] *allowance*   b. *schwa*[ɹ] *insertion*
        doo[ɹ] *outside*   *law*[ɹ] *enforcement*
        lette[ɹ]*-opener*   *salsa*[ɹ]*-evening*

There has been some debate regarding whether r-sandhi involves the deletion of an underlying /r/ in preconsonantal or pre-pausal contexts, the insertion of an [ɹ], or both (for overviews, see Giegerich 1999: §6.2; Honeybone 2017; Navarro 2017: ch. 4). I will not attempt to get into the details of the various analyses but will briefly discuss one piece of evidence. Honeybone (2017) quotes several studies on r-sandhi which have quantified the realisation rates for both linking-r and intrusive-r in speech. The figures range from 58% to 88% for linking-r and from 9% to 58% for intrusive-r, linking-r being systematically more frequent than intrusive-r. This difference in realisation rates could be interpreted in two ways. First, one could argue that linking-r has higher realisation rates because there is an <r> in the orthographic representation and that, therefore, speakers have concrete evidence that there is an /r/ at the end of certain words, which they can pronounce in appropriate contexts.³² Second, the relatively low realisation rates for intrusive-r could have to do with prescriptivism. Precisely because linking-r has orthographic support and intrusive-r does not, some speakers feel like r-sandhi should only be used when it corresponds to an orthographic <r> and proscribe it when it does not (Cruttenden 2014: 316).

Clearly, spelling can be part of the explanation, but it cannot constitute all of it. As intrusive-r occurs in words with no orthographic <r>, a mechanism of analogical restructuring independent of spelling is required to account for this phenomenon (see Bermúdez-Otero 2011).

3.4.2 Pre-r dentalisation

Honeybone (2017) describes some of the properties of English spoken in Gosforth (Cumberland). This dialect is fundamentally non-rhotic, as shown by the absence of [r] in the coda (for example *arse* [aːs], *badger* [badʒə], *chair* [tʃɛˑə]) and has the property of exhibiting pre-r dentalisation (for example *dry* [d̪raɪ], *tread* [t̪rɪəd], cp. *darning* [daːnən], *tea* [tiː]). Interestingly, it shows pre-r dentalisation for words which have no surface rhotic (for example *butter* [bʊt̪ə], *spider* [spaɪd̪ə]). Honeybone interprets this as a sign that words like *butter* and *spider* do have an underlying /r/. The acquisition of this underlying /r/ could be achieved through the exposure to forms with linking-r alternating with forms without a surface rhotic or through the learning of literacy. More evidence is required to determine which hypothesis is to be retained.

3.4.3 Vowel reduction

The question of the presence of an underlying /r/ extends to word-internal positions (for example *card*, *weird*, *articulate*). In these positions, vowels which have historically been derived from a sequence of a vowel and an /r/ never display alternations which could support the presence of an underlying /r/. Synchronically deriving [aː] or [ɪə] from an underlying /Vr/ sequence would mean positing free ride derivations which have been rejected by most phonologists in the post-*SPE* era. However, new evidence from word-internal positions calls for an explanation.

Data taken from Dabouis and J.-M. Fournier (2019)³³ shows that <rC> clusters pattern with true consonant clusters (but not with <C'C'>) with regards to vowel reduction in the initial pretonic position in non-derived words (see Figure 4.2 for figures). Vowels in open syllables very often reduce but vowels in closed syllables, including those orthographically closed by <r>, rarely do so. As pointed out by Bermúdez-Otero (personal communication), this does not necessarily mean that these words have an underlying /r/ but could be due to the fact that, historically, vowel reduction preceded the loss of coda /r/. Experimental evidence is required to see whether the blocking of vowel reduction before <rC> clusters in the initial pretonic position is still synchronically active.

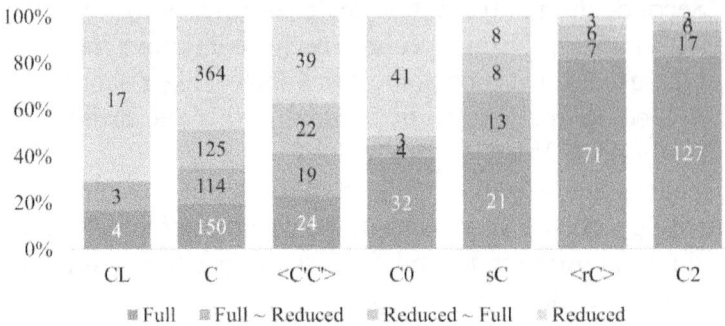

Figure 4.2 Vowel reduction in the initial pretonic position and right-hand context. C represents any consonant, L a liquid, <C'C'> orthographic geminates, C⁰ the absence of any consonants, C_2 a cluster of at least two consonants

Dabouis and J.-M. Fournier (2019) also report that vowel digraphs reduce considerably less than monographs. The effects of <rC> on vowel reduction are therefore similar to those of vowel digraphs but diverge from those of <C'C'>, which do not pattern differently from singletons. Therefore, these facts suggest that a theory in which orthographic information is translated into (surface or underlying) phonological representations would have to translate <rC> and <C'C'> differently (for example, a consonantal slot vs a mora).

4 Orthographic diacritics

Some orthographic elements can be described as diacritics, in the sense that they mark a particular behaviour of the phoneme that they represent or that they give indications about how the letters that precede them are pronounced. I will focus on the three main ones: vowel digraphs, final mute <e> and orthographic consonant geminates. It has been suggested that some of these elements are contained in underlying forms and then deleted in the derivation (Burzio 1994; *SPE*; Trevian 2003) or that words which contain them should be diacritically marked in the lexicon (Liberman and Prince 1977; Schane 1979). These elements indicate that general rules are not to be applied in words which contain them. Any theory which makes an attempt at formalising the relationship between orthography and phonology will have to take a stance on what is to be done with these diacritics.

4.1 Vowel digraphs

In (4), I presented the rule relative to vowel digraphs. It states that vowels spelled with a digraph are normally pronounced as free vowels in all contexts,[34] even contexts for which checked vowels are the norm, for example:

- before consonant clusters: *feast, augment, acoustic*
- in a stressed antepenult: *counterfeit, fraudulence, boomerang.*

Without orthographic information, it is strictly impossible to account for the multiple violations of 'shortening' rules by words with vowel digraphs.

Moreover, recent work by Dabouis and J.-M. Fournier (2019) shows that vowel digraphs tend to reduce much less than monographs in the initial pre-tonic position (for example *augmént, baptíze, eléven, routíne*).[35] This result suggests that spelling cannot be reduced to a representation of speech but that it can be a determining factor in pronunciation.

4.2 Final silent <e>

As mentioned in note 17, <-e#> appears in the structural description of the rule -V# → V̄, as it marks that the preceding vowel is a free vowel. <-e#> is most efficient when the preceding vowel is stressed, and the presence or absence of <-e#> is the only element distinguishing the pairs of words in (31a), but can also account for the unreduced final free vowels in (31b) or the free variants in (31c).

(31)   a. *fate* ~ *fat;*   *bite* ~ *bit;*   *cote* ~ *cot*
        b. *démonstr*[eɪ]*te;*   *ánecd*[əʊ]*te;*   *dýnam*[aɪ]*te*
        c. *cómpos*[aɪ ~ ɪ]*te* (adj.);   *ádvoc*[eɪ ~ ə]*te* (adj.)

Although alternations like those listed in (32) are scarce, they show that silent <-e#> behaves just as pronounced <e> does with regards to Velar Softening. Any analysis which would derive these alternations without any reference to spelling would have to assume that there is an underlying vowel at the end of the words with final [dʒ] alternating with [g].

(32)   *alle*[dʒ]*e*   →   *alle*[g]*ation*
       centrifu[dʒ]*e*   →   *centrifu*[g]*al*
       obli[dʒ]*e*   →   *obli*[g]*ation*

These two phenomena show that silent <-e#> somehow behaves like a vowel.[36] However, it is almost never pronounced and never counts as a syllable, as is shown by the examples in (33). One way to analyse this is that silent <-e#> may affect segmental processes but not suprasegmental ones.

(33)   *énvelope; páradise* (and not **envélope; *parádise*)

Therefore, the behaviour of silent <-e#> can be summed up as in Table 4.2.

Table 4.2 The behaviour of final silent <e>

Phenomenon	Behaves like a pronounced vowel?
Tenseness in (-)VCV#	✓
Triggers Velar Softening	✓
Counts as a syllable in stress assignment	✗

4.3 Orthographic consonant geminates

Orthographic consonant geminates (for example *colossus, vanilla, grammar*) are the orthographic elements which are the most commonly referred to in the literature on English phonology (see among others *SPE*: 148; Burzio 1994: 56; Giegerich 1999: 164; Stockwell and Minkova 2001: 173; Collie 2007: 134; J.-M. Fournier 2010b: 28). The reason for this might be that they are involved in four phenomena which would otherwise be considered exceptional: the behaviour of <u>, exceptions to CiV Lengthening, secondary stress placement and stressed light penults.

First, it has been noted that <u> is realised as a free vowel, except when it is followed by a consonant cluster (see (6)) or a final consonant (see (7)). However, words like those in (34a) do not contain 'true' consonant clusters, as they correspond to phonetic singletons and yet they are still pronounced with short [ʌ], just as in words with true consonant clusters like those in (34b) (Deschamps 1982).

(34) a. *butter* b. *function*
      mutter   *pustule*
      rubber   *vulture*

Second, as pointed out by Chomsky and Halle (*SPE*: 149) and Burzio (1994: 56–7), words with these orthographic geminates in (35a) also behave like words with true consonant clusters (35b) with regards to rule (11), more generally known as CiV Lengthening, and unlike those with single consonants, in (35c).

(35) a. *pot[æ]ssium* b. *c[æ]lcium*   c. *gymn[eɪ]sium*
      conf[e]ssion   *comp[e]ndium*   *magn[iː]sium*

Note that this effect seems to extend to nonce words as shown by the systematic use of [æ] for *Gussmannian* (← *Gussmann*) in the experiment reported by Giegerich (1999: 163), as opposed to the use of free vowels in the nonce words derived from bases with a single final consonant (for example *Anders[əʊ]nian* ← *Anderson*). However, there are well-known exceptions to CiV Lengthening without orthographic geminates (for example *c[æ]nyon, It[æ]lian, r[e]quiem*) and, in a recent paper, Steriade (2019) shows that CiV Lengthening only applies in derived environments when the vowel is reduced in the base (36a), but not when it is full (36b). This means that checked vowels may be preserved in the derivative, even when there are no orthographic geminates.

(36) a. *Ab[ə]l* → *Ab[iː]lian*
       Can[ə]da → *Can[eɪ]dian*
       col[ə]ny → *col[əʊ]nial*
    b. *Color[ɑː]do* → *Color[ɑː]dian*
       Louisi[æ]na → *Louisi[æ]nian*
       Rav[e]l → *Rav[e]lian*

Therefore, it appears that there are other factors at work here and that the role of orthography might actually be minor, if it has any role at all.

Then, in a study on secondary stress placement in monomorphemic words or words derived from bound roots, Dabouis et al. (2017) found that the position of secondary stress was determined by syllable closedness and by the presence or absence of an initial onset. Interestingly, orthographic consonant geminates have the same effect on the position of secondary stress as true consonant clusters:

- Pen-initial stress is always possible if the second syllable is closed: *amòntilládo, Monòngahéla, Ticònderóga* cp. *appòggiatúra, acciàccatúra, Pantèlleria*.
- Initial stress is always possible when the first syllable is closed: *èspionáge, Pàntagruél, prèstidigitátion* cp. *Càssiopéia, hùllabalóo, Wìnnipesáukee*.

Finally, following the Romance Stress Rule, which is typically adopted for main stress placement in English, stress should fall on the penult if it is heavy (37a) and on the antepenult if the penult is light. Therefore, stressed light penults are not predicted to occur, and yet they do when they are marked with orthographic geminates, as in (37b).[37]

(37)   a. *agénda, seméster, advénture, elíxir*, . . .
       b. *vanílla, colóssus, spaghétti, amarétto*, . . .

Therefore, these orthographic consonant clusters behave like true consonant clusters in all these environments, which leads Guierre (1979: 285–6) to argue that they share two of the three properties of the latter.[38] We saw that they seem to 'attract' stress in the pre-final position, and that vowels which immediately precede them are short (this is the rule $C_2 \to \breve{V}$), but they do not behave in the same way as 'true' consonant clusters with regards to vowel reduction in pretonic unstressed syllables. The latter tend to block vowel reduction in this environment[39] whereas reduction is not

Table 4.3 The behaviour of orthographic geminates

Phenomenon	Behaves like a pronounced consonant cluster?
Laxness of preceding <u>	✓
Blocking of CiV Lengthening	?
Secondary stress placement	✓
Can attract stress on the penult	✓
Less vowel reduction in the initial pretonic position	✗

systematically blocked by geminates. The results in Figure 4.1 clearly show that orthographic geminates (marked as <C'C'>) pattern with the absence of consonants, single consonants and obstruent + liquid clusters (i.e. open syllables). The behaviour of orthographic geminates can be summed up as in Table 4.3

5 Some implications for lexical stress

Most analyses of English stress in the generative literature derive the position of stresses from the segmental structure of words, vowels included. This state of affairs is not without raising a few questions. First, when native learners of English acquire their language, their input contains both vowels and stress. If the input contains both, what justifies that vowels should be seen as lexical and not stress? Why should stress be derived from lexical vowels? Why not derive vowels from lexical stress? Many analyses of English stress crucially rely on the difference between long and short vowels,[40] but they would be faced with considerable difficulty to extend the analysis to dialects such as Standard Scottish English, which does not have long vowels and yet has overall the same stress patterns as standard British or American English (Carr 2000). Second, if vowel reduction is seen as a consequence of stresslessness, then it seems difficult to argue that there are underlying reduced vowels which cannot be stressed. These issues show that the position that has been adopted in the literature regarding the relationship between vowels and stress is not unquestionable. Now, how would including spelling make things any different?

Throughout this chapter, it has been shown that a number of generalisations allow us to predict the value of a vowel in a given context quite reliably. Some of these generalisations refer to the position of stress, which suggests that the rules or constraints regulating stress placement have to dominate or precede those regulating vowel values.[41] Moreover, if one assumes that spelling restructures vowels into series such as those suggested in section 2.2, then a given orthographic vowel would not have a fixed weight which could be used to determine the position of stress. Once again, this suggests that the computation of vowel values has to be subordinated to that of stress. In a model that includes orthography (and especially in a reading grammar), vowels are fundamentally variable and depend on context. As a consequence, they cannot be part of the parameters which determine stress placement, unlike consonants, which display a far greater stability.[42]

Finally, orthographic information can be used to account for stress placement in classes of words which otherwise would remain unaccounted for. One such example is words with light penults. Pater (1994) shows that there is a considerable proportion of words with a light penult which have penultimate stress, such as those in (38).

(38)   *vanílla, Mississíppi, Kentúcky, confétti, abscíssa, Philíppa*

The stress behaviour of these words, along with some of the phenomena discussed in section 4.3, led Chomsky and Halle (*SPE*) to postulate that they had underlying 'double consonants' in the prefinal position (i.e. between the last two vowels), which would be deleted by a degemination rule after stress assignment had taken place. Taking spelling into consideration makes stress a lot more predictable and allows us to get rid of most of these exceptions, even though some persist (for example *Attila* [əˈtɪlə], *Alabama* [ˌæləˈbæmə], *Cincinnati* [ˌsɪnsəˈnæti]).

However, there is an alternative explanation to these exceptions. Pater (1994) observes that none of the words he found with light penult stress were Anglo-Saxon or other Germanic words. Instead, most of them turn out to be borrowings or proper names. This leads him to propose that light penult stress 'is a productive property of the periphery of the grammar, and antepenult stress the core' (1994: 102). Following J.-M. Fournier (2010a) and Dabouis and P. Fournier (2022), one could go further and argue that penultimate stress *in general* is a property of the periphery of the grammar.[43] However, this analysis alone would not allow us to account for the behaviour of vowels discussed in section 4.3, and the reference to spelling is still necessary to account for the high regularity of penultimate stress in words with a prefinal <C'C'>, as opposed to the variability found for words with a single prefinal consonant.

In sum, in this section I have shown that the relationship between vowels and stress is problematic and that assuming that vowels are lexical and stress is not raises a few questions, which should probably be asked more often. I have also shown there is a class of words, those with stressed light penults, which could be accounted for more easily if spelling were taken into consideration. I am not aware of any existing analyses of English stress which assign stress without using the weight of vowels while accounting for all the stress-related phenomena that weight-based analyses account for (for example, aspiration, the distribution of [h], expletive infixation), but J.-M. Fournier's (2010b) model provides a satisfactory account of stress placement, although it remains to be seen whether this analysis can incorporate those other phenomena.

6 Where does orthography stand?

There are two main options regarding the manner in which orthographic information could be brought about in phonology. I will not consider the option taken by Giegerich (1999), which consists in having phonological rules which are able to refer to orthographic information, as in (26). Instead, the first option that I will assume is a modular framework in which there would be an orthographic module. Domain specificity (Fodor 1983) requires that each module has its own vocabulary, suggesting that one way to import orthographic information into the phonological module is to translate that information into phonological vocabulary (segments, morae, prosodic boundaries, CV units, etc.). The second option, which is not necessarily incompatible with the first one, would consist in assuming that there are graphophonological representations that emerge from the system of correspondences between orthography and phonology and from which both orthographic and phonological representations could be derived.[44] There is a third option which does not involve any claims on the relationship between orthography and phonology: to study a reading grammar. As mentioned in section 0, Guierre (1979) found that this grammar was the most efficient to determine the position of stress(es) and vowel values out of all four possible grammars.

The aim of this chapter is not to say which of these options should be preferred but mainly to pave the way for future research by laying down the empirical facts that a theory willing to include orthographic information should account for and by proposing some of the ways that this could be achieved. Let me conclude on the nature of the generalisations discussed in this chapter. Recent evidence suggests that speakers do not use categorical rules but use statistical-learning, that is, 'people implicitly pick up associations between spelling and phonology through their experience with written words' (Treiman et al. 2020). Therefore, a theory seeking to model the linguistic ability of English speakers will have to use probabilistic generalisations rather than categorical ones.

7 Conclusions

This chapter has shown the necessity of taking orthographic information into account when dealing with English phonology. The reasons for doing so are numerous: psycholinguistic evidence suggests that orthography strongly influences and restructures phonological knowledge and some dead-end problems of phonology which can be resolved if orthographic information is taken into consideration. This chapter can only begin to scratch the surface of what remains largely uncharted territory: the links between orthography and phonology. Consequently, there are many additional issues which would need to be taken into consideration, such as spelling pronunciations, sometimes called the Buben effect (Chevrot 2015; Chevrot and Malderez 1999; Giegerich 1992, 1999),[45] or the role of spelling in diachronic changes (for example Neuman 2009: 395–8 on [h] in French borrowings in English).

I have also shown how integrating orthography opens the way for an analysis of English stress which does not depend on the length of vowels, and such an analysis can be taken up in frameworks which do not integrate orthographic information. However, the advantages of integrating orthography are twofold: we can correctly predict stress in words with prefinal orthographic consonant geminates; and we can provide a general account of the distribution of vowels rather than simply assume that they are lexical.

Notes

I would like to thank Ricardo Bermúdez-Otero, Jacques Durand, Jean-Michel Fournier, Silke Hamann, Sylvain Navarro, an anonymous reviewer and the participants of the 2015 PAC conference (Phonology of Contemporary English) and those of the 2015 RFP conference (French Phonology Network) for constructive remarks and discussion. All mistakes are mine alone.

1. Interestingly, she found that this effect did not extend to non-words, which suggests that the duration effect is linked to the lexical representation of words.
2. It is probably mentioned more often for research on French, especially on *liaison* or word segmentation, even though these phenomena cannot be accounted for using orthography alone (see Durand and Eychenne 2014 for discussion).
3. See also Neuman (2009: §§0.8, 1.9) for a historical review of linguists' views on orthography.
4. Carr (2000) opposes this approach to that of Chomsky and Halle (1968) which, arguably, makes implicit use of spelling.
5. See also Deschamps (1994) for a review of the 'classical' arguments used to demonstrate that English spelling is highly irregular and cannot be used to predict the pronunciation of words (for example Shaw's rewriting of *fish* into *ghoti*, Trenité's poem *Chaos* or the words in -*ough*). As the author points out, none of these arguments is actually based on any sort of statistical approach.
6. All phonemic transcriptions in this chapter are British pronunciations taken from Wells (2008).

7. Interestingly, historical Great Vowel Shift alternations may not be productive (for example [ʌ] ~ [aʊ]), and alternations which did not come from the historical Vowel Shift can be productive (for example [ʌ] ~ [(j)uː]; McMahon 2007) . This seriously weakens the view that the synchronic Vowel Shift Rule directly comes from the historical Vowel Shift. Clearly, there is something else involved, and that something else may very well be orthography.
8. The specific vowels given here reflect what we would expect from the rules detailed in section 2.3, here short vowels, as is usual before *-ic* (unless the vowel is <u>). [sɪmˈbɒlɪk] would most likely not be a possibility, as it would be blocked by the existing *symbolic*.
9. This could predict that languages which do not have an orthographic system should not have such alternations, or that these alternations should be less stable in such languages than they are in languages which do have an orthographic system. This prediction remains to be explored.
10. Green (2007: 174) underlines 'the problem of determining what the underlying phonemes are whose allophones are [aɪ, ɪ], [i, ɛ], [e, æ], [o, ɑ], because the surface allophones are featurally often more distinct from each other than they are from allophones of a different phoneme'.
11. Jaeger (1986) claims that children who learn how to spell unlearn phonetic groupings for vowels and learn to group them according to spelling, or Vowel Shift patterns, which would support the view defended here.
12. Considering vowel qualities as series is a view developed in Dabouis (2014).
13. Under the assumption that [iː] and [uː] are actually [ɪi] and [ʊu], respectively (see Wells 1982: 140, 147).
14. This table does not include reduced vowels and 'foreign' vowels, which will be discussed below, such as:

    - <a> → [ɑː], <e> → [eɪ/eə], <i> → [iː/ɪə]: *fa, re, mi*
    - French: <ou> → [uː/ʊə]: *bijou, courgette*; <eu> → [ɜː]: *danseur/danseuse*; <(e)au> → [əʊ]: *auberge, chateau*; <oi, oy> → [wɑː]: *boudoir*; <é(e), ê, è> à [eɪ/eə]: *negligée, déjà vu*
    - 'Classical': <ae, oe> → [iː]: *Caesar, foetus*; <aa> → [ɑː]: *bazaar*

15. There are additional sub-rules applying, for example <alC> and <olC> (*talk, old*), and 'exceptional subclasses', such as <ind#> words (*bind, blind, find*) or <Vste#> words (*chaste, paste, riposte*) which all have free vowels, contrary to the C_2 rule in (6).
16. J.-M. Fournier (2010b: 38) defines a C_2 as any group of two consonants (even orthographic ones) except <Ch>, <Cr>, <Cle#> and <Cre#>, but including <x>. The term 'functional consonant cluster' is used by Guierre (1979) to distinguish those referred to as C_2 and 'non-functional' clusters, which phonologically behave like singletons for stress, vowel values and vowel reduction (although orthographic consonant

geminates differ from other C$_2$s for vowel reduction, as discussed in section 4.3).
17. This context includes final mute <e>, which will be discussed in section 4.2.
18. J.-M. Fournier (1990) shows that this rule knows exceptions (sometimes as pronunciation variants) in the case of derivatives with free vowels in their base (for example *basic, cyclic, hydric*). He shows that the existence of a base with a long vowel is a necessary (but not sufficient) condition for an exceptional long vowel in the related *-ic* derivative.
19. This rule is named after Luick (1898), who first described it.
20. This rule, mostly known as Trisyllabic Shortening or Laxing in generative literature, is often questioned because it has many exceptions (for example *Oberon, obesity*) but it actually has an efficiency of over 92%, with 3632 out of 3930 words following that rule (Deschamps 1994). Building upon Prince's (1991) reformulation of Trisyllabic Shortening as Trochaic Shortening, Dabouis (2018) proposes to reformulate this rule so as to include the penultimate syllable of verbs, which is generally checked (see also Dickerson 1980 on a similar claim, but another view is proposed by Nessly 1982).
21. Crucially, 'direct computation' concerns only primary stress, as secondary stress(es) is/are often inherited from their base (Collie 2007, 2008; J.-M. Fournier 2010b: 79–80; Kiparsky 1979 and many others).
22. The online *Oxford English Dictionary* lists only two words in *-ionic* (with the suffix *-ion*, not the word *ion*), both qualified as 'rare', which do have the predicted pattern: *regionic* [ˌriːdʒiˈɒnɪk] and *visionic* [ˌvɪʒiˈɒnɪk].
23. Less common examples of foreign vowels are mentioned in note 14. Note that <o> and <u> are not realised differently in foreign vocabulary. However, Dabouis (2016: 472; 2018) lists several words with <o> realised as [əʊ] in a context where a checked vowel is expected and which can be argued to be foreign free vowels (for example *oloroso, omerta, origami*).
24. One could also use other orthographic clues to identify 'foreign' vocabulary. For example, for [i] in final position we can have either <i> or <y>, but the former is almost systematically found in 'foreign' words. This can be shown if we list the first ten words (apart from proper names) in Wells (2008) which end in <i> and the first which end in <y>:

<i>: *aduki, adzuki, agouti, aioli, alhaji, alibi, alkali, ani, annuli, anthropophagi.*
<y>: *abbacy, abbreviatory, ability, ably, abnormality, aboriginality, absently, absolutely, absorbedly, absorbency.*

25. Dabouis and P. Fournier (2022) also discuss spelling-to-sound correspondences for consonants in foreign vocabulary.
26. As pointed out by Aronoff (1976: 52), this rule needs to be restricted to [+Latinate] items as it does not apply in [−Latinate] items.

27. Following J.-M. Fournier, I assume syllabic /r/ to be realised [ə] word-finally in British English.
28. Deschamps (1994) and Deschamps et al. (2004) do include these words among those which obey Luick's rule.
29. When a word had two stress variants, only the one with phonetic antepenultimate stress was taken into consideration.
30. If one assumes that Luick's rule is in fact Trochaic Shortening (Bermúdez-Otero and McMahon 2006; Prince 1991), then these facts could be captured assuming that the syllabic /l/ is extrametrical (Hayes 1982).
31. The examples are taken from Heselwood (2009).
32. Heselwood (2009) makes a similar point when he asserts that 'There is no difference in the possible distribution of [r] at wordform boundaries in relation to *lettER* and *commA* words unless induced by knowledge of spelling and a greater prescriptive desire to avoid intrusive R over linking R.'
33. Dabouis and J.-M. Fournier (2019) is a large-scale dictionary study of vowel reduction in the initial pretonic and intertonic positions. It uses data from Jones (2006) and Wells (2008), coded for morphological and syllabic structure. It seeks to test the different parameters put forward in the literature on vowel reduction. The data presented in Figure 4.2 concern words which are not derived from another word and which do not contain any form of prefix, even etymological prefixes such as *ad-*, *con-* or *ob-*.
34. Obviously, there are exceptions with checked vowels, for example *head, bread, breath, sweat, foot, book, good, could, should*, or exceptional orthographic changes in derivatives, for example *beast → bestial; feast → festal*.
35. This observation is not new (see Dahak 2011; Deschamps 1994: 111; Deschamps et al. 2004: 217; Guierre 1984, 1987) but had not been tested with multiple variables such as syllable structure or word frequency.
36. This is actually unsurprising as most orthographic <-e#>s used to be pronounced (Bermúdez-Otero 1998; Duffell 2008; Minkova 1982, 1991).
37. They do also occasionally occur without orthographic geminates (for example *alpáca, bandána, spèrmacéti, tantívy*), although most of the relevant cases are occurrences of [æ], which often alternate with [ɑː], and are generally realised as the latter vowel in British English (for example *banána, Còlorádo, nirvána, sopráno*). Pater (1994) discusses words with light penult stress in detail.
38. This should not be surprising as there were geminates in Old English and Middle English (Britton 2011) and they triggered Shortening before Consonant Clusters, like other consonant clusters (Bermúdez-Otero 1998). Guierre (2001) also reports that when geminate consonants were simplified, the use of double orthographic consonants to indicate that the previous vowel is 'short' was systematised.

39. This reduction blocking knows one major class of exceptions: Latinate prefixes, which tend to reduce systematically (Burzio 1994: 56–7; *SPE*: 118; Collie 2007: 129, 215, 318–19; Dabouis and J.-M. Fournier 2019; Deschamps 1994; Guierre 1979: §3.4.11; Halle and Keyser 1971: 37; Halle and Vergnaud 1987: 239; Hammond 2003; Hayes 1982; Liberman and Prince 1977; Pater 2000; Selkirk 1980; Stockwell and Minkova 2001: 173).
40. Some would say tense and lax, but see Durand (2005), who argues that phonological length (be it in the form of x-slots or morae) is required to cross-classify the vowel phonemes in English.
41. At least at the lexical level. As an anonymous reviewer points out, phrase-level processes such as iambic reversal may affect stress without changing vowel values.
42. As pointed out by an anonymous reviewer, this is a simplification if one considers processes such as consonant cluster simplification, /h/ elision or glottaling. These processes are, however, highly constrained by the phonological environment and do not affect all consonants equally.
43. That claim deals with words which do not contain stress-affecting affixes such as -*ic* or semantically opaque prefixes, which are regularly associated to penultimate stress in words which are not nouns (for example *consíder, detérmine, embárrass*; see section 2.2.1 in Chapter 2 of this volume).
44. See Ryan (2011, 2017) on a writing grammar.
45. Roché (2010) gives an interesting series of examples to support his view that 'Dans une langue comme le français, la mémoire lexicale est pour une large part une mémoire de la graphie' ['In a language such as French, lexical memory is for the most part a memory of spelling']. He quotes a number of neologisms based on names of presidential candidates (for example *sarkozyment, bovément, bayroument*) and observes that these neologisms are strongly influenced by spelling. Indeed, names with final [ɛ] are derived differently according to how they are spelled: *laguillerement, bovément, buffettement, devilliersement*.

References

Anderson, S. R. (1981), 'Why phonology isn't "natural"', *Linguistic Inquiry* (12), 493–539.

Aronoff, M. (1976), *Word Formation in Generative Grammar*, Cambridge, MA: MIT Press.

Bassetti, B., P. Escudero and R. Hayes-Harb (2015), 'Second language phonology at the interface between acoustic and orthographic input', *Applied Psycholinguistics* 36, 1–6.

Bauer, L., R. Lieber and I. Plag (2013), *The Oxford Reference Guide to English Morphology*, Oxford: Oxford University Press.

Bermúdez-Otero, R. (1998), 'Prosodic optimization: The Middle English length adjustment', *English Language and Linguistics* 2, 169–98.
Bermúdez-Otero, R. (2011), 'Cyclicity', in M. van Oostendorp, C. Ewen, E. Hume and K. Rice (eds), *The Blackwell Companion to Phonology*, vol. 4, Malden, MA: Wiley-Blackwell, pp. 2019–48.
Bermúdez-Otero, R. (2012), 'The architecture of grammar and the division of labour in exponence', in J. Trommer (ed.), *The Morphology and Phonology of Exponence*, Oxford: Oxford University Press, pp. 8–83.
Bermúdez-Otero, R. (2018), 'Stratal Phonology', in S. J. Hannahs and A. R. K. Bosch (eds), *The Routledge Handbook of Phonological Theory*, Abingdon: Routledge, pp. 100–34.
Bermúdez-Otero, R. and A. McMahon (2006), 'English phonology and morphology', in J. Trommer (ed.), *The Handbook of English Linguistics*, Oxford: Oxford University Press, pp. 382–410.
Bonilla, J. C. (2003), 'The formation of syllabic consonants and their distribution in southern British English', *Atlantis* 25(2), 97–112.
Brewer, J. B. (2008), 'Phonetic reflexes of orthographic characteristics in lexical representation', PhD dissertation, University of Arizona.
Britton, D. (2011), 'Degemination in English, with special reference to the Middle English period', in D. Denison, R. Bermúdez-Otero, C. McCully and E. Moore (eds), *Analysing Older English*, Cambridge: Cambridge University Press, pp. 232–43.
Bürki, A., E. Spinelli and M. G. Gaskell (2012), 'A written word is worth a thousand spoken words: The influence of spelling on spoken-word production', *Journal of Memory and Language* 67(4), 449–67.
Burzio, L. (1994), *Principles of English Stress*, New York: Cambridge University Press.
Carr, P. (2000), 'Vowel length in Standard Scottish English', in *10ème Colloque d'Avril sur l'anglais oral*, Villetaneuse: Université Paris Nord, CELDA, diffusion APLV, 13–24.
Chéreau, C., M. G. Gaskell and N. Dumay (2007), 'Reading spoken words: Orthographic effects in auditory priming', *Cognition* 102(3), 341–60.
Chevrot, J.-P. (2015), 'Orthographe et phonologie : Réciprocité des influences et équilibration lors du développement du langage', paper presented at the 13th RFP conference (French Phonology Network) held at the University of Bordeaux-Montaigne on 29 June–1 July 2015.
Chevrot, J.-P. and I. Malderez (1999), 'L'Effet Buben: De la linguistique diachronique à l'approche cognitive (et retour)', *Langue française* 124, 104–25.
Chomsky, N. (1986), *Knowledge of Language: Its Nature, Origin and Use*, New York: Praeger.
Chomsky, N. and M. Halle (1968), *The Sound Pattern of English*, New York: Harper & Row.
Collie, S. (2007), 'English stress preservation and Stratal Optimality Theory', PhD disssertation, University of Edinburgh.
Collie, S. (2008), 'English stress preservation: The case for " fake cyclicity"', *English Language and Linguistics* 12(3), 505–32.
Cruttenden, A. (2014), *Gimson's Pronunciation of English*, 8th edn, London: Routledge.

Dabouis, Q. (2014), 'English stress and underlying representations', *Proceedings of the First Postgraduate and Academic Researchers in Linguistics at York* 1, 1–15.

Dabouis, Q. (2016), 'L'accent secondaire en anglais britannique contemporain', PhD disssertation, University of Tours.

Dabouis, Q. (2018), 'The pronunciation of vowels with secondary stress', *Corela* 16(2), <https://doi.org/10.4000/corela.7153>.

Dabouis, Q. and J.-M. Fournier (2019), 'On the role of morphology, syllable structure, frequency and spelling in English vowel reduction', Poster presented at the 27th MFM Conference, held at the University of Manchester, Manchester, UK, on 23–25 June 2019.

Dabouis, Q., J.-M. Fournier and I. Girard (2017), 'Ternarity is not an issue: Secondary stress is left edge marking', Paper presented at the MFM25 Fringe Meeting – PTA Dataset Workshop, held at the University of Manchester, Manchester, UK, on 24 May 2017.

Dabouis, Q. and P. Fournier (2022), 'English PhonologieS', in V. Arigne and C. Rocq-Migette (eds), *Modèles et modélisation en linguistique / Models and Modelisation in Linguistics*, Brussels: Peter Lang, pp. 215–58.

Dahak, A. (2011), 'Étude diachronique, phonologique et morphologique des syllabes inaccentuées en anglais contemporain', PhD disssertation, Université de Paris Diderot.

Derwing, B. L. (1992), 'Orthographic aspects of linguistic competence', in *The Linguistics of Literacy*, Amsterdam, Philadephia: John Benjamins, pp. 193–210.

Deschamps, A. (1982), 'L'orthographe de l'anglais est-elle phonologique?', in *Colloque d'avril sur l'anglais oral*, Villetaneuse: Université Paris Nord, CELDA, diffusion APLV, pp. 68–96.

Deschamps, A. (1994), *De l'écrit à l'oral et de l'oral à l'écrit*, Paris: Ophrys.

Deschamps, A. et al. (2004), *English Phonology and Graphophonemics*, Paris: Ophrys.

Dickerson, W. B. (1980), 'Bisyllabic laxing rule: Vowel prediction in linguistics and language learning', *Language Learning* 30, 317–29.

Domahs, U., I. Plag and R. Carroll (2014), 'Word stress assignment in German, English and Dutch: Quantity-sensitivity and extrametricality revisited', *The Journal of Comparative Germanic Linguistics* 17(1), 59–96.

Duffell, M. J. (2008), *A New History of the English Metre*, London: Legenda.

Durand, J. (2005), 'Tense/lax, the vowel system of English and phonological theory', in P. Carr, J. Durand and C. J. Ewen (eds), *Headhood, Elements, Specification and Contrastivity: Phonological Papers in Honour of John Anderson*, Amsterdam: John Benjamins Publishing, pp. 77–90.

Durand, J. and J. Eychenne (2014), 'Mot et phonologie en français: De la persistance d'une illusion', in J. Durand, G. Kristoffersen and B. Laks (eds), *La phonologie du français: Normes, périphéries, modélisation*, Paris: Presses Universitaires de Paris Ouest Nanterre la Défense, pp. 227–60.

Ehri, L. C. and L. S. Wilce (1980), 'The influence of orthography on reader's conceptualization of the phonemic dtructure of xords', *Applied Psycholinguistics* 2, 371–85.

Fodor, J. (1983), *The Modularity of the Mind*, Cambridge, MA: MIT-Bradford.

Fournier, J.-M. (1990), 'Analogie et isomorphisme, conflits et conspirations', in *5ème Colloque d'Avril sur l'anglais oral*, Villetaneuse: Université Paris Nord: CELDA, diffusion APLV, pp. 74–87.

Fournier, J.-M. (1998), 'Que contraignent les terminaisons contraignantes?', in *Topiques, Nouvelles recherches en linguistique anglaise, Travaux XCIII du CIEREC*, Université de Saint-Etienne, pp. 44–75.

Fournier, J.-M. (2007), 'From a Latin syllable-driven stress system to a Romance versus Germanic morphology-driven dynamics: In honour of Lionel Guierre', *Language Sciences* 29, 218–36.

Fournier, J.-M. (2010a), 'Accentuation lexicale et poids syllabique en anglais: L'analyse erronée de Chomsky et Halle', Paper presented at the 8th meeting of the French Phonology Network, held at the Université d'Orléans, Orléans, France, on 1–3 July 2010.

Fournier, J.-M. (2010b), *Manuel d'anglais oral*, Paris: Ophrys.

Giegerich, H. J. (1992), 'The limits of phonological derivation: Spelling pronunciations and schwa in English', *Linguistische Berichte* 142, 413–36.

Giegerich, H. J. (1999), *Lexical Strata in English: Morphological Causes, Phonological Effects*, Cambridge: Cambridge University Press.

Green, A. (2007), *Phonology Limited*, Linguistics in Potsdam 27, Potsdam: Universitätsverlag Potsdam.

Guierre, L. (1975), *Drills in English Stress-Patterns: Ear and Speech Training Drills and Tests for Students of English as a Foreign Language*, 3rd edn, Paris: Armand Colin-Longman.

Guierre, L. (1979), 'Essai sur l'accentuation en anglais contemporain: Éléments pour une synthèse', PhD dissertation, Université Paris 7.

Guierre, L. (1984), *Drills in English Stress-Patterns: Ear and Speech Training Drills and Tests for Students of English as a Foreign Language*, 4th edn, London: Armand Colin-Longman.

Guierre, L. (1987), *Règles et exercices de prononciation anglaise*, Paris: Longman France.

Guierre, L. (2000), 'Pourquoi la morpho-phonologie?', in P. Busuttil (ed.), *Points d'interrogation: Phonétique et phonologie de l'anglais*, Pau: Publications de l'Université de Pau, pp. 32–46.

Guierre, L. (2001), 'Cent ans de phonétique anglaise en France', *Modèles linguistiques* 43, 45–74.

Halle, M. and S. Keyser (1971), *English Stress: Its Form, Its Growth, and Its Role in Verse*, New York: Harper & Row.

Halle, M. and K. P. Mohanan (1985), 'Segmental phonology of Modern English', *Linguistic Inquiry* 16, 57–116.

Halle, M. and J.-R. Vergnaud (1987), *An Essay on Stress*, Cambridge, MA: MIT.

Hamann, S. and I. E. Colombo (2017), 'A formal account of the interaction of orthography and perception: English intervocalic consonants borrowed into Italian', *Natural Language & Linguistic Theory* 35, 683–714.

Hammond, M. (2003), 'Frequency, cyclicity, and optimality', University of Arizona, <http://www.u.arizona.edu/~hammond/kslides.pdf>.

Hayes, B. (1982), 'Extrametricality and English stress', *Linguistic Inquiry* 13(2), 227–76.

Heselwood, B. (2009), 'R vocalisation, linking R and intrusive R: Accounting for final schwa in RP English', *Transactions of the Philological Society* 107(1), 66–97.

Honeybone, P. (2017), 'Does English r-sandhi involve insertion, deletion, or both?: Evidence from opacity in pre-r dentalisation', Paper presented at the 2017 PAC conference, held at the University of Paris Nanterre, Paris, France, on 28–30 September 2017.

Hyman, L. (1975), *Phonology: Theory and Analysis*, New York: Holt, Rinehart and Winston.

Jaeger, J. J. (1986), 'On the acquisition of abstract representations for English vowels', *Phonology Yearbook* 3, 71–97.

Jones, D. (2006), *Cambridge English Pronouncing Dictionary*, 17th edn, Cambridge: Cambridge University Press.

Kaisse, E. M. and P. A. Shaw (1985), 'On the theory of Lexical Phonology', *Phonology Yearbook* 2, 1–30.

Kaye, J. (1995), 'Derivations and interfaces', in J. Durand and F. Katamba (eds), *Frontiers of Phonology: Atoms, Structures, Derivations*, London: Routledge, pp. 289–332.

Kiparsky, P. (1979), 'Metrical structure assignment is cyclic', *Linguistic Inquiry* 10(3), 421–41.

Kiparsky, P. (1982), 'From cyclic phonology to lexical phonology', in H. van der Hulst and N. Smith (eds), *The Structure of Phonological Representations I*, Dordrecht: Foris, pp. 131–75.

Kiparsky, P. (1985), 'Some consequences of lexical phonology', *Phonology Yearbook* 2, 85–138.

Kiparsky, P. (2000), 'Opacity and cyclicity', *The Linguistic Review* 17, 351–67.

Laks, B. (2005), 'La liaison et l'illusion', *Langages* 158(2), 101–25.

Liberman, M. and A. Prince (1977), 'On stress and linguistic rhythm', *Linguistic Inquiry* 8(2), 249–336.

Luick, K. (1898), 'Beiträge zur englischen Grammatik III, Die Quantitäts Veränderungen im Laufe der englischen Sprachentwicklung', *Anglia* 20, 335–62.

McMahon, A. (2007), 'Who's afraid of the Vowel Shift Rule?', *Language Sciences* 29(2–3), 341–59.

Mairano, P., B. Bassetti, M. Sokolović-Perović and T. Cerni (2018), 'Effects of L1 orthography and L1 phonology on L2 English pronunciation', *Revue française de linguistique appliquée* 1(23), 45–57.

Minkova, D. (1982), 'The environment for Open Syllable Lengthening in Middle English', *Folia Linguistica Historica* 3(2), 29–58.

Minkova, D. (1991), *The History of Final Vowels in English: The Sound of Muting*, Berlin, New York: Mouton de Gruyter.

Mohanan, K. P. (1986), *The Theory of Lexical Phonology*, Dordrecht: Reidel.

Montgomery, S. (2001), 'The case for synchronic orthographic primacy: The effect of literacy on phonological processing', PhD dissertation, University of Edinburgh.

Montgomery, S. (2005), 'Lax vowels, orthography and /ə/: The need for orthographic primacy', *Linguistische Berichte* 201, 14–64.

Myers, J. (1999), 'Lexical phonology and the lexicon', Manuscript, National Chung Cheng University.

Myers, S. (1987), 'Vowel shortening in English', *Natural Language & Linguistic Theory* 5(4), 485–518.

Navarro, S. (2017), *Le /r/ en anglais*, Dijon: Éditions universitaires de Dijon.

Nessly, L. (1982), 'Vowel tenseness in English: Another look', *Language Learning* 32(2), 393–410.

Neuman, Y. (2009), 'L'influence de l'écriture sur la langue', PhD dissertation, Université de la Sorbonne nouvelle – Paris III.

Pater, J. (1994), 'Against the underlying specification of an exceptional English stress pattern', *Toronto Working Papers in Linguistics* 13, 95–121.

Pater, J. (2000), 'Non-uniformity in English secondary stress: The role of ranked and lexically specific constraints', *Phonology* 17, 237–74.

Peereman, R., S. Dufour and J. S. Burt (2009), 'Orthographic influences in spoken word recognition: The consistency effect in semantic and gender categorization tasks', *Psychonomic Bulletin & Review* 16(2), 363–8.

Perre, L., C. Pattamadilok, M. Montant and J. C. Ziegler (2009), 'Orthographic effects in spoken language: On-line activation or phonological restructuring?', *Brain Research* 1275, 73–80.

Perre, L. and J. C. Ziegler (2008), 'On-line activation of orthography in spoken word recognition', *Brain Research* 1188, 132–8.

Pierrehumbert, J. B. (2006), 'The statistical basis of an unnatural alternation', *Laboratory Phonology* 8, 81–107.

Prince, A. (1991), 'Quantitative consequences of rhythmic organization', in M. Ziolkowski, M. Noske and K. Deaton (eds), *Papers from the Twenty-Sixth Regional Meeting of the Chicago Linguistics Society, vol. 2: The Parasession on the Syllable in Phonetics and Phonology*, Chicago: Chicago Linguistic Society, pp. 355–98.

Raffelsiefen, R. (2010), 'Idiosyncrasy, regularity, and synonymy in derivational morphology: Evidence for default word interpretation strategies', in S. Olsen (ed.), *New Impulses in Word-Formation*, Hamburg: Buske, pp. 173–232.

Roché, M. (2010), 'Base, thème, radical', *Recherches linguistiques de Vincennes* 39, 95–134.

Ryan, D. (2011), 'Grammaphonology: A new theory of English spelling', *SKASE Journal of Theoretical Linguistics* 8(2), <http://www.skase.sk/Volumes/JTL19/pdf_doc/01.pdf>.

Ryan, D. (2017), 'Principles of English spelling formation', PhD dissertation, Trinity College Dublin.

Schane, S. A. (1979), 'The rhythmic nature of English word accentuation', *Language* 55(3), 559–602.

Scheer, T. (2011), *A Guide to Morphosyntax-Phonology Interface Theories: How Extra-Phonological Information is Treated in Phonology since Trubetzkoy's Grenzsignale*, Berlin: Mouton de Gruyter.

Seidenberg, M. S. and M. K. Tanenhaus (1979), 'Orthographic effects on rhyme monitoring', *Journal of Experimental Psychology: Human Learning and Memory* 5, 546–54.

Selkirk, E. O. (1980), 'The role of prosodic categories in English word stress', *Linguistic Inquiry* 11(3), 563–605.

Siegel, D. C. (1974), 'Topics in English morphology', PhD dissertation, MIT.

Steriade, D. (2019), 'CiV lengthening and the weight of CV', in M. Bowler, P. T. Duncan, T. Major and H. Torrence (eds), *Schuhschrift: Papers in Honor of Russell Schuh*, eScholarship Publishing, University of California, pp. 161–76.

Stockwell, R. and D. Minkova (2001), *English Words: History and Structure*, Cambridge: Cambridge University Press.

Taft, M. (2006), 'Orthographically influenced abstract phonological representation: Evidence from non-rhotic speakers', *Journal of Psycholinguistic Research* 35(1), 67–78.

Taft, M. and G. Hambly (1985), 'The influence of orthography on phonological representations in the lexicon', *Journal of Memory and Language* 24, 320–35.

Toft, Z. (2002), 'The phonetics and phonology of some syllabic consonants in Southern British English', *ZAS Papers in Linguistics* 28, 111–44.

Tournier, J. (1993), *Précis de lexicologie anglaise*, 3rd edn, Paris: Nathan.

Treiman, R., J. A. Bowey and D. Bourassa (2002), 'Segmentation of spoken words into syllables by English-speaking children', *Journal of Experimental Child Psychology* 83, 213–38.

Treiman, R., N. Rosales, L. Cusner and B. Kessler (2020), 'Cues to stress in English spelling', *Journal of Memory and Language* 112, <https://doi.org/10.1016/j.jml.2020.104089>.

Trevian, I. (2003), *Morphoaccentologie et processus d'affixation de l'anglais*, Bern: Peter Lang.

Trevian, I. (2007), 'Stress-neutral endings in contemporary British English: An updated overview', *Language Sciences* 29(2–3), 426–50.

Wang, H. S. and B. L. Derwing (1986), 'More on English Vowel Shift: The back vowel question', *Phonology Yearbook* 3, 99–116.

Wells, J. C. (1965), 'The phonological status of syllabic vonsonants in English R.P.', *Phonetica* 13, 110–13.

Wells, J. C. (1982), *Accents of English: An Introduction*, Cambridge: Cambridge University Press.

Wells, J. C. (2008), *Longman Pronunciation Dictionary*, 3rd edn, London: Longman.

Zamuner, T. S. and D. K. Ohala (1999), 'Preliterate children's syllabification of intervocalic consonants', in *Proceedings of the 23rd Annual Boston Conference on Language Development*, Somerville, MA: Cascadilla Press, pp. 753–63.

5 The Stress Patterns of English Verbs: Syllable Weight and Morphology

Quentin Dabouis and Jean-Michel Fournier

0 Introduction

Most studies about English verb stress, however interesting from a theoretical point of view, seem to be based on limited sets of examples, leading their authors to assertions about the stress behaviour of English that are not actually vindicated through comprehensive data. Following Lionel Guierre's teachings, this study sets out to analyse as comprehensive a corpus as possible, based on dictionary data: though limited in some extent by the very nature of the source, it can still be seen as a first step towards a reliable description of the category. The chapter is structured as follows: first, we review the literature on English stress and distinguish two generalisations which were proposed in Chomsky and Halle's *Sound Pattern of English* (section 1). One generalisation refers to the weight of the final syllable of verbs while the other refers to the presence of a semantically opaque prefix. We then set out to evaluate the empirical validity of these two generalisations, as well as to propose a global overview of how English verbs are stressed, all morphological categories included. In section 2, we present how the data were collected, cleaned and classified. In the following section, we detail the stress distributions found in all the morphological categories found in the data (section 3). At the end of the presentation of our results, we measure the empirical validity of the two generalisations in the relevant morphological categories and show that they have similar efficiencies but different theoretical costs. Crucially, we find that the data support an analysis including semantically opaque morphological constituents among the possible determiners of stress.

1 English verbs: stress, syllable structure and morphology

1.1 The two generalisations

In Chomsky and Halle (1968, hereafter *SPE*), there are two parameters determining the position of primary stress in verbs that many morphologists would now analyse as monomorphemic. The first parameter is the segmental make-up of the final syllable. In their Main Stress Rule, a verb gets penultimate stress if the final syllable contains a 'weak cluster' (V̆C; for example *astónish, édit, consíder, imágine, intérpret*) and final stress otherwise (for example *maintáin, eráse, appéar, collápse, exháust, tormént, usúrp*). Since Kahn (1976), the terms 'weak cluster' or 'strong cluster' have been abandoned and replaced by the notion of syllable weight. Heavy syllables are now commonly defined as syllables 'which have branching anywhere within the rhyme constituent' (Carr 1999: 76), but the final consonant in verbs is usually assumed not to contribute weight to the final syllable (see section 4.1). The generalisation can thus be formulated as (1).

(1)   **The weight-based generalisation**
        In verbs, assign primary stress to:
        a. the penultimate syllable if the ultima is light, and
        b. the final syllable otherwise.

The second parameter invoked by Chomsky and Halle is morphological. 'Complex verbs', which they describe as being 'morphologically analyzable into one of the prefixes *trans-, per-, con-*, etc. followed by a stem such as *-fer, -mit, -cede, -curn* or *-pel*' (*SPE*: 94), have a different stress behaviour. They analyse these complex verbs as containing an = boundary. In their theory, this boundary has to be explicitly mentioned in the formulation of rules, which has the consequence of blocking (1a) and leads to the application of (1b), regardless of the weight of the ultima. For disyllabic verbs, this means that all complex verbs should have final stress, which allows them to account for final stress in words such as *permít, concúr, compél, detér* and *transfér*, whose final syllable is light.

Longer verbs are said to undergo the Alternating Stress Rule (ASR): if they receive final stress because of (1b), that stress is retracted to the antepenultimate syllable (for example *éxercise, ánalyze, cómplicate, clárify*). Once again, complex verbs have a different behaviour: they do not undergo the ASR when an = boundary is found between the penult and the ultima, as in *comprehénd, apprehénd, intervéne, introspéct, introdúce*. To account for that behaviour, Chomsky and Halle formulate the ASR as in (2).

(2)   **Alternating Stress Rule**
        $V \rightarrow [1\ \text{stress}]\ /\ \_\!\_\ C_0\ (=)\ C_0VC_0[1\ \text{stress}]\ C_0\ ]_{\text{NAV}}$

This rule allows for the presence of an = boundary between the antepenult and the penult (for example *com=plicate*) but not between the penult and the ultima (for example *contra=dict*). This correctly predicts antepenultimate stress in the former case and final stress (no retraction) in the latter case.

An alternative way to analyse the behaviour of complex verbs is Fournier's (2007) Germanic Law in (3).

(3) **The Germanic Law**
Overlook the prefix(es) and assign stress normally to what remains.

This law means that stress will be assigned to the root of opaque prefixed verbs, regardless of the number of prefixal syllables or the length of the root (for example *contáin, devélop, intervéne*). Note that, in Fournier's model, the Germanic Law is subordinated to the effects of stress-affecting suffixes such as *-ate*, which may impose primary stress to be placed on the prefix (for example *désignate, éxtricate, rénovate*).

Although both are used in *SPE* to account for the stress behaviour of verbs (even if the Germanic Law is not formulated as in (3)), the two generalisations have known different fates in the literature.

1.2 Two generalisations, two different fates

Most proposals since *SPE* (*SPE*: 69) claim that the stress pattern of simplex verbs is determined by the weight of their final syllable (see for example Burzio 1994: 43; Hammond 1999: 263; Hayes 1982). This is also the rule that one finds in textbooks such as Cruttenden (2014: 244–5) and Roach (2000: 110). Only the weight-based generalisation is put forward and little is said on *SPE*'s 'complex verbs'. The reason for that state of affairs might have to do with the fate of the = boundary.

Shortly after the publication of *SPE*, the = boundary was done away with by Siegel (1974, 1980), who introduced the now commonplace Class I and Class II classification of English affixes, which corresponds to the other two boundaries found in *SPE*: + and #, respectively. Her new analysis of stress placement in long verbs does not radically differ from that of *SPE*: she claims that the blocking of the ASR has nothing to do with the presence of the = boundary but with the morphological nature of the final syllable: if it is a root, the ASR does not apply (for example *interséct*) and, if it is a suffix, it does (for example *désignàte*).[1] However, disyllabic verbs are not explicitly discussed. This is problematic because doing away with the = boundary to replace it with the + boundary has the consequence that these words should behave like words with no internal structure. As a consequence, words such as *permít* or *compél* are incorrectly predicted to receive penultimate stress.

This did not stop the reference to these 'complex verbs' from progressively disappearing from generative analyses of stress placement in English verbs.

Such verbs are explicitly mentioned in early works such as Halle and Keyser (1971: 37) and Liberman and Prince (1977), but examples of 'complex verbs' have sometimes been used to illustrate the claim that verbs with a heavy final syllable have final stress (for example *prevent* and *decide* in Burzio 1994: 43). Hammond (1999: 71) observes that 'While most speakers of English are incapable of assigning any sort of meaning to elements like *ob-*, they are aware that it forms some sort of building-block in the vocabulary of English', which does not prevent him from including them in his analysis of 'monomorphemic' words in English.

SPE's analysis did not use = only for the purposes of stress assignment. It was also used to account for the specific behaviour of the prefixes introduced with the = boundary with regards to vowel reduction (sometimes called 'destressing').[2] It has often been claimed that these prefixes generally see their vowel reduces even though it is in a closed syllable, as opposed to non-prefixed words (*SPE*: 118; Halle and Keyser 1971: 37; Liberman and Prince 1977: 284–5; Guierre 1979: 253; Selkirk 1980; Hayes 1982; Halle and Vergnaud 1987: 239; Pater 2000; Hammond 2003; Collie 2007: 129, 215, 318–19), which has recently been empirically confirmed (Dabouis and Fournier 2019).

Reference to the 'complex verbs' in *SPE* and their specific stress behaviour did not disappear from all strands of the literature. It is mentioned in Fudge (1984: 165) and has been developed within the framework put forward by French linguist Lionel Guierre (Chapter 2 of this volume; Fournier 2010; Guierre 1979, 1984; Trevian 2003). Many authors have assumed that *SPE*'s = boundary applied to Latinate items only, but this seems to be an overinterpretation as it is never said explicitly in *SPE*. Following Guierre (1979), we assume that the words concerned can be Latinate (as most examples cited so far) or Germanic (for example *begin, forget, understand*) and that what characterises them is mainly their semantic opacity.

However, there is one issue which we have not yet addressed. 'Complex verbs' have often been treated alongside words with no internal structure in most post-*SPE* analyses of verb stress placement (see the examples above), so one can wonder if this departure from previous analyses was motivated by a different analysis of their structure. In other words, can *SPE*'s 'complex verbs' really be treated as morphologically complex?

1.3 Are *SPE*'s 'complex verbs' actually complex?

In the morphological literature, the status of historically prefixed verbs in contemporary English is a well-known problem (Anderson 1992: 55; Aronoff 1976: 12–15; Bauer et al. 2013: 15–16; Carstairs-McCarthy 2002: 23–6; Katamba and Stonham 2006: 23; Mudgan 2015; Plag 2003: 24–7) as they are recurring forms with meanings which are not always clearly identifiable and therefore constitute a challenge to the standard definition of the morpheme as the minimal meaningful unit. Ben Hedia and Plag clearly formulate the way that this problem can be addressed:

> Locative *in-* belongs to a set of Latinate forms in English that are often discussed in the context of morpheme-based approaches to word structure (e.g. Aronoff, 1976, 12; Bauer et al., 2013, 15f; Don, 2014, 15; Lieber, 2010, 41f; Plag, 2003, 24f). In this set we find historically Latin prefixes such as *ad-*, *con-*, *in-*, *re-*, but also bound roots, for example *-ceive*, *-mit* or *-fuse*. These forms may sometimes have a clear meaning, sometimes not. Depending on which type of definition of morpheme one adheres to, such forms are treated as morphemes (if one's theory allows for morphemes without clear semantic content), or as units below the word level that have no clear semantic content. According to the latter position these strings are called 'formatives' and are considered 'elements contributing to the construction of words' (Bauer et al., 2013, 16), and thus as some kind of morphologically relevant unit.
> (Ben Hedia and Plag 2017: 36–7)

We do not want to make any claims on the precise morphemic status of elements such as *ad-*, *con-* or *-mit* within the scope of this chapter, though they clearly need to be distinguished from productive units such as *co-* ('together'), *ex-* ('former') or *re-* ('again'). However, we argue that it is not because they might indeed not be morphemes that they are not some form of morphological unit, which some have called 'pseudo-morphemes' and others 'formatives'. Accordingly, we will retain the idea that, these elements being 'morphologically relevant', it is legitimate to assess their potential interaction with phonology.

There are various kinds of evidence which support the idea that words such as *contain* or *submit* are complex. First, there are other phonological phenomena which have been shown to be sensitive to this kind of morphological structure, such as vowel reduction (see previous section) and secondary stress placement (Dabouis 2016, 2020). Second, a number of psycholinguistic studies on lexical access in visual word recognition have shown that 'morphological decomposition is a process that is applied to all morphologically structured stimuli, irrespective of their lexical, semantic or syntactic characteristics' (Rastle and Davis 2008, in a review on the issue). This morpho-orthographic decomposition would appear to take place in the early stages of the recognition process, independently of semantics (see Marslen-Wilson et al. 2008 and references therein). Third, there is evidence from reading studies which shows that prefixes are usually not assigned stress in disyllabic words and so have to be identified in computational models of reading (Ktori et al. 2016, 2018; Rastle and Coltheart 2000; Treiman et al. 2020). Fourth, there are phonotactic sequences found in semantically opaque prefixed constructions which do not occur in morphologically simple words

(Guierre 1990; Hammond 1999: §3.3; for example [dh] in *adhere*). Finally, the distributional recurrence of prefixes and roots can be argued to provide enough evidence for morphological segmentation, independently of semantics (Fournier 1996; Pastizzo and Feldman 2004; Taft 1994).

An open question is that of the criteria that should be used to determine whether a given word contains an opaque prefix and a bound root. Indeed, classical morphological analysis crucially uses shared meaning to identify morphemes. Semantically opaque constituents may sometimes be difficult to identify and there is, to the best of our knowledge, no established procedure for doing so. Of course, one can refer to etymology but this entails two problems (Pastizzo and Feldman 2004). The first problem is that historically morphologically complex words may not be identifiable as such any more. The evolution of their pronunciation and/or spelling may have altered their shape in such a way that there is no way that they could be parsed by speakers. The second problem is that, if there are synchronic mechanisms used by speakers to parse semantically opaque complex words, these mechanisms could lead to the parsing of words which actually have no historical morphological structure. But for any such mechanism to be relevant, we first need to make sure that unaltered historical prefixation does indeed affect stress placement.

Our position will be to assume that most historically prefixed words are still potentially recognisable in contemporary English. One of the goals of this chapter is to seek to establish whether historically prefixed verbs do indeed have a stress behaviour that is distinct from that of words with no internal structure, as was claimed in *SPE*. If they do, then it would imply that phonological analyses of English stress cannot do away with what *SPE* called 'complex verbs'. It would also raise the question of learnability, which has probably led generative linguists to reject the synchronic relevance of this type of morphological structure (as pointed out by Renate Raffelsiefen, personal communication), and open the way to test out the predictions that such a model makes: loss of identifiability or assimilatory identification (things that 'look like' prefixes).

1.4 Aims of the chapter

It has been noted before that many studies on English phonology 'suffer from a scarcity of systematic empirical evidence' (Domahs et al. 2014) or are based on 'convenient samples' (Wenszky 2004: 12). McMahon (2001) also notes that 'there is undoubtedly a problem in phonology, especially the sort that rather distances itself from phonetics, of reliance on stock examples and introspection'. Consequently, the generalisations discussed in the previous sections have seldom been tested against large datasets. The only study of which we are aware is that of Guierre (1979). His study showed a strong effect of opaque prefixation, but his results did not strongly support the weight-based generalisation, even though he did find a tendency towards final stress in disyllables with a heavy ultima. Since Guierre's study, there seems to have been no empirical evaluation of the efficiencies of the two generalisations. Therefore, the first aim of this chapter will be to remedy that state of affairs. To do so, we will constitute a large corpus of pronunciation dictionary data. This will allow us to give a detailed empirical account of both the morphology and the stress patterns of English verbs.

We will test the two generalisations presented in section 1.1 and will seek to establish whether both reference to opaque morphology and syllable weight are needed to account for the placement of primary stress in English verbs. If the study does confirm Guierre's results that opaque morphology does determine the position of primary stress in these words, the question of the learnability of such structures will have to be addressed. Note that such an endeavour implies, as a first step, describing the different morphological categories found in verbs since it will allow us to isolate the morphological categories relevant to test the two generalisations by clearly identifying categories which must be excluded on account of their distinct behaviours (most notably suffixed words, with either stress-shifting suffixes or stress-neutral suffixes, whose effects have been shown to override those of opaque prefixes). It will also allow for a detailed description of stress placement in verbs (maybe most interestingly for categories which are not well described, such as compounds). Our study will thus provide a general view of the morphological and accentual characteristics of English verbs and of how they interact, which is something that, to our knowledge, has not been done before.

2 Methodology

2.1 Data collection

The data used in this study come from the Laboratoire Ligérien de Linguistique's (LLL) Dictionary Database. This is an ongoing project which gathers three reference pronunciation dictionaries (Delbridge et al. 2009; Jones 2006; Wells 2008) and contains additional information such as syntactic categories and word meaning, and will contain token frequencies and morphological analyses. The syntactic categories in the database come from the *Macquarie Dictionary*, which is the only dictionary of the three which is not only a pronunciation dictionary.

For this study, we extracted all 5236 verbs listed in Jones (2006). Only the main pronunciation for British English was extracted. Words which were marked as 'rare', 'obsolete', as belonging to another dialect of English (American, Australian, etc.) or which had no entry as verbs in the online *Oxford English Dictionary* (*OED*) were left out. This led to the exclusion of 293 words.

2.2 Conversion

One crucial issue with using the syntactic categories in the *Macquarie Dictionary* is that, like many dictionaries of its kind, it tends to attribute several categories to certain words, even when they are predominantly used within a single category. Henceforth, many of the words which are tagged as 'verbs' in the dictionary are in fact verbal uses of nouns or, more marginally, adjectives. As pointed out by Bauer et al. (2013: 279) and Bram (2011), it is not always easy to determine which member of a homophonous pair, one a verb and the other a member of another category, should be analysed as the base of the other. More generally, the question of directionality is a hotly debated topic in the literature on conversion in English. Recent work underlines the necessity of using several criteria in order to establish the directionality of conversion. The criteria which have been used in the literature, although none of them is free of limitations (see Bram 2011 for detailed discussion), include: attestation dates, frequency of occurrence, semantic range and semantic dependency. Following these previous works, we based our identification of those verbal uses on these same four criteria, all of which are based on data recorded on the *OED*.

The **dates of first attestation** were taken from the *OED*. The first member of the pair to be recorded was seen as more likely to be the base of the other. In some cases, it was not possible to compare attestation dates because the *OED* refers to undefined dates such as OE (Old English) or eOE (early Old English). As pointed out by Plag (2003: 108), historical information cannot be used alone because 'complex semantic changes may overwrite the original direction of conversion'.

The **frequency of occurrence** was taken from the *OED* Frequency Bands, which are based on Google Book Ngram data and other corpora. It was used as a rough indication of which member of the pair is used more frequently than the other, in which case the former is seen as more likely to be the base. This is based on the assumption that 'derived words tend to have a narrower range of meaning' (Plag 2003: 111) and that, as a consequence, they tend to be used in fewer contexts.

Semantic range was established by looking at the number of meanings given for each member of the pair. The member with more meanings was seen as more likely to be the base.

Semantic dependency was established using the definitions of both members of the pair. We checked whether the semantic relationship between the two members of the pair fits within one of the thirteen semantic categories listed by Lieber (2004: 92), which are largely based on those listed by Plag (1999: 220), which are themselves based on earlier literature on conversion. Such categories include the locative 'put (in)to N' (for example *jail*), the ornative 'provide with N' (for example *staff*) or the causative 'make (more) Adj' (for example *yellow*).

For all the words in our dataset, we checked whether a noun existed in the *OED* to establish a first list of potential candidates for conversion. We then collected the relevant information for each pair and made our decision based on the four criteria described above. Whenever there were inconsistencies between the four criteria, the decision was based on semantic dependency.

In the case of conversions from other categories, all fairly obvious, these criteria did not seem helpful and were not used.

This led to the identification of 1395 converted words (see examples in (4)), which were therefore excluded from the dataset as their stress patterns could be attributed to their original syntactic category.[3]

(4)   *author, baby, catalogue, engineer, input, invalid, exile, patent, ready, signature, silence, tapestry* . . .

They are mostly conversions from nouns: only 94 are conversions from other classes (adjectives, adverbs, interjections), such as those in (5).

(5)   *busy, even, narrow, oblique, opaque, overnight, farewell, hello* . . .

It is worth noting than no criterion could have been used on its own. For instance, if we consider the 1312 verbs classified as denominal, we find that the noun is more frequent than the verb in only 868 (66%) cases and similarly that only 858 (65%) of the nouns entered the language over 50 years before the verb did, according to the *OED*.

The final dataset contains 3548 words, 1918 disyllables and 1630 longer verbs.

2.3 Morphological classification

As discussed in section 1.4, one of the aims of this chapter is to investigate the relationship between obscure morphology and stress placement in English verbs. Therefore, standard analyses for morphological complexity (for example Plag 2003: §5.2.2; Stockwell and Minkova 2001: 58ff.) cannot be used. While words whose elements have identifiable semantics can confidently be analysed as morphologically complex (even though that meaning can sometimes be rather vague; for example *spect* 'looking, sight' in *inspect, suspect, spectacle*), it may not be so easy to do so for words with semantically opaque constituents. This is the case for prefixes (for example most *ob-* prefixed verbs) and for roots (for example *-pel, -fer, -mit*).

In the absence of an established procedure for an analysis of morphological structure which is not based on these definitions of the morpheme, it seems preferable that the procedure we adopt should be replicable and therefore based on accessible, verifiable data. One option for prefixed verbs could be to analyse as morphologically complex any word whose constituents occur elsewhere, even though they do not have a clear identifiable meaning. This methodology seems problematic with those cases where the potential prefix has little segmental content and the potential base[4] is not attested elsewhere (for example *attack, esteem, erase*). If one assumes that distributional recurrence of prefixes and roots is a key mechanism allowing speakers to parse semantically opaque prefixed words, then one can wonder how a synchronic analysis could actually treat those words as morphologically complex. However, there might be other properties which could still lead to their parsing as morphologically complex and such a methodology would therefore miss out on some of the data (although probably not a lot). Therefore, it was decided to use etymological information, taken from the *OED*, prior to any further, and synchronic, considerations. Doing so has the advantage that other researchers can replicate our findings using the same objective criterion, even though, at this stage, it comes at the cost of the limitations discussed in section 1.4, that is, the assessment of the conditions of learnability. But precisely, it also opens up the possibility to lead a contrastive analysis amongst these cases and thus define further criteria of relevance to contemporary speakers, entailing a more restrictive classification method. Of course, one can just as much refute the whole idea and group this category with the base (or simplex) category as distinct results will be given for each of our categories and therefore allow for such a stance.

Since an active base in contemporary English may influence the behaviour of a prefixed verb, whatever the status of its prefix, all such cases have been identified. However, even with an active prefix, the relationship between prefix and base can be either compositional (for example *disprove, rewrite, unlock*) or not (for example *compile, depose, react*): we call the latter 'opaque' constructions. The two types have therefore been further distinguished. A restrictive interpretation of compositionality led us to deem 'opaque' all cases of verbs which, though their meaning is transparent, are formed from a nominal (or marginally other non-verb classes) base, on account of category change (for example *devoice, discourage, endear*): as will be seen, whatever their classification, it does not affect the position of primary stress. We identified 144 such cases, 128 from a nominal base and 16 from an adjectival base.

Constructions whose first element is one of the following adverbial or prepositional elements have been listed separately: *back-, by-, down-, fore-, in-* (locative), *off-, out-, post-, up-, with-* (for example *backfire, foreclose, outdate*). In construction, these units seem to behave as prefixes in the case of verbs but as roots in the case of nouns (Abasq 2007). They are mostly compositional in the case of verbs.[5]

In the case of suffixed verbs, we listed all cases which contain final sequences which may be analysed (at least historically) as suffixes, even when their base is not active in contemporary English (for example *happen, vibrate, polish, compliment, fraternize*), that is, we used the same strategy as that adopted for prefixed words. We then further divided all suffixed entries between so-called stress-preserving and so-called stress-shifting suffixes,[6] the free or bound[7] status of the base being indifferent in the case of stress-shifting suffixes, as is well established (as far as main stress is concerned). Certain suffixes have been treated as being alternatively stress-preserving and stress-shifting. The verbal suffix -*ize* has often been considered as one of these 'mixed' (or 'dual-level' in Stratal Phonology) suffixes (Bermúdez-Otero 2018; Guierre 1979: 711–14; Selkirk 1982; Szpyra 1989: §2.2.3; Trevian 2007, 2015: §13.2) and will therefore be presented separately.[8]

This distinct treatment of suffixed words is crucial, as stress-preserving suffixes are irrelevant for stress assignment and stress-affecting suffixes directly determine the position of primary stress, regardless of other factors (and so may neutralise the effects of other types of morphological structures).

The 'compounds' category contains all cases formed from the association of two free bases, the most widely accepted definition (for example *blindfold*, *skyjack*, *cross-examine*). These words need to be treated separately as the previous literature has shown that compound words have a stress behaviour that is distinct from that of non-compound words.

All other constructions which did not fit into any of the previous categories, and whose numbers were too low for an independent analysis, were grouped into the 'other' category: truncations, back-formations, neoclassical formations, bound bases compounds and some other, obscure cases (for example *liaise*, *animadvert*, *choreograph*, *genuflect*, *flabbergast*).[9]

Finally, the 'simplex' (or root) category (for example *argue*, *harangue*, *listen*) consists of words for which no morphological structure can be identified.

The distribution of the data among the different categories we have just presented is shown in Table 5.1.[10]

The difference in the morphological distribution of the two inventories is striking:

- Disyllables are massively 'left-edge constructions' (they are constructed on the left of the root: compositional + opaque prefixed: 66%), while the rest is roughly equally divided between simplex and suffixed forms (about 15% each). This is clearly different from nouns; in his dataset, Guierre (1979) similarly found that 77% of verbs are prefixed while only 9% of nouns are.
- Longer verbs are mostly suffixed (60%), though left-edge constructions still represent a significant part of the inventory (35%), and long simplex verbs are extremely rare. This account is somewhat misleading, however: suffixation is mostly due to only 3 suffixes, -*ate*, -*ify* and -*ize*, and no fewer than 335 (i.e. an additional 20% of all long verbs) out of the 617 verbs with a stress-shifting suffix are also prefixed.[11] Stress determination apart, English verbs of all length thus display a remarkable proportion of left-edge constructions.

Table 5.1 Morphological distribution in the dataset

	Disyllables		Long verbs		Total	
Compositional left-edge constructions	227	*12%*	362	*22%*	589	*17%*
Opaque prefixed constructions – free base	364	*19%*	110	*7%*	474	*13%*
Opaque prefixed constructions – bound base	665	*35%*	105	*6%*	770	*22%*
Simplex	278	*14%*	15	*1%*	293	*8%*
Bound base + suffix	112	*6%*	18	*1%*	130	*3%*
Stress-shifting suffixes	40	*2%*	617	*38%*	657	*19%*
Stress-preserving suffixes – free base	114	*6%*	6	*<1%*	120	*4%*
-*ize* – free base	2	*<1%*	334	*20%*	336	*9%*
Compounds	88	*4%*	24	*2%*	112	*3%*
Other	28	*1%*	39	*2%*	67	*2%*
Total	**1918**		**1630**		**3548**	

3 The stress patterns of English verbs in British English: a comprehensive description

Results will be presented according to phonological behaviour types: first, compositional constructions, stress-shifting suffixes whatever the status of their base (active/inactive) and its morphology, stress-preserving suffixes and the mixed suffix -*ize* when they are attached to a free base, whatever its morphology; then the remaining cases, divided into five categories: compounds, other, prefixed words, non-prefixed suffixed (with stress-preserving suffixes) words with a bound base, and simplex words. Given the limits of this chapter, only samples will be displayed but the full data are available online (see note 3).

3.1 Compositional constructions (n = 589)

Semantically compositional constructions whose leftmost formative is a prefix (411 words) or an adverbial particle (178 words) tend to behave as two distinct phonological domains, as evidenced by stress clashes (for example *dèclássify, rèwríte, òutbálance*) or morphological geminates (for example *di*[ss]*atisfy, mi*[ss]*pell*).[12]

Primary stress is on the base in the vast majority of words (581/589, 99%). The only words in which that is not the case are shown in (6).

(6)   *fórecast, ínfix, óutcry, óutsource, cóuntercharge, cóuntersign, cóuntersink, óversew*

Interestingly enough, all constructions with an adverbial particle (or 'adverbial constructions') are formed from an active base, with the exception of locative *in-* (which is not surprising given its history;[13] for example *ínfer, ínject, ínspect*),[14] and are mostly semantically compositional, again except for *in-* constructions (for example *inflámе, infórm, inténd*): despite our relatively restrictive definition of compositionality, only 25 cases (for example *withdráw, outwít, understánd*) were analysed as opaque, that is < 14% of the class (*in-* constructions excluded). These cases are included within the opaque prefixation categories presented below.

3.2 Stress-shifting suffixes (n = 657)

Some suffixes determine the position of primary stress in vast parts of the data. The most common one is *-ate*, with 536 words. Verbs in *-ate* usually have final stress in 33/36 disyllables (for example *dictáte, negáte, gradáte* ... but *cúrate, fúrcate, stríate*)[15] and antepenultimate stress in 494/500 longer verbs (for example *démonstrate, oríginate, máturate* ... but *detrúncate, èquilíbrate, inspíssate, óxygenate, péregrinate, térgiversate*[16]). It seems interesting to associate to this class the 3 disyllables and 13 longer verbs in *-ite/-ute* (for example *uníte, salúte, éxpedite, cónstitute, pérsecute*), with similar stressing except the *-tribute* verbs (*attríbute, contríbute, distríbute*[17]), which seems to allow for a *-Vte* (or /-V̄t/) constraint.

The second largest class concerns the 89 verbs ending in *-ify/-efy*, which all have antepenultimate stress (for example *divérsify, glórify, rárefy, solémnify, vílify*).[18]

The dataset also contains 9 words ending with the suffix *-esce* and which all have final stress (for example *àcquiésce, èfflorésce, lùminésce*). We have associated the verb *rèminísce* to this category because, although it is does not formally contain the suffix *-esce*, it seems to owe its final stress to an (orthographic?) analogy with this category.

The 6 remaining verbs contain various Class I suffixes and follow the regular patterns associated with these suffixes: *cashiér, bùccanéer, elèctionéer, appórtion, dìsillúsion, envísion*.

Let us finish this section by pointing out that words with opaque prefixes behave in the same way as words without such prefixes, even when that entails stressing on the prefix (for example *ácclimate, cómpensate, dédicate, émigrate, ímplicate, óbfuscate, prómulgate, súbjugate* cp. *álternate, círculate, dóminate, émulate, ímitate, óscillate, póstulate, stránguale*): the rules or constraints which regulate stress placement in words with stress-shifting suffixes clearly dominate the potential 'stress-repelling' effects of prefixes, just as much as they interfere with the potential effect of the weight of the final syllable.

3.3 Stress-preserving suffixes – free base (n = 120)

Contrary to stress-shifting suffixes, whose associated stress-pattern is systematic whatever the status of the base, stress-preserving suffixes preserve the pronunciation of free bases. Apart from a few exceptions, no stress shifts are observed.

The most commonly found stress-preserving suffix is *-en* with 59 verbs transparently derived from a free base (for example *awáke → awáken, fát → fátten, shórt → shórten*).

The second most common stress-preserving suffix is *-le*. It is found in only 42 disyllables. Stress, obviously enough, never shifts to the second syllable (for example *cráckle, hándle, súckle*). Although the frequentative (and sometimes diminutive) meaning of this historical verbal suffix is often still apparent, the suffix is clearly no longer active in contemporary English: these cases could alternatively be analysed as non-derived.[19] Additionally, 10 of these words display important alterations of the root, which further questions their derived status: *boom → bumble, daze → dazzle, game → gamble, joust → jostle, nose → nuzzle, prate → prattle, stride → straddle, throat → throttle, wade → waddle*.

Finally, we find 19 other words containing stress-preserving suffixes. Among those, the 17 shown in (7) fully preserve the stress pattern of their base.

(7)   *banish, blandish, bumper, burnish, distinguish, flitter, jigger, moulder, mullock, multiply, notice, pester, prophesy, putter, skitter, upholster, whimper*

The other two show an exceptional stress shift: *bómb → bombárd* and *ímage → imágine*. However, considering the semantic drift between the two words, *imagine* might be better analysed as a deradical formation. Similarly, *bombard*, originally converted from the noun referring to the military engine, has now lost that reference in favour of a direct but somewhat loose relationship with *bomb*, with an intensive value that has been lost in all the other derivatives in *-ard*. Additionally, these derivations are both one of a kind.

3.4 -ize – free base (n = 336)

The dataset contains 318 *-ize* derivatives which may be analysed as stress-preserving constructions considering that the position of stress is identical to that found in the base (for example *cánon → cánonize, cháracter → cháracterize, pròpagánda → pròpagándize, stýle → stýlize*). The remaining 18 words do show stress shifts, as shown in (8).

(8)   *advért → ádvertize*   *épilogue → epílogize*
            àlumínium → alúminize   *épigram → èpigrámmatize*
            ànaesthésia → anáesthetize   *Galváni → gálvanize*
            ánthropomorph → ànthropomórphize   *gélatin → gelátinize*
            apòtheósis → apótheosize   *hypnósis → hýpnotize*

áttitude → àttitúdinize	immúne → ímmunize
canál → cánalize	pànegýric → panégyrize
cátholic → cathólicize	vólatile → volátilize
émblem → emblématize	+ parasynthetic demóralize ← morale

However, for a number of these cases the derivation can be questioned in contemporary English and some might prefer to classify these among bound base constructions.[20]

3.5 Compounds (n = 112)

Main stress tends to be on the first constituent in disyllables (75% of 88 words):

(9)   *blíndfold, hándcraft, kídnap, skýjack* ... vs *dèep-frý, hànd-píck, vòuchsáfe* ...

but is equally divided between first and second constituents in words of three syllables or more (24 words):

(10)   *bábysit, wíndow-shop* ... vs *cròss-exámine, stàge-mánage* ...

Let us examine the data more closely to see which factors could explain the position of stress in these compounds.

Previous research has shown that verbal compounds are quite uncommon and that they are often formed through conversion or backformation (Carstairs-McCarthy 2002: 60–1; Marchand 1969: 100ff.; Plag 2003: 154–5). The 271 converted compounds present in the initial dataset have already been excluded (see section 2.2). Following Bauer et al. (2013: 280–1), we identified 26 cases of backformation based on the dates of attestation (taken from the *OED*) of verbal compound and its base and the semantic dependency between them.[21] These cases are shown in (11).

(11)   *air-condition, back-pedal, brainwash, bulldoze, chain-smoke, crash-land, cross-refer, dive-bomb, freeload, freeze-dry, gatecrash, ghostwrite, headhunt, jaywalk, jerry-build, lip-read, mass-produce, plea-bargain, shoplift, shrink-wrap, spring-clean, stage-manage, steamroll, touch-type, typewrite, windsurf*

We then compared the stress patterns of these compounds with those of their bases and found that the position of primary stress is systematically identical. Therefore, we cannot exclude the possibility that the stress patterns of these verbal compounds actually reproduce those of their bases, and so they were excluded from further analyses.

Most studies on compound stress have focused on noun + noun constructions and there is no previous extensive work on verbal compounds that we know of. Previous work on nominal compounds has shown the importance of lexicalisation, the semantic relationship between the two elements, length, informativity and analogy (see among others Bell and Plag 2013; Giegerich 2009; Plag 2006). The data were therefore coded as follows:

- Lexicalisation was approached using two variables:
  - SPELLING: more lexicalised compounds tend to be spelled as one word while less lexicalised compounds tend to be spelled hyphenated or as two words (Plag et al. 2007, 2008).[22]
  - FREQUENCY: the frequency of the whole construction was extracted from SUBTLEX-UK (Van Heuven et al., 2014) and log-transformed, as is standard procedure.
- Less informative elements have been found to be less likely to be stressed (Bell and Plag 2013). Following Bell and Plag (2013), these are assumed to be more frequent and have a greater number of senses. Therefore, we used two measures of informativity:
  - FREQUENCY of each of the two constituents, following the same procedure as that used for the whole construction.
  - SYNSETS for the two constituents. Synsets correspond to sets of words with similar meanings. We used the WordNet lexical database to manually extract the number of synsets for each constituent.[23]
- We coded for the number of syllables of the first and second constituents, of the whole construction, and of syllables following the last strong syllable of the first constituent.
- The syntactic categories of Constituent 1 and Constituent 2 were coded for.

Given the limited size of our dataset and the diversity of the semantic relationships found in it, we chose not to study this variable, for it would seem difficult to draw any conclusions with such small samples. For the same reasons, it is difficult to study analogy as few constructions share a constituent, but this parameter is discussed below.

These factors were tested in a binary logistic regression model with the position of main stress in the compound as the dependent variable.[24] Two variables were found to be significant predictors of the position of stress: the syntactic category of Constituent 1 and spelling. The results are shown in Table 5.2 and the distribution of the data is shown in Figure 5.1.

As can be seen in Figure 5.1, stress on Constituent 2 is more likely if Constituent 1 is not a noun and if the compound is hyphenated. The absence of effects from the other factors such as informativity could be due to the restricted size of the dataset.

Table 5.2 Binary logistic regression for the position of main stress in verbal compounds

	95% C.I.			p-value
	Lower	**OR**	**Higher**	
CatC1-Noun	0.010	0.053	0.224	0.000163
CatC1-Adj	0.034	0.272	1.809	0.183954
CatC1-Verb	0.0725	0.372	1.680	0.211397
Spelling-OneWord	0.053	0.194	0.627	0.008040

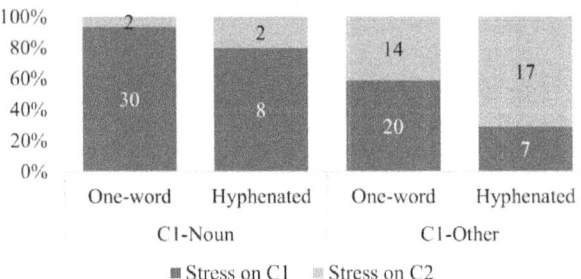

Figure 5.1 Position of main stress in verbal compounds depending on the syntactic category of Constituent 1 and spelling

Let us finish with the question of analogy. It has long been observed that, in noun–noun compounds, compounds which share a constituent tend to be stressed in the same way. For example, compounds which end in *street* are stressed on their first constituent while those which end in *avenue* are stressed on their second element (Arndt-Lappe 2011). As mentioned above, our dataset being quite small, there are few instances of compounds sharing a constituent. However, we have grouped those which do in Table 5.3.

As can be seen from Table 5.3, no clear picture emerges from this variable alone. Although this is consistent with previous research, which has shown that analogy is not the only factor at play, additional research using more extensive data might allow for a clearer picture on the importance of analogy in verbal compounds and how it might interact with the other factors seen previously.

In sum, we have found that the position of main stress in verbal compounds can be related to lexicalisation, as compounds which are spelled as one word are more likely to get stress on their first constituent than those spelled with a hyphen. We have also found effects of syntactic categories, with compounds whose first constituent is a noun being more likely to get stress on this element than those whose first constituent has another category. However, because of the small number of observations and the number of tested variables, the results that we report are to be taken with caution and should be replicated using larger datasets based on speech data.

Table 5.3 Position of main stress in compounds which share a constituent

	Shared constituent	Stress on Constituent 1	Stress on Constituent 2
Constituent 1	about	Ø	about-face, about-turn
	air	air-cool, air-dry	Ø
	back	backcomb, backfill, backslide, backtrack, backwash	backdate, backfire
	cross	crossbreed, crosscut, crosshatch	crosscheck, cross-examine, cross-fertilize, cross-question
	hand	handcraft	hand-pick
	side	sideslip, sidestep	Ø
Constituent 2	cast	broadcast, typecast, webcast	Ø
	dry	air-dry, drip-dry	spin-dry
	fill	backfill	fulfil
	fry	pan-fry, stir-fry	deep-fry
	jack	highjack, skyjack	Ø
	start	jump-start, kick-start	Ø
	surf	bodysurf, windsurf	Ø

3.6 'Others' (n = 67)

As stated above, this inventory includes truncations, back-formations, neo-classical formations, bound bases compounds and some other, obscure cases such as those listed in (12).

(12)   cónfab, liáise, vìviséct, ànimadvért, quádruple, chóreograph, génuflect, mànufácture, flábbergast, cáterwaul . . .

Given the heterogeneity of this inventory, the stress distribution (41 on the first element, 26 on the second) is most probably of no significance.

So far, none of the categories we described is sensitive to opaque pre-fixation, either by nature in the case of compositional constructions or compounding, or because the parameter is superseded by stress-shifting or stress-preserving suffixes. From here on, both the weight parameter and the opaque prefixation parameter can come into play: let us take a detailed look at each sub-category.

3.7 Opaque prefixation (n = 1244)

We treated as 'opaque' any construction whose meaning is not compositional. For example, *exact* does not transparently inherit its meaning from the prefix *ex-* and the free base *act*, nor does *proclaim* transparently inherit its meaning from the prefix *pro-* and the free base *claim*.

As stated in section 2.3, this includes semantically transparent cases but whose base is not a verb, on account of category change such as the cases shown in (13).

(13)   *debag, de-ice, derail, dismast, enchain, enlist, ensnare* . . .

As will be seen through the examples, a number of these cases are also suffixed with a stress-preserving suffix (34 as part of a free base, and 20 as part of a bound base): they do not seem to play any part in the placement of primary stress either on the prefix or on the base, which explains why they were included here.

3.7.1 Free base (n = 474)
The stress-pattern of the base is not affected; primary stress is on the base in 99% of cases, as shown with the examples in (14). This includes 2 parasynthetic formations: *aggrandize, embolden*.

(14)   *accústom, accóunt, becóme, besprínkle, defáult, elápse, emblázon, expórt, preóccupy, rècolléct, redréss, ùnderstánd*

Stress is not base-initial in six words. In five of them, primary stress falls on the prefix (*cómpass, párboil, tréspass, cóunterpoise, rétrograde*), and in the last one, primary stress falls on the second syllable of the base (*àscertáin*).

3.7.2 Bound base (n = 770)
In 733/770 (95%) of cases, stress is on the base.

(15)   *abhór, commít, distráct, ejéct, obtáin, persíst, refér, survíve*
       còntradíct, ìntercépt, ìntermít, rètrogréss
       amórtize, contínue, demólish, elícit, inhábit, remémber

This rate is higher in disyllables, with base stress found in 643/665 (97%) of cases, than in longer verbs, with base stress found in 91/105 (87%) of cases. The words in which primary stress is not on the base are shown in (16).

(16)   Disyllables: *ábseil, cómbat, cómfort, cónjure, cónquer, cóver, déstine, díffer, édit, énter, ínjure, óffer, pérjure, próffer, prósper, rálly, rélay, rével, séver, sójourn, súffer, súmmon*

Long verbs: *círcumcise, círcumscribe, cómpliment, cóuntenance, discómfit, éxorcize, ímplement, ìmportúne, ímprovise, intérpret, óccupy, récognize, réconcile, súpervise*

3.8 Bound base + suffix (n = 130)

In disyllables, stress is initial in 102/112 words (91%), such as those shown in (17).

(17) *chérish, chúckle, glísten, glítter, héarken, mánage, pótter, slíther, sprínkle, vánish . . .*

The ten words with final stress are *augmént, chastíse, divíne, fermént, fomént, frequént, lamént, levánt, rampáge* and *tormént*.

In longer verbs, 17/18 (94%) have antepenultimate stress. These includes 16 words in *-ize* (for example *fráternize, órganize, sánitize*) and *mónitor*. The only word with penultimate stress is *etérnize*.

Following on the observations about the *-le*, *-er* and *-ish* verbal suffixes in section 3.3, this class contains a number of cases whose historical suffixes have been inactive for quite a long time, notably *-it* (*merit, posit, visit, vomit*) and nominal *-le* (*nettle, ripple, spindle, tackle, trundle, whittle*): semantically completely opaque, and, contrary to those in section 3.3, never suffixed to a free base, they would probably be best considered as extinct and the verbs analysed as simple roots. We only kept them here for the sake of consistency at this point. This decision, however, does not affect the contrastive analysis between theories that follows since this class of verbs is grouped with the simplex class anyhow.

3.9 Simplex verbs (n = 293)

In disyllables, stress is initial in 262/278 words (94%), as in the words listed in (18).

(18) *árgue, cáncel, cópy, fóllow, góvern, hállow, lísten, rénder, scúrry, swállow, vómit . . .*

The 16 words with final stress are all listed in (19).

(19) *blasphéme, cajóle, caréen, caréss, caróuse, cavórt, equíp, maráud, molést, opíne, ordáin, patról, piáffe, posséss, shampóo, usúrp*

In longer verbs, we have:

- 8 words with penultimate stress: *bamboozle, canoodle, finagle, malinger, manoeuvre, sequester, skedaddle, solicit*

- 7 with antepenultimate stress: *damascene, gallivant, manacle, manifest, massacre, minister, orient.*

3.10 Interim summary

At the end of this detailed presentation of stress and the morphological distribution of British English verbs, and before confronting both treatments of stress placement in the relevant categories, we believe it important to repeat the observation prompted by the figures in Table 5.1 above: English verbs are quite obviously morphologically characterised as heavily built 'on the left'. The first two categories, obvious to the speaker because of semantic compositionality or the presence of a free base, represent no less than 30% of the whole class and, as such, constitute quite a strong incentive to identify the same left-edge morphology in the 22% (up to 35% in the case of disyllables) of the opaque prefixed constructions with a bound base. In such a context, hypothesising a role to opaque morphology appears rather consistent with the data.

4 Syllable weight and opaque prefixation

The aim of this section is to evaluate the scope and efficiency of the weight-based generalisation and of the Germanic Law and to determine whether both are needed to account for stress placement in English verbs. Before this evaluation, it is necessary to go through the proposals which have been made in the literature on what counts as a heavy syllable and, more specifically, what counts as a heavy syllable at the end of verbs.

4.1 On syllable weight

Nowadays, most practitioners use Moraic Theory (Hayes 1989; Hyman 1985; McCarthy and Prince 1996) to deal with weight-related phenomena. Moraic Theory claims that rhyme constituents possess something which onset constituents do not: they can project morae, that is, weight-bearing units. The possible weight configurations in Moraic Theory are represented in (20).

(20)

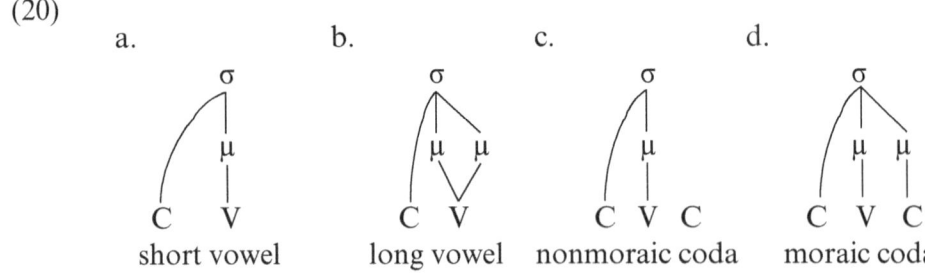

The distinction between light and heavy syllables is represented by the number of morae which syllables carry. A syllable is said to be heavy when it carries at least two morae (it is said to be bimoraic) and light when it carries only one (it is monomoraic). Short vowels project only one mora (20a), long vowels project two morae (20b), and coda consonants may (20d) or may not (20c) project a mora, depending on the language (or, as we will see below, on the nature of the coda).

In English, final syllables have been claimed to have specific properties, as is illustrated mostly by stress and by the distribution of segments (see Hammond 1999: §4). Most analyses consider the final consonant of verbs to be invisible to stress-assignment rules or constraints. This can be achieved through final consonant extrametricality (Hayes 1982), which means that that consonant is invisible to the stress-assigning mechanism. Another option is catalexis, which is the introduction of a final null vowel (Burzio 1994; Hammond 1999), which makes the final consonant the onset of a syllable with an empty nucleus.[25] These two options are represented in (21) with the examples of *adapt* and *edit*.

(21) a. extrametricality   b. catalexis

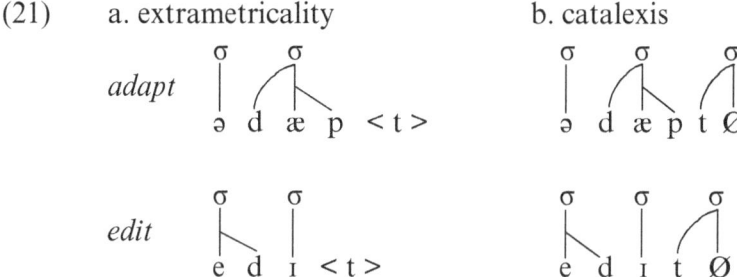

In both cases, the final consonant does not contribute weight to the preceding syllable. For English verbs, the claim is therefore that final syllables which contain a short vowel may be heavy only if they are followed by at least two consonants.

Moreover, there have been further proposals as to the number of morae that a given segment may or may not project. Hammond (1999: 147) proposes the mora counts in (22), based on distributional regularities in English and on the assumption that stressed syllables should contain at least two morae and three morae at the most.[26]

(22) **Consonants**   **Vowels**[27]
      Coronals   (μ)[28]   Lax   μ
      Noncoronals   μ   Tense   μμ
      [ʒ, ŋ]   μμ   [aʊ, ɔɪ]   μμμ
      [ð]   Ø

Additionally, it has been proposed that coda sonorants have variable weight (Burzio 1994: §3.4; Giegerich 1999: 371; Halle and Vergnaud 1987:

257; Selkirk 1984: 127), which we will assume to be the variable projection of a mora, as Hammond proposes for coronals. Therefore, these more recent proposals suggest that stress placement in verbs is not simply determined by the number of consonants following the last vowel but also by the nature of these consonants.

Finally, certain vowels have been argued to be lighter than can be observed on the surface. For instance, [ə] has been argued to be less heavy than full vowels (Burzio 2007) or even nonmoraic (Hammond 1999: 206–7).[29] Another case is that of unstressed final [əʊ],[30] which has been argued to be underlyingly lax (*SPE*: 75; Hammond 1999) and, therefore, which can be interpreted as being monomoraic. Hammond (1999) also extends that claim to final [i].[31]

Consequently, a lot of potential drawbacks for the weight-based analysis can be excluded on the grounds that the surface weight is not the actual weight. In order to test the weight-based generalisation in its most favourable conditions, the following assumptions were adopted to code the weight of the final syllables in our dataset:

- [ə] is moraless.
- Final unstressed [i] and [əʊ] are monomoraic (but final stressed [əʊ] is treated along with the other long/tense vowels).
- Short/lax vowels are monomoraic.
- Long/tense vowels are bimoraic, except [aʊ, ɔɪ], which are trimoraic.
- The last consonant is moraless.
- Preconsonantally, sonorants and [s] are moraless if unstressed and have one mora if stressed, with the exception of [ŋ], which is bimoraic.
- Preconsonantally, other consonants are treated as monomoraic.

This set of assumptions gives us the weights in Table 5.4. Syllables which are at least bimoraic were treated as heavy and are shown in grey. An empty cell means that the configuration is not attested in the dataset.

4.2 Relevant data and results

In order to evaluate the role of syllable weight and that of opaque prefixation, we kept only the relevant data: simplex and deradical verbs. We distinguished two categories:

- prefixed: opaque prefixed constructions with bound bases (see section 3.7.2)
- non-prefixed: bound base + suffix (see section 3.8) and simplex verbs (see section 3.9).

These categories were selected because they are those which many practitioners would treat as 'monomorphemic' and so potentially free of morphological

Table 5.4 Weight coding adopted

Final consonant(s) Vowel	_#	_C#	_C[+son]C# _sC#	_[ŋ]C#	_C[-son]C#
[ə]	0μ	0μ	0μ	–	1μ
[i]	1μ	–	–	–	–
[əʊ]	1μ	–	–	–	–
[aʊ, ɔɪ]	3μ	3μ	3μ	–	–
V̆	–	1μ	2μ[a]	3μ	2μ
V̄	2μ	2μ	3μ	–	3μ

[a] The only attested cases have final stress.

influences. The dataset thus contains 1193 items: 1055 disyllables and 138 longer verbs.

4.2.1 Disyllables

Most of the relevant data concern disyllabic verbs, in which the study of the position of stress with regards to the two generalisations is relatively easy: the weight-based generalisation predicts final stress in verbs with a heavy ultima while the Germanic Law predicts final stress in the presence of an opaque prefix. Note that they do not necessarily make contradictory predictions: they are actually convergent in 90% of cases, as will be seen below. The two parameters were tested in a binary logistic regression with the position of stress as the dependent variable. The predictor variables were implemented as MORPHOLOGY (with two possible values: PREFIXED and NON-PREFIXED) and FINAL WEIGHT (with two possible values: LIGHT if the weight of the final syllable has 0 or 1μ and HEAVY if it has 2μ or more). The results are shown in Table 5.5. The stress distribution of the data with regards to prefixation and the weight of the final syllable is shown in Figure 5.2.

Figure 5.2 shows that syllable weight is mostly inoperant in prefixed verbs, which almost systematically have stress on their base regardless of the weight of the final syllable. Crucially, the weight-based generalisation is contradicted

Table 5.5 Binary logistic regression with morphology (prefixed vs non-prefixed) and syllable weight (heavy vs light) as predictor variables and the position of primary stress (initial vs final) as the dependent variable

	95% C.I.			p-value
	Lower	OR	Higher	
MORPHOLOGY-PREFIXED	0.002	0.006	0.014	< 2e-16
FINAL WEIGHT-LIGHT	74.007	180.867	558.917	< 2e-16

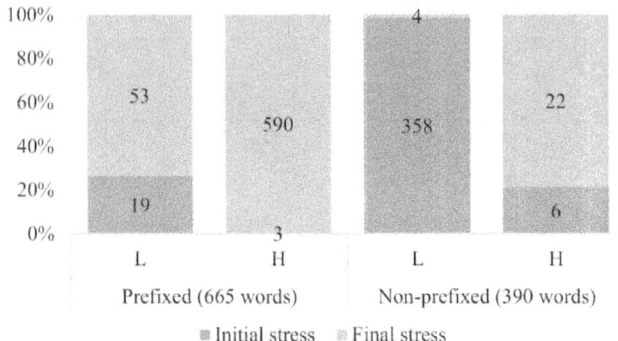

Figure 5.2 Stress distribution of disyllabic verbs depending on the weight of the final syllable (H = heavy and L = light) and of the presence or absence of an opaque prefix

by 74% of prefixed verbs with a light final syllable which have final stress, such as those shown in (23).

(23)   abásh, asséss, condémn, detách, emít, propél, obséss, succúmb . . .

However, it should be noted that there is a statistically significant difference between prefixed verbs with a light ultima and those with a heavy ultima (Fisher's exact test, $p < 0.01$). The full inventory of prefixed words with initial stress is shown in (24).

(24)   abseil, combat, comfort, conjure, conquer, cover, destine, differ, edit, enter, injure, offer, perjure, proffer, prosper, rally, relay, revel, sever, sojourn, suffer, summon

It should be noted that these include words for which historical prefixation is probably highly difficult to perceive because of the lack of paradigmatic support of the base, of the absence of phonotactic cues pointing to the presence of a morphological boundary or of historical change which have altered the segmental content of the prefix, making it unrecognisable.

The effect of syllable weight is clearer in non-prefixed verbs. There too, the difference between verbs with a light ultima and those with a heavy ultima is statistically significant (Fisher's exact test, $p < 0.01$).

Strikingly, the two generalisations make identical predictions in the vast majority of cases (955/1055, 90%), that is, the second and third columns in Figure 5.2, as most prefixed verbs have a heavy final syllable and most non-prefixed verbs have a light final syllable. If we evaluate the efficiency of each generalisation independently, both have an efficiency of 97%. Therefore, both can be said to be efficient descriptive generalisations of the disyllabic verbs data.

Finally, as noted above, 30% of the verb category are compositional constructions or opaque constructions with a free base: given this characteristic proportion, it seems plausible to surmise that speakers of English should be more sensitive to the presence of prefixes even in constructions with bound bases.

4.2.2 Longer verbs

As we have seen in section 3.7.2, only 14 words (13%) do not have base-initial primary stress: *círcumcise, círcumscribe, cómpliment, cóuntenance, discómfit, éxorcize, ímplement, impórtune, ímprovise, intérpret, óccupy, récognize, réconcile, súpervise*. In non-prefixed words, Fournier's (2007) Normal Stress Rule predicts that non-prefixed verbs should have antepenultimate stress. As was seen in section 3.9, this is only confirmed in 7 simplex words out of 15 and in 17/18 verbs made up of a bound root and a suffix. Overall, the Germanic Law and the Normal Stress Rule correctly predict the position of primary stress in 115/138 (83%) of long verbs.

The weight-based generalisation also fails to account for the prefixed words listed above, except for *discómfit, impórtune* and *intérpret*. Moreover, it fails to account for an additional seven words: *amórtize, contínue, impóverish, intermít, intromít, prètermít* and *rètrogréss*. In simplex verbs, all eight words with penultimate stress are accounted for as they all have a light final syllable (*bamboozle, canoodle, finagle, malinger, manoeuvre, sequester, skedaddle, solicit*). However, the seven words with antepenultimate stress are unaccounted for (*damascene, gallivant, manacle, manifest, massacre, minister, orient*). In verbs made up of a bound root and a suffix, all are unaccounted for as 17 contain the heavy suffix *-ize* /-aɪz/ which never receives final stress, and the remaining word, *monitor*, has a light ultima but antepenultimate stress. Let us note that there is no attested case of non-prefixed word with a heavy ultima and final stress. Overall, the weight-based generalisation makes correct predictions in 95/138 (69%) of long verbs.[32]

However, it has been claimed that the suffix *-ize* is a strong retractor when it attaches to roots (see Bermúdez-Otero 2018)[33] and so one might want to exclude it from the counts. If we do so, the first approach makes correct predictions in 97/118 (82%) of cases while the weight-based generalisation does so in 95/118 (80%) of cases. Therefore, as in disyllabic verbs, both generalisations have similar efficiencies.

4.3 Discussion

The results presented in the previous section have shown that both generalisations have high efficiencies, especially in disyllabic verbs. Therefore, both can be said to constitute accurate descriptive generalisations of the dataset. If one were to choose one of the two generalisations, two elements should be taken into consideration: the theoretical cost and the empirical scope of both generalisations. Let us briefly go through these elements.

Positing the Germanic Law only requires one to assume that opaque prefixes are somehow recognised by speakers. Some may argue that this is already too great a cost but, as discussed in section 1.3, there is independent evidence that this is indeed the case. On the other hand, positing the weight-based generalisation in a way that allows it to reach levels of efficiency close to those of the Germanic Law requires one to accept the assumptions detailed in section 4.1. Some of these assumptions may be independently motivated (for example by phonotactics; see Hammond 1999) while others are more problematic (for example moraless schwa).

Both generalisations have empirical scopes which go beyond the current dataset. The Germanic Law applies to all opaque prefixed words that are not nouns (Fournier 2010; Guierre 1979) and, more generally, allowing the phonology to see opaque prefixes is necessary for other phenomena evoked in section 1.3. The weight-based generalisation extends to other categories, notably nouns, under final syllable extrametricality (Hayes 1982), although that claim has been challenged by Fournier (2007), who claims that weight-sensitivity is only a property of certain subsets of the vocabulary: borrowings and learned words. English secondary stress assignment has also been claimed to be weight-driven (Burzio 1994; Hammond 1999; Pater 2000), but the number of relevant words is extremely small and the claim can only be supported by examples with closed syllables, not long vowels, as shown by Dabouis et al. (2017) in an exhaustive dictionary-based study.

Therefore, anyone wishing to choose between the two generalisations will have to take these elements into consideration. An alternative could be to integrate both generalisations, considering that they are not necessarily contradictory. As we have seen in the previous section, they often make identical predictions. The Germanic Law should simply be stated to override the weight-based generalisation so that verbs with light final syllables get final stress. Stress assignment in verbs could then be summed up as in (25).

(25) **Stress assignment in simplex or deradical verbs**
Overlook the prefix(es) and assign stress to what remains as follows: assign primary stress to the final syllable if it is heavy and to the penultimate otherwise.

Interestingly, if one assumes a constraint-based probabilistic model such as Max-Ent-OT (Goldwater and Johnson 2003) in which both generalisations are expressed through independent constraints, such a model would predict that the two generalisations may conspire and yield higher regularity when they make the same predictions. This is precisely what was found in the data, as shown in Figure 5.2.

Even though we have seen that the two generalisations are useful in describing the distribution of stress in verbs, we have also seen that they overlap considerably. This might lead speakers to use only one of the two generalisations and overgeneralise it. There are several ways in which this could be done. Speakers could just assume the weight-based generalisation, or they could adopt a simple generalisation regarding prefixed words according to which prefixes should not get primary stress. This second option has some support from Guierre (1979), as he found that, in his dataset, 76% of prefixed disyllabic words have final stress while only 7% of non-prefixed disyllabic words do. This could explain the relatively high rate of final stress in prefixed disyllabic nouns (19% in Guierre's dataset, as opposed to 7% for non-prefixed nouns). Another option would be for speakers to assume, as asserted by Moore-Cantwell (2020), that 'verbs prefer final stress'. In the dataset used in section 4.2, we found final stress in 64% of disyllabic verbs and in 30% of longer verbs (36% if the verbs in *-ize* are excluded). The evidence from our study to support this last option is rather weak. Once again, if we consider Guierre's (1979) data, 92% of disyllabic nouns have initial stress while only 20% of verbs do, but he also shows that only 9% of nouns are prefixed while 77% of verbs are. As we have argued in this chapter, the explanation for the greater tendency of verbs to have final stress seems to lie partly in their morphological characteristics. Moore-Cantwell supports her assertion by quoting three papers, Sereno and Jongman (1995), Sonderegger and Niyogi (2013) and Kelly and Bock (1988). Let us briefly go through the findings of these papers and see to what extent they can be used as evidence that 'verbs prefer final stress'.

First, let us note that all the cited papers only deal with disyllabic words and that, if any preference for final stress is to be observed for verbs, it has to be restricted to disyllabic verbs, as found in our data. Sereno and Jongman (1995) report acoustic differences between homophonic disyllabic verb–noun pairs (for example *answer*), with a preference for trochaic patterns for nouns and iambic patterns for verbs. However, their data sample is very restricted, and their results did not reach statistical significance. Their study was recently replicated by Lohmann (2020) with more extensive data and he did not confirm their findings. Sonderegger and Niyogi (2013) report on the diachronic evolution of homographic verb–noun pairs (for example *convict, concrete, exile*). They report that most stress changes lead to pairs in which the noun has initial stress and the verb has final stress. However, they note that most pairs do not change, as long as they are in 'stable states' (both initial stress, both final stress, or noun with initial stress and verb with final stress), the only unstable state being when the noun has final stress and the verb has initial stress. However, the vast majority of the pairs which they study are prefixed, so we can cast doubt on whether their results can be extended to non-prefixed words. Moreover, Sonderegger and Niyogi observe that words which share a prefix tend to evolve in similar directions, which they comment is 'particularly interesting because they suggest that it is a shared morphological prefix rather than simply shared initial segments which correlates with trajectory similarity' (2013: 276). Finally, Kelly and

Bock (1988) report that the rhythmic context in which words appear might explain the stress difference between nouns and verbs, as they find that nouns tend to appear more often in trochaic-biasing contexts than verbs. They also report evidence from nonword experiments that rhythmic context and syntactic category are indeed determining for the placement of stress in disyllabic pseudowords. However, there are several limitations to this study and what can be drawn from it. First, there was no control of the structure of pseudowords, and some of them could be assimilated to compounds (for example *pomset, ransfoe, solray*) or prefixed words (for example *pernew, covact, premit*), while others contained final sequences which are found in real prefixed words (for example *ponset, rendict, deltain*) and yet others contained double vowels in their last syllable (for example *delpeen, ronvoon, bontoon*), which are known to be associated to final stress (see Chapter 2 of this volume). It is unclear how this lack of control of the stimuli used affected the results. The second limitation of the paper is the size of the difference which Kelly and Bock report. In their second experiment, they report 75% of trochaic patterns for pseudowords in verbal contexts, against 86% for pseudowords in nominal contexts (trochaic-biasing and iambic-contexts confounded). Although the difference does go in the expected direction, nouns being more likely to be trochaic than verbs, this difference is nowhere near that found in the lexicon: the authors themselves report a dictionary study in which 94% of disyllabic nouns were found to be trochaic while only 31% of disyllabic verbs were. In her dissertation, Moore-Cantwell (2016) reports that speakers' productions tend to reflect the probabilistic distribution of patterns found in the lexicon. The considerable gap between the dictionary data and the production data should be accounted for. Our hypothesis is that the difference can be explained because of the morphology of the stimuli used by Kelly and Bock, as only 12% of their stimuli were prefixed, and therefore we would indeed expect less final stress than what is found in the lexicon, which contains a greater proportion of prefixed words.

There are other studies which have sought to test whether disyllabic verbs do prefer final stress as compared with nouns. The results appear to confirm this hypothesis, although the effects of syllable structure were also found to be significant. However, the effects of prefixation were not tested thoroughly enough (Turcsan and Herment 2015) or not at all (Guion et al. 2003). Therefore, it is possible that speakers, or at least some of them, assume that verbs should have final stress more often than nouns, and such a tendency could be one of the factors explaining the existence of alternating noun/verb pairs such as *récord ~ recórd* (see Chapter 3 of this volume), but in the light of the findings reported in this chapter, it seems to us that prefixation should be controlled for along with the other factors tested in previous studies. Moreover, the findings reported by Kelly and Bock (1988) raise interesting research questions: could it be that the contexts in which individual words usually appear determine their stress patterns? Could some of the exceptions to the generalisations studied in this chapter be accounted for in that way? Castanier (2016: 611) notes that this could be the case for a word like *ally*, which may have seen its stress pattern shift to first-syllable stress as an effect of stress shift in expressions such as *allied forces*.

5 Conclusion

In this chapter, we have shown that stress assignment in 'monomorphemic' verbs has been described through two generalisations, one referring to semantically opaque prefixation and another one referring to the weight of the final syllable. We saw that these two generalisations have known different fates in the literature, as the former has only been maintained in a specific strand of literature – the framework introduced by Guierre – while the latter has become the standard generalisation on verb stress in the generative literature. The reference to semantically opaque elements is controversial, and words as *contain* or *submit* have often been treated as morphologically simplex. We have put forward arguments from phonology, phonotactics and psycholinguistics which support the idea that the constituents in these words are 'morphologically relevant', even though they may not be called morphemes. Consequently, we argued that it is legitimate to include semantically opaque constituents among the possible determiners of stress placement.

Therefore, we have sought to evaluate the empirical validity of the two generalisations through a large dictionary-based study on English verbs in British English. In order to narrow our study down to the relevant morphological categories, we first gave a detailed description of stress placement in verbs. The first question we have had to deal with is that of conversion, as a large proportion of our dataset was found to be verbal uses, mainly of nouns, rather than actual verbs. These were left aside from the present study and we then detailed the methods used to classify the remaining 3550 verbs morphologically. The main, striking fact which emerged from this morphological classification is the large proportion of left-edge constructions in verbs, which in itself is an argument to assume that speakers may be more sensitive to prefixation in verbs, even if it is semantically opaque.

We gave a detailed descriptive account of the stress pattern of English verbs based on our extensive dataset of 3350 verbs. To our knowledge, this is the most detailed description to date with a systematic quantification of each category, of exceptions and of stress regularities. Then, we detailed how the weight of the final syllable was coded in our data to measure the empirical validity of the two generalisations. A striking result is that the two generalisations make identical predictions for a large majority of the data and can only be compared within a relatively marginal proportion. Overall, we found that both generalisations have similar efficiencies. In order to tease apart these two generalisations, we detailed the theoretical cost of each generalisation as well as its empirical scope beyond the present dataset. We argue that the results reported in this chapter constitute strong support in favour of the inclusion of semantically opaque constituents among morphologically relevant units for phonological computation. We showed that it is possible to keep both generalisations for a more accurate description of the stress pattern of English verbs. Finally, we discussed other possible analyses which speakers might make and have reviewed some of the evidence and limitations for each of the three alternatives considered.

Notes

We would like to thank Ricardo Bermúdez-Otero, Patrick Honeybone, Jacques Durand, Philip Carr, Renate Raffelsiefen, Ingo Plag, Sabine Arndt-Lappe and the audiences of the several conferences at which sections of this chapter have been presented for their useful comments and suggestions. We also warmly thank Véronique Abasq, Pierre Fournier, Marjolaine Martin and Nicolas Trapateau, who contributed to the early stages of the data analysis. All mistakes are ours alone.

1. Incidentally, Siegel's criticism is based on dubious examples that she describes as 'the ones I have been able to find' (without mentioning how the search had been conducted) such as *bicuspid, inhibit, prohibit, inhabit, evanesce, immature, premature* or *determine.* She claims that *SPE* predicts that these verbs would receive stress on their prefix. This is clearly wrong: *SPE* predicts stress retraction only in the case where the verbs receive final stress. Apart from *immature* and *premature*, all of these verbs have a light ultima and are correctly predicted to receive penultimate stress. Moreover, *bicuspid, immature* and *premature* all have semantically transparent prefixes and would have been described more accurately using # than +.
2. They also use it to account for /s/-voicing (*SPE*: 95), which will not be discussed here.
3. The datasets used in the chapter are available at <https://lll.cnrs.fr/actualite/the-stress-patterns-of-english-verbs/>.
4. We will use the term 'base' rather than 'root' since in a number of cases, the right-hand constituent (or the left-hand one in the case of suffixed form) is morphologically complex (for example *abbreviate, embellish, emulsify*), at least in the view adopted here.
5. These adverbial constructions are grouped with prefixed constructions within the 'compositional' and 'opaque prefixed' categories in Table 5.1. See also section 3.1.
6. This terminology, used by Fudge (1984), distinguishes classes of suffixes based on their stress behaviour (although other works have shown that differences in stress behaviour are correlated with other characteristics).

It is largely co-referent with other terminologies such as the + vs # boundary distinction in *SPE*, 'Class-I' vs 'Class-II' suffixes (Siegel 1974), 'Level-I' vs 'Level-II' suffixes (Kiparsky 1982) or 'stem-level' vs 'word-level' suffixes (Bermúdez-Otero 2018): 'stress-preserving' suffixes generally have stress on the same syllable as that which bears stress in the base (for example *símilar → símilarly*) while 'stress-shifting' suffixes are associated to a fixed position of primary stress, which can be either on themselves (for example *kítchen → kitchenétte*) or on a syllable which precedes them (for example *équal → equálity*).

7. Following Bauer et al. (2013: 14), we assume that a free morph is 'a morph which has the ability to be a word-form on its own' and that a bound morph is one 'that lacks this ability'.
8. Giegerich (1999) claims that all suffixes have a dual affiliation and that, in a stratal model, stratal affiliation is base-driven, not affix-driven.
9. It is clearly a kind of 'leftovers' group, but it seems more convincing to admit them as such within an effort at a comprehensive description of the English verb category.
10. Relevant examples are given in the text above.
11. The verbs with stress-preserving suffixes are not taken into consideration since these suffixes do not affect the pronunciation of the base. In other words, the structure before the suffix is that of the base, not that of the verb itself.
12. See Dabouis (2016); Raffelsiefen (1993). In Prosodic Phonology, this is commonly analysed as evidence that the prefixes have their own prosodic words (Booij and Rubach 1984; Raffelsiefen 1993, 1999, 2007; Szpyra 1989; Wennerstrom 1993).
13. As stated in the *OED* in the entry on the *in-* prefix borrowed from Latin, 'Since this prefix and IN- *prefix*[1] [from Germanic] are identical in form, and to a great extent in sense, they come in later use to be felt as one and the same prefix', both also adverbs in their original languages though the modern adverb comes from Germanic. This explains why the corpus contains mostly forms inherited from Latin (through French in a number of cases) with opaque bases like the examples above, despite the active adverb.
14. And *upbraid*, its relationship with *braid* being nowadays farfetched at best.
15. Note that in American English, there is a significant difference ($\chi^2 = 14.45$, $df = 1$, $p < .001$) between prefixed verbs ending in <-ate> (for example *ablate, collate, debate, inflate, relate, translate*) and suffixed verbs ending in *-ate* (for example *castrate, dictate, gradate, migrate, rotate, vibrate*), as the former have final stress as their main pronunciation in 13/14 words, while the latter have final stress in 9/35 words.
16. Words containing a hiatus (for example *álienate, améliorate, detériorate, orientate*) can be analysed as either being stressed /(-)1000/ or /(-)100/. We are treating them here as being stressed /(-)100/.

17. Both *contribute* and *distribute* have variants with antepenultimate stress.
18. Including *satisfy*, with the very same historical suffix *-fy*, but the only one in contemporary English not preceded by either *e* or *i* (the latter being either part of the stem in loanwords or connective in English formations).
19. Though such is not the position we have adopted here, it must be noted that the same observation also applies to frequentative verbal *-er*, and verbal *-ish* inherited from French infinitive *-ir*; see examples in (7).
20. The derivation is also not simply *-ize* in the cases of *attitud/inize*, *emblem/atize* and *epigram(m)/atize*.
21. We treated as semantically dependent compounds whose definition in the *OED* or Dictionary.com mentions the base (for example *bulldoze* 'to clear away by or as if by using a *bulldozer*').
22. See also Guierre (1979) on the observation that compounds spelled as one word usually have more initial stress than compounds which are hyphenated or spelled as two words.
23. <https://wordnet.princeton.edu/citing-wordnet>.
24. Some variables were correlated (synset count and frequency, spelling and frequency) and so they were tested separately.
25. See also Harris and Gussmann (1998), who argue that all final consonants should be analysed as onsets.
26. His proposal concerns American English. We are here using the British equivalents. Hammond also gives additional constraints which may render coronals heavy depending on the moraicity of the neighbouring consonants which are not relevant here.
27. In British English, the lax vowels are [æ, e, ɪ, ʊ, ɒ, ʌ] and the reduced vowels [ə, i, u], the tense vowels are [aɪ, eɪ, iː, (j)uː, əʊ, ɔː, aʊ]. In later sections, we will assume the r-coloured vowels [ɑː, ɜː] to be bimoraic.
28. There have been proposals to account for the particular case of /s/ in /sC/ clusters in terms of variable syllabification (tautosyllabic or heterosyllabic) because it can function as an onset word-initially (Kager 1989: 117–18). Burzio (1994: 61–2) describes the /s/ in /sC/ clusters as having variable weight.
29. Note that this creates circularity in the analysis, which is perfectly identified and claimed by Burzio (2007: 170–1), who argues that it is a strength of parallel evaluation models, such as Optimality Theory (Prince and Smolensky 1993), over rule-based models: 'stress and vowel reduction stand in a mutual dependency relation: stress is a determinant of vowel reduction (if stress, no reduction), but at the same time reduction controls syllable weight, and hence the position of stress. Such mutual dependencies are ordering paradoxes for ordered rules, and thus provide a direct argument for the parallel interaction of surface constraints.'
30. A vowel that our American colleagues are used to represent with [o] in American English.

31. A possible explanation is proposed in *SPE*: [i] would be an underlying glide /j/, which would explain the fact that words ending in -C$_2 y$ have antepenultimate stress and prefenestral stress in words such as *orthodoxy*, *téstimony* or *áuditory*.
32. Let us note that the Alternating Stress Rule (see section 1.1) is no longer used in recent analyses. Most of the words to which it was applied contain stress-shifting suffixes and so their stress patterns are accounted by referring to the suffixes.
33. Although doubts can be shed on this claim. In our dataset, five root-derived words have a heavy penultimate syllable, and they are almost equally divided among penultimate and antepenultimate stress: *amórtize*, *etérnize* vs *éxorcize*, *fráternize*, *récognize*.

References

Abasq, V. (2007), 'Préfixation et particules adverbiales en anglais contemporain: Étude du comportement accentuel', PhD dissertation, Université de Tours.

Anderson, S. R. (1992), *A-Morphous Morphology*, Cambridge: Cambridge University Press.

Arndt-Lappe, S. (2011), 'Towards an exemplar-based model of stress in English noun–noun compounds', *Journal of Linguistics* 47(3), 549–85.

Aronoff, M. (1976), *Word Formation in Generative Grammar*, Cambridge, MA: MIT Press.

Bauer, L., R. Lieber and I. Plag (2013), *The Oxford Reference Guide to English Morphology*, Oxford: Oxford University Press.

Bell, M. and I. Plag (2013), 'Informativity and analogy in English compound stress', *Word Structure* 6(2), 129–55.

Ben Hedia, S. and I. Plag (2017), 'Gemination and degemination in English prefixation: Phonetic evidence for morphological organization', *Journal of Phonetics* 62, 34–49.

Bermúdez-Otero, R. (2018), 'Stratal phonology', in S. J. Hannahs and A. R. K. Bosch (eds), *The Routledge Handbook of Phonological Theory*, Abingdon: Routledge, pp. 100–34.

Booij, G. and J. Rubach (1984), 'Morphological and prosodic domains in Lexical Phonology', *Phonology Yearbook* 1, 1–27.

Bram, B. (2011), 'Major total conversion in English: The question of directionality', PhD dissertation, Victoria University of Wellington.

Burzio, L. (1994), *Principles of English Stress*, New York: Cambridge University Press.

Burzio, L. (2007), 'Phonology and phonetics of English stress and vowel reduction', *Language Sciences* 29(2–3), 154–76.

Carr, P. (1999), *English Phonetics and Phonology*, Oxford: Basil Blackwell.

Carstairs-McCarthy, A. (2002), *An Introduction to English Morphology: Words and Their Structure*, Edinburgh: Edinburgh University Press.

Castanier, J. (2016), 'L'évolution accentuelle du lexique anglais contemporain appréhendée à travers les dictionnaires de prononciation (XVIIIe–XXIe siècles)', PhD dissertation, Université de Poitiers.

Chomsky, N. and M. Halle (1968), *The Sound Pattern of English*, New York: Harper & Row.
Collie, S. (2007), 'English stress preservation and Stratal Optimality Theory', PhD dissertation, University of Edinburgh.
Cruttenden, A. (2014), *Gimson's Pronunciation of English*, 8th edn, London: Routledge.
Dabouis, Q. (2016), 'L'accent secondaire en anglais britannique contemporain', PhD dissertation, Université de Tours.
Dabouis, Q. (2020), 'Secondary stress in contemporary British English: An overview', *Anglophonia* 30, <https://doi.org/10.4000/anglophonia.3476>.
Dabouis, Q. and J.-M. Fournier (2019), 'On the role of morphology, syllable structure, frequency and spelling in English vowel reduction', Poster presented at the 27th MFM Conference, held at the University of Manchester, Manchester, UK, on 23–25 June 2019.
Dabouis, Q., J.-M. Fournier and I. Girard (2017), 'Ternarity is not an issue: Secondary stress is left edge marking', Paper presented at the MFM25 Fringe Meeting – PTA Dataset Workshop, held at the University of Manchester, Manchester, UK, on 24 May 2017.
Delbridge, A. et al. (eds) (2009), *The Macquarie Dictionary, Australia's National Dictionary Online*, Sydney: Macquarie Library, <http://www.macquariedictionary.com.au>.
Domahs, U., I. Plag and R. Carroll (2014), 'Word stress assignment in German, English and Dutch: Quantity-sensitivity and extrametricality revisited', *The Journal of Comparative Germanic Linguistics* 17(1), 59–96.
Fournier, J.-M. (1996), 'La reconnaissance morphologique', in *8ème Colloque d'Avril sur l'anglais oral*, Villetaneuse: Université Paris Nord, CELDA, diffusion APLV, pp. 45–75.
Fournier, J.-M. (2007), 'From a Latin syllable-driven stress system to a Romance versus Germanic morphology-driven dynamics: In honour of Lionel Guierre', *Language Sciences* 29, 218–36.
Fournier, J.-M. (2010), *Manuel d'anglais oral*, Paris: Ophrys.
Fudge, E. (1984), *English Word-Stress*, London: George Allen & Unwin.
Giegerich, H. J. (1999), *Lexical Strata in English: Morphological Causes, Phonological Effects*, Cambridge: Cambridge University Press.
Giegerich, H. J. (2009), 'The English compound stress myth', *Word Structure* 2(1), 1–17.
Goldwater, S. and M. Johnson (2003), 'Learning OT constraint rankings using a maximum entropy model', in J. Spenader, A. Eriksson and Ö. Dahl (eds), *Variation within Optimality Theory: Proceedings of the Stockholm Workshop on 'Variation within Optimality Theory'*, Stockholm: Stockholm University, pp. 111–20.
Guierre, L. (1979), 'Essai sur l'accentuation en anglais contemporain: Éléments pour une synthèse', PhD dissertation, Université Paris 7.
Guierre, L. (1984), *Drills in English Stress-Patterns: Ear and Speech Training Drills and Tests for Students of English as a Foreign Language*, 4th edn, London: Armand Colin-Longman.
Guierre, L. (1990), 'Mots composés anglais et agrégats consonantiques', in *5ème Colloque d'Avril sur l'anglais oral*, Villetaneuse: Université Paris Nord, CELDA, diffusion APLV, pp. 59–72.

Guion, S. G., J. J. Clark, T. Harada and R. P. Wayland (2003), 'Factors affecting stress placement for English nonwords include syllabic structure, lexical class, and stress patterns of phonologically similar words', *Language and Speech* 46(Pt 4), 403–27.

Halle, M. and S. Keyser (1971), *English Stress: Its Form, Its Growth, and Its Role in Verse*, New York: Harper & Row.

Halle, M. and J.-R. Vergnaud (1987), *An Essay on Stress*, Cambridge, MA: MIT.

Hammond, M. (1999), *The Phonology of English: A Prosodic Optimality-Theoretic Approach*, Oxford: Oxford University Press.

Hammond, M. (2003), 'Frequency, cyclicity, and optimality', University of Arizona, <http://www.u.arizona.edu/~hammond/kslides.pdf>.

Harris, J. and E. Gussmann (1998), 'Final codas: Why the west was wrong', in E. Cyran (ed.), *Structure and Interpretation: Studies in Phonology*, Lublin: Folium, pp. 139–62.

Hayes, B. (1982), 'Extrametricality and English stress', *Linguistic Inquiry* 13(2), 227–76.

Hayes, B. (1989), 'Compensatory Lengthening in Moraic Phonology', *Linguistic Inquiry* 20, 253–306.

Hyman, L. (1985), *A Theory of Phonological Weight*, Dordrecht: Foris.

Jones, D. (2006), *Cambridge English Pronouncing Dictionary*, 17th edn, Cambridge: Cambridge University Press.

Kager, R. (1989), 'A metrical theory of stress and destressing in English and Dutch', PhD dissertation, University of Utrecht.

Kahn, D. (1976), 'Syllable-based generalizations in English phonology', PhD dissertation, MIT.

Katamba, F. and J. Stonham (2006), *Morphology*, Basingstoke: Palgrave Macmillan.

Kelly, M. H. and J. K. Bock (1988), 'Stress in time', *Journal of Experimental Psychology: Human Perception and Performance* 14(3), 389–403.

Kiparsky, P. (1982), 'From cyclic phonology to lexical phonology', in H. van der Hulst and N. Smith (eds), *The Structure of Phonological Representations I*, Dordrecht: Foris, pp. 131–75.

Ktori, M., P. Mousikou and K. Rastle (2018), 'Cues to stress assignment in reading aloud', *Journal of Experimental Psychology* 147(1), 36–61.

Ktori, M., J. J. Tree, P. Mousikou, M. Coltheart and K. Rastle (2016), 'Prefixes repel stress in reading aloud: Evidence from surface dyslexia', *Cortex* 74, 191–205.

Liberman, M. and A. Prince (1977), 'On stress and linguistic rhythm', *Linguistic Inquiry* 8(2), 249–336.

Lieber, R. (2004), *Morphology and Lexical Semantics*, Cambridge: Cambridge University Press.

Lohmann, A. (2020), 'No acoustic correlates of grammatical class: A critical re-examination of Sereno and Jongman (1995)', *Phonetica* 77(6), 429–40.

McCarthy, J. J. and A. S. Prince (1996), 'Prosodic Morphology 1986', *Linguistics Department Faculty Publication Series*, University of Massachusetts, Amherst, 13.

McMahon, A. (2001), Review of *The Phonology of English: A Prosodic Optimality-Theoretic Approach* by M. Hammond (1999), Oxford: Oxford University Press, *Phonology* 18, 421–6.

Marchand, H. (1969), *The Categories and Types of Present-Day English Word-Formation*, Munich: C.H. Beck.

Marslen-Wilson, W. D., M. Bozic and B. Randall (2008), 'Early decomposition in visual word recognition: Dissociating morphology, form, and meaning', *Language and Cognitive Processes* 23(3), 394–421.
Moore-Cantwell, C. (2016), 'The representation of probabilistic phonological patterns: Neurological, behavioral, and computational evidence from the English stress system', PhD dissertation, University of Massachussetts Amherst.
Moore-Cantwell, C. (2020), 'Weight and final vowels in the English stress system', *Phonology* 37(4), 657–95.
Mudgan, J. (2015), 'Units of word-formation', in P. O. Müller, I. Ohnheiser, S. Olsen and F. Rainer (eds), *Word-Formation: An International Handbook of the Languages of Europe*, vol. 1, Berlin: Mouton de Gruyter, pp. 235–301.
Pastizzo, M. J. and L. B. Feldman (2004), 'Morphological processing: A comparison between free and bound stem facilitation', *Brain and Language* 90(1–3), 31–9.
Pater, J. (2000), 'Non-uniformity in English secondary sress: The role of ranked and lexically specific constraints', *Phonology* 17, 237–74.
Plag, I. (1999), *Morphological Productivity: Structural Constraints in English Derivation*, Berlin: Mouton de Gruyter.
Plag, I. (2003), *Word-Formation in English*, Cambridge: Cambridge University Press.
Plag, I. (2006), 'The variability of compound stress in English: Structural, semantic and analogical factors', *English Language and Linguistics* 1(10), 143–72.
Plag, I., Kunter, G. and S. Lappe (2007), 'Testing hypotheses about compound stress assignment in English: A corpus-based investigation', *Corpus Linguistics and Linguistic Theory* 2(3), 199–232.
Plag, I., G. Kunter, S. Lappe and M. Braun (2008), 'The role of semantics, argument structure, and lexicalization in compound stress assignment in English', *Language* 84(4), 760–94.
Prince, A. and P. Smolensky (1993), 'Optimality Theory: Constraint interaction in Generative Grammar', Manuscript, Rutgers University and University of Colorado.
Raffelsiefen, R. (1993), 'Relating words: A model of base recognition', *Linguistic Analysis* 23, 3–161.
Raffelsiefen, R. (1999), 'Diagnostics for prosodic words revisited: The case of historically prefixed words in English', in T. A. Hall and U. Kleinhenz (eds), *Studies on the Phonological Word*, Current Issues in Linguistic Theory 174, Amsterdam: John Benjamins Publishing, pp. 133–201.
Raffelsiefen, R. (2007), 'Morphological word structure in English and Swedish: The evidence from prosody', in G. Booij, L. Ducceschi, B. Fradin, E. Guevara, A. Ralli and S. Scalise (eds), *Online Proceedings of the Fifth Mediterranean Morphology Meeting (MMM5)*, Fréjus, 15–18 September 2005, pp. 209–68.
Rastle, K. and M. Coltheart (2000), 'Lexical and nonlexical print-to-sound translation of disyllabic words and nonwords', *Journal of Memory and Language* 42, 342–64.
Rastle, K. and M. H. Davis (2008), 'Morphological decomposition based on the analysis of orthography', *Language and Cognitive Processes* 23(7–8), 942–71.
Roach, P. (2000), *English Phonetics and Phonology: A Practical Course*, 3rd edn, Cambridge: Cambridge University Press.
Selkirk, E. O. (1980), 'The role of prosodic categories in English word stress', *Linguistic Inquiry* 11(3), 563–605.

Selkirk, E. O. (1982), *The Syntax of Words*, Cambridge, MA: MIT Press.
Selkirk, E. O. (1984), *Phonology and Syntax: The Relation between Sound and Structure*, Cambridge, MA: MIT Press.
Sereno, J. A. and A. Jongman (1995), 'Acoustic correlates of grammatical class', *Language and Speech* 38(1), 57–76.
Siegel, D. C. (1974), 'Topics in English morphology', PhD dissertation, MIT.
Siegel, D. C. (1980), 'Why there is no = boundary', in M. Aronoff and M.-L. Kean (eds), *Juncture*, Saratoga: Anma Libri, pp. 131–4.
Sonderegger, M. and P. Niyogi (2013), 'Variation and change in English noun/verb pair stress: Data and dynamical systems models', in A. C. L. Yu (ed.), *Origins of Sound Change*, Oxford: Oxford University Press, pp. 262–84.
Stockwell, R. and D. Minkova (2001), *English Words: History and Structure*, Cambridge: Cambridge University Press.
Szpyra, J. (1989), *The Morphology–Phonology Interface: Cycles, Levels and Words*, London: Routledge.
Taft, M. (1994), 'Interactive-activation as a framework for understanding morphological processing', *Language and Cognitive Processes* 9(3), 271–94.
Treiman, R., N. Rosales, L. Cusner and B. Kessler (2020), 'Cues to stress in English spelling', *Journal of Memory and Language* 112, <https://doi.org/10.1016/j.jml.2020.104089>.
Trevian, I. (2003), *Morphoaccentologie et processus d'affixation de l'anglais*, Bern: Peter Lang.
Trevian, I. (2007), 'Stress-neutral endings in contemporary British English: An updated overview', *Language Sciences* 29(2–3), 426–50.
Trevian, I. (2015), *English Suffixes: Stress-Assignment Properties, Productivity, Selection and Combinatorial Processes*, Bern: Peter Lang.
Turcsan, G. and S. Herment (2015), 'Making sense of nonce word stress in English', in J. A. Mompean and J. Fouz (eds), *Investigating English Pronunciation: Current Trends and Directions*, Basingstoke: Palgrave Macmillan, pp. 23–46.
Van Heuven, W. V. J., P. Mandera, E. Keuleers and M. Brysbaert (2014), 'Subtlex-UK: A new and improved word frequency database for British English', *Quarterly Journal of Experimental Psychology* 67(6), 1176–90.
Wells, J. C. (2008), *Longman Pronunciation Dictionary*, 3rd edn, London: Longman.
Wennerstrom, A. (1993), 'Focus on the prefix: Evidence for word-internal prosodic words', *Phonology* 10(2), 309–24.
Wenszky, N. (2004), *Secondary Stress in English Words*, Budapest: Akadémiai Kiadó.

6 Lexical Stress in Varieties of Australian English: A Corpus-Based Exploration

Anne Przewozny and Marjolaine Martin

0 Introduction

Australian English has received much attention with a view to describe and model the components of its lexicon and phonology while assessing its role and status in the English-speaking world. Recently, possibly because the Australian science of linguistics thoughtfully relies on national programmes of spoken corpus-making as well as on a broad landscape of laboratory phonology, some perceptual and acoustic analyses of stress and pitch accent have regularly been published, notably about High Rising Terminal (HRT) (for example Guy and Vonwiller 1989; Fletcher and Harrington 2001; Fletcher et al. 2002; Horvath 2004; Jespersen 2016). Other linguistic works have investigated the issue of lexical stress in Australian English phonology (Tabain et al. 2004).

Australian English is no homogeneous variety. The demonstration that multiple British dialectal origins at the root of its endogenous development led to a common systemic core (one transported English) under a determined evolutionary process of native Englishes must be balanced with the contemporary reality of phonological variation in Australian English (Przewozny and Viollain 2016). Furthermore, while language contact between British dialects of English has constantly played a crucial role from the early days of Proto-Early Australian English (for example Mitchell 1940; Turner 1966; Hill 1967; Bernard 1969; Fielding and Ramson 1973; Horvath 1985; Gunn 1992; Przewozny 2016), the influence of the Aboriginal input has to be considered too, both from the point of view of lexical stress in Aboriginal loanwords in Standard Australian English (Dixon 2002; Dixon et al. 2006; Martin 2011b) and that of the lexicon of Standard Aboriginal English (Malcolm and Kaldor 1991; Eades 1993; Vinson 2008 among others).[1]

The scope of this chapter is (i) to analyse the nature of lexical stress patterns in Aboriginal loanwords in Standard Australian English (SAusE), (ii) to present a systemic account of lexical stress in SAusE based on dictionary data, and (iii) to examine the common hypothesis that speakers of

Standard Australian Aboriginal English (SAbE) have a tendency to stress words initially in contemporary spoken data.

Our theoretical stance is a Guierrian one (see Chapters 2 and 5 of this volume) inasmuch as dictionary data, morphological and orthographic information can support the systematic study of the Australian lexicon. Thus, a treatment of the reference dictionary of Australian English as well as major reference dictionaries of pronunciation is provided (*Macquarie Dictionary, Longman Pronunciation Dictionary, Cambridge English Pronouncing Dictionary*). We revisit previous analyses of a set of about 3700 words chosen because they may display lexical stress variation in contemporary English (Duchet 1994; Deschamps 2000; Collins and Mees 2008; Martin 2010; Martin 2011a). The words under study are disyllabic verbs, prefixed multicategorial words, words known as exceptions in the Guierrian context, as well as loanwords from Aboriginal languages in Australian English. We then rely on the framework of corpus phonology to examine the tendency of speakers of SAbE to stress words initially in spoken corpora (Carr et al. 2004; Delais-Roussarie 2008; Burnham et al. 2011; Durand et al. 2014; Przewozny et al. 2020).

1 Standard Australian English and heterogeneity in Australia

From the 1960s onwards, Australian linguistics has been committed to documenting and modelling the stages of internal development that Antipodean English had been undergoing, up to a phase of endonormative stabilisation (Schneider 2007). Another dynamic which was founded on Eurocentric principles of thought has traditionally described the Australian and New Zealand varieties as one block of 'Australasian' English. However, it is crucial to remember that the two varieties are linguistically, historically, socially and culturally distinct (Przewozny and Viollain 2016). In fact, a mosaic of English varieties that linguistically display plural statuses and functions covers the Asia-Pacific and Australasian zones of the globe, and such a global vision in favour of homogeneity in Australasia would be wholly unsatisfactory.

As far as Australia is concerned, recent research has been dedicated to investigating linguistic realities throughout Australia, thus bringing to light its internal evolution along with other settler varieties (Peters 2014), the wealth of language variation at each level of linguistic inquiry (for example Blair and Collins 2001; Burridge and Kortmann 2008) and the dynamic system at work that has been shaped by the interface between internal (linguistic) processes and phenomena and external (broadly social, demographic, geographic and cultural) parameters. In this dynamic, SAusE constitutes a basis from which researchers can investigate Australian diversity and linguistic subsystems. Several varieties of Australian English are officially attested and linguistically described in contemporary multicultural Australian society. Although the rates have been in constant evolution, Lo Bianco's (1990) typology of six types of populations from different origins within the Australian linguistic community remains valid:

1. Aboriginal and Torres Strait Islander (1% of the total population in 1990)
2. Australians of British or Irish origin going back more than three generations (60%)
3. Australians of non-English-speaking origin going back more than three generations (5%)
4. First- and second-generation Australians of English-speaking origin (14%)
5. Second-generation non-English speaking Australians (8%)
6. First-generation non-English-speaking Australians (12%)

SAusE is generally understood as Mainstream AusE, the common language of Australians. In fact, the term 'SAusE' is used in a number of ways. It is the official linguistic reference for the entire Australian language community, both at written and spoken levels ('the variety of spoken and written English language in Australia used in more formal settings such as for official or public purposes, and recorded in dictionaries, style guides and grammars', ACARA 2011). It is

> that form of English that originated early in the nineteenth century among those children of British settlers who were born and raised in the colony. Australian English has had a continuous tradition since then as the mother tongue of a very large proportion of the Australian community. It is the national variety of English, and the variety which speakers of other varieties, or indeed of other languages, meet when they come to Australia, either as visitors or as immigrants.
> (Delbridge 1983: 36–7)[2]

Since our focus in this chapter is to investigate and compare lexical stress and variation among some spoken varieties of Australian English, the term 'SAusE' will conveniently cover two meanings, namely (i) a spoken system displaying stabilised lexical stress patterns and (ii) a norm for endonormative comparison within Australia, with SAbE as a key component that is defined below.[3]

2 From Australian Aboriginal Englishes to Standard Aboriginal English

Alongside the Australian English of originally Anglo-Celtic speakers stands another living linguistic memory which is rooted in the history of the country:

Australian Aboriginal English. It is the outcome of a complex language maintenance process which encompasses different realities today: the loss of many indigenous languages as well as the necessity to interact with the English language and European culture, through both adaptation to the colonial variety and integration into the media environment, justice system and education (Walsh 1991; Eades 2013).

In spite of the loss of some 200 indigenous languages, the original and contemporary diversity of Aboriginal linguistic substrata and underpinning cultural richness (Horton 1994) could not but influence English in Australia, with pidgins as its historical roots and a fruitful and complex spectrum of regional and social dialects and creoles as its contemporary outcome ('from a mild accent to a full-blown creole language', according to Benterrak et al. 1984: 270; see also Sutton 1991). Contact phenomena, code-switching and interference processes have helped document variation at all linguistic levels. In fact, there is a whole continuum from 'light' to 'heavy' Aboriginal English dialects which differ in terms of degree of 'Aboriginality' (following the terminology of Malcolm and Koscielecki 1997). Speech communities also display much diversity in terms of geographical and sociolinguistic environments, from metropolitan to rural settings. The linguistic consequences of this diversity can be detected, for example, in the phonology of Aboriginal Englishes with a narrower vowel space across acrolectal and basilectal varieties (Butcher 2008; Butcher and Anderson 2008). Still, it is helpful to rely on a Standard variety as 'one major variety of Aboriginal English, which embraces a number of regional varieties. It is spoken within the context of Aboriginal and Torres Strait Islander communities in all parts of Australia' (Malcolm 2008: 124).

In this linguistic landscape, Aboriginal loanwords in SAusE come from about 80 Aboriginal languages such as Dyirbal in Queensland or Jingulu and Warlpiri in the Northern Territory (Dixon 2008). Out of 430 loanwords from Aboriginal languages into Australian English in the area of Sydney, 56 originate from the Dharuk language (for example *koala*, *dingo*, *wallaby*, *boomerang*). Loanwords account for one part of the lexicon at stake in the assessment of lexical stress in 'light' to Standard Aboriginal varieties and more generally speaking in SAusE.

3 Aboriginal substratum stress pattern hypothesis vs integration into the SAusE system

Regarding this specific issue, Martin (2011b) checked two hypotheses about the stress patterns of loanwords from Aboriginal languages in SAusE: (i) is the stress pattern from the original linguistic substrata maintained in SAusE, or (ii) is it integrated into SAusE and can the Guierrian approach of English stress rules account for these words today?

A number of authors note that stress can usually be found on the first syllable of a word in Aboriginal languages (Butcher 1994: 17; Dixon 2011: 128; see below for a more detailed account). So as to study the initial stress hypothesis, Martin (2011b) built a corpus of more than 280 words using Dixon et al. (1990) and Dixon et al. (2006), completed by the pronunciations provided in the *Macquarie Dictionary* for SAusE. Martin (2011b) applied the Guierrian rules for English stress assignment[4] to the entire corpus. Table 6.1 shows the results for Hypothesis (i).[5]

Overall, the initial stress hypothesis is effective 78% of the time and is particularly so for disyllabic words (97%) but does not work well for words of three syllables (49%). As for Hypothesis (ii), the synthesis in Table 6.2 shows that the rules of stress assignment in English applied to loanwords from Aboriginal languages are effective in 83% of the cases. This result is five points higher than that of the initial stress hypothesis.

Table 6.1 Initial stress hypothesis: results (source: Martin 2011b)

No. of syllables	No. of items	Effective	Not effective	% effective
2	172	166	6	97
3	87	43	44	49
4	11	3	8	27
5	2	0	2	0
Total	272	212	60	78

Table 6.2 English stress pattern hypothesis (source: Martin 2011b)

Rule applied	No. of items	Efficient	Not efficient	Efficiency %
$-V'V'(C_0(e)) \rightarrow -1$	26	10	16	38%
$-V'V'(C_0(e)) \rightarrow -1$ (disyllables)	15	2	13	13%
$-V'V'(C_0(e)) \rightarrow -1$ (3 or more syllables)	11	8	3	73%
$-[i, e, u] + V(C_0(e)) \rightarrow /(-)100/$	4	4	0	100%
Disyllable $\rightarrow /10/$	157	153	4	97%
Prefinal $C_2 \rightarrow /-10/$	31	22	9	71%
'Italian' word $\rightarrow /-10/$	5	5	0	100%
Normal Stress Rule $\rightarrow /(-)100/$	49	32	17	65%
Total	272	226	46	83%

4 Lexical stress in Standard Australian English

4.1 Intervarietal variation in the literature

In her examination of lexical stress variation between standard varieties of English, Martin (2011a) underlines a lack of extensive data-supported research on the matter. Martin's study is dedicated to Standard British English (SBE), Standard American English (SAmE) and Standard Australian English (SAusE) on the basis of dictionary data. Other works such as Mitchell and Delbridge (1965), Duchet (1994), Cruttenden (2001), Peters (2007) and Collins and Mees (2008) rely on diverse theoretical and methodological stances with varied comparative patterns between the three standards. For Collins and Mees (2008: 154), the differences in terms of stress patterns are significant: 'There are some significant differences between British and American in (1) allocation of stress, (2) the pronunciation of unstressed syllables'; while Duchet (1994: 118) concludes that 'There are few systematic differences between the British stressing system and the American one.' The differences mainly occur in disyllabic verbs ending in *-ate*, which tend to be stressed on their final rather than initial syllable, and in nouns and adjectives ending in *-ative*, *-ary*, *-ery* and *-ory*, for which a secondary stress can be observed in SAmE (for example *military, arbitrary, mandatory* being stressed /1020/ in SAmE and /1000/ in SBE following Collins and Mees 2008). For Martin (2011a: 111–14), the fact that 148 words have at least one variant with a stress pattern present in at least one of the other two varieties at stake is a sign of intervarietal lexical stress stability.

4.2 Further examination on a specifically built dictionary corpus

So as to check intervarietal lexical stress variety, Martin (2011a) brings together a specifically built extensive corpus (3742 lexical items) made up of four complementary sub-corpora which display 2550 disyllabic verbs (complete class), 370 prefixed multicategorial words, 542 exceptions to the rules of word-stress assignment in a Guierrian context (Fournier 2010) and 280 loanwords from Aboriginal languages. These 3742 items are known to show lexical-stress variation in contemporary English: 50% of disyllabic verbs are initially stressed while the other 50% bear stress on their final syllable; prefixed multicategorials undergo a tension between the verbal logic in which the prefix is ignored (/01/) and the substantive logic in which it is taken into account (/10/); exceptions to the rules of word-stress assignment could inherently be different in diverse varieties of English; loanwords could undergo a tension between the Aboriginal source language and English.

Martin (2011a) follows Guierre (1979, 1985) with a dictionary-type treatment drawing on data from the *Longman Pronunciation Dictionary* (Wells 2008, hereafter *LPD3*), the *Cambridge English Pronouncing Dictionary* (Jones 2006, hereafter *CEPD17*) and the *Macquarie Dictionary* (Delbridge et al. 2009, hereafter *MD Online*). As for loanwords from Aboriginal languages, the research relies not only on *MD Online* but also on Dixon et al. (2006) and Dixon et al. (1990) as an expansion of the corpus.[6] Martin's study demonstrates that lexical stress[7] is unequivocally stable between SAusE, SBE and SAmE. We outline the results for each sub-corpus below.

As for disyllabic verbs, the assessment of all main pronunciations shows that out of 2549 verbs, 94% display a stable stress pattern between the three varieties (*MD Online/LPD3/CEPD17*) with only 152 verbs which differ. Martin's classification of verbs articulates intervarietal variation between SAusE, SAmE and SBE in Table 6.3 in a quantitative approach (Appendix 6.1 gives a detailed account of the words at stake). Five main types of words can be identified here: 37 verbs ending in –V*te*, 36 compounds, 38 prefixed multicategorials, 11 words in *up-*, *down-* and *out-*, and 26 loanwords, the other 4 words being 2 prefixed verbs and 2 verbs ending in *-ent*.

The data for disyllabic verbs in –V*te* (see Table 6.3) confirm a clear trend to initial stress in SAmE (36 out of 37 verbs), an opposite trend in SBE (1 out of 37 verbs) and a more balanced situation in SAusE (25 verbs follow a /01/ stress pattern while 12 verbs follow a /10/ pattern).[8]

Table 6.3 Verb stress pattern variation /01/–/10/ in SAusE, SAmE and SBE (source: Martin 2011a)

Type of word	Total	SAusE /01/	SAusE /10/	SBE LPD /01/	SBE LPD /10/	SAmE LPD /01/	SAmE LPD /10/
Disyllabic verbs in –V*te*	37	25	12	36	1	1	36
Compounds	36	13	23	29	7	22	14
Prefixed multicategorials	38	22	16	20	18	20	18
Other prefixed verbs	2	2	0	1	1	0	2
Out, down, up verbs	11	7	4	4	7	3	8
V *-ent*	2	1	1	2	0	1	1
Loanwords	26	6	20	9	17	21	5
Total	152	76	76	101	51	68	84

Martin's study of prefixed multicategorials takes into account 357 disyllabic verbs and 13 trisyllabic ones. Both main and attested variant stress patterns were considered in the three varieties of English at stake in both *MD Online* and *LPD3*. The results shown in Table 6.4 display three types of lexical items: *concern* (noun and verb stressed on the final syllable), *convict* (noun in /10/ and verb in /01/) and *offer* (both noun and verb stressed initially).

First of all, both *LPD3* and *MD Online* strictly display the same stress patterns for all three varieties: all main pronunciations and variants are identical, no variant being absent for any variety for all 260 items although they belong to a category of words that proves to be unstable in terms of lexical stress.

Second, when considering only main stress patterns, no intervarietal variation can be detected in 90% of the data. The three types are not equally stable: the *concern* type and the *convict* type are stable in 93% of the lexical items when the *offer* type displays stability in 84% of those. Appendix 6.2 gives a detailed account of the words at stake.

Table 6.4 Distribution of prefixed multicategorials by type (source: Martin 2011a)

	concern type	*convict* type	*offer* type	Adj	3 syllables and more	Total
No attested difference	130 (89%)	65 (53%)	51 (68%)	6 (46%)	8 (62%)	260 (70%)
Variant in one or two varieties	6 (4%)	49 (40%)	12 (16%)	3 (23%)	5 (38%)	75 (20%)
Different stress pattern in main pronunciation	10 (7%)	9 (7%)	12 (16%)	4 (31%)	0 (0%)	35 (10%)
Total	146	123	75	13	13	370

Finally, regarding prefixed multicategorials it should be noted that 15 words are stressed differently in SAusE and in the two other varieties studied for their main stress pattern (*annex* (V), *collect* (N), *contract* (V), *decoy* (V), *discount* (V), *downgrade* (V), *eject* (N), *intrigue* (N), *prolapse* (V), *rebate* (V), *recall* (N), *relay* (V), *remit* (N), *transport* (V), *upsurge* (V)), and 4 for their secondary stress pattern (*incline* (N), *rebore* (N), *rebound* (N), *upset* (Q)). It was also shown that SAusE shows greater intravarietal stability. Indeed, 57 items have no stress pattern variants in SAusE when they have one in the other varieties. These words are:

abstract (V), *access* (V), *adept* (NQ), *alloy* (N), *ally* (VN), *commune* (V), *compound* (V), *conflict* (V), *contest* (V), *contrast* (V), *decline* (N), *decrease* (V), *detail* (VN), *discount* (V), *dispute* (N), *essay* (V), *excess* (Q), *excise* (N), *exhibit* (N), *impact* (V), *imprint* (V), *increase* (VN), *indent* (N), *ingrate* (NQ), *inset* (V), *miscount* (N), *outlay* (V), *premise* (V), *presage* (N), *protest* (V), *recount* (N), *redress* (N), *refill* (N), *refit* (N), *refund* (V), *rehash* (N), *remount* (N), *reprint* (N), *retail* (V), *retouch* (N), *rewind* (N), *subject* (V), *sublease* (VN), *suffix* (V), *surmise* (V), *survey* (N), *transfer* (V), *update* (N), *upgrade* (VN), *uplift* (V).

Martin's set of exceptions to stress rules was tested in terms of (i) the rules they violate and (ii) their level of variation, with parameters such as those displayed in Table 6.5.

For this sub-corpus, we observe more stability than for multicategorials, as 86% of them show no sign of variation and only 8% display a main pronunciation with a different stress pattern in one of the three varieties. Intervarietal lexical stress variation can be established for 41 lexical items (see Appendix 6.3 for more details). For the 542 items studied, Martin (2011a) observes high lexical stress stability.[9]

Generally, in the case of exceptions to stress rules, the general tendency is that variation leads to regularisation: for instance, words such as <u>carburettor</u>,

Table 6.5 Distribution of lexical items in terms of rule violation (source: Martin 2011a)

	Disyllable → /10/	Prefinal C$_2$ → /–10/	'Italian' word → /–10/	NSR[a] → /(–)100/	Total
No attested difference	166 (82%)	98 (90%)	7 (100%)	195 (87%)	**466 (86%)**
Variant in one or two varieties	18 (9%)	6 (5%)	0 (0%)	11 (5%)	**35 (6%)**
Different stress pattern in main pronunciation	18 (9%)	5 (5%)	0 (0%)	18 (8%)	**41 (8%)**
Total	202	109	7	224	542

[a] Normal Stress Rule.

<u>pro</u>testant or <u>bene</u>factor, which are initially stressed exceptions to the rule prefinal C$_2$ → /–10/, have a variant stressed on the penultimate syllable, that is, a regular stress pattern.

In the analysis of intervarietal lexical stress variation in loanwords from Aboriginal languages, 47 out of the 280 items taken from Dixon et al. (2006) and Dixon et al. (1990) were tested, that is, only the items present in *LPD3* and *CEPD17* and those which did not have homographs in English.

Of the 47 words, 43 display perfect stability in terms of stress pattern and only 1 shows intervarietal variation: *waratah* is stressed on the final in SAusE (for more details, see Appendix 6.4). Table 6.7 provides a quantitative synthesis for each sub-corpus and for the whole corpus.[10]

Using words which are prone to lexical stress variation, Martin (2011a) shows that 94% of the 3500 words are stressed identically in SAusE, SBE and

Table 6.6 Distribution of loanwords from Aboriginal languages in terms of word length (source: Martin 2011a)

	Monosyllables	Disyllables	Three-syllable words	Four-syllable words	Five-syllable words	Total
No attested difference	1 (100%)	21 (100%)	16 (90%)	4 (67%)	1 (100%)	**43 (91%)**
Variant in one or two varieties	0 (0%)	0 (0%)	1 (5%)	2 (33%)	0 (0%)	**3 (6%)**
Different stress pattern in main pronunciation	0 (0%)	0 (0%)	1 (5%)	0 (0%)	0 (0%)	**1 (3%)**
Total	1	21	18	6	1	47

Table 6.7 A quantitative synthesis of SAusE, SBE and SAmE stress patterns intervariation (source: Martin 2011a)

	Disyllabic verbs	Multicategorial prefixed words	Exceptions to stress rules	Aboriginal loanwords	Total
No attested difference	2397 (94%)	264 (71%)	467 (86%)	44 (94%)	**3172 (91%)**
Variant in one or two varieties	Not studied	76 (20%)	36 (7%)	2 (4%)	*Not relevant*
Different stress pattern in main pronunciation	152 (6%)	30 (9%)	39 (7%)	1 (2%)	**222 (6%)**
Total	2549	370	542	47	3508

SAmE. Intervarietal lexical stress variation is limited and not specific to word types, thus lexical only.[11]

5 Lexical stress in Standard Aboriginal English

The scope of this chapter so far has been (i) to examine the nature of lexical stress patterns in Aboriginal loanwords in SAusE, and (ii) to account for lexical stress in SAusE and intervarietal variation as based on dictionary data in a Guierrian framework. We turn to spoken corpora (Burnham et al. 2011) and to the framework of corpus phonology (Carr et al. 2004; Delais-Roussarie 2008; Durand et al. 2014; Przewozny et al. 2020) to test the hypothesis that, in the Australian English system, speakers of SAbE tend to produce initial stress in the lexicon of contemporary Australian English, which would constitute a case of intravarietal variation within SAusE. Our approach in this chapter was built up following the concomitant exploration of the two corpora that offered reliable spoken data, namely the AusTalk corpus (Burnham et al. 2011) and PAC-Australia [Ulladulla] corpus (Przewozny and Fabre 2018).

5.1 Patterns and variation in Aboriginal English dialects

Along with some Caribbean Creoles, most West and South African varieties, as well as some Asian Englishes and Pacific contact varieties, varieties of Aboriginal English are said to display a tendency towards a syllable-timed rhythm while SBE, SAmE and SAusE are all stressed-timed (Schneider 2004: 1126), thus confirming the distinctive rhythm of Standard to heavier Aboriginal English varieties.

Most if not all accounts of the segmental and suprasegmental features of Aboriginal English claim that Aboriginal English notably diverges from

SAusE in terms of lexical stress patterns. Malcolm (for example 1995, 2018) states that just like stress patterns vary in SAusE categories (*ˈcommon, perˈmitted, enterˈtain*), Aboriginal AusE displays variation in patterns with a preference for such a pattern as 'primary stress on the initial syllable of lexical words' (*ˈguitar*) (Malcolm 2018: 3–4). This is in line with many documented descriptions of Aboriginal indigenous languages (such as Douglas 1976) in which primary stress falls on the initial syllable of words in accordance with syllable timing, although Malcolm (2004: 666) argues that only some of the Western Desert languages tend towards such syllable timing, which in turn reflects the stress patterns of Aboriginal English speakers in these areas.[12] Dixon offers a clear overview of Australian indigenous languages:

> In most Australian languages word stress is predictable. Most commonly, primary stress goes onto the first syllable of a word; there is then often secondary stress on the third, fifth, etc. syllables, excepting that the final syllable of a word does not usually bear stress. Using ´ for primary and ` for secondary stress we would have díban, yálŋgay, báyimbam, gúbimbùlu. There are some variations on this basic pattern, and each does tend to recur in a number of different languages. For instance, if long vowels can occur in non-initial syllables, they may bear primary stress – e.g., gimáal.
>
> (Dixon 2011: 128)

The phonotactics of the phonological word in Australian indigenous languages can be a clue to lexical stress patterns in SAbE and how it can be accounted for through corpus data. As Butcher (2008: 629) reminds us, from the prototypical phonological word $C_{INIT}VC1(C2)V(C_{FIN})$ it ensues that complex syllable onsets are absent from most Australian indigenous languages or else may be subject to schwa epenthesis, while complex codas are generally reduced in some specific environments, as in the examples in Table 6.8.

Drawing on a foot-based approach, Butcher (2008: 631) thoroughly accounts for the prototypical pattern (primary stress on the initial syllable of a word) in basilectal AbE in the terms in Table 6.9.

Table 6.8 Complex syllable onsets and codas in basilectal AbE (source: Butcher 2008: 629)

Aus. Indigenous languages	AAE basilectal variation		
	Reduction/ simplification	[ə] epenthesis	Reduction
$C_{INIT}VC1(C2)V(C_{FIN})$	*stopping* [ˈdɔpɪn] *driving* [ˈdɐbɪn]	*sleeping* [səˈlipɪn] *splashing* [pəˈlɐʃɪn]	*fast* [fɐs, pɐs] *cask* [kɐs]

Table 6.9 Elision and stress shift to the initial syllable in AbE (source: Butcher 2008: 631)

Standard AusE wS pattern	AAE wS	SAE swS pattern	AAE Sws
along	[lɔŋ]	operation	[ˈɔpɹɛʃɐn]
suppose	[spɔz]	referee	[ˈɹɛfɹɪ]
explain	[splɛn]	kangaroo	[ˈkɛŋɡɹʊ]
collect	[klɛk(t)]	cup of tea	[ˈkɐpɐtɪ]

Butcher argues that

> certain categories of prosodic word which require final stress in SAE [hence SAusE in our own terminology], such as acronyms and road names, have initial stress in AAE [hence AbE]: thus, *CD* and *DVD*, for example, are pronounced [ˈsɪ dɪ] and [ˈdɪ bɪ dɪ], while 'Bagot Road' is [ˈbɛɡət ɹɔd] and 'Traeger Park' is [ˈtɹ [ɡɐ pɐk] [*sic*]. This preference for trochaic (or dactylic) feet gives a very distinctive rhythm to AAE speech.
>
> (Butcher 2008: 631)

Malcolm (2018, 2021) confirms Butcher's analyses.

5.2 A reanalysis of lexical stress in Standard Aboriginal English through spoken data

The rationale for the present study on stress assignment in SAbE is directly linked to the fact that the above-mentioned authors have pointed out the tendency of speakers of Aboriginal Englishes to stress words initially as well as to elide unstressed initial vowels (apheresis). Yet to our knowledge, hardly any dataset of spoken Australian English was ever used to test the small sets of lexical items which support those previous analyses. The sections which follow are therefore devoted to testing the tendency for speakers of Aboriginal English to shift primary stress to the left on larger numbers of lexical items using either dictionary data or spoken data. First, we give our methodological options to make up for the scarcity of contemporary data in SAbE. We then provide the details of our analyses and results, before offering some quantitative interpretation of the data and further views on potential markers of Aboriginality.

In an initial phase of our study, our dictionary-based dataset focused on all items labelled as 'Aboriginal English' or 'Chiefly AbE' in *MD Online*. *MD Online* displays 184 words and phrases together with each item's spelling, category, definition, pronunciation and stress pattern (although, unfortunately, no transcriptions of SAbE pronunciation are available):

afternoon time, all time, ashes bread (or *ashes dumper*), *aunty/auntie, ay, bala, balanda, be drinking up, be rowing, big, Big Sunday, bimeby/bimebye, bin, blackfella, bone, booliman, boss, boss man, boss woman, bro, brother, brudda, bullock, bunji/bunjie/bungee/bunge, business, camp, caught up in yarns, cheeky, clever, coldsick, come in, cooldrink, council, cousin brother, cousin sister, cultural, cut, cuz, dancing, darkfella, dat, debil-debil, disco dancing, doctor, dog-eye, double-bank, dust, father, featherfoot, fella/ fulla, finger-talk, finish, fire, flash, footwalk, footwalker, get over this side, get shame, go for, goditcha, goom, goona/guna/kuna, goongadji, grandfather, grandmother, granny, grog-free, grow someone up, grow up in the ashes, growl, growling, gubba/gubbah/gubber/gubb/gub, guna, gunjabal/gunjie/goongadji, hear, homeland, honey bee, honeybee sugar, horsy tail, humbug, im, jar, jealous, kaikai, kangaroo marriage, kuna, kurdaitcha, language, lation, laughing up, law, learn, legs-up, lift, lingo, longa, longtime, longway, maa, mai, make someone a* (*young*) *man, make someone weak, manager, marlu, married up, Mary, maya, mayi, mayla week, minya, mob, modaga, morning supper, morning time, mother, mulba, nikiti, nother one, nuba, off country, old people, olgomen, olmen, on country, one, onetime, own, owner, ownership, paint up, painted up, payback, pitcher-pitcher, poison, poor, proper, pyin, rear up, red band, rinse up, roller, row breeder, rubbish, ruk, rule, saltwater, scratch, secret, shame, shame job, shy off, side, sister/titja/tidda/thitha, sit-down money, sorry business, sorry cut, speak, stiff* (N, def: a conceited and overconfident young person, usually an adolescent male), *stiff* (V, def: to kill), *stopper, story, sugarbag, sugarbag fly, sulky, swim, take away, talk, thitha, tidda, titja, tjamu, tjilbi, trouble, tuck-out, tumble down, uncle, uncle David, unna, walypala, wanim/wanem, way, waybala, wetjala, white lingo, white Mary, whitefella dancing, yandi.*

Four of *MD Online*'s lexical items display elision of initial unstressed syllable in the English original word (*lations* for *relations*, *longa* for *belong*, *long time* for *a long time*, and *long way* for *a long way*).

Another attempt to enhance an already existing AbE lexicon has relied on Malcolm and Koscielecki (1997) (again, no pronunciations of the items in AbE are given by the authors):

Alah ('halloo'), *all* (pl. pr.), *all* ('only'), *all a same* (*all same/all same like/all the same as*, 'like'), *all time* ('constantly'), *along* ('belonging to'), *amanning, baal, bad mobs, Bael* (*Bail, bel,* 'no, not'), *Ballanda, bang-all, being Nyungar, belcoula, belongit, bereewolgal, bidegree, big Father, big-fella church, big mob, big water, big wheelbarrow, bingeye, black money, blackfeller* (*blackfellow,* 'Aborigine, Aboriginal'), *boodgeree* (*boodgorer,* 'good'), *boorak, boss, boy, brother, budgeree* ('lucky'), *budgery* ('good'), *budjari* ('pregnant'), *bull* ('alcohol'), *bulla* ('two'), *bunji* ('darling, mate'), *bunji* ('whore, dirty old man'), *bush black pellow* (*busk black*, 'wild Aborigines'), *by and bye* (*bye and bye*, 'after that, in the past'), *cabou, camping about, capital, choogar bag, close up, cobawn* (*cobbaun*, 'big'), *cobbera* (*cobrer*, 'head'), *cobra* ('witchety grub'), *coe* (*coo-ee*, 'come hither'), *come along, cool(a)* (*coolar*, 'anger'), *coolar* ('pick a quarrel'), *corban* ('very'), *corbon* ('large'), *corbon water, corees, corrobbory* (*corroberry, corrobery*, 'native dance'), *coulor, crammer, croppy, cudgel, dable, dable* (*debble, debble, devil-devil, dibble-dibble, dibil dibil*, 'evil spirit, Potayan, malignant apparition'), *dee-in, demons, dingo, direckaly, dousand, dreckle, dugais, durri* ('smoke'), *durri* ('copulate'), *Englat, fellow* ('man, animal'), *finish, fire stick, flog, gammon, geban geban wheelbarrow, gerret, gib berram, gidjey, gin* (*jin*, 'wife, woman'), *giving, goat, gone, good boy, goodfella, gooreebeera, granny, grasse, grind, gubba* (*gubbas*, 'white person'), *gunya* ('Aboriginal makeshift home'), *gunya* ('European'), *gunyon* ('kennel, container'), *gurrier, hang, him* (*im*), *Jackey Jackey* ('a white lackey'), *jacky jacky talk* ('broken English'), *jarrah* (*jerran, jirrand*, 'afraid'), *jump up, jump up white fellow* ('enter the afterlife'), *Kanguroo, Karrady, katawara, keening, kibra men, kill, king* ('wine, alcohol'), *knock up, koori* (*koories*, 'south-east Aborigines'), *learn, like it, lingo, listen to, long time, look out, lubra, maan, Marmon, Marnameek, marry* (*merry, muree, murray, murry*, 'very'), *massa, megalet* (*megalizt*, 'see'), *might be, mikloo, moak, mob, monarch, moon, moroo, moru, most, mun, mundoey, murri* ('koori'), *murri* (*murries*, 'Aborigine'), *musquito* (interj.), *myall pellow* (*myalls*, 'wild blackfellow'), *nangora* ('asleep'), *nangri* (*nangry*, v. 'sleep'), *Narang, narrawan, new way, no good, now, nyandi, nyook, old girl, ole man, ommina, owrangey bit, paddy melon, pai-alla, paper talk, patta, patter, phim, piccanini* (*pickaninney, pickaninny, pikenini*, 'child'), *piola, plenty* ('frequently'), *plenty sixpence, poor fellow, possum, pyook, quicktime, quipple, reared up, roast, rush, set down, shame, shame job, shamed, sing magic, sing out, sister, sit down, some fella, sorry, sorryfella, stop, stupid fellows, sulky, sundown, take off, taken away, talk up* (*talkin up*, 'use Aboriginal language'), *that-a-way, thieves, this place, tit down, tong, too* 'very'), *too much* ('many'), *thousand, towsan, tucker, tumble down, tumble down pickaninny, uncle, urokah, viddy, waddle, waddy, waijela, wandas, Warredya, waw!waw!, werie, werie, what for* ('why'), *Whehill, white bread* (*white fellow, White man*, 'non-Aboriginal fellow'), *white money, wickeye, winyarn, wunda, wunga, yabba, yabber, Yahoo Yarhoo, yorga*.

We then turned to spoken data. Those are less exhaustive in terms of the numbers of available items but, in most cases, they display operable information regarding the pronunciation of an item. Given the scarcity of speakers and corresponding relevant sociolinguistic information, data from two different spoken corpora had to be used: the AusTalk corpus and the PAC-Australia [Ulladulla] survey.

5.2.1 The AusTalk audio-visual corpus

AusTalk, an audio-visual corpus of Australian English (Burnham et al. 2011), is part of the national Big ASC project which was set up in 2011 to provide the largest ever audio-visual collection of spoken Australian English. In its final version (2016), AusTalk offers audio-visual data for 915 adult speakers from 15 areas across Australia. It aims at representing the dialectal and sociolinguistic diversity of contemporary Australian English, thus deliberately taking into account Aboriginal English (originally with speakers from Darwin and Alice Springs) and ethnolectal varieties as sheer parts of the Australian English-speaking community. AusTalk speakers represent age groups ranging from 18 to 83 years old. Their participation was validated provided they had completed their schooling in the Australian context. The protocol consists of an online questionnaire about the background of the speaker and the recording of three one-hour sessions of read and spontaneous speech production tasks. The reading tasks include wordlists (see below), digit strings (for example *two oh nine four*), sentences (such as *Who says itches are always so tempting to scratch?*) and a story to be read, while the spontaneous tasks include yes/no answers, the retelling of a story, an interview, a maptask and a conversation. In terms of variability, Burnham et al. (2011: 841) built a protocol of three one-hour sessions to be recorded at intervals of at least one week so as to 'capture potential variability over time, while geographical variability is guaranteed by recording at 17 locations, covering all capital cities of Australian states and territories and several regional centres'. The protocol ensures stylistic and social variability of the speakers.

Out of the 915 adult speakers from 15 areas across Australia, we selected all (19) speakers who declared being from Aboriginal cultural heritage,[13] having at least one parent from Aboriginal cultural heritage (5 speakers have both parents declared from an Aboriginal cultural heritage), whose spoken data is available on the Alveo Query Engine,[14] and whose quantity of data would allow for comparability with *MD Online* (SAusE data) and with the PAC-Australia [Ulladulla] data (SAbE data and corresponding sociolinguistic metadata, see below). Appendix 6.5 synthesises the sociolinguistic descriptors which support the AusTalk spoken corpus for our set of 19 AbE speakers: 11 female speakers (aged between 22 and 60 years old) and 8 male speakers (aged between 23 and 53 years old).

The two guiding hypotheses for our analysis were (i) the 'stress shift to initial syllable' hypothesis, and (ii) the possibility of variation within AbE and subsequent speaker variation. As detailed below, the analysis of the data was carried out in both auditory and acoustic perspectives.

The auditory component of our analysis relates to 1560 sound files with 40 words in citation form for each of the 19 speakers (corresponding to Part 1

'Words Component' of the Read Speech section of the AusTalk protocol) recorded in one, two or three sessions (WS1, WS2, WS3).[15] In order to test our hypothesis, we checked the pronunciation of the 322 words in the AusTalk list in *MD Online*. We selected the 40 words that are non-initially stressed for their main pronunciation and have no variant showing initial-stress in *MD Online* (i.e. since *manufacture* and *vaccine* have an initially stressed variant, they were discarded from our study):

- 8 words stressed as 01 (Type-1 words): *adapt, adjust, comply, delete, fatigue, gazelle, guitar, kazoo*
- 8 words stressed as 001 (Type-2 words): *bassinette, Halloween, kangaroo, masquerade, serenade, silhouette, souvenir, tangerine*
- 9 words stressed as 010 (Type-3 words): *abandon, alfalfa, bazooka, coyote, imagine, mascara, museum, pyjamas, tomato*
- 6 words stressed as 0010 (Type-4 words): *avocado, diabetes, epidemic, influenza, macaroni, paranoia*
- 7 words stressed as 0100 (Type-5 words): *amphibian, anaemia, anatomy, Australia, conspicuous, curriculum, evaporate*
- 2 words stressed as 00100 (Type-6 words): *aluminium, constellation*

Intentionally, the notation scheme regarding stress patterns does not include secondary stress, as *MD Online* rarely mentions secondary stress. Furthermore, as can be seen in Appendix 6.6, *MD Online* only mentions 1 of them (i.e. *aluminium*) in the 16 words which bear a secondary stress in *LPD3* and *CEPD17* (i.e. all the words given in Appendix 6.6 that have two unstressed syllables initially). The exploitation of the 1560 sound files enabled us to test three assumptions: (i) the 'stress shift to initial syllable' hypothesis, (ii) variation within SAbE, and (iii) possible intraspeaker variation.

In terms of stress pattern identification, the auditory analysis proved to be an easy task for Type-1/3/4/5/6 words (*abandon, avocado, aluminium*). The Type-2 word stress pattern (three-syllable words bearing stress in final position such as *bassinette/kangaroo/silhouette*, noted /201/ in the Guierrian approach) proved to be more difficult to identify in terms of primary/secondary stress discrimination and required further acoustic analysis with Praat (Boersma and Weenink 2014, 2021).

For each token isolated in each sound file, a number of criteria were processed with Praat so as to determine the position and nature of stress. The sound measurements were performed according to pitch variation mainly, as well as intensity, vocalic reduction and elision (Cutler 2005; Yuan et al. 2008; Eriksson and Heldner 2015). Vocalic duration was not tested as the data clearly display alternation of weak and strong syllables, putting aside the hypothesis of syllable-timed production; intensity remained insufficient to discriminate between primary and secondary stress. For each word, pitch measurement was performed, corresponding to the vocalic prominences

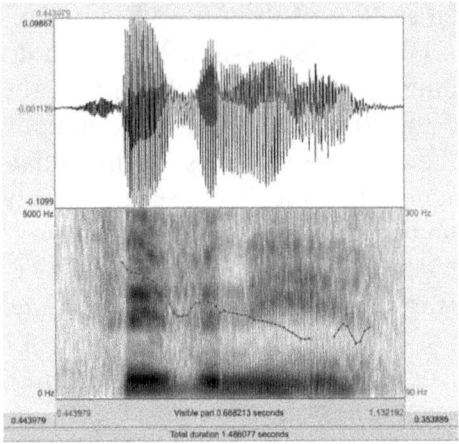 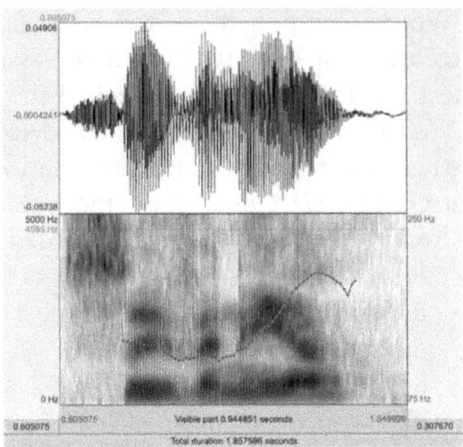

Figure 6.1 Stress pattern /100/ Speaker 1-1172, WS1, *souvenir*

Figure 6.2 Stress pattern /201/ Speaker 1-2770, WS3, *souvenir*

within the initial and final syllables of each token of the lexical items. For each speaker, the pitch parameters were specified in accordance with gender and voice quality (for example Speaker 3_1056 = pitch range <150–350Hz> and Speaker 4_389 = pitch range <65–200Hz>). One speaker had a very low voice during one of the sessions and some of the tokens had to be ruled out since they could not be processed through Praat with significant accuracy. Each token was analysed collecting pitch measurements corresponding to the vocalic prominences of initial and final syllables and checked against spectrographic information. Every single measurement was double-checked by the two authors and thoroughly discussed on the basis of spectrographic and auditory information.

The AusTalk corpus was not built to test lexical stress specifically. Thus, a series of constraints have emerged from the AusTalk dataset. The wordlist format induces phenomena such as reading list effect (for example 4_421, WS2 *kangaroo*) with rising intonation movements and numerous instances of hyperarticulation occasionally resulting in incidental syllable-timed occurrences (for example *bassinette* 2-945-1-43-001.wav). Moreover, the number of tokens per speaker was sometimes too small to ensure any reliable conclusion about intra- or inter-speaker variation of the stress patterns. For example, Speaker 3_1056 pronounces *aluminium* with a /01000/ stress pattern, but the fact that the corpus gives only one recording for this speaker prevented us from determining whether it was indeed a bias of the test or an occasional or usual feature of that speaker. Still, such cases were considered for both the qualitative and quantitative aspects of our study. We also detected instances of interfering interactions between the technician and some speakers during some of the recordings (for example *gazelle* 2-1142-2-23-285.wav) and these instances were discarded.

5.2.2 Results from AusTalk

Appendix 6.6 gives a detailed account of stress patterns as determined auditorily for Type-1/3/4/5/6 words, or else using Praat for Type-2 words (per item per speaker).

Out of the 760 tokens which were taken into account for the present study, 26 of them could not be used for want of good sound quality, 28 others because of biased interferences on the part of the technician, and another 1 had to be ruled out, which left us with 705 tokens (see Appendix 6.6). Several observations can be drawn from our exploration. First and foremost, the great majority of stress shifts to initial syllable is to be found in Type-2 words, with the exception of *coyote* initially stressed by speaker 1_1172 on one of the three occurrences. From a SAusE point of view (using *MD Online*), it has to be underlined that some of the words at stake do have initially stressed variants in SBE or in SAmE (for example *coyote*, as well as *serenade*, *silhouette*, *souvenir* and *tangerine*, all followed by * in Appendix 6.6.2); it would therefore not be surprising to encounter lexical stress variation for these words in SAusE as well. Appendix 6.6 also displays three other cases of stress shifts in non-Type-2 words: *aluminium* in /01000/ (Speaker 3_1056_1_2_038-ch6-speaker.wav), *curriculum* in /2010/ (Speaker 1_678_2_22_173-ch6-speaker.wav; the other two sound samples show an elision of the initial vowel and no stress shift) and *coyote* in /100/ (Speaker 1_1172_2_22_292-ch6-speaker.wav), *curriculum* and *coyote* being found in situations of intraspeaker variation. In two instances, speakers produce unexpected consonants (i.e. *conspicuous* for speaker 4_882 pronounced [kənˈspɪʃuəs] and *anatomy* for speaker 1_678 pronounced [əˈnænəmi]). Still, these two examples show no stress shift towards the left. On other occasions some speakers hesitate when pronouncing a word (for example *alfalfa* 1_127, *bassinette* 2_945). Finally, we observe several cases of elision of the initial syllable. These are discussed later in this chapter.

Overall, 80.7% of the 705 tokens studied do not display stress shift at all and 12.6% show stress shift to the initial syllable (see Figure 6.3).

As displayed in Appendix 6.6, the vast majority (89 out of 90) of stress shifts to initial syllable are found in Type-2 words. Indeed, out of the 562 other tokens studied, only 3 show a stress shift (*aluminium*, *curriculum* and

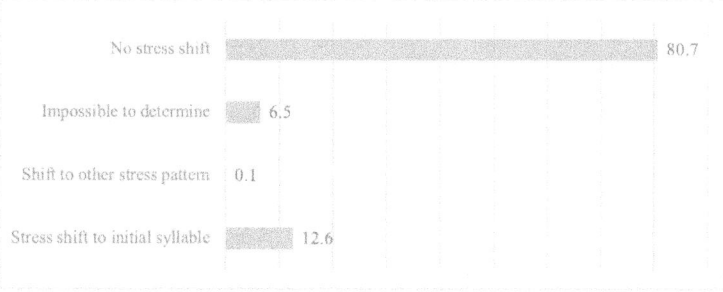

Figure 6.3 Distribution of the 705 tokens studied, in %

coyote as explained above). Overall, Type-1/3/4/5/6 words are 99.5% stable in terms of lexical stress between AusTalk SAbE speakers and *MD Online*.[16]

5.2.3 Interpretation of Type-2 words

The analysis of all the occurrences of Type-2 words leads to five possible interpretations of the lexical stress pattern:

- words showing no stress shift: /201/ pattern
- words showing stress shift to the initial syllable: /100/ pattern
- words for which it was not possible to discriminate between primary and secondary stresses: Stressed-Unstressed-Stressed pattern (SUS), as in Figure 6.4 (Speaker 2_642, WS2, *tangerine*), where the measurement of both pitch prominences (151/151.1Hz) prevents any discrimination between a primary and a secondary stress
- words where no prominence could be found: 'flat' pattern, which cannot be viewed as a sign of any syllable-timed trend because of the *ad hoc* nature of such occurrences per speaker, as in Figure 6.5 (Speaker 4_882, WS1, *silhouette*)
- items for which we detected persistent intraspeaker variation across the wordlist sessions.

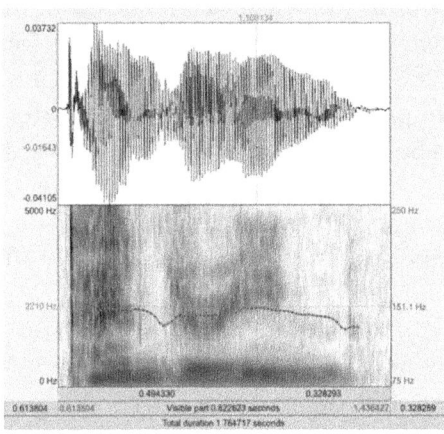
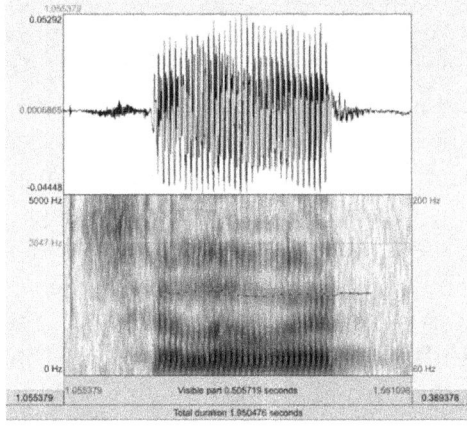

Figure 6.4 Stress pattern /SUS/ Speaker 2-642, WS2, *tangerine*

Figure 6.5 'Flat' stress pattern Speaker 4-882, WS1, *silhouette*

Type-2 words display 152 tokens. Ten tokens were discarded because of poor sound quality or the technician's interference with the speaker. The other 142 tokens are distributed as in Figure 6.6.

Of the Type-2 words, 62.7% show stress shift to initial syllable. All 8 words studied display this phenomenon and the 19 speakers produce initial stress in at least one word. Speaker 2_770 does not shift stress initially in most cases except in the case of *serenade*, that is, a word that has a /100/ variant in SBE

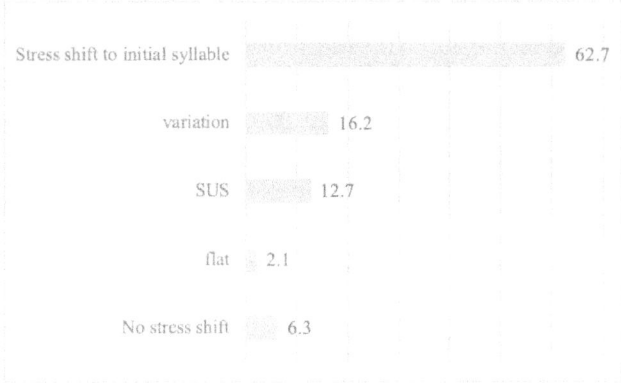

Figure 6.6 Distribution of the 142 tokens studied for intraspeaker variation, in %

and in SAmE. Despite the attractiveness of this interpretation, when thoroughly listening to the 54 sound files available to study the 23 tokens showing variation, we notice that, interestingly, the four words (*serenade*, *silhouette*, *souvenir* and *tangerine*) which have a variant with initial primary stress in SBE and SAmE do not display more variation than the other words.

Of the sound files for which intraspeaker variation was determined, 50% correspond to a shift towards the left (26 cases of primary stress on the first syllable, 1 case of /010/ in the word *bassinette*). Final stress is shown in 8 occurrences, and the 19 other recordings display either a flat picture (no pitch variation) or the impossibility of distinguishing secondary and primary stress (SUS).

5.2.4 The PAC-Australia [Ulladulla] corpus
The Phonology of Contemporary English: Usage, Varieties, Structure programme is an interdisciplinary research programme rooted in corpus phonology (Durand et al. 2014; Durand 2017) which aims at making sense of the observed linguistic heterogeneity and variation among native (and non-native) English-speaking communities around the world (Durand and Przewozny 2012; Przewozny et al. 2020). Since 2003, the PAC corpus has been developed to support (i) the study of the English language in its phonological structure, (ii) the description of English varieties in their specific dialectal and sociolinguistic contexts, and (iii) the exploration of various theoretical models accounting for variation and language change. Within the PAC database, the PAC-Australia corpus (37 informants) was developed through three surveys in 2003, 2015 and 2018 with specific interests such as real-time sociophonetic analysis and urban/post-urban dialectological issues in historical and contemporary contexts (Przewozny and Viollain 2016; Przewozny 2016; Przewozny and Fabre 2018).

The set of linguistic data and corresponding sociolinguistic metadata which were selected for our study was extracted from the 2018 Ulladulla (New South Wales) PAC survey, with a focus on two female Aboriginal speakers who participated in the reading tasks and the interactional tasks of the PAC protocol, namely the reading of two wordlists and a text ('A Christmas Interview'), answers to a sociolinguistic questionnaire, a semi-guided conversation with the investigator and informal conversation within the speaker's own network (without the PAC investigator).

As far as sociolinguistic indicators are concerned, the speakers are mother (anonymised as *ausnsulbnm1*, aged 79) and daughter (*ausnsulbnm2*, aged 46) who belong to the Budawang people of the Yuin Nation. *Ausnsulbnm1* was born in Nowra (NSW) and spent her whole childhood there. Her daughter *ausnsulbnm2* was born in Penrith (Sydney, NSW) as the family nucleus was living and working in Sydney (for 13 years), and soon spent her childhood in Ulladulla. Both speakers are fluent readers of English, which corresponds to their respective careers: *ausnsulbnm1* was a School Learning Support Officer and *ausnsulbnm2* is a high school teacher in English.

5.2.5 Results from PAC-Australia [Ulladulla]

Along with the two guiding hypotheses for analysis – (i) the 'stress shift to initial syllable' hypothesis, and (ii) the possibility of variation within SAbE and subsequent speaker variation – our analysis was performed both auditorily and acoustically (see Appendix 6.7). In accordance with the description of Malcolm (2008), *ausnsulbnm1* and *ausnsulbnm2*'s phonological system is typical of a 'light' SAbE, and some of their diphthongal realisations correspond to a General AusE pronunciation on the stylistic continuum of SAusE. As far as consonants are concerned, the glottal fricative is systematically produced by the two speakers as expected in SAusE, while /t/ can be realised as a dental in the conversation task (though not in the reading tasks). High Rising Tones can be heard in the interaction between the informants and the investigator, as revealed in Jespersen (2016) for Sydney varieties of AbE (ausnsulbnm1t.wav, ausnsulbnm2t.wav, ausnsulbnm1f.wav).

Because of the small number of the lexical items with an unstressed initial syllable in the PAC wordlists (*decree, degree, behave*), we chose to focus on a set of 22 lexical items extracted from the text 'A Christmas Interview'. Overall, the words are as follows:

- 13 words stressed in /01/ (Type-1 words): *agreed, behave* (Wordlist 1 and Text), *decree, degree, describes, disguise, employs, expects, fourteen, himself, polite, remarks*
- 4 words stressed in /010/ (Type-3 words): *dilemma, exactly, relating, whenever*
- 4 words stressed in /0100/ (Type-5 words): *behaviour, indifference, religious, society*
- 3 words stressed in /20100/ (Type-6 words): *Christianity, personalities, personality*
- 1 word stressed in /200100/ (Type-7 words): *organisations*

No Type-2/4 words were available in the data.[17] Out of the 48 tokens considered in the reading tasks (wordlists and text), 1 occurrence of a stress shift was found on *whenever* (ausnsulbnm1t.wav) as well as 1 instance of hyperarticulation on *decree* (ausnsulbnm1c.wav).

5.3 On the Aboriginality of stress patterns in spoken data

A perception test was implemented using the judgements of 6 non-Aboriginal native speakers of SAusE on the speech of 18 of the 19 AusTalk SAbE speakers. The subjects were asked to listen to the AusTalk text reading task or, if not available, to the sentence reading task, and declare if speakers were Aboriginal, non-Aboriginal, or if they did not know. The results were as follows: 8 speakers were perceived as non-Aboriginal (5 out of 6 listeners agreed), while another set of 8 speakers were perceived as Aboriginal (4 out of 6 listeners agreed). A closer look at these perceptive results within the scope of our AusTalk spoken data shows that speakers perceived as Aboriginal show 80.8% of no stress shift, while speakers perceived as non-Aboriginal show 78.5% of no stress shift. Therefore, the perceived Aboriginality of the speakers' performance is not to be related to the production of stress shift, and other (segmental) features certainly play a role in the perception judgements. Table 6.10 presents a synthesis of salient segmental and suprasegmental markers (from the WS task) among five speakers in the AusTalk corpus.

Some occurrences of elision of the initial vowel can be observed among four AusTalk speakers only and exclusively on Type-5 words /0100/: *(Au)stralia* [ˈstreɪljə] (Speaker 4_882, WS1), *c(u)rriculum* [ˈkrɪkjələm] (Speakers 1_678, WS1/2/3, 2_642, WS1/2/3 and 4_791, WS1) and *(e)vaporate* [ˈvæpəreɪt] (Speaker 4_882, WS3). Only Speaker 2_642 presents both suprasegmental and segmental markers of Aboriginality in coherence with previous descriptions (although SUS occurrences may not be easily linked to such a profile).

The PAC-Australia [Ulladulla] data display a number of explicit linguistic markers which can help strengthen the description of SAbE segmental markers in spoken data, and provide input to contribute to the idea of correlating SAbE segmental markers with relevant stress pattern shifts from our comparative study between dictionary-based and spoken-based data.

The two speakers from the PAC-Australia [Ulladulla] survey present a segmental system which is typical of a 'light' SAbE. Some diphthongal realisations correspond to a General AusE vocalic subsystem. A glottal fricative /h/ is systematically produced by the two speakers as is normally expected in SAusE, and /t/ is sometimes realised as a dental consonant in the semi-guided conversation task (never in the reading tasks). At the suprasegmental level, High Rising Tones can also be identified in the interaction between the informants and the investigator, which is in line with their variety of Aboriginal English. Despite the fact that the two PAC SAbE speakers display some features of General AusE which may correspond to the definition of a

Table 6.10 Salient segmental and suprasegmental markers for five AusTalk speakers

id	Suprasegmental	Segmental	Perceived as SAbE speaker	Age	Gender	First language	Other languages
2_642	Type-2 words variation: 1) shift *bassinette*, 2) shifts *masquerade*, 3) SUS patterns	1 elision *curriculum*, apical /ɹ/ *kangaroo*, dental /d/ *masquerade*	Always	39	female	English	Bardi
4_421	none	none	Always	48	female	English	
3_1056	1 shift *aluminium*	none	Never	59	female	English	
2_770	none	none	Not tested	40	male	English	AbE
4_271	Flat pattern *silhouette*	none	Always	53	male	English	

'light' SAbE with specific segmental Aboriginal markers, the two speakers show no sign of stress shift to the left in the spoken data in the types of words which could be analysed.

6 Conclusion

The purpose of this chapter was (i) to examine lexical stress patterns in Aboriginal loanwords in SAusE, (ii) to present a systemic account of lexical stress in SAusE based on dictionary data with an intervarietal scope, and (iii) to explore the hypothesis of 'stress shift to initial syllable' in contemporary spoken data in SAbE, for it would constitute an interesting case of lexical stress variation in contemporary English, within the context of both SAusE and English worldwide.

Regarding the issue of Aboriginal loanwords' stress patterns in SAusE, the initial stress hypothesis as a sign of maintenance of the original linguistic substrata is valid, yet it is a weaker hypothesis than the rules of stress assignment in English as applied to loanwords. Overall, this tends to show that, in terms of lexical stress, Aboriginal loanwords in SAusE are possibly more influenced by English stress rules than by stress patterns originating from Australian indigenous languages. Crucially, such a provisional conclusive remark calls for a dedicated corpus which would be inclusive of both Aboriginal loanwords and toponyms (see Leitner 1984; Australian National Placenames Survey;[18] Hercus et al. 2002).

In terms of intervarietal variation between SAusE, SAmE and SBE, it is found that, in a corpus of more than 3700 words which are sensitive to word-stress variation in contemporary English, the vast majority (94%) show no intervarietal stress variation for their main pronunciation. Our study also shows that when taking into account variation at large (i.e. including the existence or even the absence of a variant when comparing *MD Online* and *LPD3/CEPD17*), 90% of these same words show no lexical stress variation. We also conclude that, in the case of multicategorial words, SAusE tends to show less variation, with 57 words (15% of the class) having variants in SBE and SAmE displaying no variation in SAusE.

When testing the 'stress shift to initial syllable' hypothesis in SAbE in the framework of corpus phonology, we showed that the hypothesis is not valid among the AusTalk speakers of SAbE for 80.7% of the 40 words tested. This figure increases unequivocally to 99.5% when only taking into account Type-1/3/4/5/6 words. Type-2 words (*bassinette, Halloween, kangaroo, masquerade, serenade, silhouette, souvenir, tangerine*) do display stress shift in 62% of the cases, and half of the cases in which we found intraspeaker variation account for a shift to the initial syllable as well. These results are consistent with what Deschamps claims on this particular type of words:

Often assimilated to French endings: **C'C'e** or **V'V'** [sic] (geminated consonants or vowels most often **-tte, sse, nne** or **oo** et **ee**) **ese, que, Vsce, aire** or **ade** [sic], they statistically correspond to a final stress rule, although there are a large number of exceptions with or without stress variation which are generally characterised by a retraction from /01/ to /10/ and from /201/ to /100/ (*coffee, omelette, igloo* . . .). A number of words are found with a double pattern: disyllables stressed on the last or on the penultimate syllable (*colleen, pongee, ranee, lychee, impasse, pratique* . . .), trisyllables or longer words stressed on the last or on the antepenultimate syllable (*dungaree, silhouette cigarette, espadrille, pipistrelle, cavalcade, escalade, barricade, officialese* . . .). These variants emphasise the particular situation of final stress rules often complemented by incomplete phonetic integration of the corresponding items (as seen for instance in words with **-ade** endings pronounced [ɑː] instead of [eɪ].

(Deschamps 2001: 49–50)

This leads us to call into question the claim of SAbE speakers to shift stress to the initial syllable of Type-2 words as a typical feature of SAbE. Rather, we suggest that, within the system of SAusE, this confirms a general tendency of SAbE to behave coherently with the final stress rule and possible variants in words displaying (assimilated) French endings. Our cohort of SAbE speakers from AusTalk and PAC-Australia [Ulladulla] seem to follow this trend. As for the Aboriginality of these 'light' AbE speakers, we provisionally conclude that the evidence of stress shift to initial syllable in our exploration of spoken data is not central to the perception of AusE speakers as Aboriginal speakers.

Of course, we acknowledge the transitional property of this conclusion. It is now crucial to undertake the same test with non-Aboriginal speakers and with speakers of other varieties in the first place, more particularly for Type-2 words. It is also essential to consider that these first tests were conducted with currently available data and that a new corpus dedicated to the study of lexical stress and variation in SAbE and SAusE remains to be developed.[19] Such a corpus needs to integrate quantitative and qualitative parameters of inter- and intraspeaker variation, and be supported by a larger set of sociolinguistic descriptors to validate (or invalidate) possible correlations between qualitative and quantitative sociophonetic analyses on SAbE and degrees of Aboriginality. This in turn could contribute to a refined definition of SAbE as integrated into the system of SAusE and its distinctive function alongside General AusE.

Appendixes

Only 152 disyllabic verbs have intervarietal variation, which represent 6% of the verbs at stake. There are 163 differences in total and 11 verbs show 2 differences for they do not have the same stress patterns in *CEPD17* and *LPD3* (*concrete, curate, detox, downgrade, downplay, dumbfound, fragment, freewheel, prefix, rebate, shanghai*).

A6.1 Verbs displaying intervarietal stress pattern variation between SAusE, SAmE and SBE (source: Martin 2011a)

SAusE	Dictionary	No.	/1–/	No.	/–1/	Total
Specific	both	18	*alloy, annex, baksheesh, blue-sky, clear-cut, concave, contract, decoy, fast-talk, front-page, halal, occult, offset, ragout, snafu, soft-soap, tomfool, upload*	13	*citrate, clip-clop, haw-haw, infix, inlet, misfit, outbox, outcrop, outcry, relay, remix, tie-dye, upsurge*	31
	CEPD17	1	*concrete (solidify)*	3	*curate, pinch-hit, reflex*	4
	LPD3	16	*deadhead, detox, downgrade, downplay, dumbfound, fragment, free-fall, freeload, freewheel, freeze-dry, grimace, hot-wire, prolapse, rebate (deduct), shanghai, stir-fry*	7	*backfire, compact, discount (disregard), outgo, outwork, perpend, prefix*	23
= SBE ≠ SAmE	both	13	*chassé, chauffeur, combat, crochet, croquet, filet, garage, massage, parquet, plateau, roquet, sashay, sauté*	30	*bisect, blaspheme, capsize, chastise, cremate, dictate, dilate, donate, download, fellate, frustrate, gradate, gyrate, lactate, lasso, locate, migrate, mutate, narrate, notate, orate, placate, prostrate, pulsate, recess, resource, segment, truncate, vacate, vibrate*	43

A6.1 (continued)

SAusE	Dictionary	No.	/ˈ–/	No.	/–ˈ/	Total
	CEPD17	5	barrage, detail, detox, presage, travail	11	crosscheck, descant, dry-clean, no-ball, off-load, precast, prefix, quick-freeze, rebound, spin-dry, waylay	16
	LPD3	1	sojourn	6	accent, combine, curate, quadrate, translate, unquote	7
= SAmE ≠ SBE	both	17	backdate, castrate, chelate, DJ, fixate, gestate, hotfoot, hydrate, mandate, palpate, phonate, prospect, stagnate, stonewall, strip-search, top-dress, weekend	3	chagrin, flambé, harass	20
	CEPD17	12	co-star, crash-land, downgrade, downplay, downsize, dumbfound, fragment, freewheel, premise, rebate (deduct), shanghai, two-time	0		12
	LPD3	2	concrete (solidify), decal	5	converse, decoke, perfume, reheat, remake	7
Total		85		78		163

Most of the intervarietal differences imply stress pattern variation in only one category, either the verb or the noun (Appendix 6.2). Thus, 11 variations belong to a *concern/convict* type with variation of the stress pattern on the noun; 17 variations follow a *convict/offer* type with stress pattern variation on the verb; 2 items display full variation (*concern/offer* type), which implies a different stress pattern for both the verb and the noun; and only 1 pair has a different type in the 3 varieties (i.e. *occult*).

A6.2 Intervarietal variation for multicategorials – a detailed account (source: Martin 2011a)

Spelling (order used: V, N, Q)	Stress pattern MD online SAusE	Result of the dictionary study for main and variant pronunciation in SAusE	Stress pattern LPD3 SBE (* for CEPD17)	Result of the dictionary study for main and variant pronunciation in SBE	Stress pattern LPD3 SAmE (* for CEPD17)	Result of the dictionary study for main and variant pronunciation in SAmE
decoke	/01/	***concern* type**	V/21/-N/10/, /21/	*convict* type, N/-1/ variant	V/21/-N/10/	*convict* type
pretend/ pretence	/01/	*concern* type	/01/	*concern* type	V/01/-N/10/	***convict* type**
rebore	/01/	***concern* type**	V/21/-N/10/	*convict* type	V/21/-N/10/	*convict* type
reheat	/01/	***concern* type**	V/21/-N/10/	*convict* type	V/21/-N/10/	*convict* type
remit	/01/	***concern* type**	V/01/-N/10/, /01/	*convict* type, N/-1/ variant	V/01/-N/10/, /01/	*convict* type, N/-1/ variant
rethink	/01/	*concern* type	V/21/-N/10/, /21/	*convict* type, N/-1/ variant	V/21/-N/10/, /21/	*convict* type, N/-1/ variant
collect ('bet')	V/01/-Q/01/-N/01/, /10/ - A/01/	***concern* type, NQA align variant N/10/**	V/01/-Q/01/-N/10/-A/01/	*convict* type, NQA not aligned	V/01/-Q/01/-N/10/-A/01/	*convict* type, NQA not aligned
intrigue	V/01/-N/01/, /10/	***concern* type, N/10/ variant**	V/01/-N/10/, /01/	*convict* type, N/-1/ variant	V/01/-N/10/, /01/	*convict* type, N/-1/ variant
recess	V/01/-N/01/, /10/	*concern* type, N/10/ variant	V/01/, /10/-N/01/, /10/	*concern* type, /10/ variant	V/10/, /01/-N/10/, /01/	***offer* type, /01/ variant**
recoil	V/01/-N/01/, /10/	***concern* type, N/10/ variant**	V/01/-N/10/, /01/	*convict* type, N/-1/ variant	V/01/-N/10/, /01/	*convict* type, N/-1/ variant

A6.2 (continued)

Spelling (order used: V, N, Q)	Stress pattern *MD* online SAusE	Result of the dictionary study for main and variant pronunciation in SAusE	Stress pattern *LPD3* SBE (* for *CEPD17*)	Result of the dictionary study for main and variant pronunciation in SBE	Stress pattern *LPD3* SAmE (* for *CEPD17*)	Result of the dictionary study for main and variant pronunciation in SAmE
accent	V/01/-N/10/	*convict* type	V/01/-N/10/	*convict* type	V/10/, /01/-N/10/	***offer* type, V/01/ variant**
eject	V/01/-N/10/	***convict* type**	/01/	*concern* type	/01/	*concern* type
perfume	V/01/-N/10/	*convict* type	V/10/, /01/-N/10/	***offer* type, V/01/ variant**	V/01/, /10/-N/10/, /01/	*convict* type, V/10/ variant, N/-1/
recall	V/01/-N/10/	***convict* type**	V/01/-N/01/, /10/	*concern* type, N/10/ variant	/01/	*concern* type
upsurge	V/01/-N/10/	***convict* type**	absent V, N/10/, V/10/? /N/10/*	*offer* type	absent V, N/10/, V/10/?-N/10/*	*offer* type
prostrate	V/01/-Q/10/	*convict* type VQ	V/01/-Q/10/, /01/	*convict* type VQ, Q/-1/ variant	V/10/-Q/10/	***offer* type VQ**
discount ('rule out')	V/01/-N/10/-Q/10/	***convict* type, NQ align**	V/10/, /01/-N/10/	*offer* type, V/01/ variant	V/10/, /01/-N/10/	*offer* type, V/01/ variant
prefix	V/01/, /10/-N/10/	***convict* type, V/10/ variant**	V/10/, /01/-N/10/	*offer* type, V/01/ variant	V/10/, /01/-N/10/	*offer* type, V/01/ variant
relay	V/01/, /10/-N/10/	***convict* type, V/10/ variant**	V/10/, /01/-N/10/	*offer* type, V/01/ variant	V/10/, /01/- N/10/	*offer* type, V/01/ variant
prospect	/10/	*offer* type	V/01/-N/10/	***convict* type**	/10/	*offer* type

rebate ('a discount')	/10/	**offer type**	V/01/, /10/-N/10/, /01/	convict type, V/10/ variant, N/-1/	convict type, V/10/ variant, N/-1/
sojourn	/10/	offer type	/10/	offer type	/01/, /10/
concrete ('solidify')	/10/	offer type, NQ align	V/01/-N/10/-Q/10/	**convict type, NQ aligned**	V/10/, /(2)1/-N/10/, /(2)1/-Q/21/, /10/
downgrade	V/10/, /01/-Q/10/-N/10/	**offer type, NQ aligned, V01 variant**	V/21/,/10/-N/10/	convict type, V/10/ variant	V/21/,/10/-N/10/
occult	/10/, /01/	offer type, /01/ variant	V/01/-N/10/, /01/-Q/10/, /01/	**convict type, NQ -1/ variant**	V/01/-N/01/, /10/-Q/01/, /10/
annex	V/10/, /01/-N/10/	**offer type, V/01/ variant**	V/01/-N/10/	convict type	V/01/-N/10/
combat	V/10/, /01/-N/10/	offer type, V/01/ variant	V/10/, /01/-Q/10/-N/10/	offer type, NQ aligned, V/01/ variant	V/01/, /10/-Q/10/-N/10/
contract	V/10/, /01/-N/10/	**offer type, V/01/ variant**	V/01/, /10/-N/10/	convict type, V/10/ variant	V/01/, /10/-N/10/
decoy	V/10/, /01/-N/10/	**offer type, V/01/ variant**	V/01/-N/10/, /01/	convict type, N/-1/ variant	V/01/-N/10/, /01/
offset	V/10/, /01/-N/10/	**offer type, V/01/ variant**	V/21/, /10/ N/10/	convict type, V/10/ variant	V/21/, N/10/
prolapse	V/10/, /01/-N/10/	**offer type, V/01/ variant**	V/01/, /10/-N/10/, /01/	convict type, V/10/ variant, N/-1/	V/01/, /10/-N/10/, /01/
No. of specificities		22 (67%)		4 (12%)	7 (21%)

	convict type, V/10/ variant, N/-1/
	concrete type, /10/ variant
	offer type, NQ not aligned, VN /-1/ variant, Q /10/
	convict type, V/10/ variant
	concrete type, NQ /10/ variant
	convict type
	convict type, NQ aligned, V/10/ variant
	convict type, V/10/ variant
	convict type, N/-1/ variant
	convict type
	convict type, V/10/ variant, N/-1/

A6.3 Intervarietal variation regarding exceptions to the stress rules of English in a Guierrian context: a detailed account (Martin 2011a)

A6.3.1 Exceptions to the rule Disyllabic word →/10/: 18 words

Spelling	Variation at stake	Stress pattern
adult	main in SBE	/10/
impasse	main in SBE	/01/
Mamma	main in SBE	/01/
capsize	main in SAmE	/10/
schottische	main in SAmE	/10/
baptize	main in SAmE	/10/
Malay	main in SAmE	/10/
recourse	main in SAmE	/10/
rupee	main in SAmE	/10/
resource	main in SAmE	/10/
recluse	main in SAmE	/10/
segment V	main in SAmE	/10/
papa	main in SAmE	/10/
esquire	main in SAmE	/10/
garage	main in SAmE	/01/
maidan	main in SAusE	/10/
finance	main in SAusE	/10/
grimace	main in SAusE	/10/

A6.3.2 Exceptions to the rule prefinal C_2 →/–10/: 5 words

Spelling	Variation at stake	Stress pattern
palanquin	main in SBE and SAmE	/100/
tergiversate	main in SBE	/1000/
carburettor	main in SBE	/–10/, regular
gaberdine	main in SAmE	/100/
subaltern	main in SAmE	/–10/, regular

The following items have a regular stress pattern in the variety mentioned in brackets: *astrakhan* (SAusE), *aureola* (SBE), *curator* (SAmE), *dictator* (SAmE), *embouchure* (SAusE), *in/extrados* (SAmE), *testator* (SAmE).

The other 11 items are presented below.

A given word (for example *parmesan*) is exceptional in the variety present in the column 'Variation at stake' (for example SBE) displaying a main stress pattern as given in the column on the right of the table.

A6.3.3 Exceptions to the Normal Stress Rule: 18 words (11+7)

Spelling	Variation at stake	Main stress pattern in variation
parmesan	main SBE	/(−)1/
canzonet	main SBE	/(−)10/
verrucose	main SBE	/(−)10/
epsilon	main SBE	/(−)10/
upsilon	main SBE	/(−)10/
antepenult	main SAmE	/(−)10/
viola ('flower')	main SAmE	/(−)10/
substratum	main SAusE	/(−)10/
catamaran	main SAusE	/(−)1000/
orthopaedy	main SAusE	/(−)1000/
laboratory	main SAmE	/(−)10000/

A6.4 Loanwords from Aboriginal languages and intervarietal stability (source: Martin 2011a)

Main spelling	Other spellings	No. of syllables	Stress pattern in Dixon et al. (2006)	Stress pattern in *LPD3* and *CEPD17** if different	Intervarietal variation
quoll	x	1	/1/	/1/	
bilby	*bilbi*	2	/10/	/10/*	
bunya	*bunya-bunya, bunya-bunya pine*	2	/10/	/10/	
bunyip	x	2	/10/	/10/	
cooee	x	2	/10/, /01/	/10/, /21/	
dingo	x	2	/10/	/10/	
euro	*euroo, uroo, yuro*	2	/10/	/10/	
galah	x	2	/01/	/01/	
gilgai	*ghilgai, gilgi, gilgie*	2	/10/	/10/	
gundy	*goondie*	2	/10/	/10/	
gunyah	*gunya*	2	/10/	/10/	
jarrah	x	2	/10/	/10/	
mallee	x	2	/10/	/10/	
mulga	*malga, mulgah, mulgar*	2	/10/	/10/	
myall	*mial, miall, myal*	2	/10/	/10/	

A6.4 (continued)

Main spelling	Other spellings	No. of syllables	Stress pattern in Dixon et al. (2006)	Stress pattern in *LPD3* and *CEPD17** if different	Intervarietal variation
nardoo	x	2	/01/	/21/	
numbat	x	2	/10/	/10/	
quandong	quondong, quandang, quantong	2	/10/	/10/	
quokka	x	2	/10/	/10/	
wallum	x	2	/10/	/10/	
wombat	x	2	/10/	/10/	
yakka	yacca, yacka, yacker, yakker	2	/10/	/10/	
billabong	x	3	/100/	/100/	
boomerang	x	3	/100/	/100/	
brigalow	x	3	/100/	/100/	
burrawang	buddawong, burrawong, burwan	3	/100/	/100/	
coolamon	coolaman, cooliman, kooliman	3	/100/	/100/	
coolibah	coolabah, coolobar, coolybah	3	/100/	/100/	
currawong	x	3	/100/	/100/	
koala	x	3	/010/	/010/	
nannygai	nannagai, nannygy	3	/100/	/100/	
perentie	parentie, parinti, perenty, prenti, printhy, printy	3	/010/, /(0)10/	/010/	
pituri	pitcheri, pitcherie, pitchery, pitury	3	/100/	/100/	
potoroo	x	3	/001/	/201/	
wallaby	x	3	/100/	/100/	

A6.4 (continued)

Main spelling	Other spellings	No. of syllables	Stress pattern in Dixon et al. (2006)	Stress pattern in *LPD3* and *CEPD17** if different	Intervarietal variation
wallaroo	x	3	/001/	/201/	
warrigal	x	3	/100/	/100/	
witchetty	*witchetty grub, widgery, witchety, witjuti*	3	/100/	/100/	
alcheringa	*alchuringa*	4	/0010/	/2010/	
didgeridoo	*didjeridu, didjiridu, didjerry*	4	/0001/	/2001/	
kookaburra	x	4	/1000/	/1000/	
pademelon	*paddymelon, pademella, paddymalla, paddymellon*	4	/1000/	/1020/	
Jindyworobak	x	5	/00100/	/20100/	
waratah	*warata, warratah, warrataw, warrettah*	3	/001/, /100/	/100/	Main stress pattern specific in SAusE
barramundi	*barramunda, burramundi*	4	/0010/, /1000/	/2010/	Variant in SAusE
kangaroo	x	3	/001/	/201/ – /201/, /100/*	Absence of variant in SAusE
corroboree	x	4	/0100/	/0100/ – /0100/, /0201/*	Absence of variant in SAusE

A6.5 Sociolinguistic typology of AusTalk speakers

Note that all speakers have English as their first language and have declared having an Aboriginal Australian cultural heritage.

A6.5.1 Sociolinguistic descriptors per speaker

id	age	gender	other_languages	pob_country	pob_state	pob_town	is_student	education_level
1_1172	39	female	French	AU	NSW	Armidale	true	bachelor degree
1_127	60	female	Kriol	AU	QLD	Mt Isa	false	graduate diploma
1_5	28	male		AU	NT	Darwin	false	school certificate
1_678	22	female		AU	NSW	Kempsey	true	higher school certificate
2_1142	28	female		AU	NT	Darwin	true	associate degree
2_1171	21	female	Japanese	AU	NT	Darwin	true	higher school certificate
2_208	31	male	None	AU	NSW	Cobar	false	higher school certificate
2_567	51	female		AU	NT	Darwin	true	bachelor degree
2_642	39	female	Bardi	AU	WA	Broome	false	school certificate
2_770	40	male	Aboriginal English	AU	NT	Darwin	true	graduate certificate
2_945	37	male		AU	NT	Darwin	false	school certificate
3_1056	59	female	Spanish	AU	NSW	Sydney	false	associate degree
3_1081	28	male		AU	NT	Darwin	false	diploma
3_1236	57	female	Aboriginal English	AU	QLD	Mt isa	false	diploma
3_719	36	female		AU	SA	Adelaide	false	higher school certificate
4_271	53	male		AU	NT	Darwin	true	TAFE certificate
4_389	23	male	Tiwi	AU	NT	Darwin	true	higher school certificate
4_421	48	female		AU	NT	Katherine	true	bachelor degree
4_648	22	female	German; Japanese	AU	NT	Katherine	true	higher school certificate
4_791	59	female	Yugumbeh	AU	QLD	Mt Morgan	false	doctoral degree
4_882	41	male	Anmatjerre	AU	NT	Alice Springs	false	school certificate

A6.5.2 Sociolinguistic descriptors per speaker's mother

id	mother_first_language	mother_cultural_heritage	mother_pob_country	mother_pob_state
1_1172	English	Australian	AU	NSW
1_127	English	Aboriginal Australian	AU	SA
1_5	English	Aboriginal Australian	AU	QLD
1_678	English	Australian	AU	NSW
2_1142	English	Aboriginal Australian	AU	NT
2_1171	English	Aboriginal Australian	AU	WA
2_208	English	Australian	AU	NSW
2_567	English	Aboriginal Australian	AU	NT
2_642	English	Aboriginal Australian	AU	WA
2_770	English	Aboriginal Australian	AU	NT
2_945	English	Australian	AU	SA
3_1056	English	Aboriginal Australian	AU	NSW
3_1081	English	Aboriginal Australian	AU	NSW
3_1236	English	Aboriginal Australian	AU	QLD
3_719	English	Aboriginal Australian	AU	NT
4_271	English	Aboriginal Australian	AU	NT
4_389	English	Aboriginal Australian	AU	NT
4_421	English	Aboriginal Australian	AU	WA
4_648	English	Australian	AU	VIC
4_791	English	Aboriginal Australian	AU	QLD
4_882	English	Aboriginal Australian	AU	NT

A6.5.3 Sociolinguistic descriptors per speaker's father

id	father_first_language	father_cultural_heritage	father_pob_country	father_pob_state	father_pob_town	father_professional_category	father_education_level
1_1172	English	Aboriginal Australian	AU	NSW	Ashfield	tradesperson	bachelor degree
1_127	English	Australian	AU	SA	Port Lincoln	labourer	primary to junior high
1_5	English	North-West European	GB		Haverfordshire	elementary clerical	higher school certificate
1_678	English	Aboriginal Australian	AU	NSW	Armidale	manager and admin	school certificate
2_1142	Greek, Modern (1453–)	Southern and Eastern European	GR		Corfu	intermediate clerical and service	primary to junior high
2_1171	English	Aboriginal Australian	AU	NT	Darwin	intermediate production	school certificate
2_208	English	Aboriginal Australian	AU	NSW	Cobar	labourer	primary to junior high
2_567	English	Australian	AU	WA	Maylands	tradesperson	primary to junior high
2_642	English	Aboriginal Australian	AU	WA	Lobadina	labourer	primary to junior high
2_770	English	Australian	AU	WA	Meckering	intermediate clerical and service	school certificate
2_945	English	Aboriginal Australian	AU	NT	Tenant Creek	intermediate production	school certificate
3_1056	English	Australian	AU	NSW	Hurstville	unemployed	primary to junior high
3_1081	English	Aboriginal Australian	AU	QLD	Inisfail	manager and admin	school certificate
3_1236	English	Australian	AU	QLD	Cloncurry	labourer	primary to junior high
3_719	English	Aboriginal Australian	AU	NSW	Sydney	intermediate production	school certificate
4_271	English	Aboriginal Australian	AU	NT	Darwin	elementary clerical	school certificate
4_389	Dutch	North-West European	NL		Unknown	clerical and service	higher school certificate
4_421	English	Australian	AU	QLD	Prosepine	intermediate production	school certificate
4_648	English	Aboriginal Australian	AU	NSW	Newcastle	tradesperson	TAFE certificate
4_791	English	Australian	AU	QLD	Brisbane	intermediate production	primary to junior high
4_882	English	Australian	AU	SA	Adelaide	intermediate production	school certificate

A6.6 Results from the AusTalk corpus

A6.6.1 Results per speaker and item, AusTalk corpus: legend

S	Shift to initial stress	
O	Shift to another stress pattern	
N	No shift	
P	Sound problem	
T	Technician interference	
V	Intraspeaker variation	
R	Ruled out	
U	Stress-unstressed-stressed	
F	Flat	

* /100/ Variant in SBE

Remark: for the reading task (wordlists), 6 speakers were recorded 3 times (Speakers 1_1172, 1_678, 2_1142, 2_208, 2_642, 4_421), 8 speakers were recorded twice (Speakers 1_127, 1_5, 2_567, 2_945, 3_1081, 3_719, 4_389, 4_882) and 5 speakers were recorded only once (Speakers 2_770, 3_1056, 3_1236, 4_271 and 4_791) and were therefore not eligible to intraspeaker variation in the present study.

A6.6.2 Results per speaker and item, AusTalk corpus

Word type	Item	Acc MD	1-1172	1-127	1-5	1-678	2-1142	2-208	2-567	2-642	2-770	2-945	3-1056	3-1081	3-1236	3-719	4-271	4-389	4-421	4-791	4-882
1	adapt	/01/	N	N	N	N	N	N	N	N	N	N	P	N	N	N	N	N	N	N	N
1	adjust	/01/	N	N	N	N	N	N	N	N	N	N	P	N	N	N	N	N	N	N	N
1	comply	/01/	N	N	N	N	N	N	N	N	N	N	P	N	N	N	T	N	N	N	N
1	delete	/01/	N	N	N	N	T	N	N	N	N	N	N	N	N	N	N	N	N	N	N
1	fatigue	/01/	N	N	N	N	T	N	N	N	N	N	N	N	N	N	N	N	N	N	N
1	gazelle	/01/	N	N	N	N	N	N	N	N	N	N	P	N	N	N	N	N	N	N	N
1	guitar	/01/	N	N	N	N	N	N	N	N	N	N	P	N	N	N	N	N	N	N	N
1	kazoo	/01/	N	N	N	N	N	N	N	N	N	N	N	N	N	N	T	N	N	N	N
2	bassinette	/001/	S	T	S	S	U	S	V	U	N	V	N	S	S	S	U	V	T	S	U
2	Halloween	/001/	S	F	V	S	S	S	S	U	N	S	P	S	T	S	U	V	V	S	V
2	kangaroo	/001/	S	F	S	S	S	S	U	S	S	S	S	S	S	S	S	S	V	S	V
2	masquerade	/001/	S	N	V	S	U	S	S	V	U	T	S	S	S	S	U	U	U	S	S
2	serenade*	/001/	S	S	S	S	S	V	S	S	S	S	S	S	S	S	F	S	V	S	S
2	silhouette*	/001/	S	F	V	S	T	V	V	S	N	V	U	S	S	S	U	S	V	S	S
2	souvenir*	/001/	S	T	S	S	S	S	S	V	N	V	P	S	S	S	U	S	S	S	T
2	tangerine*	/001/	S	S	S	S	S	S	S	U	N	N	P	S	S	S	U	S	U	S	U
3	abandon	/010/	N	N	N	N	N	N	N	N	N	N	P	N	N	N	N	N	N	N	N
3	alfalfa	/010/	N	N	N	N	N	N	T	N	N	N	P	N	N	N	T	N	T	N	T

A6.6.2 (continued)

σ	word	pattern																
3	bazooka	/010/	N	N	N	N	N	N	N	P	N	N	N	N	N	N	N	N	N
3	coyote*	/010/	V	N	N	N	N	N	N	P	N	N	N	N	N	N	N	N	N
3	imagine	/010/	N	N	N	N	N	N	N	P	N	N	N	N	N	N	N	N	N
3	mascara	/010/	N	N	N	N	N	N	N	N	N	N	N	N	N	N	N	N	N
3	museum	/010/	N	N	N	N	N	N	N	P	N	N	N	N	N	N	N	N	N
3	pyjamas	/010/	N	N	N	N	N	N	N	P	N	N	N	N	N	N	N	N	N
3	tomato	/010/	N	N	N	N	N	N	N	P	N	N	N	N	N	N	N	N	N
4	avocado	/0010/	N	N	N	N	N	N	T	P	N	N	N	N	N	N	N	N	N
4	diabetes	/0010/	N	N	N	N	N	N	N	P	N	N	N	N	T	N	N	N	N
4	epidemic	/0010/	N	N	N	N	N	N	N	P	N	T	T	N	N	N	N	N	N
4	influenza	/0010/	N	N	N	N	N	N	T	N	N	T	N	N	N	N	N	N	N
4	macaroni	/0010/	N	N	N	N	N	N	N	P	N	N	T	N	T	N	N	T	N
4	paranoia	/0010/	N	N	N	N	N	N	N	P	N	N	N	N	N	N	N	N	N
5	amphibian	/0100/	N	N	N	N	V	N	N	P	N	N	N	N	N	N	N	N	N
5	anaemia	/0100/	N	N	N	N	N	T	N	N	T	N	T	N	N	N	N	N	N
5	anatomy	/0100/	N	N	N	N	N	N	N	P	N	N	N	N	N	T	T	N	T
5	Australia	/0100/	N	N	N	N	N	N	N	N	N	N	N	N	N	N	N	N	N
5	conspicuous	/0100/	N	N	N	N	N	T	N	P	N	N	T	N	T	N	N	N	N
5	curriculum	/0100/	N	N	N	N	N	N	N	P	N	N	N	N	T	N	N	N	N
5	evaporate	/0100/	N	N	N	N	N	N	N	P	N	N	N	N	N	N	N	N	N
6	aluminium	/20100/	N	N	N	N	N	N	N	O	N	N	N	N	N	N	T	N	N
6	constellation	/00100/	N	N	N	N	N	N	N	P	N	N	N	N	N	N	N	N	N

The number of wordlist sessions for each speaker has little influence on intraspeaker variation. Indeed, for the 3 speakers (out of 6 who have been recorded 3 times) who show such variation, only 1 item (*bassinette*) out of 8 displays a different type for each recording and for 2 speakers only (Speaker 2_642: /201/, /100/, SUS; Speaker 4_421: SUS, Flat, /100/).

A6.7 Results from the PAC-Australia [Ulladulla] corpus

A6.7.1 Results per speaker and item, PAC-Australia [Ulladulla] corpus: legend

S	Shift to initial stress
N	No shift
H	Hyperarticulation

A6.7.2 Results per speaker and item, PAC-Australia [Ulladulla] corpus

Word type	Item	Acc MD	ausnsulbnm 1	ausnsulbnm 2
1	behave	/01/	N	N
1	decree	/01/	H	N
1	degree	/01/	N	N
1	agreed	/01/	N	N
1	behave	/01/	N	N
1	describes	/01/	N	N
1	disguise	/01/	N	N
1	employs	/01/	N	N
1	expects	/01/	N	N
1	fourteen	/01/	N	N
1	himself	/01/	N	N
1	polite	/01/	N	N
1	remarks	/01/	N	N
3	dilemma	/010/	N	N
3	exactly	/010/	N	N
3	relating	/010/	N	N
3	whenever	/010/	S	N
5	behaviour	/0100/	N	N
5	indifference	/0100/	N	N
5	religious	/0100/	N	N
5	society	/0100/	N	N
6	Christianity	/00100/	N	N
6	personality	/00100/	N	N
6	personalities	/00100/	N	N
7	organisations	/000100/	N	N

Notes

1. We wish to acknowledge and pay respect to Aboriginal people past and present as the traditional owners of the land, namely the Gadigal people of the Eora Nation, the Bunurong Boon Wurrung and Wurundjeri Woi Wurrung peoples of the Eastern Kulin Nation and the Budawang people of the Yuin Nation whose ancestral lands Sydney, Melbourne and Ulladulla are built upon and on which Lison Fabre conducted the PAC-Australia [Ulladulla] fieldwork, as well as to peoples of the nations on which members of the AusTalk corpus conducted their fieldwork.
2. For standards and written usage in Australia, see the annual revision of the *Australian Government Style Manual* and the many reference publications edited by the Macquarie Dictionary Research Centre (for example Peters 2007).
3. Within the system of Australian English, ethnocultural varieties (or ethnolects) cannot be ignored. Although they do not embrace the scope of the present chapter, let us simply remind the reader of the general definition of Australian ethnolects provided by Clyne et al. (2001: 225): 'The term "ethnolect" is used here to denote a variety of a language that marks speakers from groups which originally had another first language. Thus, we may recognise, for instance, a Greek ethnolect of AusE (while at the same time excluding from this definition the Greek spoken in Australia). The phenomenon has been described in various other ways. For example, Clyne (1968) refers to the "stabilised transference" of lexical items, features and structures from the substratum language or variety (that is, the language originally spoken by the community). Clyne (1981) also speaks of second generation "foreigner talk" (that is, a register employed by the second generation to first generation users whose English may be characterised as "foreign" or "non-mainstream", often their parents or other older relatives.' German AusE, Lebanese AusE or Vietnamese AusE are famous examples that have been analysed from sociolinguistic and linguistic points of view in recent decades (for example in Clyne 1970, 1976; Horvath 1985; Warren 1999; Kiesling 2001; Leitner 2004; Cox and Palethorpe 2006).
4. See Chapter 2 of this volume for details.
5. Eight monosyllabic words were not taken into account in this part of the study.
6. Martin's study (2011a) on dictionary data was checked against a series of oral tests on specific items of the corpus (following a protocol close to that of the PAC research programme; see Durand and Przewozny 2012), as well as frequency results extracted from the *Corpus of Contemporary American English*. This spoken-data-based approach is little used by Guierre's school, although Guierre himself stated that 'Il y a des années

que j'appelle de mes vœux des recherches in vivo. Grâce à des linguistes comme Labov, Derwing, Prideaux, Neslly, ... la recherche en linguistique redevient ce qu'elle n'aurait jamais dû cesser d'être: une science humaine à la fois théorique et empirique' (Guierre 1983: 136).

7. Lexical stress is described as stable because in the vast majority of cases, a given word has the same stress pattern in SAusE, SBE and SAmE (and most of the time the same variants as well) in the pronunciation dictionaries considered in Martin (2011a).
8. Strong endings of disyllabic verbs in −V*te* fit SBE perfectly, which comes as no surprise since the linguists who unveiled this trend worked specifically on SBE. These results are only average in SAusE and poor in the context of SAmE. In SAmE, the rule Disyllable → /10/ is more efficient for non-prefixed items.
9. The lists of exceptions to the English stress rules that Martin (2011a) builds on here were compiled by authors largely working on SBE. Further study on lists taking into account SAusE and SAmE would be welcome.
10. These figures include the work led on spoken data in Martin (2011a).
11. Following Cling (1984: 200), Martin (2011a: 371) hypothesises for inner circles varieties that stress pattern 'must be retained as fundamental invariants of any English accent variety'.
12. Fletcher et al. (2015) argue that not all Aboriginal languages can be described as stress languages, with pitch being possibly the major acoustic cue to prominence.
13. These 19 Aboriginal speakers account for 2% of the AusTalk 915 speakers, slightly under the 3% proportion of Aborigines and Torres Strait Islanders in the Australian population (727 485 inhabitants for a total population of 24,190,907 inhabitants, according to the 2016 Census).
14. <https://austalk-query.apps.alveo.edu.au>.
15. <https://austalk.edu.au/about/corpus/>.
16. Contrary to Malcolm (1995, 2018, 2021), AusTalk SAbE speakers do not shift stress initially when pronouncing the word *guitar*.
17. This is certainly due to our use of a reading text passage instead of a wordlist in this corpus, as the number of /201/ words could be overrepresented in the selection of non-initially stressed words found in the AusTalk wordlist (8 out of 40).
18. <https://www.anps.org.au/>.
19. This will include disyllabic verbs in −V*te* and -*ment* (*create, migrate, ignite, unite, salute, segment, torment* . . ., and exceptions to disyllable → /10/). Apart from words with strong endings (often assimilated to French endings), a few exceptions to the Normal Stress Rule could be added but they usually are of genuine or assimilated French origin as well.

References

ACARA (2011), *The Australian Curriculum*, Sydney: Australian Curriculum, Assessment and Reporting Authority (ACARA).
Benterrak K., S. Muecke and P. Roe (1984), *Reading the Country: Introduction to Nomadology*, Liverpool: Liverpool University Press.
Bernard, J. R. L. (1969), 'On the uniformity of spoken Australian English', *Orbis* 18(1), 62–73.
Blair, D. and P. Collins (eds) (2001), *Varieties of English around the World: English in Australia*, Amsterdam: John Benjamins.
Boersma, P. and D. Weenink (2014), 'The use of Praat in corpus research', in J. Durand, U. Gut and G. Kristoffersen (eds), *The Oxford Handbook of Corpus Phonology*, Oxford: Oxford University Press, pp. 342–60.
Boersma, P. and D. Weenink (2021), 'Praat: doing phonetics by computer' [Computer program], version 6.1.40, <http://www.praat.org/>.
Burnham, D., D. Estival, S. Fazio, J. Viethen, F. Cox, R. Dale, S. Cassidy, J. Epps, R. Togneri, M. Wagner, Y. Kinoshita, R. Göcke, J. Arciuli, M. Onslow, T. Lewis, A. Butcher and J. Hajek (2011), 'Building an audio-visual corpus of Australian English: Large corpus collection with an economical portable and replicable Black Box', in *Proceedings of the 12th Annual Conference of the International Speech Communication Association, Interspeech 2011*, pp. 841–4, doi: 10.21437/Interspeech.2011-309.
Burridge, K. and B. Kortmann (2008), *Varieties of English: The Pacific and Australasia*, Berlin: Mouton de Gruyter.
Butcher, A. (1994), 'The phonetics of neutralization: The case of Australian coronals', in J. Windsor Lewis (ed.), *Studies in General and English Phonetics: Essays in Honour of J. D. O'Connor*, London: Routledge, pp. 10–39.
Butcher, A. (2008), 'Linguistic aspects of Australian aboriginal English', *Clinical Linguistics and Phonetics* 22(8), 625–42.
Butcher, A. and V. B. Anderson (2008), 'The vowels of Australian Aboriginal English', in *Proceedings of the 9th Annual Conference of the International Speech Communication Association, Interspeech 2008*, pp. 347–50, doi: 10.21437/Interspeech.2008-145.
Carr, P., J. Durand and M. Pukli (2004), 'The PAC project: Principles and methods', *Tribune internationale des langues vivantes* 36, 24–35.
Cling, M. (1984), 'Vers l'archisystème phonologique de l'anglais', in M. Cling and J. Humbley (eds), *Actes du 2ème colloque d'avril sur l'anglais oral*, Villetaneuse: Université Paris Nord: CELDA, diffusion APVL, pp. 193–204.
Clyne, M. (1968), 'Transference patterns among English–German bilinguals', *ITL* 2, 5–18.
Clyne, M. (1970), 'Migrant English in Australia', in W. S. Ramson (ed.), *English Transported*, Canberra: Australian National University Press, pp. 123–36.
Clyne, M. (ed.) (1976), *Australia Talks: Essays on Australian Immigrant and Aboriginal Languages*, Series D, No. 23, Pacific Linguistics, Canberra: Australian National University Press.
Clyne, M. (1981), '"Second generation" foreigner talk in Australia', in M. Clyne (ed.), *Foreigner Talk*, The Hague: Mouton, pp. 69–80.

Clyne, M., E. Eisikovits and L. Tollfree (2001), 'Ethnic varieties of Australian English', in D. Blair and P. Collins (eds), *Varieties of English around the World: English in Australia*, Amsterdam: John Benjamins, pp. 221–38.

Collins, B. and I. Mees (2008), *Practical Phonetics and Phonetics: A Resource Book for Students*, London, New York: Routledge.

Cox, F. and S. Palethorpe (2006), 'A preliminary acoustic phonetic examination of Lebanese Australian English', in L. Cupples (ed.), *Abstracts of the 15th Australian Language and Speech Conference. Australian Journal of Psychology* 58, 5.

Cruttenden, A. (2001), *Gimson's Pronunciation of English*, 6th edn, London: Edward Arnold.

Cutler, A. (2005), 'Lexical stress', in D. Pisoni and R. Remez (eds), *The Handbook of Speech Perception*, Malden, MA: Blackwell, pp. 264–89.

Delais-Roussarie, E. (2008), 'Corpus et données en phonologie post-lexicale: Forme et statut', *Langages* 3(171), 60–76.

Delbridge, A. (1983), 'On national variants of the English dictionary: The English dictionary in different parts of the world', in R. R. K. Hartmann (ed.), *Lexicography: Principles and Practice*, London: Academia Press, pp. 23–40.

Delbridge, A. et al. (eds) (2009), *The Macquarie Dictionary, Australia's National Dictionary Online*, Sydney: Macquarie Library, <http://www.macquariedictionary.com.au>.

Deschamps, A. (2000), 'La logique des variantes accentuelles de l'anglais', in P. Busuttil (ed.) *Points d'interrogation. Actes du colloque de décembre 1998 sur l'anglais oral*, Pau: Publications de l'Université de Pau et des Pays de l'Adour, pp. 82–98.

Deschamps, A. (2001), 'Stress-patterns, rules and variants: Can stress variation be accounted for?', *Anglophonia* 9, 41–57.

Dixon, R. M. W. (2002), *Australian Languages*, Cambridge: Cambridge University Press.

Dixon, R. M. W. (2008), 'Australian Aboriginal words in dictionaries: A history', *International Journal of Lexicography* 21(2), 129–52.

Dixon, R. M. W. (2011), *The Languages of Australia*, Cambridge: Cambridge University Press.

Dixon, R. M. W., B. Moore, W. S. Ramson and M. Thomas (2006), *Australian Aboriginal Words in English: Their Origin and Meaning*, 2nd edn, South Melbourne: Oxford University Press.

Dixon R. M. W., W. S. Ramson and M. Thomas (1990), *Australian Aboriginal Words in English: Their Origin and Meaning*, Melbourne: Oxford University Press.

Douglas, W. H. (1976), *The Aboriginal Languages of the South-West of Australia*, Canberra: Australian Institute of Aboriginal Studies.

Duchet, J.-L. (1994), *Code de l'anglais oral*, Paris: Ophrys.

Durand, J. (2017), 'Corpus phonology', in M. Aronoff (ed.), *Oxford Research Encyclopedia of Linguistics*, Oxford: Oxford University Press, pp. 1–20.

Durand, J, U. Gut and G. Kristoffersen (eds) (2014), *The Oxford Handbook of Corpus Phonology*, Oxford: Oxford University Press.

Durand, J. and A. Przewozny (2012), 'La phonologie de l'anglais contemporain: Usages, variétés et structure', *Revue Française de Linguistique Appliquée* 17(1), 25–37.

Eades, D. (1993), *Aboriginal English*, PEN 93, Newtown, NSW: Primary Teaching Association.

Eades, D. (2013), *Aboriginal Ways of Using English*, Canberra: Aboriginal Studies Press.

Eriksson, A. and M. Heldner (2015), 'The acoustics of word stress in English as a function of stress level and speaking style', in *Proceedings of the 16th Annual Conference of the International Speech Communication Association, Interspeech 2015*, pp. 41–5, doi: 10.21437/Interspeech.2015-9.

Fielding, J. and W. S. Ramson (1973), 'Settlers and convicts: Firste fynderes of our faire longage', *Southerly* 33(2), 200–16.

Fletcher, J. and J. Harrington (2001), 'High-rising terminals and fall-rise tunes in Australian English', *Phonetica* 58, 215–29.

Fletcher, J., H. Stoakes, D. Loakes and R. Singer (2015), 'Accentual prominence and consonant lengthening and strengthening in Mawng', in *Proceedings of the 18th International Congress of Phonetic Sciences*, ICPhS, Glasgow: University of Glasgow.

Fletcher, J., R. Wales, L. Stirling and I. Mushin (2002), 'A dialogue act analysis of rises in Australian English map task dialogue', in *Proceedings of Speech Prosody 2002*, Aix-en-Provence: Laboratoire Parole et Langage, pp. 299–302.

Fournier, J.-M. (2010), *Manuel d'anglais oral*, Paris: Ophrys.

Guierre, L. (1979), 'Essai sur l'accentuation en anglais contemporain: Éléments pour une synthèse', PhD dissertation, Université Paris 7.

Guierre, L. (1985), 'Remarques sur les conflits en morphophonologie', in M. Cling and J. Humbley (eds), *Actes du 2ème colloque d'avril sur l'anglais oral*, Villetaneuse: Université Paris Nord: CELDA, diffusion APVL, pp. 139–52.

Guierre, L. (1983), 'Grammaire et lexique en phonologie, les oppositions accentuelles catégorielles', in M. Cling and J. Humbley (eds), *Actes du 2ème colloque d'avril sur l'anglais oral*, Villetaneuse: Université Paris Nord: CELDA, diffusion APVL, pp. 127–40.

Gunn, J. S. (1992), 'Social contexts in the history of Australian English', in T. W. Machan and C. T. Scott (eds), *English in Its Social Contexts: Essays in Historical Sociolinguistics*, Oxford: Oxford University Press, pp. 204–29.

Guy, G. and J. Vonwiller (1989), 'The high rising tone in Australian English', in P. Collins and D. Blair (eds), *Australian English: The Language of a New Society*, St Lucia: University of Queensland Press, pp. 21–34.

Hercus, L., F. Hodges and J. Simpson (2002), *The Land is a Map: Placenames of Indigenous Origin in Australia*, Canberra: Pandanus Books/Australian National University Research School of Pacific and Asian Studies.

Hill, R. P. (1967), 'Prospects of the study of early Australian pronunciation', *English Studies* 48(1), 43–52.

Horton, D. (ed.) (1994), *The Encyclopedia of Aboriginal Australia: Aboriginal and Torres Strait Islander History, Society and Culture*, vol. 1, Canberra: Aboriginal Studies Press for the Australian Institute of Aboriginal and Torres Strait Islander Studies.

Horvath, B. (1985), *Variation in Australian English: The Sociolects of Sydney*, Cambridge: Cambridge University Press.

Horvath, B. (2004), 'Australian English: Phonology', in B. Kortmann, E. W. Schneider, K. Burridge, R. Mesthrie and C. Upton (eds), *A Handbook of Varieties of English: A Multimedia Reference Tool*, Berlin: Mouton de Gruyter, pp. 625–44.

Jespersen, A. B. (2016), 'A first look at declarative rises as markers of ethnicity in Sydney', *Proceedings of Speech Prosody 2016*, pp. 143–7, doi: 10.21437/SpeechProsody.2016-30.

Jones, D. (2006), *Cambridge English Pronouncing Dictionary*, 17th edn, Cambridge: Cambridge University Press.

Kiesling, S. F. (2001), 'Australian English and recent migrant groups', in D. Blair and P. Collins (eds), *Varieties of English Around the World: English in Australia*, Amsterdam: John Benjamins, pp. 239–58.

Leitner, G. (1984), 'Australian English or English in Australia: Linguistic identity or dependence in broadcast language', *English World-Wide* 5(1), 55–85.

Leitner, G. (2004), *Australia's Many Voices: Ethnic Englishes, Indigenous and Migrant Languages. Policy and Education*, Berlin: Mouton De Gruyter.

Lo Bianco, J. (1990), 'Making language policy: Australia's experience', in R. B. Baldauf Jr and A. Luke (eds), *Language Planning and Education in Australasia and the South Pacific*, Multilingual Matters 55, Philadelphia: Clevedon.

Malcolm, I. (1995), *Language and Communication Enhancement for Two-Way Education: Report*, Perth, WA: Edith Cowan University.

Malcolm, I. (2004), 'Australian creoles and Aboriginal English: Phonetics and phonology', in B. Kortmann, E. W. Schneider, K. Burridge, R. Mesthrie and C. Upton (eds), *A Handbook of Varieties of English: A Multimedia Reference Tool*, Berlin: Mouton de Gruyter, pp. 656–70.

Malcolm, I. (2008), 'Australian creoles and Aboriginal English: Phonetics and phonology', in K. Burridge and B. Kortmann (2008), *Varieties of English: The Pacific and Australasia*, Berlin: Mouton de Gruyter, pp. 124–41.

Malcolm, I. (2018), 'Australian Aboriginal English and links with culture', in *The TESOL Encyclopedia of English Language Teaching*, pp. 1–7, <https://doi.org/10.1002/9781118784235.eelt0306>.

Malcolm, I. (2021), 'Australian Aboriginal English and linguistic inquiry', in M. Sadeghpour and F. Sharifian (eds), *Cultural Linguistics and World Englishes*, Singapore: Springer.

Malcolm, I. and S. Kaldor (1991), 'Aboriginal English – an overview', in S. Romaine (ed.), *Language in Australia*, Cambridge: Cambridge University Press, pp. 67–83.

Malcolm, I. and M. Koscielecki (1997), *Aboriginality and English: Report to the Australian Research Council*, Mount Lawley, WA: Edith Cowan University.

Martin, M. (2010), 'Lexical stress variation: Key disyllable classes in Australian English', *The Australian Linguistics Society Annual Conference 2010*, Brisbane: University of Queensland.

Martin, M. (2011a), 'De l'accentuation lexicale en anglais australien standard contemporain', PhD dissertation, University of Tours.

Martin, M. (2011b), 'Lexical stress of loanwords from Aboriginal languages in contemporary standard Australian English', paper presented at the 42nd Australian Linguistic Society Conference at Australian National University, Canberra ACT, on 2–4 December 2011.

Mitchell, A. G. (1940), *The Pronunciation of English in Australia: A Lecture Delivered before the Australian English Association on April 1st, 1940*, Sydney: Australasian Medical Publishing.

Mitchell, A. G. and A. Delbridge (1965), *The Pronunciation of English in Australia*, Sydney: Angus and Robertson.
Peters, P. (2007), *The Cambridge Guide to Australian English Usage*, Melbourne: Cambridge University Press.
Peters, P. (2014), 'Differentiation in Australian English', in S. Buschfeld, T. Hoffmann, M. Huber and A. Kautzsch (eds), *The Evolution of Englishes: The Dynamic Model and Beyond*, Amsterdam: John Benjamins.
Przewozny, A. (2016), *La Langue des Australiens: Genèse et description de l'anglais australien contemporain*, Limoges: Lambert-Lucas.
Przewozny, A. and L. Fabre (2018), 'Promouvoir les variétés ethnolectales pour consolider le socle linguistique national australien: Réalité sociolinguistique et enjeux contemporains du New Australian English', Paper presented at the symposium Promoting or Demoting: The Transmission of Minority Languages from Past to Present, held at the Université de Poitiers – Laboratoire FoReLL, Poitiers, France, on 6–7 April 2018.
Przewozny, A. and C. Viollain (2016), 'On the representation and evolution of Australian English and New Zealand English', *Anglophonia: French Journal of English Linguistics*, 21, https://doi.org/10.4000/anglophonia.727.
Przewozny, A., C. Viollain and S. Navarro (eds) (2020), *The Corpus Phonology of English: Multifocal Analyses of Variation*, Edinburgh: Edinburgh University Press.
Schneider, E. W. (2004), 'Global synopsis: Phonetic and phonological variation in English world-wide', in B. Kortmann, E. W. Schneider, K. Burridge, R. Mesthrie and C. Upton (eds), *A Handbook of Varieties of English: A Multimedia Reference Tool*, Berlin: Mouton de Gruyter, pp. 1111–37.
Schneider, E. W. (2007), *Postcolonial English: Varieties Around the World*, Cambridge: Cambridge University Press.
Sutton, P. (1991), 'Language in Aboriginal Australia: Social dialects in a geographic idiom', in S. Romaine (ed.), *Language in Australia*, Cambridge: Cambridge University Press, pp. 49–66.
Tabain, M., G. Breen and A. R. Butcher (2004), 'VC vs CV syllables: A comparison of Aboriginal languages with English', *Journal of the International Phonetic Association* 34(2), 175–200.
Turner, G. W. (1966), *The English Language in Australia and New Zealand*, London: Longman.
Vinson, T. (2008), 'Some lexical variations of Australian Aboriginal English', *Griffith Working Papers in Pragmatics and Intercultural Communication* 1(1), 1–6.
Walsh, M. (1991), 'Overview of indigenous languages of Australia', in S. Romaine (ed.), *Language in Australia*, Cambridge: Cambridge University Press, pp. 27–48.
Warren, J. (1999), 'Wogspeak: Transformations of Australian English', *Journal of Australian Studies* 23(62), 85–94.
Wells, J. C. (2008), *Longman Pronunciation Dictionary*, 3rd edn, Harlow: Pearson Education.
Yuan, J., S. Isard and M. Liberman (2008), 'Different roles of pitch and duration in distinguishing word stress in English', in *Proceedings of the 9th Annual Conference of the International Speech Communication Association, Interspeech 2008*, pp. 885–8.

7 Melodic Complexity and Lexical Stress in Singapore English: An Experimental Study

Gabor Turcsan and Oriana Reid-Collins

0 Introduction

Emerging Englishes, New Englishes or outer-circle Englishes such as Singapore English (SgE) may sound markedly different from native or inner-circle varieties. One of the main perceptive features that distinguishes SgE from inner-circle Englishes is claimed to be its staccato, machine-gun-like rhythm due to its distinctive rhythmic properties, namely syllable timing instead of stress timing. Stressed syllables may not be substantially longer nor pronounced with higher pitch; moreover, vowel reduction in unstressed syllables may not be systematic either (Levis 2005; Bao 1998). The absence of quantity raises an interesting question: while inner-circle Englishes all organise their stress algorithm partly around quantity sensitivity, at least for the non-derived part of the lexicon, how do SgE speakers assign lexical stress (accent) if their system lacks quantity?

This chapter looks at lexical stress patterns in standard SgE. The evidence comes from two types of complementary corpora: (i) recordings following the PAC[1] protocol (informal and formal conversations, text reading), and (ii) findings from a nonce experiment testing SgE native speakers' intuition about the stress of disyllables, which we carried out in 2016. Our nonce experiment follows the protocol of Turcsan and Herment (2015), inspired by Krämer (2009) and Bárkányi (2002). The experiment involves reading tasks with embedded nonce words displaying different phonological and morphological structures forced by the spelling. The exact duplication of the protocol allows us to compare SgE speakers with inner-circle speakers in their stress placement and to shed light to SgE speakers' internalised system with respect to lexical prominence.

In section 1 we briefly discuss some necessary background elements for evaluating the results of the nonce-word test. In section 1.1, we present our object of study by locating the variety of SgE we have access to through our PAC recordings. Section 1.2 is concerned with lexical prominence: we compare findings in the literature with those from our PAC recordings.

Section 2 gives the rationale for our nonce-word test by explaining our methodology. Section 3 describes the results from various points of view: first with respect to other statistical approaches based on the lexicon in 3.1, then by looking at speakers' preferences in 3.2. The link to quantity sensitivity is established in 3.3, constraints on unstressed syllables are explained in 3.4 and finally, possible analogical patterns are discussed in 3.5. Section 4 contains our conclusions. The Appendix shows the bare results of the experiment.

1 Background

The study of any outer-circle[2] (Kachru 1990) or emerging variety of English, and especially that of New Englishes, raises considerable theoretical and methodological problems, and SgE is no exception. Clearly, the intimate relationship between SgE and Standard British English (SBE) cannot be denied. On the one hand, Singapore was a British colony from 1819 to 1963 and, owing to this historical connection, SBE has had a decisive influence on how English is spoken in Singapore today. In addition, SBE still serves as a reference point for education. However, taking SBE as a frame of reference while studying SgE can be misleading since it may obfuscate native emerging patterns. Taking the example of stress, for instance, if SgE has indeed switched to a syllable-timed system, the whole frame of analysis based on the stress-timed system of SBE becomes rather dubious. Clearly, a self-contained descriptive approach abstracting away SBE biases should be favoured over a derived one, provided one manages to define the object of study, which is not an easy task.

Any description of SgE should acknowledge the dynamic nature of the system. Indeed, SgE represents an impressive lectal continuum, ranging from acrolectal to mesolectal and basilectal varieties the like of which we encounter in the description of Standard Aboriginal English (see Chapter 6 of this volume). Acrolectal, prestige varieties are very close to the SBE standard, while Brown (1988) dismisses basilectal Singlish varieties[3] as too inconsistent for any systematic analysis. The object of study, then, should be the conversational mesolects. According to Brown,

> However, considerable variation exists in mesolectal EMS (English in Malaysia and Singapore) speech, dependent on a variety of sociolinguistic factors, notably education and age. For example, there are EMS speakers who consistently distinguish [Received Pronunciation] RP's /i/ and /ɪ/. Others keep these vowels separate most of the time, but there is some overlap, while still others make no distinction, completely conflating the two RP vowels.
>
> (Brown 1988: 132–3)

The speakers we recorded for this experiment were university students at Nanyang Technological University in their early twenties. Educated young speakers such as these clearly have access to the acrolect. In the following two sections we present features that help to situate our speakers' productions on the lectal continuum. This positioning is crucial for an honest interpretation of the experimental data in section 3. We begin first by sketching the vocalic system of SgE in section 1.1. This sketch will be our litmus test for a tentative placement of our speakers' vernacular on the lectal range. Then, in section 1.2, we highlight some rhythmic features of SgE and compare them with our non-experimental productions.

1.1 Vowel systems

The description of SgE vowel systems is critical for understanding the relationship between phonological form and lexical stress preference in the experimental data. Figure 7.1 displays one possible depiction of SgE, based on traditional descriptions (see Bao 1998 for an overview) and on our observations on PAC corpus data.

We can split the vowels in Figure 7.1 first into two major categories: (i) monophthongs and (ii) diphthongs. The five diphthongs are quite similar to those of SBE. We chose to transcribe them with the /j/ and /w/ glides to underline their diphthongal nature and to highlight the notable consonantal reflexes in the centring diphthongs. The monophthong set contains three vowels that alternate between genuine diphthongal realisations and somewhat lengthened monophthongs: /ej/, /ow/ and /æə/. The glide part is presented in parentheses to indicate the variable nature of these pronunciations: the more acrolectal the speaker is, the more diphthongal reflexes they have. Triphthongs are absent from the chart since they are split into two syllables in SgE: *fire* /fajə/ and *hour* /awə/ (Sieuw and Low 2005).

One noticeable feature of this system is the absence of the central lax vowels /ɪ/, /ʊ/ and /ʌ/ of inner-circle Englishes in particular and the somewhat depleted lax set in general. The only 'genuine' lax vowel as far as phonological

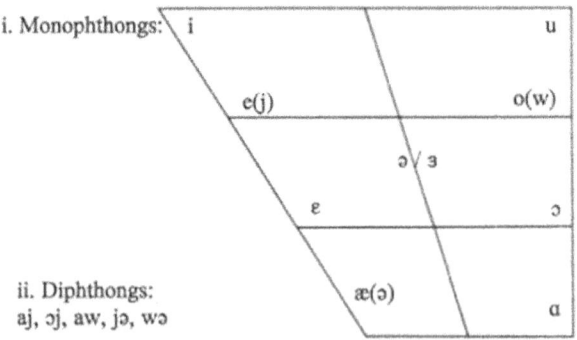

Figure 7.1 SgE (conversational) vowel system

distribution is concerned (for example the ban on occurring in an open monosyllable) is /ɛ/. It seems the system is rebalanced in favour of peripheral and phonologically tense vowels. In section 1.2 a similar rebalancing is described with respect to rhythmic properties of utterances: strong realisations seem to be favoured over weak ones, hence the relative scarcity of reductions. We do not have an explanation for the reasons for these rebalancings, but we surmise that the importance of notions like salience, markedness and perceptual cues in a multi-ethnic and multi-lingual society must have something to do with them.

In order to have a clearer understanding of the systemic properties of vowels in SgE, we have included a correspondence table between SgE and RP. We contend that the comparison with RP is a necessary step, given that educated speakers have early access to it. Figure 7.2 lists the correspondences exemplified with lexical items.

According to Figure 7.2, in conversational SgE, closer to the mesolectal range, the contrast between tense or peripheral /i/ and /u/ and lax or central /ɪ/ and /ʊ/ is neutralised in favour of the tense vowel. The degree of neutralisation clearly depends on the register (see the quote from Brown 1988: 132–3 above): SgE speakers may use the BEAT/BIT and BOOT/BOOK contrasts in formal speech. The conflating of the tense central vowel and schwa does not make much sense to us if we want to separate phonetic realisation from systemic considerations, given their functional differences: schwa denotes a behaviour (reduction) and not a specific quality. Three other contrasts may be neutralised: BET vs BAT, CAUGHT vs COT and STAFF vs STUFF.

Our PAC recordings confirm the variable nature of neutralisations. In conversational data, closer to the mesolect, speakers readily neutralise, especially the contrast in high vowels. However, in more formal tasks, like the text or especially the wordlist readings, speakers make these contrasts, notably with minimal pairs. An extract from the PAC wordlist is shown in Figure 7.3.

The first item in the list is invariably pronounced with a neutralised /i/. However, when our SgE speakers reach examples 20 and 21 in the list, they all differentiate the two, clearly pronouncing /i/ and /ɪ/. The same is true for items 24 /ʊ/ and 25 /u/: when confronted with minimal pairs, speakers seem to

BEAT	iː →	i		BOOT	uː →	u	
BIT	ɪ ↗			BOOK	ʊ ↗		
BET	ɛ →	ɛ		CAUGHT	ɔː →	ɔ	
BAT	æ ↗			COT	ɒ ↗		
BIRD	ɜː →	ə		STAFF	ɑː →	a	
ABOUT	ə ↗			STUFF	ʌ ↗		
BAY	eɪ	e(j)		HOW	aʊ	aw	
BOAT	əʊ	o(w)		BOY	ɔɪ	ɔj	
BARE	ɛə	æ(ə)		HERE	ɪə	jə	
BUY	aɪ	a(j)		POOR	ʊə	wɔ	

Figure 7.2 RP and conversational SgE compared (adapted from Bao 1998)

1. pit	7. sea	13. stairs	19. moor	25. fool
2. pet	8. say	14. err	20. feel	26. fail
3. pat	9. sigh	15. far	21. fill	27. foal
4. pot	10. sue	16. war	22. fell	28. file
5. put	11. stir	17. more	23. fall	
6. putt	12. steer	18. purr	24. full	

Figure 7.3 PAC reading list, extract

have full access to the acrolect, very close to an RP-like system. Nevertheless, some neutralisations seem to have made their way into the acrolect of our speakers: the PET (2) vs PAT (3) contrast is totally absent. Item number 7 is also interesting inasmuch as speakers pronounce it with a fairly long /iː/. This takes us to the question of vowel length in SgE. Traditional descriptions, like the one depicted in Figure 7.1, dispense with phonemic vowel length altogether, based on the assumptions that the contrast is neutralised. The validity of the phonemic length feature has been debated for inner-circle varieties as well from the very early stages of description, and authors vary according to whether they follow: (i) Daniel Jones's tradition and subscribe to a system organised by length, (ii) a more 'phonetic' approach based on quality (for example the American descriptive tradition), or (iii) the mixed system of Gimson, followed by dictionaries in the British tradition. This debate is largely orthogonal to the present study. Our speakers have access to an inner-circle-like acrolectal system with a nearly full set of contrasts. Besides, even the simplified mesolectal system in Figure 7.1 contains phonologically long/tense vowels: in actual fact, 8 out of the 14 vowels are variably or invariably diphthongal. Clearly, it is secondary whether these contrasts are expressed in terms of short/long or lax/tense. We would tentatively use the tense/lax contrast phonologically and reserve length to the phonetics. Phonetic length depends on many factors that are completely independent from the lexicon, such as syllabic position: SgE vowels are substantially longer in open syllables (Brown 1991).

1.2 Lexical stress

The notion of stress is a problematic one in the literature on SgE. Some researchers prefer to substitute the notion of 'stress' with the more neutral term 'prominence' when talking about rhythmic properties, be they word, tone-unit or utterance level. As the focus of this chapter is the discovery of SgE speakers' intuitions underlying the assignment of lexical prominence and limited to disyllabic words only, we have kept the label 'stress' or 'lexical stress' for this behaviour. Obviously, by using the term 'stress' we do not claim that the SBE pattern of stressed syllables being 'longer, louder, higher' or 'unstressed = reduced' directly translates into the SgE system. We henceforth use the term 'stress' only as a convenient label for any manifestation of lexical prominence and not as a shorthand expression for a collection of specific acoustic properties. Section 2 discusses the acoustic cues taken into account when analysing the nonce productions.

1.2.1 Prominence in SgE

One of the distinctive perceptual properties of SgE is its staccato-like rhythm. This perception may give the impression of a certain flatness and *in fine*, the lack of distinction between stressed and unstressed prosodic units, leading to the strong hypothesis that SgE lacks stress altogether. This lack of distinction may come from either (i) the absence or lesser incidence of prominent items or (ii) the absence or lesser incidence of non-prominent items. Levis (2005) shows that the second option is the one that describes SgE best. Levis (2005) compares readings of *The North Wind and the Sun* by SgE speakers from the Singapore English corpus (Deterding and Low 2001) with productions of General American (GA) speakers and finds that SgE speakers use a much larger number of prominent syllables. SgE speakers produce 3.9 prominent syllables for an average tone-unit comprising 10 words of text while the figure drops to 2.7 with GA speakers. Prominence is established on the basis of acoustic cues (pitch protrusion and movement, energy level) complemented by perception tests. The significant difference in the proportion of prominent syllables is due to two major factors. First, the final lexical item of a tone-unit tends to be prominent with a high pitch contour, regardless of lexical category ('*the traveller fold his coat around HIM*'): there are very few non-final tonics. Second, more generally, grammatical or function words behave as lexical words inasmuch as they are (i) not reduced and (ii) display some kind of an acoustic prominence (pitch or intensity).

Bearing all this in mind, the claim that SgE lacks distinctive prominence relations does not seem to be true: there is an average of 6.1 non-prominent syllables out of 10 words. Levis (2005) does not give a detailed description of these non-prominent syllables, but based on a similar text-reading task in the Singapore English PAC corpus, we observe that the non-prominent units largely correspond to the recessive syllables of polysyllabic words, be they pronounced with a reduced vowel or not: ''*Be 'on your 'best be 'haviour and 'be 'happy 'all the 'time*'. Again, in this example, not all grammatical words show prominence either: the pronoun '*your*', the article '*the*' and the conjunction '*and*' are non-prominent with respect to the neighbouring units. On the other hand, an inner-circle speaker would not stress '*on*' and the second '*be*' in a neutral sentence.

To sum up, there seems to be a conspicuous difference between SgE prominence patterns and inner-circle English stress patterns: namely, SgE displays more prominence than SBE or GA. The main difference stems from the propensity of SgE to treat some grammatical words as lexical items and the general lack of de-accenting at the utterance level. However, there seems to be clearly established prominence patterns within lexical items.

These prominence patterns may be further obfuscated by the somewhat different vowel-reduction patterns, discussed in the next section.

1.2.2 Vowel reduction
Vowel-reduction patterns of SgE are significantly different from inner-circle Englishes (Low 1998): most notably, SgE has a marked tendency to use full vowels. This tendency has some important bearings on word stress perception and production in SgE. In inner-circle Englishes, vowel reduction is one of the cues for stress, inasmuch as unstressed vowels tend to lose their distinctive phonological properties and reduce to schwa. Note that while it is true that schwa can only occur in an unstressed position, not all unstressed positions correspond to reduced vowels. Distributional constraints based on syllable structure ('proj[ɛ]ct, st[ɑː]r'vation, ch[eɪ]'otic, 'men[juː]) or lexical marking ([ɔː] 'thentic) may overwrite reduction even in inner-circle Englishes.

Owing to SgE's propensity to treat grammatical words as lexical items, the number of reduced vowels is automatically curtailed in utterances. Now, looking at longer words, the correlation between vowel reduction and non-prominence, albeit present to some extent, is weaker than in inner-circle Englishes. Gek and Deterding (2005) give a statistical analysis of reduced vowels in the first syllable of polysyllabic words, based on SgE conversational data. Their tokens include words spelled with *a*, *o*, and *u*. The remaining letters *i* and *e* are discarded since they are invariably pronounced [ɪ], neutralising the difference between a full and a reduced vowel. They prefer an auditory analysis, given that no reliable acoustic measurements seem to exist for vowel reduction because of the unstable character of F2 according to following consonants. Their results show that although the incidence of reduced vowels is lower than in SBE, 45% of them are still reduced. This figure hides considerable differences between the propensity of individual vowels to reduce: *a*-type vowels almost always reduce (81%), *u* is reduced across the board, while *o*-types tend to keep a full quality with only 31% reduction. In the case of *o*, half of the tokens belong to the prefix *con-/com-* in morphologically complex words (*consider, convinced, computer*): in these words, only 8% of vowels are reduced. The generalisation on *o* seems very strong to us, independently from morphology: unstressed *o* in our nonce tokens is very rarely reduced either (see section 3).

Our PAC recordings confirm the observations about reduction. TIL and YAN, the speakers with the most mesolectal features with respect to their phonemic inventory, are the ones who have the fewest number of reductions. Strikingly, they do not reduce even many of the *a*-type vowels in the reading task, certainly corresponding to the formal register: *ago, collar, vicar, agreed* or *appear* all pronounced with an [ɑ]. The other speakers, despite their closer proximity to the acrolectal range, do not reduce vowels and never syncopate: JER *temporary* [tɛmpɔrɛri], *evenly* [iːvɛnli], *family* [fɛmili] or *behaviour* [bihɛɪviə]. Finally, KEV, the most acrolectal speaker in terms of his phonemic inventory, pronounces the phrase *would have come out* [ˈwʊd ˈhɛf ˈkʌm ˈaʊt] with prominence on each item.

In sum, the lesser incidence of vowel reduction, in part due to the stressing of grammar words, in part lexical, is one of the main rhythmic features of SgE as it contributes to syllable timing. Nevertheless, vowels inside lexical items may and do reduce in recessive positions. Reduction may not be the most important cue to word stress, but it certainly remains one of them.

2 Methodology

This study was conducted with 10 participants at Nanyang Technological University in Singapore by the first author in November 2014. The 10 participants (9 female and 1 male) were students in their early twenties at the time of the recording. They were all of Chinese ethnicity with English as their first language. Two of the participants were also recorded for a full PAC survey, consisting of wordlist and text readings, and formal and informal interviews. The participants did not receive any payment for their participation.

2.1 Materials

The experiment consisted in a reading task of carrier sentences in which 53 nonce words were embedded, as described in Turcsan and Herment (2015). Each nonce word was presented twice, once positioned as a noun and once as a verb, for a total of 106 tokens per participant or 1058 tokens in total[4] (see Appendix).

The nonce words were created based on the principle of syllable shape potentially translating into weight. For a thorough discussion of the concept of weak and strong clusters and their evolution into phonological weight we refer to Chapter 1 of this volume, while the intricate relationship between spelling and stress assignment is explained in Chapter 4. The reader will also find an interesting discussion of the explanatory adequacy of weight vs morphology-based approaches in Chapter 5, although the role of morphology is necessarily diminished in our experimental approach. Given that nonce words do not have lexical properties or marking, the only testable parameters were phonological properties. Turcsan and Herment (2015) explored different combinations of heavy (H) and light (L) syllables as described in Table 7.1 to form nonce words such as LL *befin*, LH *recane*, HL *furna*, or HH *hastelk* following standard syllabification rules (Harris 1994). The backbone of the nonce list contains strings corresponding to the general or regular pattern (in bold). Systematic irregularities linked to the lexicon are present only marginally, notably with prefix-stem structures like *befin* mentioned above. Different spellings were retained to encourage the pronunciation of diphthongs and

Table 7.1 Constraints on English stressed syllables, general pattern in bold, with systematic exceptions in italics

Stress pattern	Nouns		Verbs	
	10	01	10	01
LL	**city**	*abyss*	**vomit, carry**	*omit*
LH	**fellow, missile, menu**	*debate, July, parade*	**swallow**	*cajole, neglect, defend*
HL	**paper**	*hotel*	**feature**	*success*
HH	**hero, disco**	*trombone*	**franchise**	**baptize**

long vowels, and equal numbers of potentially heavy syllables were placed in VV and VC rhymes. As for Turcsan and Herment (2015), our analysis was based on production data. Some forms were pronounced consistently across speakers in the two studies, while others varied either across speakers or between the two studies. For instance, *disper* (/dɪspə/) was routinely produced with a HL structure, while *divey* was realised as either LL (/dɪvi/), LH (/dɪveɪ/), HL (/daɪvi/) or HH (/daɪvɪ/ or /diːveɪ/). This variation is discussed in more detail in section 3.1.

As discussed in section 3.3, the nonce words also included a number of words formed with common prefix + root structures such as *ad* + *nop*, *be* + *pult*, *re* + *cane* or *ex* + *bain*. Although the nonce words lack semantic content, we included these structures to provide an initial look at how they were stressed and as a comparison with Turcsan and Herment (2015).

Other words were formed in order to test Hammond's (1999) claim (illustrated in Table 7.2) that certain word-final structures are not found in English unstressed syllables, namely final clusters and schwa plus noncoronal

Table 7.2 Non-existent final unstressed syllables (*)

		N	A	V
Penult	ə			*
	ə + COR			
	ə + NONCOR		*	*
	ə + C + COR			*
	i o u			
Antepenult	ə			*
	ə + COR		*	*
	ə + NONCOR	*	*	*
	ə + COR + COR		*	*
	I			
	o u		*	*

sequences. These structures are included respectively in our nonce words *meluct* and *lanop* which were thus expected to be stressed on the ultimate syllable.

The carrier sentences used for the task framed each word either as a noun (common noun or proper noun) or as a verb:

My mum likes these _____ / *My mum lives in* _____.
She often _____ *when she's tired.*

The nouns were presented in a plural form and the verbs in the third person singular so as to better integrate them into the language and partially conceal the aim of the experiment.

2.2 Procedure

The nonce words were initially tested in Turcsan and Herment (2015) by three native speakers; the Turcsan and Herment (2015) experiment was then carried out with ten native speakers of English working at Aix-Marseille University. We kept the same experiment design as it yielded interesting results and as a means of comparison between varieties. The sentences were given to each participant just before the recording started, and each sentence was read once. The participants did not guess the aim of the task.

2.3 Annotation

The productions were analysed separately by the two authors. For 3 of the 10 speakers, the authors agreed on approximately 90% of the tokens and easily put to rest any doubts on other cases. For 5 of the other subjects, the authors disagreed on 30% of the tokens, and for 2 subjects, on 40% of the tokens. Perceiving prominence is far from being a trivial issue in SgE compared with the productions of inner-circle speakers. In Turcsan and Herment (2015) only a tiny minority of forms had to be put to further scrutiny.

The disagreements generally involved which acoustic correlates were to be taken into account. Bao (1998), following Tay (1982), claims that the main correlates used in SgE are length and loudness. Tan (2005) finds that length and pitch are taken into account in prominence perception by SgE speakers. Our experiment found that pitch, length, loudness, vowel quality and even aspiration of preceding plosives were all potential correlates to prominence. The speakers who used several correlates proved to be less subject to disagreement, especially those who produced more vowel reduction. The three speakers in this latter case all tended to use an acrolectal variety of SgE, confirmed by PAC recordings of conversational and read data. In other cases of disagreement, the first author noted different pitch patterns, in particular a specific L HL pattern (see example in Figure 7.4). These patterns differ from those generally expected in native varieties of English, especially American

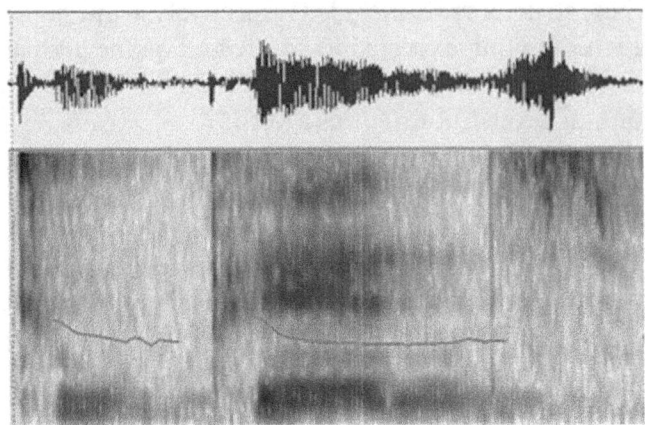

Figure 7.4 SgE iambic pitch pattern (NAO_tupan_verb)

English. This result conforms to the literature on SgE (Tan 2005) and, more widely, to other new varieties of English (for example Wiltshire and Moon 2003 for Indian English compared with American English word stress).

3 Results

3.1 Overall results

Table 7.3 compares figures for trochees found in the present study with those from three other corpus-based quantitative approaches on inner-circle varieties of English, including Turcsan and Herment (2015). The percentages of trochees (/10/) for verbs and nouns are listed with number of word tokens in parentheses. As can been seen in Table 7.3, the SgE corpus revealed a markedly different pattern from the other three corpora.

Hammond's (1999) study is based on a random sample of 20,000 words of different texts in American English. Descloux et al. (2010) only give figures for verbs; their data are based on electronic versions of the *Cambridge English Pronouncing Dictionary* (Jones 2011), the *Longman Pronunciation Dictionary* (Wells 2008) and the *Macquarie Dictionary* (Delbridge 2005).

Table 7.3 Penult stress in disyllables

/10/	Turcsan and Reid-Collins	Turcsan and Herment (2015)	Hammond (1999)	Descloux et al. (2010)
V + N	40% (1058)	62% (1060)	71% (7018)	NA
V	26% (529)	48% (530)	50% (2072)	46.6% (Dict.)
N	54% (529)	76% (530)	80% (3652)	NA

As seen in Table 7.3, the inner-circle preference for trochees shown in the three other corpora does not hold for our SgE data. SgE nouns can be stressed on either the penultimate or the ultimate syllable, whereas for inner-circle varieties, nouns are preferably trochees. Verbs, which are alternatively trochees or iambs in inner-circle varieties, are preferably iambs for SgE speakers. These results confirm observations in the literature that stress in SgE tends to shift towards the end of the word (Tongue 1979; Platt and Weber 1980; Tay 1982, cited in Bao 1998). This result also reflects perceptual patterns: SgE speakers expect to hear prominence on final syllables (Tan 2005). Interestingly, this iambic preference is the exact opposite of what we can find in Standard Aboriginal English, where the vernacular feature would be trochaic preference (see Chapter 6 of this volume).

These results confirm the rationale for using experimental data in order to better understand underlying patterns. The speakers of this experiment, all close to the acrolectal range, follow inner-circle 'standard' word stress patterns in their conversational and read data. Just by analysing these productions, we do not learn much about their intuitions. One only uses words in conversation that one knows, hence the absence of any difference between our SgE data and inner-circle English with respect to word stress. However, once stripped of lexical, stored information, mesolectal features inevitably surface. We surmise that had it been possible to test speakers with unknown but existing English words, the results would have been similar, with a marked shift towards iambs.

3.2 Speakers' preference

One of our research questions concerns the extent to which the English system of word stress is lexically based or phonologically based. In a fully lexically based system, a nonce test would produce random answers and no agreement as speakers would have no cues as to what to stress. In a purely phonological system, speakers would fully agree on stress. Previous literature points to a typologically mixed system for English, as did Turcsan and Herment (2015). We thus expected to find a mixed system in SgE, and this finding was confirmed.

We split the data into three groups depending on the number of participants who agreed on items:

- Set A (no agreement): 4, 5 or 6 out of 10 speakers disagreed (5_5, 6_4, 4_6)
- Set B (agreement): 0 or 1 out of 10 speakers disagreed (0_10, 10_0, 1_9, 9_1)
- Set C (preference): 2 or 3 out of 10 speakers disagreed (2_8, 8_2, 3_7, 7_3).

The percentages of agreement were calculated using the total number of tokens (1058 words). Agreement figures were found to be remarkably close to those calculated for the inner-circle participants in Turcsan and Herment (2015). This similarity is a welcome result since it indicates that our ten SgE speakers share strong feelings about the rhythmic structure of these words, to the same extent as inner-circle speakers do. As we have seen above, these preferences contrast markedly with respect to right or left stress; nevertheless, they point to the existence of a certain, albeit different, system.

Set A, the smallest set, includes 22% of items (compared with 23.5% in the inner-circle group), including 15 nouns and 7 verbs. These figures include three of the same noun and verb tokens: *calben, manem* and *trotint*. These items turned out to be the most difficult when it comes to assigning stress, possibly because their final syllables end in a nasal. However, on closer inspection, we can find strings with a similar phonological shape in Set B (*befin* V, *anem* N) thus the reason must lie elsewhere. All four possible weight configurations (LL, HH, HL, LH) are distributed among these items with LH representing only two items.

The participants agreed on 34% of the items (Set B), compared with 30% for inner-circle speakers. These include 13 trochee nouns, 6 iamb nouns, 17 iamb verbs and 1 trochee verb. Five noun/verb pairs are included. The speakers tended to agree on trochee nouns (13 vs 6) and felt very strongly about iambic-patterned verbs (17 vs 1). There are four /01/ agreement verbs (*befin, clantew, foslaint, tupan*). However, the corresponding nominal forms all belong to the random Set A. Conversely, four agreement nouns (*adna, apel, disper, furna*) switch to the random set in their verbal form. This shows that the strong verb vs noun dichotomy of inner-circle Englishes exists in SgE as well, as speakers do not hesitate or agree on a specific phonological string, but on a specific verbal or nominal form. There are five words (*begoin, calbain, ducasp, recane, tupane*) with iambic agreement in both their nominal and verbal forms, with a predominant LH structure.

Finally, 44% of the items reached 'preference' (Set C), or 70–80% agreement, compared with 46.5% preference for inner-circle speakers. By conflating Set C with Set B we obtain the superset that excludes the random productions of Set A. This superset represents 78% of tokens, indicating that SgE speakers have strong intuitions about three quarters of the items.

3.3 Quantity sensitivity

The issue of syllable weight in SgE is more complex than in inner-circle varieties due in part to SgE's emerging system. We considered various options in determining syllable weight. One possibility was to assign weight resting on RP considerations, based on the proof from the PAC wordlists and texts that SgE speakers have access to the RP-like acrolectal SgE variety as discussed in section 1.1 above. However, as noted in section 3.1, a number of mesolectal features surface in speakers' productions in the nonce experiment. We thus based weight assignments on the conversational SgE system

(Figure 7.1) combined with evidence from speakers' productions; our results are shown in Table 7.4.

It should be noted that our SgE speakers' productions were more variable than Turcsan and Herment's (2015) inner-circle data. For instance, the nonce token *assey* was produced alternatively as /ˈɛsi/, /ɛˈsi/, /ˈɛseɪ/ and /ɛˈseɪ/, and *abmone* was produced as /ɛbˈmown/, /ˈɛbmown/, /ˈɛbmən/ and /əbˈmown/. Variation in back vowels in the tokens *folaint*, *rotel*, *trosey* and *trotint* tended to correspond to different phonological parsings of the word. For example, when the token *trosey* was pronounced as a trochee, a lax vowel[5] tended to be followed by a voiceless coronal sibilant /ˈtrɔsi/, whereas a tense vowel was followed by a voiced sibilant /ˈtrowzi/. These cases were all counted accordingly as either heavy or light occurrences in Table 7.4. However, all in all, the issue of syllable weight in SgE is far from being resolved, and our results should be taken with caution.

Generally, syllable weight influences stress placement (63% of all HL tokens vs 19% of LH tokens are trochees) but does not override the overall SgE preference for right stress. This iambic preference is especially strong for verbs in all categories, including HL verbs.

All the occurrences of LH trochee verbs are dispreferred: *assey* (3_7), *bickean* (1_9), *capult* (2_8), *galeaft* (1_9), *linue* (2_8), *meluct* (2_8), *nabbast* (3_7), *nabelk* (2_8), *plegoin* (2_8), *tupane* (1_9), *trotint*[6] (2_5). Only *assey*, *nabbast* and *nabelk* have a slightly higher percentage of trochee occurrences.

HL iamb verbs include *adna* (6_4), *adnop* (3_7), *apel** (0_1), *disper* (5_5), *divey** (1_1), *fisper* (8_2), *furna* (6_4), *ganton* (3_7), *rotel** (1_5), *tincton* (3_7), *trosey** (3_3), *urfin* (3_7), *urfy* (3_7). Adnop, ganton, rotel, tincton, urfin and urfy all have preferred stress on the right despite their HL syllable structure. Note that four out of these six items end in a sonorant, more specifically, a nasal consonant. Iambic preference may indicate that not all final consonants are extrametrical in English (Hayes 1982) and that sonorants may be moraic after all and project a weight unit.

Nouns seem to be more sensitive to syllable weight – or less sensitive to the 'right-stress' SgE pattern. LL and HH nouns are split between left and right stress, with a slight to moderate left-stress preference. Three quarters of LH nouns are preferably right-stressed, whereas three quarters of HL nouns are left-stressed.

Table 7.4 SgE trochees according to syllable weight

Grammatical category of trochees	Total	LL	HH	LH	HL
V + N	**40%**	47%	41%	19%	63%
V	**26%**	30%	24%	12%	45%
N	**53%**	64%	57%	26%	81%

LH trochee nouns include *assey* (9_1), *bepult* (2_8), *bickean* (2_8), *capult* (5_5), *debilk* (2_8), *galeaft* (2_8), *linue* (6_4), *meluct* (2_8), *nabbast* (3_7), *nabelk* (2_8), *plegoin* (3_7), *recane* (1_9), *tupane* (1_9), and *trotint** (2_1). Only *assey*, *capult*, and *linue* secure a larger share of trochee occurrences.

The group of HL iamb nouns lists the following items: *calben* (6_4), *ganton* (6_4), *rotel** (1_5), *tincton* (1_9), *trosey** (1_6), *urfin* (8_2) and *urfy* (4_6). *Rotel* (possibly by analogy with *hotel*, see section 3.5), *tincton*, *trosey* and *urfy* are predominantly iambs. Though trochee LH and iamb HL occurrences are generally dispreferred, verbs in particular somewhat override syllable weight, whereas nouns are more split.

Now, let us compare the degree of weight sensitivity between the SgE and the inner-circle (IC) data. Table 7.5 includes percentages from both corpora.

As compared with inner-circle data, the significant shift towards iambs becomes apparent in every category except for HL nouns, where the figures are similar in both varieties. Heavy final verbs are overwhelmingly iambic in SgE compared with inner-circle English, while the difference is somewhat lesser for nouns. When there is no difference in weight, with an HH structure, there is a slight preference for trochaic nouns. The preference for trochees is more pronounced with LL nouns. The differing figures for noun tokens show that the inner-circle strong preference for trochaic nouns influences SgE speakers and counterbalances their iambic parsing.

3.4 Constraints on unstressed syllables

The English lexicon contains various gaps as far as the phonological make-up of words is concerned. Some of these gaps seem to be accidental, while others may be linked to deeply rooted structural properties of phonological strings. Table 7.2 in section 2.1, inspired by Hammond (1999), lists certain non-existent combinations of a rhythmic structure coupled with a specific melodic content. We included two of these combinations in our tokens. First, we considered the ban on sequences of a final schwa plus two consonants in verbs. Translated into positive terms, in order to get rid of these configurations, one would have to stress the final syllable and turn the schwa into a full vowel.[7] Indeed, in a rule-based approach, one rule would state that 'verbs ending in a consonant cluster are stressed on their last syllable', a stance taken by Carr (2013), for instance. Table 7.6 displays ten words ending in a consonant

Table 7.5 SgE and inner-circle (IC) trochees according to syllable weight

/10/	LL		HH		LH		HL	
Corpus	SgE	IC	SgE	IC	SgE	IC	SgE	IC
V	42%	30%	57%	24%	19%	12%	78%	45%
N	84%	64%	83%	57%	56%	26%	89%	81%

Table 7.6 Number of trochees in SgE (bold) and inner-circle varieties (in parentheses) for CC final verbs

bepult	capult	dilact	finlact	galeaft	hastelk	meluct	nabbast	nabelk	trotint
2 (0)	**2** (0)	**3** (6)	**8** (7)	**1** (2)	**3** (7)	**2** (4)	**3** (3)	**2** (3)	**4** (6)

cluster together with the number of trochees when produced in a verbal position in SgE. We also include the number of trochees produced by inner-circle speakers from the Turcsan and Herment (2015) experiment.

If the generalisation were a very strong constraint in English, we would expect across the board iambic stress in our data. The results show that although trochees are the clear minority in our speakers' productions, we do find some nevertheless. In this respect, these productions are quite similar to inner-circle intuitions. Taking into account both corpora, some tokens stand out: *finlact, trotint, hastelk* and perhaps *dilact*. All these strings are potential HH structures, which explains their propensity for a trochaic rhythm. Syllable weight may be the real clue even for the well-behaved iambic set: they all display potential LH structures and, following regular stress rules for verbs (see Table 7.1), they are end-stressed. Disyllabic verbs ending in a consonant cluster may all have LH structure in the lexicon, a hypothesis which should be tested on dictionary data. The behaviour of HH words sheds some doubt on the validity of the constraint that requires iambs for CC# verbs: it may be the result of a static distributional regularity in the lexicon instead of an active phonological constraint.

Table 7.7 shows the behaviour of the tokens potentially corresponding to a final syllable containing a schwa + noncoronal obstruent. According to the generalisations of Table 7.2, disyllabic verbs in English never end in ə + C (-cor), meaning that these types of words are expected to display iambic stress instead. The only exception, according to Hammond (1999), is the verb *gallop*. There are two possible interpretations of this static lexical regularity: either it is a historical accident or there are hard-wired phonological reasons underlying the pattern. If the latter is true, we may give a rhythmic interpretation to this state of affairs. It may well be the case that word-final noncoronals contribute to syllable weight by projecting a mora after all. Since heavy final verbs are right-stressed, we expect iambic productions. The data in Table 7.7 are interesting in this respect.

Table 7.7 Number of trochees in SgE (bold) and inner-circle varieties (in parentheses) for VC noncoronals

Token	Adnop V	Adnop N	Lanop V	Lanop N
Trochees SgE **(IC)**	**3** (3)	**10** (7)	**2** (3)	**8** (9)

First, note that the SgE and inner-circle productions, although not identical, point to similar conclusions. Second, the verbal pattern is markedly different from the nominal one, with verbs showing a clear preference for iambs and, conversely, nouns tending to be trochees. For SgE speakers this is especially the case with *adnop*, probably because the first heavy syllable attracts stress in the nominal form in a uniform fashion, while the verbal form is right-stressed 7 times out of 10. These productions seem to indicate that the special status of noncoronal final verbs is far from being a mere lexical accident and that an active phonological pattern is well in operation.

3.5 Lexical effects

Despite the lack of meaning of the nonce words, it is possible that an analogical effect was present either from the English lexicon (standard or specifically SgE terms) or from the nonce tokens themselves. In addition, it is possible that speakers applied morphological analogies to the nonce words by way of a Latinate prefix + bound root structure. As we note in section 2, a number of nonce words were intentionally created with the purpose of testing if and when speakers would rely on analogies to stress these morphologically opaque items. Results are shown in Table 7.8 for SgE, with a comparison with inner-circle varieties in Table 7.9.

Knowing that SgE prefers right stress, especially for verbs, it is difficult to separate out the items that may be influenced by analogical internal morphology. In addition, a number of items have syllable weights that further confound the question. Surprisingly, the six equally weighted nouns in the prefixed-like words are actually all predominantly left-stressed (compared with 30% of LL nouns and 24% of HH nouns overall), except for *exbain*

Table 7.8 Behaviour of prefixed-like words in SgE

BE+N: 8_22	EX+N: 3_6*	DE+N: 2_8	A+N: 27_3	AB+N: 9_1
BE+V: 1_29	EX+V: 1_9	DE+V: 0_10	A+V: 11_19	AB+V: 2_8
DI+N: 8_2	DIS+N: 10_0	AD+N: 20_0	RE+N: 1_9	
DI+V: 2_8	DIS+V: 5_5	AD+V: 9_11	RE+V: 0_10	

Table 7.9 Behaviour of prefixed-like words in inner-circle varieties (Turcsan and Herment 2015)

BE+N: 17_13	EX+N: 8_2	DE+N: 5_5	A+N: 24_6	AB+N: 7_3
BE+V: 0_30	EX+V: 2_8	DE+V: 1_9	A+V: 7_23	AB+V: 2_8
DI+N: 6_4	DIS+N: 9_1	AD+N: 17_3	RE+N: 2_8	
DI+V: 6_4	DIS+V: 7_3	AD+V: 11_9	RE+V: 3_7	

(LL *befin* 6_4, *anem** 8_1, *apel** 6_1; HH *abmone** 8_1, *disper* 10_0 and *exbain* 3_6). In any case, more extensive data would be necessary to draw meaningful conclusions.

It is possible that some tokens were influenced by lexical analogies, such as *rotel*–hotel. *Rotel* produced as a noun was right-stressed in 9 out of 10 productions but also pronounced with a tense back vowel in the first syllable / ro(w) 'tɛl/, unlike most of the right-stressed productions of *folaint*, *trosey* and *trotint*. In addition, *fisper* and *disper* were uniformly left-stressed, especially in their nominal forms (10_0 for each), perhaps evoking *whisper*. *Sonnel* was also highly preferred as a trochee (9_1 for both nominal and verbal forms), perhaps due to an analogy with *sonnet*, though the verbal form is more elusive. *Capult* (5_5) does not seem to have been influenced by the possible *catapult*.

A final possibility is that analogies would occur within the experiment, as each form appeared twice, once as a noun and once as a verb. We attempted to prevent this by separating the tokens from each other as best we could in the list, and the speakers did not read over the sentences before the experiment began. We thus did not find any strong analogical patterns in our data.

4 Conclusions

This chapter set out to characterise lexical stress or prominence patterns of Singapore English based on two types of evidence: conversational and read data following the PAC protocol and a nonce word test following a similar experiment with inner-circle speakers (Turcsan and Herment 2015). Our speakers, university students, belong to the acrolectal range and show no notable difference with inner-circle speakers in the PAC data as far as the placement of word stress is concerned. However, the lack of vowel reduction in grammatical words in general and a lesser incidence of reduction in recessive positions of lexical words in particular all contribute to a vernacular rhythm resembling a syllable-timed system.

The nonce word experiment proved very useful to uncover mesolectal patterns pertaining to SgE. Indeed, our speakers' intuitions are markedly different from those of inner-circle speakers in several respects. Notwithstanding these differences, our speakers' productions point to the existence of a coherent system. The ten speakers show strong preference for three quarters of the tokens, leaving just a quarter of them in the random set. In this respect, the robustness of their system is very close to what we can find with inner-circle speakers. Moreover, the verb vs noun dichotomy remains critical in establishing stress patterns for SgE speakers as well.

The major difference in prominence patterns can be attributed to a generalised switch towards final, iambic stress, especially for verbs. Three quarters of the verbal tokens are iambs compared with only a half for inner-circle speakers. Approximately half of the nouns show iambic preference while the inner-circle speaker experiment only resulted in one quarter of iambs. Verbs can be iambs with a light final syllable, while nouns tend to be trochaic with a light ult.

The nonce word test allowed us to test the validity of some static distributional lexical patterns as well. The majority of verbs ending in a consonant cluster are right-stressed, but the data seem to indicate a strong tendency instead of an absolute ban, the like of which we can find in the lexicon. Verbs ending in a noncoronal consonant tend to have iambic stress confirming that the absence of *gallop*-like trochaic verbs is not an accidental gap in the lexicon.

Our findings give support to the use of experimental data, especially in the discovery of hidden patterns like mesolectal features hidden under an acrolectal cover. Experiments may also help to separate active dynamic patterns from static distributional accidents. We thus believe that experimental evidence, despite its 'unnatural' character, may be a useful complement to corpora based on 'natural' speech data.

Appendix

A7.1 Results of a nonce experiment testing SgE native speakers' intuition about the stress of disyllables

	JAC	JAS	JER	KEV	NAO	PHY	SAM	SIR	TIL	YAN	
abmone (n)	L	L	R	L	L	L	L	L	L	L	9_1
abmone (v)	R	R	R	R	L	L	R	R	R	R	2_8
adna (n)	L	L	L	L	L	L	L	L	L	L	10_0
adna (v)	R	L	R	L	L	L	L	L	R	R	6_4
adnop (n)	L	L	L	L	L	L	L	L	L	L	10_0
adnop (v)	R	L	R	R	L	R	R	R	R	L	3_7
anem (n)	L	L	R	R	R	R	R	L	R	L	4_6
anem (v)	L	R	R	R	R	R	R	L	R	L	3_7
apel (n)	L	L	R	L	L	L	L	L	L	L	9_1
apel (v)	R	L	R	L	R	L	R	L	R	L	5_5
assey (n)	L	L	L	L	L	L	L	L	R	L	9_1
assey (v)	R	L	R	L	R	R	L	R	R	R	3_7
befin (n)	L	R	R	L	L	L	L	L	R	R	6_4
befin (v)	R	R	R	R	L	R	R	R	R	R	1_9
begoin (n)	R	R	R	R	R	R	R	R	R	R	0_10
begoin (v)	R	R	R	R	R	R	R	R	R	R	0_10
bepult (n)	R	R	R	L	R	L	R	R	R	R	2_8
bepult (v)	R	R	R	R	R	R	R	R	R	R	2_8
bickean (n)	R	R	L	L	R	R	R	R	R	R	2_8
bickean (v)	R	R	R	L	R	R	R	R	R	R	1_9
calbain (n)	R	R	R	R	L	R	R	R	R	R	1_9

A7.1 (continued)

	JAC	JAS	JER	KEV	NAO	PHY	SAM	SIR	TIL	YAN	
calbain (v)	L	R	R	R	R	R	R	R	R	R	1_9
calben (n)	L	R	L	L	L	R	R	L	L	R	6_4
calben (v)	R	L	L	L	R	R	R	L	R	R	4_6
capult (n)	L	L	R	R	R	R	R	L	L	L	5_5
capult (v)	R	L	R	R	R	R	R	R	R	L	2_8
clantew (n)	R	L	R	L	L	R	R	L	R	R	4_6
clantew (v)	R	R	R	L	R	R	R	R	R	R	1_9
debilk (n)	R	R	R	L	R	L	R	R	R	R	2_8
debilk (v)	R	R	R	R	R	R	R	R	R	R	0_10
dilact (n)	L	L	R	L	R	L	R	L	L	L	7_3
dilact (v)	R	L	R	L	R	R	R	L	R	R	3_7
disper (n)	L	L	L	L	L	L	L	L	L	L	10_0
disper (v)	L	L	L	R	R	R	L	L	L	L	7_3
divey (n)	L	L	R	L	L	R	L	L	L	L	8_2
divey (v)	R	R	R	L	R	R	L	R	R	R	2_8
divvey (n)	R	L	R	L	R	R	L	L	R	R	4_6
divvey (v)	R	R	R	L	R	R	L	R	R	R	2_8
ducasp (n)	R	R	R	R	R	R	R	R	R	R	0_10
ducasp (v)	R	R	R	R	R	R	R	R	R	R	0_10
exbain (n)	R	R	R	L	R	L	R	R	R	L	3_7
exbain (v)	R	R	R	L	R	R		R	R	R	1_8
finlact (n)	L	L	L	L	L	L	L	L	R	L	9_1
finlact (v)	L	R	R	L	L	L	L	L	L	L	8_2
fisper (n)	L	L	L	L	L	L	L	L	L	L	10_0
fisper (v)	L	L	L	L	R	L	L	L	R	L	8_2
folaint (n)	R	R	L	L	R	L	R	R	R	R	3_7
folaint (v)	R	R	R	R	R	R	R	R	R	R	0_10
foslaint (n)	L	R	R	L	L	L	R	R	L	L	6_4
foslaint (v)	R	R	R	R	R	R	R	R	R	R	0_10
furna (n)	L	L	L	L	L	L	L	L	L	L	10_0
furna (v)	L	L	R	L	R	L	L	L	R	R	6_4
furnoy (n)	L	L	L	L	L	R	R	L	L	L	8_2
furnoy (v)	R	R	R	R	R	R	L	L	R	R	2_8
galeaft (n)	R	R	R	L	R	R	R	R	R	L	2_8
galeaft (v)	R	R	R	R	R	R	R	R	R	L	1_9
ganton (n)	R	L	R	L	L	L	R	L	R	L	6_4
ganton (v)	R	R	R	L	L	R	R	R	L	R	3_7
gapel (n)	L	L	R	L	L	L	R	L	R	L	7_3
gapel (v)	R	R	R	L	L	R	R	L	R	R	3_7
gaton (n)	R	R	R	L	L	R	R	R	R	L	3_7
gaton (v)	R	R	R	R	R	R	R	R	R	R	0_10
hastelk (n)	R	R	R	L	L	R	L	L	R	L	5_5
hastelk (v)	R	R	R	L	R	L		R	R	L	3_6
lanop (n)	L	L	L	L	L	L	R	L	R	L	8_2

A7.1 (continued)

	JAC	JAS	JER	KEV	NAO	PHY	SAM	SIR	TIL	YAN	
lanop (v)	R	R	R	R	R	L	R	L	R	R	2_8
linue (n)	L	R	R	L	L	L	R	L	R	L	6_4
linue (v)	R	L	R	R	R	L	R	R	R	R	2_8
manem (n)	L	R	L	L	R	R	R	L	R	L	5_5
manem (v)	L	R	L	L	R	L	R	L	R	L	6_4
meluct (n)	R	R	R	L	R	L	R	R	R	R	2_8
meluct (v)	R	R	R	L	R	R	R	L	R	R	2_8
nabbast (n)	L	R	R	R	L	L	R	R	R	R	3_7
nabbast (v)	L	R	R	L	R	L	R	R	R	R	3_7
nabelk (n)	R	R	R	L	R	R	R	R	R	L	2_8
nabelk (v)	R	R	R	R	R	R	R	L	R	L	2_8
plegoin (n)	R	R	L	L	R	L	R	R	R	R	3_7
plegoin (v)	R	L	R	L	R	R	R	R	R	R	2_8
relbene (n)	R	R	L	L	R	R	R	R	R	L	3_7
relbene (v)	R	R	R	L	R	R	R	R	R	L	2_8
recane (n)	R	R	R	L	R	L	R	R	R	R	2_8
recane (v)	R	R	R	R	R	R	R	R	R	R	0_10
rotel (n)	R	R	R	L	R	R	R	R	R	R	1_9
rotel (v)	R	R	R	L	R	L	R	L	R	R	3_7
sonnel (n)	L	L	R	L	L	L	L	L	L	L	9_1
sonnel (v)	L	L	R	L	L	L	L	L	L	L	9_1
sturmone (n)	R	L	L	R	L	L	L	L	L	L	8_2
sturmone (v)	R	R	R	L	R	L	R	L	R	R	3_7
tatick (n)	L	R	L	L	L	L	R	R	R	L	6_4
tatick (v)	R	R	R	R	R	L	R	R	R	R	1_9
tinctain (n)	L	R	L	L	L	L	R	L	R	R	6_4
tinctain (v)	L	R	R	L	L	R	R	L	R	R	4_6
tincton (n)	L	R	L	L	L	L	L	L	L	L	9_1
tincton (v)	R	R	L	L	R	R	L	R	R	R	3_7
trosey (n)	L	L	L	L	L	L	L	L	R	L	9_1
trosey (v)	R	R	R	L	R	R	L	R	L	R	3_7
trotint (n)	L	L	L	L	L	R	L	R	R	L	7_3
trotint (v)	R	R	L	L	L	R	R	L	R	R	4_6
tupan (n)	R	L	R	L	R	L	R	R	L	R	4_6
tupan (v)	R	R	R	L	R	R	R	R	R	R	1_9
tupane (n)	R	R	R	L	R	R	R	R	R	R	1_9
tupane (v)	R	R	R	L	R	R	R	R	R	R	1_9
urfin (n)	L	L	L	L	L	L	L	R	R	L	8_2
urfin (v)	R	R	L	L	L	R	R	R	R	R	3_7
urfy (n)	L	R	L	L	R	R	L	R	R	R	4_6
urfy (v)	R	L	R	R	R	R	L	R	R	L	3_7

Notes

1. Phonologie de l'Anglais Contemporain – Phonology of Contemporary English, see Durand and Przewozny (2012, 2015).
2. Recent literature on varieties of English challenges the traditional native/non-native dichotomy as presenting an overly simplistic view of the myriad ways in which English is used throughout the world. A number of different terms have been proposed to better describe this complex linguistic reality. Kachru (1990), for instance, proposes a widely adopted scalar view with an intermediate category he calls 'outer circle' to describe emerging second language varieties, as opposed to the two extremes: 'inner circle' (L1/native) and 'expanding circle' (non-native). In Singapore, English is clearly not a non-native language; in fact, the younger generation are essentially inner-circle English speakers. However, in line with current literature on SgE, we have adopted the label 'outer-circle' as a means of comparison with other work on this variety.
3. For a discussion of the fairly complicated language-use scene in Singapore and the place of Singlish, see Bao (2015).
4. One participant inadvertently omitted two sentences and thus two nonce words in the reading.
5. Note that /ɔ/ corresponds to RP lax /ɒ/.
6. The items marked by an asterisk were counted in two (or more) different categories depending on speaker productions, as discussed above.
7. Clearly, there are many possible repair strategies; getting rid of one of the consonants would be an equally possible move in languages other than English.

References

Bao, Z. (1998), 'The sounds of Singapore English', in J. Foley, T. Kandiah, Z. Bao, A. F. Gupta, L. Alsagoff, C. L. Ho, L. Wee, I. S. Talib and W. Bokhorst-Heng (eds), *English in New Cultural Contexts: Reflections from Singapore*, Singapore: Singapore Institute of Management, pp. 152–74.

Bao, Z. (2015), *The Making of Vernacular Singapore English: System, Transfer, and Filter*, Cambridge: Cambridge University Press.

Bárkányi, Z. (2002), 'A fresh look at quantity sensitivity in Spanish', *Linguistics* 40, 375–94.

Brown, A. (1988), 'The staccato effect in the pronunciation of English in Malaysia and Singapore', in J. Foley (ed.), *New Englishes: The Case of Singapore*, Singapore: Singapore University Press, pp. 115–28.

Brown, A. (1991), *Pronunciation Models*, Singapore: Singapore University Press.

Carr, P. (2013), *English Phonetics and Phonology*, 2nd edn, Oxford: Wiley Blackwell.

Delbridge, A. (2005), *The Macquarie Dictionary*, 5th edn, Sydney: Macquarie University.
Descloux, E., I. Girard, J.-M. Fournier, P. Fournier and M. Martin (2010), 'Structure, variation, usage and corpora: The case of word stress assignment in disyllabic verbs', Paper presented at the PAC 2010 Conference, Montpellier, France, on 13–14 September 2010.
Deterding, D. and E. L. Low (2001), 'The NIE corpus of spoken Singapore English (NIECSSE)', *SAAL Quarterly* 56, 2–5.
Durand, J. and A. Przewozny (2012), 'La phonologie de l'anglais contemporain: Usages, variétés et structure', *Revue Française de Linguistique Appliquée* 17(1), 25–37.
Durand, J. and A. Przewozny (2015), 'La variation et le programme PAC: Phonologie de l'anglais contemporain', in I. Brulard, P. Carr and J. Durand (eds), *La prononciation de l'anglais contemporain dans le monde: Variation et structure*, Toulouse: Presses Universitaires du Midi, pp. 55–91.
Gek, H. M. and D. Deterding (2005), 'Reduced vowels in conversational Singapore English', in D. Deterding, A. Brown and L. E. Ling (eds), *English in Singapore: Phonetic Research on a Corpus*, Singapore: McGraw Hill Asia (Education), pp. 54–63.
Hammond, M. (1999), *English Phonology*, Oxford: Oxford University Press.
Harris, J. (1994), *English Sound Structure*, Oxford: Blackwell.
Hayes, B. (1982), 'Extrametricality and English stress', *Linguistic Inquiry* 13, 227–76.
Jones, D. (2011), *Cambridge English Pronouncing Dictionary*, 18th edn, ed. by P. Roach, J. Setter and J. Esling, Cambridge: Cambridge University Press.
Kachru, B. B. (1990), *The Alchemy of English: The Spread, Functions and Models of Non-native Englishes*, Urbana: University of Illinois Press.
Krämer, M. (2009), 'Main stress in Italian nonce nouns', in D. Torck and W. L. Wetzels (eds), *Romance Languages and Linguistic Theory 2006*, Amsterdam: John Benjamins, pp. 127–41.
Levis, J. M. (2005), 'Prominence in Singapore and American English: Evidence from reading aloud', in D. Deterding, A. Brown and L. E. Ling (eds), *English in Singapore: Phonetic Research on a Corpus*, Singapore: McGraw Hill Asia (Education), pp. 86–94.
Low, E. L. (1998), 'Prosodic prominence in Singapore English', PhD dissertation, University of Cambridge.
Platt, J. and H. Weber (1980), *English in Singapore and Malaysia*, Kuala Lumpur: Oxford University Press.
Sieuw, L. S. and E. L. Low (2005), 'Triphthongs in Singapore English', in D. Deterding, A. Brown and L. E. Ling (eds), *English in Singapore: Phonetic Research on a Corpus*, Singapore: McGraw Hill Asia (Education), pp. 64–71.
Tan, Y. Y. (2005), 'Observations on British and Singaporean perception of prominence', in D. Deterding, A. Brown and L. E. Ling (eds), *English in Singapore: Phonetic Research on a Corpus*, Singapore: McGraw Hill Asia (Education), pp. 95–103.
Tay, W. J. M. (1982), 'The phonology of educated Singapore English', *English World-Wide* 3(2), 135–45.
Tongue, R. K. (1979), *The English of Singapore and Malaysia*, 2nd edn, Singapore: Eastern Universities Press.

Turcsan, G. and S. Herment (2015), 'Making sense of nonce word stress in English', in J. A. Mompeàn and J. Fouz (eds), *Investigating English Pronunciation: Trends and Directions*, London: Palgrave Macmillan, pp. 23–46.

Wells, J. C. (2008), *Longman Pronunciation Dictionary*, 3rd edn, Harlow: Pearson Education.

Wiltshire, C. and R. Moon (2003), 'Phonetic stress in Indian English vs. American English', *World Englishes* 22, 291–303.

8 Input Optimization and Lexical Stress in English

Michael Hammond

0 Introduction

In this chapter, we investigate the hypothesis that exceptional stress properties of English are under-represented in a systematic fashion.

What does under-representation mean here? It means that some phonological property occurs less often than expected. For example, in a sample of 19,528 English words, we find 3949 words with trochaic stress (σ́σ̆) and 1416 words with final stress (σ̆σ́).[1] On the assumption that both patterns should be equally likely, the latter class is clearly under-represented with respect to the former and a statistical comparison confirms this: $\chi^2(1, N = 5365) = 1195.916$, $p < 0.05$, Cramér's $V = 0.472$.[2]

If we assume feet in English are generally trochaic, as argued, for example, by Hayes (1981), and assume the general framework of Optimality Theory (OT) (Prince and Smolensky 1993; McCarthy and Prince 1993b), then in the case of a disyllable with final stress, its markedness could stem from the fact that the initial syllable is unfooted (Parse-σ) or it could stem from the fact that a monosyllabic foot is built (FtBin): σ̆[σ́]. Both constraints would be violated by the winning candidate.

If we assume that it is avoidance of unfooted syllables that makes iambs marked and less common, then this predicts that forms like σ́σ̆σ̆ should also be under-represented; if what is driving the under-representation of σ̆σ́ is avoidance of monosyllabic feet, then no such prediction is made about forms like σ́σ̆σ̆. Interestingly, when we turn to three-syllables words, the facts confirm that it is monosyllabic feet that are avoided, not unparsed syllables. Forms like σ́σ̆σ̆ are much more frequent (1233) than words like σ̆σ́σ̆ (159).[3]

This is consistent with the general claim of Input Optimization (Hammond 2013, 2014, 2016, 2017) and thus provides an argument for that framework. The claim there is that input representations are skewed so as to reduce phonological complexity, the rank and number of violations exhibited by winning candidates. This chapter offers a statistical analysis of the distribution of exceptional stress in English, demonstrating that the distribution can be unified by assigning a penalty to constraint violations commensurate with the rankings of the constraints.

The organization of this chapter is as follows. In the following section, we outline a partial analysis of English stress, focusing on the rightmost stressed syllable in nouns. We then provide an analysis in terms of classical OT. Next, we go on to review Input Optimization and how it is relevant to English stress. We make explicit the predictions that this framework makes. We then test those predictions using corpus data.[4] Finally, we summarize our results and discuss how these data might be treated by other quantitative phonological frameworks.

1 English stress

In this section, we outline the descriptive generalizations concerning the rightmost stress in English nouns and provide an analysis.[5] We set aside the distribution of stresses in other parts of speech and the distribution of stresses further to the left in nouns. The general facts are clear from classical treatments like Chomsky and Halle (1968) and Hayes (1981), but also more recent constraint-based treatments, for example Hammond (1999b).[6]

Note that these generalizations apply without regard to the origin of a word; the generalizations here extend to borrowed items readily.[7]

Let us begin with the effect of syllable weight on the rightmost stress in nouns. First, final underlying long vowels attract stress.[8]

(1)　　kangaroo　[kʰæ̀ŋgərú]
　　　　careen　　[kʰərín]
　　　　cartoon　　[kʰàrtʰún]
　　　　shampoo　　[ʃæ̀mpʰú]

Final closed syllables do not necessarily bear stress.

(2)　　helix　　[híləks]
　　　　torrent　　[tʰórənt]
　　　　tempest　　[tʰɛ́mpəst]
　　　　mollusc　　[máləsk]

Otherwise, if the ultima is stressless, stress must fall on the penult if it is long or closed.

(3)　　agenda　　[ədʒéndə]
　　　　synopsis　　[sənópsəs]
　　　　placenta　　[pʰləséntə]
　　　　aroma　　　[ərómə]

balalaika [bæ̀lǝlájkǝ]
horizon [hǝrájzǝn]

If none of the preceding conditions holds, stress exhibits a certain degree of variability and can fall on any of the last three syllables. This variability applies both to individual items and across items of the same phonological shape.⁹ If stress does fall on the ultima, it must be closed.

(4) Final:
    syringe [sǝríndʒ]
    violin [vàjǝlín]
    sedan [sǝdǽn]
    result [rǝzʌ́lt]
    occult [ǝkʰʌ́lt]
    minaret [mìnǝrét]

(5) Penult:
    vermicelli [vr̩mǝtʃéli]
    vanilla [vǝnílǝ]
    sultana [sʌltǽnǝ]
    spaghetti [spǝgéti]
    siesta [siéstǝ]
    professor [pʰrǝfésr̩]

(6) Antepenult:
    orchestra [órkǝstrǝ]
    algebra [ǽldʒǝbrǝ]
    America [ǝmérǝkǝ]
    Canada [kʰǽnǝdǝ]
    javelin [dʒǽvǝlǝn]
    analysis [ǝnǽlǝsǝs]

The rightmost stress in nouns can violate these generalizations only under certain conditions. First, words that end in [i] or [r̩] can skip over a heavy penult and stress an antepenult. Interestingly, this can happen regardless of whether that final syllable is a separate morpheme or not.¹⁰

(7) warranty [wárn̩ti]   allergy   [ǽlr̩dʒi]
    calumny [kʰǽlǝmni] infantry [ínfn̩tri]
    jeopardy [dʒépr̩di] puberty   [pʰjúbr̩ti]
    gallantry [gǽln̩tri] monarchy [mánr̩ki]

(8) cylinder [sílndr̩]   calendar [kʰǽlndr̩]
    sepulchre [séplkr̩]   comforter [kʰʌ́mfr̩tr̩]

governor [gʌ́vr̩nr̩] harbinger [hárbn̩d͡ʒr̩]
lavender [lǽvn̩dr̩] derringer [dérn̩d͡ʒr̩]

Morphology plays a clear role. A second related and overlapping class of exceptions involve cases when the final syllable is one of a specific class of suffixes (or a reduced monosyllabic word in a compound). These also allow antepenultimate stress when the penultimate syllable is heavy. For example:

(9) -y   galaxy   [gǽləksi]
            fervency   [fŕ̩vn̩si]
            frequency   [fríkwənsi]

(10) -er   carpenter   [kʰárpn̩tr̩]
            messenger   [mésn̩d͡ʒr̩]
            passenger   [pʰǽsn̩d͡ʒr̩]

(11) -ment betterment [bétr̩mn̩t]
            management [mǽnəd͡ʒmn̩t]
            measurement [méʒr̩mn̩t]

(12) -ton   simpleton   [símpl̩tn̩]
            singleton   [síŋgl̩tn̩]

(13) -ist   columnist   [kʰáləmnɪst]
            liturgist   [lítr̩d͡ʒɪst]
            monarchist [mánr̩kɪst]

(14) -man   congressman [kʰáŋgrəsmn̩]
            fisherman   [fíʃr̩mn̩]

(15) -ness fixedness   [fíksədnəs]
            wilderness [wíldr̩nəs]

(16) -land hinterland [híntr̩ln̩d]

(17) -ly   northerly   [nóðr̩li]
            orderly   [órdr̩li]
            quarterly   [kʰwórtr̩li]

These same elements also allow preantepenultimate stress.

(18) -ness variableness [vǽriəbl̩nəs]
            suitableness [sútəbl̩nəs]
            mutableness [mjútəbl̩nəs]

(19) -ist arialist   [ériəlɪst]
         naturalist [nætʃrəlɪst]
         alienist   [éliənɪst]

Finally, certain final long vowels do not attract stress: word-final [o] and [i]. These need not attract stress like the examples in (1) above.

(20) tomato   [tʰəméto]   pimento   [pʰəménto]
     magneto   [mægníto]   piccolo   [pʰíkəlo]
     indigo   [índəgo]   bungalow [bʌ́ŋgəlo]

(21) martini   [màrtʰíni]   effendi   [èféndi]
     coyote   [kʰàjóti]   symphony [símfəni]
     simile   [síməli]   sesame   [sésəmi]

Notice that the [i] case overlaps some with the final -*y* cases we cited in (7) above. The ones that allow preantepenultimate stress are all spelled with final *y*, but otherwise they have identical properties.[11]

Summarizing, we have seen that stress is assigned to one of the last three syllables subject to the following quantity restrictions. First, a final long vowel is stressed. If the ultima is not stressed, a heavy penult is stressed. If neither condition applies, stress can fall on any of the last three syllables. The final syllable can be skipped over entirely if one of two conditions holds. First, a final [i] or [r] can be entirely skipped over, allowing the three-syllable window to move a step to the left and moving the quantity restrictions over as well. Second, certain suffixes allow the stress window to move to the left as well. Finally, a word-final long [o] or [i] can be treated as light.[12]

2 Analysis

In this section, we develop a simple OT analysis of the facts above.

Since, in the general case, stress can fall at most three syllables from the right, we need NONFINALITY and a trochaic foot.

(22)   NONFINALITY (NONFIN)
       The rightmost syllable is not footed.

The foot is trochaic and sensitive to syllable weight, so using the foot typology of Hayes (1987) and Hayes (1995), we specify it as a moraic trochee.

(23) $\Sigma = [\acute{\mu}\mu] \, ([\acute{\mu}\mu])$
       The foot is a moraic trochee.

Input Optimization and Lexical Stress in English

We must also, of course, require feet be built.

(24)   LxWd=PrWd (L=P)
        Words must be stressed.

With these constraints formalized like this, we get several effects. First, we get that, in the absence of heavy syllables, the antepenultimate syllable will get stressed.[13]

(25)

/America/	NonFin	[μμ]	L=P
☞ A[méri]<ca>			
Ame[rí]<ca>		*	
Ameri<ca>			*
America	*		*
Ame[ríca]	*		
Ameri[cá]	*	*	

If the penult is heavy, we also correctly get penultimate stress.

(26)

/agenda/	NonFin	[μμ]	L=P
☞ a[gén]<da>			
[ágen]<da>		*	
agen<da>			*
agenda	*		*
a[gén]da	*		
a[génda]	*	*	
agen[dá]	*	*	

Since the winning candidates violate no constraints, there is no evidence for the ranking of constraints thus far.

Feet must also be built from the right edge and this must be enforced by constraint.

(27)   AlignFtRt (AΣR)
        All feet are aligned with the right edge.

When we factor in the effects of AΣR, we see evidence of rankings. First, the availability of antepenult stress shows that NonFin supersedes AΣR.

(28)

/America/	NonFin	AΣR
☞ A[méri]<ca>		*
Ame[ríca]	*!	

If NonFin did not outrank AΣR, the foot would have to appear on the right edge and antepenultimate stress would be impossible. The [μ́μ] constraint must also outrank AΣR.

(29)

/porcelain/	[μ́μ]	AΣR
☞ [pór]ce<lain>		*
por[cé]<lain>	*!	
[pórce]<lain>	*!	

With the basic system in place, let us now consider the empirical complications established in the previous section:

1. A final closed syllable does not have to be stressed.
2. Final [i] and [o] do not have to be stressed.
3. Certain affixes are outside the stress domain.
4. Final *er* and *y* are outside the stress domain.

To allow final closed syllables to evade stress, we must allow NonFin to apply to closed syllables, but not to syllables containing a long vowel. We follow Prince and Smolensky (1993) in parametrizing NonFin so as to specify what kind of syllables it can apply to. We will henceforth use NonFin[V,VC] to mean that NonFin applies to light syllables and closed syllables. On this analysis, the optimal footing for key cases is like this:

(30) long   [kànga][róo]
       light   a[gén]<da>
       closed   [tém]<pest>

We saw that a word-final [i] or [o] could also evade stress, through word-final syllables with long vowels generally do not (1). The simplest move here is to assume that parametric NonFin can refer to these as well, that is, NonFin[V,VC,i,o]. This gives us footings as in: [pícco]<lo> [pʰíkəlo] and [sésa]<me> [sésəmi].

Certain suffixes also fall outside the stress domain. These are different from the NonFin cases above in that the trisyllabic stress domain occurs to the left of any such suffixes. To account for the role of morphology in such cases, we make use of generalized alignment (McCarthy and Prince 1993a) and morpheme-specific constraints (Hammond 1999a; Pater 2000). The following constraint forces the right edge of the prosodic word to the left of certain elements.

(31)   AlignPrWd[...] (APW[...])
         The right edge of a prosodic word is aligned with the left edge of ....

This constraint is an instance of generalized alignment and parametrized to refer to specific suffixes, for example APW[-ness, -ist, . . .]. This gives us representations as follows.[14]

(32) [nátu]<ral>}ist
      [mó]<narch>}ist

APW must of course outrank NONFIN and AΣR so it has first crack at the relevant affixes.

In the general case, the right edge of the prosodic word aligns with the right edge of the morphological word.

(33) ALIGN(PW,R,MW,R) (APM)
      The right edge of a prosodic word is aligned with the right edge of the morphological word.

APW must outrank this as well.

Finally, we saw that final *er* and *y* also allowed for preantepenultimate stress and for a penultimate closed syllable to be treated as light; the simplest move here would be to simply extend APW to include them as well, that is, APW[-ness,-ist, . . . ,er,y]. We thus assume APW can refer to morphemes or syllable types.[15]

To summarize, we have proposed an OT analysis of the rightmost stress in English that includes these constraints: NONFIN[V,VC,i,o], [$\acute{\mu}\mu$], L = P, AΣR, and APW[-ness,-ist,. . . ,er,y]. The data do not give us a complete ranking, but we have at least the following ranking information.

(34) NONFIN[V,VC,i,o]   ≫   AΣR
      [$\acute{\mu}\mu$]   ≫   AΣR
      APW[-ness,-ist,. . . ,er,y] ≫   AΣR
      APW[-ness,-ist,. . . ,er,y] ≫   NONFIN[V,VC,i,o]
      APW[-ness,-ist,. . . ,er,y] ≫   APM

We can combine these rankings restrictions in a number of ways and so we do not present a unique complete ranking.

There is still one thing to account for: The system as given predicts antepenultimate stress whenever possible. On this analysis, forms like *vanílla* or *violín* should be impossible.

Our account of these follows from two generalizations, generalizations that hold regardless of the origin or history of the word. First, final stress is only possible if the final syllable is closed (or long); it is impossible for a final light open syllable to attract stress. Similarly, a light penultimate syllable can be stressed only if there is an immediately following consonant.

Together, these suggest that the exceptionality of such forms should inhere in the final/following consonant(s).[16]

This general idea is confirmed when we note that exceptional penult stress is far more likely if the following consonant is *not* a voiced obstruent. Forms like those in (35) are far more prevalent than forms like those in (36).[17]

(35) spaghetti [spəgéti]
      professor [pʰrəfésr̩]
      vermicelli [vɹ̩mətʃéli]
      sultana   [sʌ̀ltʰǽnə]

(36) macadam   [məkʰǽdəm]
      kohlrabi   [kʰòlrǽbi]

The same opposition applies to final syllables. There are very few examples of final stressed short vowels followed by voiced stops, though other final consonant types are possible.[18]

(37) shellac   [ʃəlǽk]
      minaret   [mìnərét]
      obit   [òbít]
      madam   [mədǽm]
      sedan   [sədǽn]

We can capture both of these facts if what attracts stress is a moraic coda consonant that is exceptionally treated as vocalic.

Recall that the NONFIN[V,VC,i,o] constraint must distinguish light and closed syllables from long vowels other than word-final [i,o]. Let us assume a moraic version of the syllable (Hayes 1989) and that coda consonants in English are moraic (Hammond 1999b).

(38)

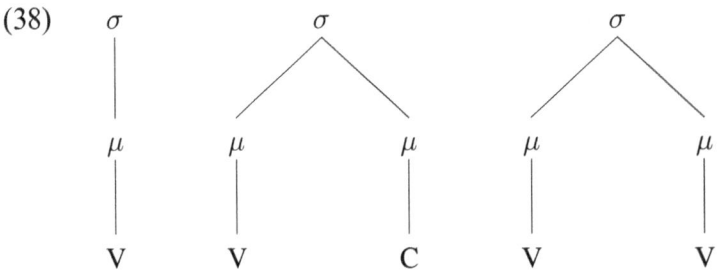

Let us treat the difference between long vowels and closed syllables by distinguishing formally between consonantal and vocalic morae. We base this on the fact that vocalic material attracts stress more aggressively than consonantal material (Hayes 1995). We therefore posit *M* as a heavier mora associated with vocalic material.

(39)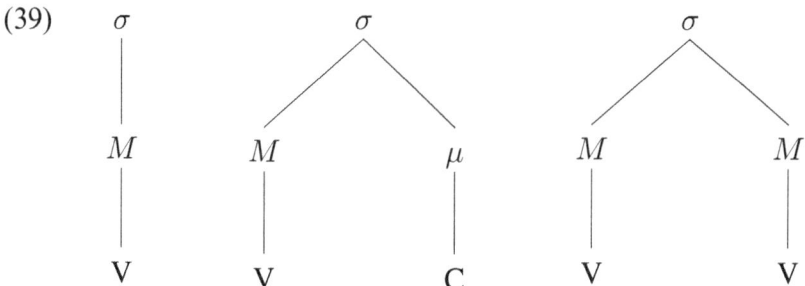

We then reformulate NONFIN to be sensitive to this distinction, rather than directly referring to the segmental content of the rhyme: NONFIN only applies to a syllable that has less moraic content than *MM*.

So far, this is merely a direct encoding of the typological claim that long vowels attract stress more than closed syllables, but we can make this do some work for us. This does not handle word-final [i,o], but we can treat these in like fashion. Let us assume that while normally a long vowel has the moraic content *MM*, word-final [i,o] have the moraic content *Mμ*, just like a coda consonant.

(40)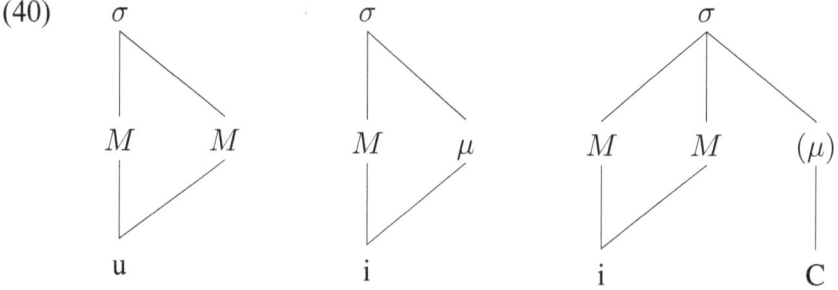

If NONFIN is sensitive to this distinction, then while a final long vowel (*MM*), as in *taboo* [tʰæbú], generally resists NONFIN, a final [i,o] (*Mμ*), as in *willow* [wílo], does not. Since this representation is specific to word-final [i,o], a final closed syllable with [i,o], as in *cologne* [kʰəlón], will still resist NONFIN. This makes the empirical prediction that final [i,o] are not as long as other long vowels. This echoes previous analyses where these vowels are underlyingly short (Chomsky and Halle 1968) or phonetically lax (Halle and Mohanan 1985).

We can use this same machinery to deal with word-final syllables that are exceptionally stressed, for example as in *violín*. Recall that a final short vowel in a closed syllable may be stressed, but does not have to be stressed. What we say is that final exceptional stress is a function of these words having a final *MM*, rather than *Mμ*.

(41)
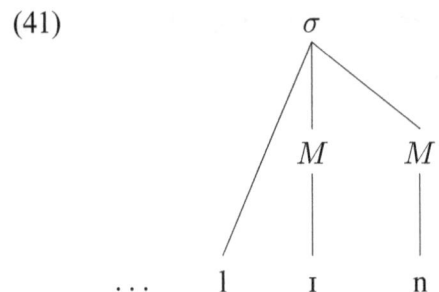

These exceptionally marked words will then resist NONFIN and surface with final stress. Words without this marking like *villain* will not escape NONFIN.

This treatment of final exceptional stress has two advantages. First, it entails that only a final closed syllable can bear exceptional stress. Second, it makes use of the same formal machinery we use to treat [i,o].

We can use this same general strategy for dealing with forms that have exceptional penult stress, for example *vanilla*. We can represent these as having a mora (M or μ) linked to the consonant after the penult.

(42)
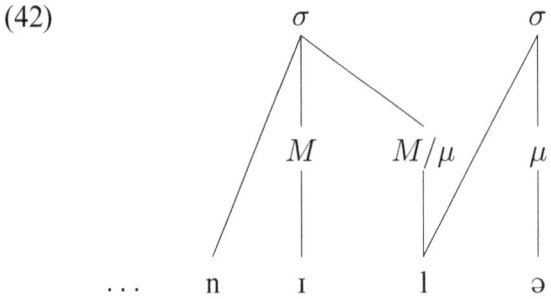

That such a syllable should be bimoraic is argued by Hammond (1997, 1999b). The analysis here uses that surface form in the input to force stress on that syllable. Confirmation of this approach comes from the observation, due originally to Chomsky and Halle (1968), that the relevant consonants are skewed just as we would expect if they were truly geminates. That is, penult stress or final stress on a light syllable in nouns is avoided when the relevant consonant is a voiced stop, echoing the general rarity of voiced geminate stops, for example as in Japanese.

3 Input Optimization

Input Optimization (Hammond 2013, 2014, 2016) is the claim that the statistical distribution of input representations is skewed so as to reduce the overall complexity of a phonological system measured in terms of ranked or weighted constraint violations over winning candidates. Let us first look at some of the arguments for this and then how it is formalized. The goal here is to outline this system in sufficient detail so that we can examine empirically the predictions it makes with respect to the analysis developed in the preceding section.

Building on earlier work by Bolinger (1962) and Hayes (1984), Hammond (2013) cites the English Rhythm Rule as an example of this kind of skewing. The basic facts are that a stress will shift leftward if it is at an inappropriate distance from a following stress.

(43) thìrtéen   thírtèen mén
      Mìnnesóta   Mínnesòta Máry
      Tènnessée   Ténnessèe Tím

Liberman and Prince (1977) argue that this is an instance of stress clash; Hayes (1984) argues for a more complex characterization in terms of optimal distance between stresses. One clear restriction on the process is that the displaced stress can only move to a position otherwise occupied by a secondary stress. Thus we get:

(44) nàíve   naíve Níck
      mùndáne   múndàne Míke
      ălóof   ălóof Állen   *álòof Állen
      sĕdáte   sĕdáte Sám   *sédàte Sám

Stress cannot shift in the last two cases because the initial syllable does not otherwise bear secondary stress. To characterize this formally, we would have some sort of clash constraint that drives the shift and some sort of constraint on whether there is a preceding secondary stress that bounds it.

Hammond (2013) examines the distribution of prenominal modifiers in the Brown corpus (Kučera and Francis 1967) with respect to modifiers in other positions and shows that forms that undergo the stress shift are under-represented prenominally; they occur significantly less often than we would expect from their distribution elsewhere. This is taken as evidence that the faithfulness violations that result from stress shift are avoided. In addition, however, forms like *aloof* are also significantly under-represented prenominally, establishing that the markedness violations that result from unresolved clash are also avoided. The table in (45) gives counts for all adjectives with the relevant stress patterns and syllable counts from the Brown corpus.

(45)
Pattern	Example	Non-prenom. tokens	Prenom. tokens
ǿŏ	happy [hǽpi]	7081	11819
ŏǿ	aloof [əlúf]	997	1001
ǿŏ	retail [rítʰèl]	171	507
òǿ	naive [nàív]	118	144

There are, of course, many factors that affect word choice and word order. The claim is that there is also a significant effect of the sort described.

To capture facts like these, Phonological Complexity is formalized as (46):

(46) **Phonological complexity**

The output or surface forms of a language comprise a set that we can denote as $O = \{O_1, O_2, \ldots, O_n\}$. Every member of that set has a corresponding (optimal) input form $I = \{I_1, I_2, \ldots, I_n\}$. There is, for any phonology, a finite sequence or vector of constraints $C = \langle C_1, C_2, \ldots, C_n \rangle$. Any input–output pairing then defines a vector of violation counts, some number of violations for each constraint earned by the winning candidate for that input. These vectors can, in turn, be summed (constraint by constraint) producing a single vector which is a measure of the phonological complexity of a set of words. To produce a relative measure of phonological complexity given some set of n forms, we divide by n.

Phonological complexity basically says that a set of occurring forms can be assessed in terms of the number of constraint violations those forms exhibit and the rank of those violations. Input Optimization is then formalized in terms of (46).

(47) **Input Optimization**

All else being equal, phonological inputs are selected that minimize the phonological complexity of the system.

Hammond (2014) and Hammond (2016) exemplify this as follows. Let us look at this schematically. Imagine we have the array of forms in (48) that do and do not undergo nasal assimilation. If we evaluate the complexity of this (partial) system with the definition above, we get the calculations in (49).

(48) on pi   an ba   un bo │ en do   on ta   un ti │ an ku   in ga   on ke
      ⇓   ⇓   ⇓   ⇓   ⇓   ⇓   ⇓   ⇓   ⇓
      om pi   am ba   um bo   en do   on ta   un ti   aŋ ku   iŋ ga   oŋ ke

(49)

Input	Output	NAS	IO-FAITH
/on pi/	om pi		*
/an ba/	am ba		*
/un bo/	um bo		*
/en do/	en do		
/on ta/	on ta		
/un ti/	un ti		
/an ku/	aŋ ku		*
/in ga/	iŋ ga		*
/on ke/	oŋ ke		*
		0	6

The relative complexity of this system is: ⟨0, 6⟩ / 9 = ⟨0, 0.67⟩.

Compare this with the hypothetical system in (50), which is *less* complex. This reduction in complexity is a function of the number of forms in each category. We give the calculations in (51).

(50) on pi   an ba | en do   on ta   un ti   in di | an ku   in ga
      ⇓   ⇓ | ⇓   ⇓   ⇓   ⇓ | ⇓   ⇓
      om pi   am ba | en do   on ta   un ti   in di | aŋ ku   iŋ ga

(51)

Input	Output	NAS	IO-FAITH
/on pi/	om pi		*
/an ba/	am ba		*
/en do/	en do		
/on ta/	on ta		
/un ti/	un ti		
/in di/	in di		
/an ku/	aŋ ku		*
/in ga/	iŋ ga		*
		0	4

The relative complexity of this system is: ⟨0, 4⟩ / 8 = ⟨0, 0.5⟩. Input Optimization (47) prefers the latter system over the former.

This hypothetical example is simplified in that we effectively only consider violations of one constraint: IO-FAITH. In a full system, we would have to consider violations of multiple constraints, and Input Optimization has to be sensitive to the relative ranking, or weighting, of those constraints.

Let us now look specifically at rhythm. Recall that there must be some high-ranked constraint that prevents stress from shifting leftward onto an otherwise stressless syllable; for convenience, let us call this 2NDARY. There must also be a constraint against clash: CLASH. Finally, there must be faithfulness, presumably faithfulness not to the input but to the independent adjective with unshifted stress: FAITH.[19]

For our purposes, all that FAITH requires is the same stress, but a more nuanced approach might take vowel reduction into account as well. On this alternative story, we replace 2NDARY with a constraint requiring faithfulness with respect to vowel quality.[20]

In (52a), we see that the winning candidate has no constraint violations; hence there is nothing to optimize and no skewing. In (52b), the winning candidate does violate CLASH, so we see the effects of Input Optimization here. Finally, in (52c), the winning candidate violates FAITH, so again there is skewing.

(52) a.

	2NDARY	CLASH	FAITH
☞ háppy Hánk			

b.

	2NDARY	CLASH	FAITH
☞ ălóof Állen		*	
álòof Állen	*!		

c.

	2NDARY	CLASH	FAITH
☞ naîve Níck			*
nàíve Níck		*!	

4 Predictions

We have seen that Input Optimization predicts that winning candidates with constraint violations will be avoided. What predictions does this make about the analysis of English developed in section 2? As we showed in the previous section, Input Optimization minimizes constraint violations for winning candidates. Hence we will see its effects when there is critical constraint ranking, in cases where winning candidates violate lower-ranked constraints in order to satisfy higher-ranked constraints.

Below in (53) we give the pattern of violations for winning candidates with different properties. The L = P, $[\acute{\mu}\mu]$, and APW constraints are never violated by winning candidates and so we leave them out below. We gave the individual rankings justified in (34), and the ranking below is one partial ranking consistent with that. Here NONFIN must outrank AΣR, but APM is unranked with respect to those two.

(53)

		APM	NF	AΣR
1	[cát]}		*	
2	[zé]<bra>}			*
	[wál]<rus>}			*
	[yúcca]}		*	
	ve[néer]}		*	
	she[llác]}		*	
3	[zéppe]<lin>}			*
	a[gén]<da>}			*
	a[ró]<ma>}			*
	[pór]ce<lain>}			**
	[ví]ta<min>}			**
	kanga[róo]}		*	
	vio[lín]}		*	
2+	X}+ist,…	*	?	?

All else being equal, Input Optimization predicts that winners with higher-ranked violations should be dispreferred to winners with no or lower-ranked violations. Thus we should get an overall pattern of skewing like the following:

(54) $\left\{\begin{array}{c}\text{zebra}\\\text{walrus}\\\text{zeppelin}\\\text{agenda}\\\text{aroma}\end{array}\right\} > \left\{\begin{array}{c}\text{porcelain}\\\text{vitamin}\end{array}\right\} > \left\{\begin{array}{c}\text{cat}\\\text{yucca}\\\text{veneer}\\\text{shellac}\\\text{kangaroo}\\\text{violin}\end{array}\right\}$

The cases subject to APM would accrue a cost for APM, but also for any violations of the other two constraints, and interleave accordingly.

To assess these, we must factor in other effects. That is, the statistical skewings that might affect words like these may be due to other factors that we need to attend to. For example, the number of syllables in a word can also have an effect.[21]

In (55) below, we give the type counts for syllables from the same dataset used in section 0.

(55)

Syllables	Type count
1	3685
2	7060
3	4746
4	2903
5	949
6	162
7	22
8	1

Notice how the number of types is skewed with two-syllable words having the largest share. Since there is an independent frequency effect having to do with the number of syllables, we need to factor this out of the proposed comparison above. In other words, we need two separate comparisons, one for two-syllable words and a separate one for three-syllable words.

(56)   Two syllables:

$$\left\{ \begin{array}{c} \text{zebra} \\ \text{walrus} \end{array} \right\} > \left\{ \begin{array}{c} \text{yucca} \\ \text{veneer} \\ \text{shellac} \end{array} \right\}$$

(57)   Three syllables:

$$\left\{ \begin{array}{c} \text{zeppelin} \\ \text{agenda} \\ \text{aroma} \end{array} \right\} > \left\{ \begin{array}{c} \text{porcelain} \\ \text{vitamin} \end{array} \right\} > \left\{ \begin{array}{c} \text{kangaroo} \\ \text{violin} \end{array} \right\}$$

We have the last category in (53): stress-neutral final syllables. There are two predictions here. First, we should expect to find the same relative skewing for the patterns that occur to the left of the final syllable as we do for words without that final syllable (56).

(58)   Two syllables with skipped final syllable:

$$\left\{ \begin{array}{c} \text{diarist} \\ \text{organist} \end{array} \right\} > \left\{ \begin{array}{c} \text{strategist} \\ \text{embroider} \\ \text{commander} \end{array} \right\}$$

We should also see that forms without that final syllable are more frequent than ones with.

(59) Two syllables with skipped final syllable vs. two syllables without:

$$\left\{\begin{array}{c}\text{zebra}\\\text{walrus}\\\text{yucca}\\\text{veneer}\\\text{shellac}\end{array}\right\} > \left\{\begin{array}{c}\text{diarist}\\\text{organist}\\\text{strategist}\\\text{embroider}\\\text{commander}\end{array}\right\}$$

Similar patterns should apply to four-syllable words with a skipped final syllable.

5 Corpus analyses

In this section, we test the predictions outlined in the previous section using dictionary/corpus data. To recap, the basic hypothesis is that there is Input Optimization: that input representations are skewed so as to minimize phonological complexity as outlined in section 3. Specifically, there are four general predictions:

1. Two-syllable nouns should skew as in (56).
2. Three-syllable nouns should skew as in (57).
3. Affixed nouns should skew as in (58).
4. Affixed nouns should skew with respect to unaffixed nouns as in (59).

Let us consider two-syllable forms first.[22] If we take all two-syllable nouns in our same sample and break them down by stress and syllable type we get the following. Words with final stress appear in (60) and words with initial stress in (61). The different (syllabic) weights for the first syllable are given along the left; those for the second syllable along the top.

(60) Iambic words:

σ_1	σ_2		
	...V	...C	...V̄...
...V	0	119	248
...C	0	72	83
...V̄...	0	66	100

(61) Trochaic words:

		σ_2		
		...V	...C	...V̄...
σ_1	...V	15	851	206
	...C	23	888	397
	...V̄...	71	1339	623

The following table shows how we calculate the values for each of the cases in (56). The symbol "X" stands for a syllable of any weight.

(62)
Example	Type	Calculation	Total
zébra	V̄ X	71 + 1339 + 623	2033
wálrus	C X	23 + 888 + 397	1308
yúcca	V X	15 + 851 + 206	1072
venéer	X V̄	248 + 83 + 100	431
shellác	X C	119 + 72 + 66	257

The prediction is that forms in the second group should be under-represented with respect to the first. This is true and the difference is significant: $\chi^2(1, N = 5101) = 490.014$, $p < 0.05$, Cramér's $V = 0.310$.

Let us now consider three-syllable forms. Recall that Input Optimization predicts the skewing in (57). We get these counts for these types from our corpus:

(63)
	Example	Type	Total
a.	zéppelin	V X X	753
	agénda	X C X	301
	aróma	X V̄ X	458
b.	pórcelain	C X X	482
	vítamin	V̄ X X	764
c.	kangaróo	X X V̄	100
	violín	X X C	94

We consider each comparison separately. First, we compare groups (63a) and (63b); the difference is significant: $\chi^2(1, N = 2758) = 25.655$, $p < 0.05$, Cramér's $V = 0.096$, though the effect size is small. The difference is also significant between groups (63b) and (63c): $\chi^2(1, N = 1440) = 768.544$, $p < 0.05$, Cramér's $V = 0.731$.

Input Optimization also predicts the skewing in (58). We give the counts below in (64). Note that counts here are approximate and inflated by morphological misanalyses, for example *baroness*, and so on. Such cases would have to be excluded by hand and our assumption is that such misanalyses occur in both categories.

(64)

	Example	Type	Total
a.	díarist	V̆ X X	243
	órganist	C X X	121
b.	strátegist	V X X	150
	embróider	X V̄ X	32
	commánder	X C X	20

This difference is also significant: $\chi^2(1, N = 566) = 46.367, p < 0.05$, Cramér's $V = 0.286$.

Finally, Input Optimization predicts the skewing in (59). Raw counts for the relevant cases are summarized below.

(65)

Example	Type	Total
zébra	V̆ X	2033
wálrus	C X	1308
yúcca	V X	1072
venéer	X V̄	431
shellác	X C	257
díarist	V̆ X X	243
órganist	C X X	121
strátegist	V X X	150
embróider	X V̄ X	32
commánder	X C X	20

This difference is also significant: $\chi^2(1, N = 5667) = 3629.120, p < 0.05$, Cramér's $V = 0.800$.

6 Conclusion

In this chapter, we have developed an analysis of the rightmost stress in English nouns within a basic Optimality Theory framework. We then reviewed the Input Optimization framework and laid out the predictions that system makes with respect to the analysis developed. In particular, it predicts that lexical items should be skewed so as to reduce phonological complexity by reducing the number of forms that violate high-ranked constraints.

We then examined these predictions with respect to dictionary data and saw that they were borne out. In each case, where Input Optimization predicts an asymmetry, a statistically significant skewing in the relevant direction was detected.

These results confirm that Input Optimization is an organizing principle in phonological systems. Phonological generalizations, as expressed by ranked constraints, are mirrored by statistically significant regularities in how the phonological system is used.

There are other systems with superficially similar properties, for example Maxent grammars (Hayes and Wilson 2008). The basic logic of that system is that weighted constraints that describe the relative distribution of phonotactic patterns can be automatically induced from training data. Constraints of this sort do extremely well in modeling experimental well-formedness data.

The approaches are similar in some regards and dissimilar in others. Like the current approach, Maxent relates constraint weights to frequency of distribution. In Maxent, constraints with very high weights are effectively unviolated and thus effectively the same as unviolated constraints in a constraint system like OT with strict ranking. That said, all constraints in a Maxent system can be violated in principle; in an OT system, only constraints that are outranked by conflicting constraints can be violated.

Another difference between the models is that in a Maxent system there are only these frequencies and there is no attempt to connect these weights to the categorical constraint grammar. Thus, there would be no conflict if the categorical phonology had constraints A and B ranked A $\gg$ B and the Maxent system developed contained the same constraints but where B had a greater weight than A.

Finally, Maxent only applies to phonotactic systems, not to phonological alternations. There is no analog to FAITH in a Maxent system. On the other hand, FAITH constraints are also subject to Input Optimization. The rhythm example reviewed in section 3 above is an example of this. Input Optimization also applies to morphology and phrasal distribution, well beyond the domain of phonotactics.

The analysis developed here reveals new aspects of the Input Optimization system as well. While it is true that the predictions made by Input Optimization for the analysis of the rightmost stress are borne out, if we examine those predictions at a different level of granularity, things are more complex. We saw that (64a) is over-represented when compared with (64b), but note that the *órganist* class is under-represented with respect to *strátegist* class. It is unclear what predictions are made at this lower level and this should be pursued further.

Another effect here is that Input Optimization predicts that affixation should be under-represented in the case of stress-neutral suffixes. These can thus be added to the morphological effects treated in depth by Hammond (2016) and Hammond (2017).

Finally, the cases treated here were all in the lexicon and morphology. One might argue that Input Optimization is an historical effect, governing the contents of the lexicon of a language. While this is true for the data here, note that it is not true for all cases covered by Input Optimization; the phrasal rhythm cases reviewed above cannot be treated as historical accretion in the lexicon.

Notes

Thanks to Diane Ohala and George-Michael Pescaru for useful discussion and to an anonymous reviewer for helpful feedback. All errors are my own.

1. This dataset is available at <http://dingo.sbs.arizona.edu/~hammond/ling410-f15/newdic.txt>.
2. See Chapter 7 of this volume for experimental data that show a similar pattern.
3. This of course assumes that σ̆σ̆σ̆ is footed as σ̆[σ̆σ̆].
4. See Chapter 2 of this volume for another approach to integrating corpus data in the analysis of English stress.
5. See Chapter 5 of this volume for a discussion of English verbs.
6. See Chapter 1 of this volume for a thorough review and summary of the facts.
7. In fact, some generalizations about stress in English are really only apparent with borrowings. For example, the pattern of secondary stresses on monomorphemes can really only be determined by looking at very long borrowed words, for example forms like *hamamelidanthemum* or *Apalachicola*. See Chapter 2 of this volume for another approach to borrowings and Chapter 6 for a discussion of borrowings with respect to Australian English.
8. We refer to phonological length here, not phonetic length. So, for example, the length induced by a following voiced segment vs. a voiceless segment is not relevant to the distribution of stress. Following Chomsky and Halle (1968), we also exclude certain underlying short vowels that surface as long in final position, for example in *happy* [hǽpi] or *elbow* [élbo]. We return to these latter cases below.
9. There is also variability in terms of the general shape of words, specifically with respect to variables that control the distribution of stress. For example, the word *sultana* is cited here with penultimate stress. For speakers for whom the penultimate vowel is [æ], penultimate stress is possible, but not required by the phonology. For speakers for whom the vowel is long [a], the phonology dictates penult stress.
10. This raises a very interesting possibility that the superficially unsuffixed forms are reanalyzed as being suffixed and that this is a morphological effect.
11. See Chapter 4 of this volume for a treatment of English phonology that exploits orthographic regularities like this.
12. All of these generalizations are discussed in Chomsky and Halle (1968) and Hayes (1981).
13. In this and subsequent tableaux, feet are marked with square brackets and syllables skipped by NONFIN with angled brackets.

14. Here and following, we use right curly braces to mark the right edge of the prosodic word.
15. It seems hardly an accident that the relevant syllable types are the same shape as independent suffixes of English. One approach to this might be a more generous notion of what a morpheme is.
16. Very similar logic in rule-based terms is developed by Chomsky and Halle (1968).
17. Note that forms like *avocado* [àvəkʰádo], *tornado* [tʰòrnédo], *armada* [àrmádə], *cicada* [səkʰédə], and so on are irrelevant; the penultimate vowel is long in these cases.
18. Using the same resource cited at the beginning of the chapter, if we search for polysyllabic nouns with final stress, we find 225 examples of final voiceless stops, but only 61 examples of final voiced stops in this context. This difference is significant: $\chi^2(1, N = 286) = 94.042, p < 0.05$, Cramér's $V = 0.573$.
19. Output-output correspondence for (cyclic) stress was first proposed by Kenstowicz (1996).
20. Thanks to an anonymous reviewer for interesting discussion on this point.
21. There are, of course, many other factors that might play a role. Our hope is to control for those that have a significant effect here. For example, we do not consider semantic factors here; see Chapter 3 of this volume for discussion.
22. Secondary stress is ignored in these calculations.

References

Bolinger, D. (1962), 'Binomials and pitch accent', *Lingua* 11, 34–44.
Chomsky, N. and M. Halle (1968), *The Sound Pattern of English*, New York: Harper & Row.
Halle, M. and K. P. Mohanan (1985), 'Segmental phonology of modern English', *Linguistic Inquiry* 16(1), 57–116.
Hammond, M. (1997), 'Vowel quantity and syllabification in English', *Language* 73(1), 1–17.
Hammond, M. (1999a), 'Lexical frequency and rhythm', in M. Darnell, E. Moravcsik, F. Newmeyer, M. Noonan and K. Wheatley (eds), *Functionalism and Formalism in Linguistics*, Amsterdam: John Benjamins, pp. 329–58.
Hammond, M. (1999b), *The Phonology of English*, Oxford: Oxford University Press.
Hammond, M. (2013), 'Input Optimization in English', *Journal of the Phonetic Society of Japan* 17, 26–38.
Hammond, M. (2014), 'Phonological complexity and Input Optimization', *Phonological Studies* 17, 85–94.
Hammond, M. (2016), 'Input Optimization: Phonology and morphology', *Phonology* 33(3), 459–91.

Hammond, M. (2017), 'Morphological complexity and Input Optimization', in C. Bowern, L. Horn and R. Zanuttini (eds), *On Looking into Words (and Beyond): Structures, Relations, Analyses*, Berlin: Language Science Press, pp. 155–70.

Hayes, B. (1981), *A Metrical Theory of Stress Rules*, New York: Garland, 1980 MIT doctoral dissertation.

Hayes, B. (1984), 'The phonology of rhythm in English', *Linguistic Inquiry* 15(1), 33–74.

Hayes, B. (1987), 'A revised parametric metrical theory', in J. McDonough and B. Plunkett (eds), *Proceedings of NELS 17*, Amherst, MA: Graduate Linguistics Students Association, pp. 274–89.

Hayes, B. (1989), 'Compensatory lengthening in moraic phonology', *Linguistic Inquiry* 20(2), 253–306.

Hayes, B. (1995), *Metrical Stress Theory*, Chicago: University of Chicago Press.

Hayes, B. and C. Wilson (2008), 'A maximum entropy model of phonotactics and phonotactic learning', *Linguistic Inquiry* 39(3), 379–440.

Kenstowicz, M. (1996), 'Base-identity and uniform exponence: Alternatives to cyclicity', in J. Durand and B. Laks (eds), *Current Trends in Phonology: Models and Methods*, Salford: University of Salford Publications, pp. 363–93.

Kučera, H. and W. N. Francis (1967), *Computational Analysis of Present-Day American English*, Providence, RI: Brown University Press.

Liberman, M. and A. Prince (1977), 'On stress and linguistic rhythm', *Linguistic Inquiry* 8(2), 249–336.

McCarthy, J. J. and A. Prince (1993a), 'Generalized alignment', in G. Booij and J. van Marle (eds), *Yearbook of Morphology 1993*, Dordrecht: Kluwer, pp. 79–153.

McCarthy, J. J. and A. Prince (1993b), 'Prosodic morphology I: Constraint interaction and satisfaction', Manuscript, University of Massachusetts, Amherst and Rutgers University.

Pater, J. (2000), 'Non-uniformity in English secondary stress: The role of ranked and lexically specific constraints', *Phonology* 17(1), 237–74.

Prince, A. and P. Smolensky (1993), 'Optimality Theory: Constraint interaction in generative grammar', Manuscript, Rutgers University and University of Colorado, Boulder. [(2004), *Optimality Theory: Constraint Interaction in Generative Grammar*, Oxford: Blackwell.]

 # A Solution to Theoretical Shortcomings in the Stress Assignment of Words in English

Eiji Yamada

0 Introduction

This chapter compares the two main groups of theories of word stress assignment in American English (General American, hereafter English), highlighting certain exceptional treatments in their accounts and identifying their limitations. It then briefly introduces a new approach that attempts to explain both exceptional and core (i.e. non-exceptional) examples in a unified way, together with an attempt to refine some of the new theory's limitations.

In section 1, we will look at certain types of exceptions to the theories. We will discuss one group of exceptional words to word stress treatments in *The Sound Pattern of English* (Chomsky and Halle 1968) and subsequent studies (section 1.1), followed by discussion of a converse group of exceptional words to treatments in classic Optimality Theory (section 1.2). In section 2, by applying the recently developed Positional Function Theory (PFT) of Yamada (2010, 2013a), we will suggest a solution to these two groups of exceptional words relating to *subsidiary* stress assignment (section 2.1), followed by a brief introduction to the treatment of *main* stress assignment within the PFT framework (section 2.2). In section 3, we will consider a number of remaining issues in PFT: first, we will solve a problematic word type by employing the concept of Coordinate Axis Shift (section 3.1); second, we will look at the treatment of another problematic word type using the concept of Stress Domain in tandem with Stress Retraction (section 3.2); and third, we will examine the motivations for the two types of 'primary–secondary' word-stress treatments discussed in 3.1 and 3.2 (section 3.3). The advantages of PFT will be outlined in section 4. The chapter ends with conclusions in section 5.

1 Exceptions

1.1 One type of exception to treatments in *SPE* and subsequent studies

First to be mentioned here is *The Sound Pattern of English* (Chomsky and Halle 1968, hereafter *SPE*). In *SPE*, main and subsidiary stress assignment are comprehensively accounted for by the Main Stress Rule (MSR) and auxiliary rules with the help of the cyclic application of stress rules.

Take the *còndênsátion* word type,[1] (1a) below, for example. This is a noun derived from the verb *condénse*.

(1) a. *còndênsátion* (Noun) < *condénse* (Verb)
     b. [[*condens*]$_V$ *ation*]$_N$
     c. *còn.dên.sá.tion* (2310)
            2   3   1   0
     d. *condénse* (01) ⟶ *còn.dên.sá.tion* (2310)
         0   1   2   3   1   0
     e. Stress inheritance by cyclicity with structural transparency

The internal constituent structure of the word is taken to be [[*condéns*]$_V$ *ation*]$_N$, (1b), that is, the verb *condénse* plus the noun-forming affix *-ation*. The MSR and auxiliary rules provide the stress pattern *còndênsátion* (1c), with primary stress on the penultimate vowel *sá*, secondary stress on the first syllable *còn*, and tertiary stress on the antepenultimate syllable *dên*. Note that all the data in this chapter are based on the data clarification method in Yamada (2010) in addition to the American English pronunciation descriptions in Wells (2008). Stress patterns are shown by numerals and sometimes enclosed in parentheses: '1' is a primary stressed vowel, '2' secondary, '3' a tertiary or full vowel without stress reduction to schwa, and '0' is schwa or its equivalent.[2] These are accompanied by acute and grave stress marks, and the circumflex indicating a full vowel.[3] (For an alternative view of tertiary stress, see Chapter 2 of this volume.)

In the derivation from the verb to the noun, (1d), the position of primary stress in the verb is inherited by the noun as tertiary stress in the cyclic application of MSR from the innermost constituent, the verb, to the next higher level of the word structure, the noun. In other words, with structural transparency in (1b) we find stress inheritance by the cyclic application of stress rules.

As is well known, the cyclic account is supported by the contrastive example of *còmpensátion*, as shown in (2).

(2)	a. còmpensátion (Noun) < cómpensàte (Verb)
	b. [[compensat]$_V$ ion]$_N$
	c. còm.pen.sá.tion (2010)
	   2 0 1 0
	d. cómpensàte (102) ⟶ còm.pen.sá.tion (2010)
	   1 0 2 2 0 1 0

As in (2c), the antepenultimate syllable *pen* does not bear any stress, which is illustrated in (2d) by the cyclic *non*-stress inheritance of the base verb *cómpensàte* with no stress on the second syllable *pen*. The stress non-inheritance on the second syllable of the base leads to zero stress on the antepenultimate syllable of the noun in this type of word. These cyclic accounts in (1) and (2) are analysed by the following familiar convention based on *SPE*, in (3).

(3)	Cyclicity (= *cyclic inheritance* or *recursion*)
	Rules are applied cyclically from the innermost constituents to the outermost, by means of a universal transformational cycle. Thus, we can retain cyclic stress inheritance.

However, this account meets a serious problem in the *informátion* word type. It seems natural in (4a, b) below to consider the noun *informátion* to be derived from the base verb *infórm* as in [[infórm]$_V$ ation]$_N$:[4]

(4)	a. informátion (Noun) < infórm (Verb)
	b. [[inform]$_V$ ation]$_N$
	c. *in.fòr.má.tion (*2310)
	   *2 3 1 0
	d. infórm (01) —?⟶ e. *in.fòr.má.tion (*2310)
	   0 1 *2 3 1 0

	                    f. in.for.má.tion (2010)
	                       2 0 1 0

As the rules and convention stand now, however, they incorrectly predict a stress pattern **infôrmátion* with *tertiary* stress on the *antepenultimate* syllable (4e). In fact, as (4f) shows, *informátion* does not have tertiary stress (i.e. does not have a full vowel) on that position but schwa. Words of this class are exceptions to stress inheritance by cyclicity and transparency.

Thus, in *SPE*, words of this type are postulated to have a 'flat' structure (like [*information*]$_N$) without an internal base verb (*SPE*: 112n64, 161) in the underlying phonological representation from the lexicon. However, this kind of treatment of exceptions creates another 'plastered transparency' problem in the theory in addition to the cyclicity problem, as in (5).

(5) Problem with 'plastered transparency'[5] (in relation to *rule ordering*)
In a plastered structure, where the internal constituent structure is invisible, we cannot apply rules *first* to the *invisible* innermost constituents. Thus, the rule ordering will be indecisive.

In other words, by plastering over the internal structure and making it invisible to the stress rules, we can ensure apparent 'transparency' and prevent unnecessary stress from appearing. There seems to be nothing wrong with this since the correct stress pattern can be predicted from the currently given structure. However, it is not clear why we should make the internal structure invisible. In subsequent studies, the issue of exceptional treatment of this class of words does not seem to be solved entirely, for example in Liberman and Prince (1977), Hayes (1980, 1982), Halle and Vergnaud (1987: 251, hereafter *HV*) and many others.[6] In other words, this type of exception remains unaccounted for in a unified fundamental rule system.[7] The following, (6), shows typical exceptions of this type.

(6) Exceptional types of words to the MSR in *SPE* and others
àffirmátion, cònfirmátion, cònservátion, cònsultátion, cònversátion, ìnflammátion, ìnformátion, làmentátion, prèservátion, trànsformátion, trànsportátion, ùsurpátion

(*SPE*: 161; *HV*: 251)

To summarise the discussion briefly, the *còndênsátion* word type (1) is concerned with cyclicity and transparency, and this word type is well accounted for by cyclic stress inheritance. In contrast, the *ìnformátion* word type (4), postulated to be without an internal base verb, is not well accounted for in *SPE* and others – the plastered transparency problem. Therefore, the *ìnformátion* word type constitutes an exceptional category to the cyclic stress inheritance account.[8]

1.2 Another type of exception to treatments in OT

Optimality Theory (OT) (Prince and Smolensky 1993; McCarthy and Prince 1993a, 1993b and others) overturns the previous approaches. Rules and their cyclic application are abolished in favour of violable constraints and parallel treatment. In effect, the *ìnformátion* word type becomes the norm, (7a), while the *còndênsátion* word type is made the exception, (7b).

(7) a. ìn.for.má.tion word type: Norm in OT
     b. còn.dên.sá.tion word type: Exception in OT
        lexical 'constraint indexation' in Pater (1995, 2000, 2010) (cf. 'lexical accent' in Hammond 1999)
     c. lexically marked set S_1 = {condénsation, augméntation, authénticity, condémnation, impórtation, ...}[9]
     d. ID-STRESS-S_1

Since there are no derivations in classic OT, the infórmátion word type seems to fit best for their purposes, as the word does not show any stress inheritance effect on the antepenultimate syllable. On the other hand, the còndênsátion word type with a stress inheritance effect on the second syllable poses a difficulty, an opacity problem, as shown by the exceptional treatment of this type of word in classic OT in (8).

(8) còndênsátion, àugmêntátion, àuthêntícity, còndêmnátion, impôrtátion, ...

For this class of exceptional words, Pater (2000), for instance, suggests that they should be placed in a *lexically* marked set in the lexicon as S_1 (i.e. a set-1), (7c). Only one type of highest-ranked, specially assumed constraint 'ID-STRESS-S_1', (7d), will then be activated for this set of words, giving the required output as in (9ciii) in contrast to (9bii) for the word infórmátion on the tableau (see similar discussion in Chapter 1, section 5.2):[10]

(9) ìn.for.má.tion vs còn.dên.sá.tion
     a. ID-STRESS-S_1 >> *CLASH-HEAD >> ID-STRESS
     b.

	ID-STRESS-S_1	*CLASH-HEAD	ID-STRESS
i. infórmation (input)			
☞ ii. [infor][má]tion			*
iii. [ìn][fòr][má]tion		*!	

     c.

	ID-STRESS-S_1	*CLASH-HEAD	ID-STRESS
i. condénsation (input) in S_1 (i.e. condénsation in S_1)			
ii. [cònden][sá]tion	*!		*
☞ iii. [còn][dèn][sá]tion		*	

This, too, is an exceptional treatment. Later in OT, the theory was modified to accept the derivational aspect in the stress assignment of words; however, this causes another problem, which will not be discussed here due to the space limitations of the chapter (see the relevant discussion in Chapter 1, sections 5.2 and 5.3).

1.3 Opposite treatments

The discussion in this chapter may appear to be a narrow one in which only two types of exceptional analyses in *SPE* and Pater (1995, 2000) are compared. However, this is not the case: it is based on the detailed discussions in Yamada (2010). The reader is referred to that study to see how this issue and others have been handled in *SPE* and subsequent analyses (including OT). Among these various analyses, for the sake of brevity, the treatment in *SPE* is taken up here as a representative of the so-called pre-OT analysis of subsidiary stress(es), and that in Pater (1995, 2000) as a representative of the analysis in classic OT.

The reason for this selection is that this problem (i.e. how to handle *information*-type words) first appears in *SPE*, and its exceptional handling has not yet been resolved, even by *HV*. In other words, the *SPE* approach has continued unresolved, and this type of word has continually been 'neglected' in a sense, as exceptional or peripheral. Thus, no unified theory has been proposed yet to systematically incorporate this type of word into the core data to which the basic stress rules apply directly.

Meanwhile and conversely, since OT, words of the *information* type have become those that can be explained without issue. They have accordingly been treated as the core group supporting theories in classic OT. However, classic OT seems then to be obliged to categorise *còndênsátion*-type words as exceptional, meaning that the latter are not the central or core words supporting classic OT but the periphery.

More recently, within OT, for example in Bermúdez-Otero (2012), a non-exceptional explanation is put forward using the idea of 'relative frequency of the base and its derivative'. However, the problems of this relative frequency analysis have been quantitatively pointed out in Yamada (2016) using the CELEX2 (Baayen et al. 1995) database.

Thus, the problem of *information* vs *còndênsátion* has been challenging to explain in a unified way within a theoretical system, both in *SPE*, *HV* and others and in classic OT. One group of words constitutes an exception in one theoretical framework, while the same group of words constitutes the core within another framework.

2 A solution

2.1 A solution to exceptional word types by Positional Function Theory (PFT) for subsidiary stress assignment

In the face of these and other issues, a new treatment for the stress assignment of words in English was put forward in Yamada (2010), entitled Positional Function Theory (PFT), followed by Yamada (2011a, 2011b, 2012, 2013a,

2013b, 2014, 2015a, 2015b, 2016, 2018), Takeda (2011), Liu (2012, 2016) and Tomioka (2019). In Yamada (2010), the *subsidiary* stress rule of American English (General American) is postulated to be composed of 16 Positional Functions (PFs), as in (10), selected from a universal set of Functions through the linguistic experience.[11] Subsidiary stresses are then computed by the combination of PFs activated on the specific syllables by each condition.

(10)　16 Positional Functions for *subsidiary* stress assignment of English words[12]
  a. *Farness (F)*　$f(x) = *$
  b. *Heaviness (H)*　$h(x) = +$
  c. *Trace (T)*　$t(x) = +$
  d. *Binarity (B)*　$b(x) = +$
  e. *Rhythm (R)*　$r(x) = +*$
  f. *Alveolar Consonant Sequence (ACS)*　$acs(x) = *$
  g. *Velar–Alveolar Sequence (VAS)*　$vas(x) = *$
  h. *Bare Nucleus Avoidance (BNA)*　$bna(x) = -$
  i. *Edge Exemption I (EE-I)*　$eeI(x) = *$, accompanied by $b(x) = +$
  j. *Edge Exemption II (EE-II)*　$eeII(x) = *$
  k. *Double Stop (DS)*　$ds(x) = *$
  l. *Category Selection (CS)*　$cs(x) = *$
  m. *Free Binarity (FB)*　$fb(x) = +$
  n. *Rhythmic Adjustment (RA)*　$ra(x) = *$
  o. *Stress Reduction (SR)*　$sr(x) = -$ (or $\neg *$)
  p. *Sole Stress Resistance (SSR)*　$ssr(x) = @$

For each English word, any number of Positional Functions are activated according to their specified conditions for application *whenever* those conditions are satisfied. Each Positional Function gives its designated stress value to the specified syllable position. Subsidiary stress assignment is thereby reduced to the interaction of these closely related universal Functions. Almost all the words discussed in the previous literature in English phonology can be appropriately accounted for by means of these 16 Functions put forward in Yamada (2010).

2.1.1 Analysis of subsidiary stress in còndênsátion
Let us now look at an actual analysis and representation of subsidiary stress assignment in PFT, for example in *còndênsátion* in (11).

(11)   còndênsátion (2310) (< condénse (01))

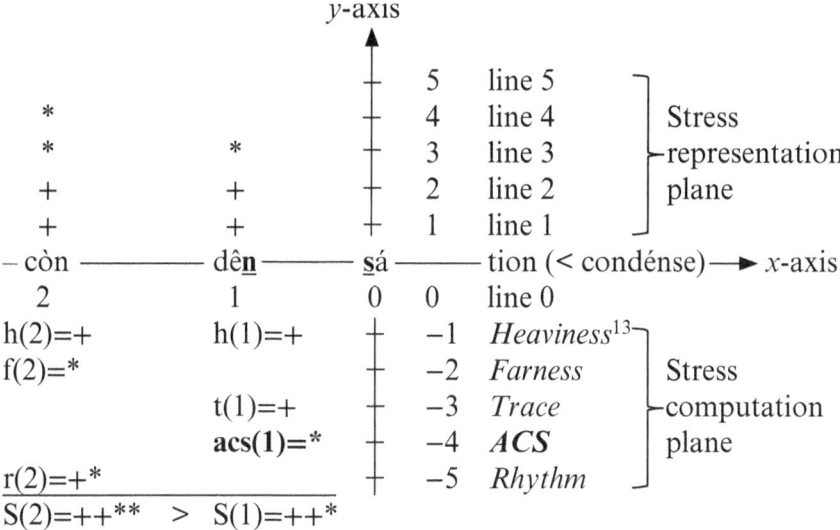

PFs activated in (11): [h(2)=+, f(2)=*, r(2)=+*, h(1)=+, t(1)=+, acs(1)=*][14]

The analysis shows stress inheritance on the second syllable, *dên*, represented by the three levels of stress values indicating tertiary stress in this case (in contrast to four levels of stress values on the first syllable *còn*, indicating secondary stress). On the stress computation plane below the *x*-axis, five Positional Functions (*Heaviness, Farness, Trace, ACS* and *Rhythm*) are activated under each syllable at six positions.[15] The sum of the stress value under each syllable is mapped onto the stress representation plane above the *x*-axis. The subsidiary stress value is represented by the height of the column on each syllable. Thus, the tertiary stress on the antepenultimate syllable *dên* caused by stress inheritance is shown by the accumulated three stress values '+, +, *' on *dên* on the stress representation plane, in contrast with the secondary stress on the first syllable *còn* with four accumulated stress values '+, +, *, *'; the three stress values of *dên* are weaker than the four of *còn*. The position of primary stress is expressed by the origin of the coordinate axes.

2.1.2 Analysis of subsidiary stress in ìnformátion
For the word *ìnformátion* below, (12), on the other hand, *ACS* is *not* triggered on the second syllable *for* since its coda is *not* an alveolar consonant, in distinct contrast with the analysis of *còndênsátion* in (11).[16]

(12)   informátion (2010) (< infórm (01))

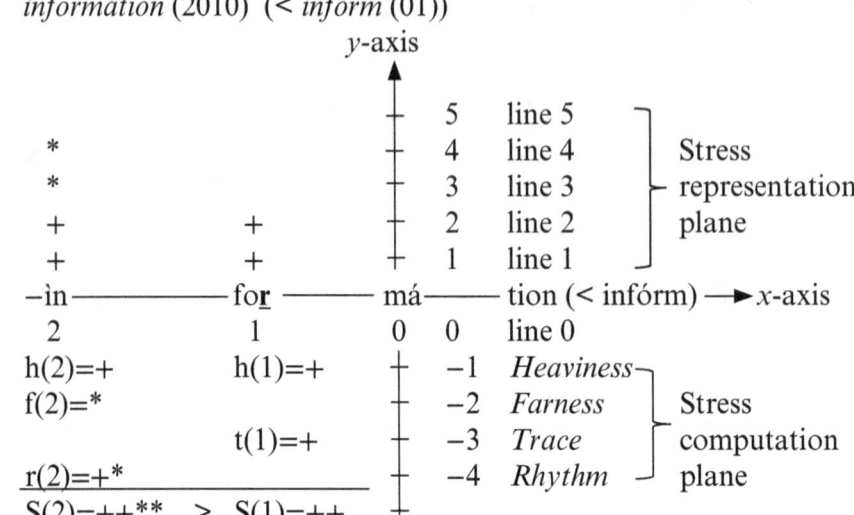

PFs activated in (12): [h(2)=+, f(2)=*, r(2)=+*, h(1)=+, t(1)=+]

Except for *ACS*, all other Functions activated for this word are identical to those of *còndênsátion* in (11). The loss of stress on the antepenultimate syllable *for* in *informátion* is attributed to this difference, that is, to the *non-application of ACS*. Note that, as seen in the antepenultimate syllable *for* here, we assume as a null hypothesis that if the stress value of one syllable differs from another by two or more, we can disregard the weaker value phonologically, that is, the stress on the antepenultimate syllable becomes zero in this case.[17]

Thus, in PFT, the *informátion* and *còndênsàtion* word types can both be equally accounted for within the same system, without recourse to exceptional treatment. I would like to emphasise one point here. This section has explained the subsidiary stress assignment of the word types of *còndênsátion* and *còmpensátion* only. However, with the PFT framework of Yamada (2010), by the systematic activation of 16 Positional Functions we can account for the subsidiary (secondary and tertiary) stress assignment of most words in English without a problem and principally without exceptional treatment.[18]

2.2 Main stress assignment in PFT

In this section, let us look at how we can account for the *main* stress assignment of words within the PFT framework.[19] As discussed in Chapter 1 of this volume, the basic tendency of the main stress assignment of words in English is as follows: in the case of nouns, if the *final syllable* is treated as *invisible* to stress rules, that is, extrametrical, main stress is placed on the last *visible* syllable when the last visible syllable is *heavy*, and on the penultimate visible syllable when the last visible syllable is *light*. These are illustrated by the main stress position of words such as *a.gén.<da>*, *co.nún.<drum>*, *ma.rí.<na>*, *a.lú.mi.<num>* and *Cá.na.<da>*, with the extrametrical invisible syllable enclosed by angled brackets. In addition, verbs and adjectives can be explained by the same principle if the *final consonant* is extrametrical, invisible to the stress rules. Words such as *só.li.<d>*, *cér.tai.<n>*, *as.tó.ni.<sh>*, *su.pré.<me>*, *a.chíe.<ve>* and *i.ná.<ne>* are typical examples. Further, adjectives with specific suffixes are considered *nominally*, that is, they behave like nouns: *pér.so.<nal>*, *à.nec.dó.<tal>*, *re.púg.<nant>* and *mô.mén.<tous>*. The exceptions to these generalisations are words whose final syllable is heavy, such as *po.líce*, *brô.cáde* and *re.gíme*. These observations are generalised into stress rules starting with *SPE* and subsequently integrated into *HV* (see Chapter 8 of this volume).[20]

Thus, based on these familiar observations and generalisations, it will be sufficient to assume just three Positional Functions (13a, b, c) with Extrametricality (13d) for the *main* stress assignment of English words within the framework of PFT in Yamada (2010, 2013a) (see Chapter 5 of this volume for Extrametricality).

(13) Three Positional Functions for the *main* stress assignment (MSA) of English words with Extrametricality (Yamada 2013)
   a. *Heaviness (H)* $h(x) = +$
   b. *Bounded Binarity (BB(L)-M)* $bb(x) = +$
   c. *Rhythmic Adjustment (RA(R)-M)*[21] $ra(x) = +$
   d. Extrametricality (from Hayes 1980, 1982, 1995; *HV* and others)

Note that these three Positional Functions are almost identical to those postulated for *subsidiary* stress assignment, with parametric differences in (14b, c): for (14b) the head is *left*; for (14c), it is *right*. Their definitions are as follows:

(14) a. *Heaviness (H)*: Assign stress '+' to the heavy syllable by the formula $h(x) = y$ with the stress value '+', i.e. $h(x) = +$.
   b. *Bounded Binarity* (obligatory) for *main* stress assignment *(BB(L)-M)*: In a successive sequence of two light syllables metrically adjacent to the origin (0, 0) of the coordinate axes,[22] an intrinsic[23] Positional Function *Bounded Binarity (BB)* is obligatorily triggered on the *left* head of the binary constituent, placing stress for the binary constituent by the formula $bb(x) = +$.
   c. *Rhythmic Adjustment* (obligatory) for *main* stress assignment *(RA(R)-M)*:

When an even stressed pattern appears metrically adjacent to the origin (0, 0), augment the *right*most of the relevant syllables by one obligatorily, by means of the formula $ra(x) = *$.

d. Extrametricality (from Hayes 1980, 1982, 1995; *HV*)
   i. A final syllable with a short vowel is not counted in nouns and in certain suffixes.[24]
   ii. A word-final consonant is not counted in non-nominals, i.e. verbs, adjectives, or others [partly adopted from a condition of the *Accent Rule* in *HV*].

As just mentioned, the functions of these three PFs in *main* stress assignment – *Heaviness*, *Bounded Binarity* and *Rhythmic Adjustment* – are essentially the same as those of *Heaviness*, (*Free*) *Binarity* and *Rhythmic Adjustment* in the *subsidiary* stress assignment rule. The difference is that the parameters of the direction in which they act and the environment in which they are activated are set differently. *Heaviness* (14a) for main stress assignment is the same Function as used for subsidiary stress assignment. The head parameter of the *Rhythmic Adjustment* Positional Function (10n and Appendix n) is set to the left and applied *optionally* for subsidiary stress assignment (Yamada 2010: 289), but in (14c) it is set to the right and applied *obligatorily* for main stress assignment. On the other hand, *Bounded Binarity* in (14b) is a Positional Function unique to main stress assignment, and its head parameter is set to the left. When a parameter is set uniquely for main stress assignment, '-M', meaning 'for main stress assignment', is suffixed.

In other words, even though the rules are different – main or subsidiary stress rules – they are common components of the overall system, as the same types of commonly assumed PFs contain parameters as part of their definitions. It should be noted that Extrametricality, by its very nature, cannot be seamlessly encoded into the overall system as one of the PFs at present. This is discussed in Yamada (2014). It would be ideal if Extrametricality could be incorporated as a PF, but this is a subject for further research.

Now, let us show actual examples for each Positional Function. In the computation of main stress assignment, unlike subsidiary stress assignment, the origin of the coordinate axes (0, 0) is set at the word boundary at the end of the word, following Yamada (2013a). In the *agénda* word type (15), for example, the last syllable of the word satisfies the condition for Extrametricality (14di). Eventually, *Heaviness* in (14a) becomes the only Function that satisfies any of the invoking conditions in (14) and brings main stress to the last visible heavy syllable *gen*, as in (15).

(15)   a.gén.da (010)²⁵

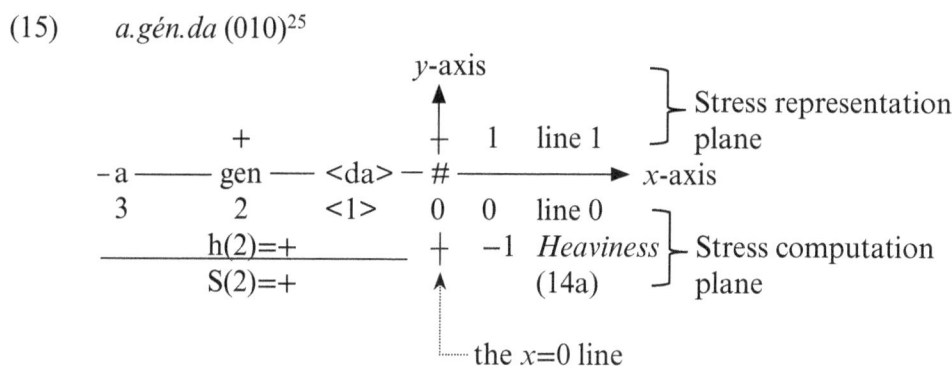

PF activated in (15): [h(2)=+]

In the case of the *Canada* word type in (16) below, *Bounded Binarity* in (14b) is also the only Function that satisfies any of the invoking conditions in (14), yielding main stress on the first syllable, *Ca*. The key to the activation of this Function is that there are two consecutive light syllables to the left of the *invisible* final syllable, which is extrametrical by (14di) in (16). This Function provides a left-headed binary foot according to (14b).²⁶

(16)   Cá.na.da (100)²⁷

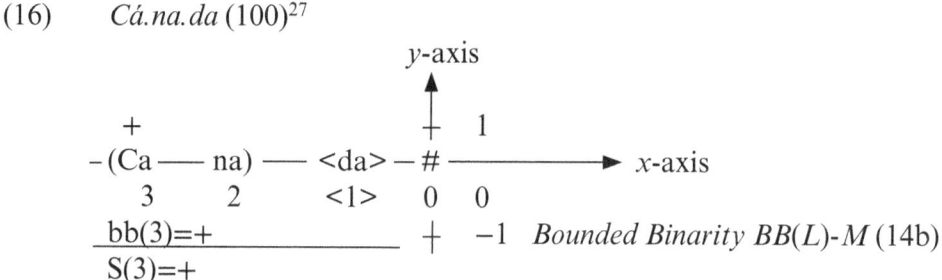

PF activated in (16): [bb(3)=+]

In the case of the word type *mô.mén.tous* (310) (i.e. *m[ʊ].men.tous*) in (17) below, the analysis is a little more complicated. Extrametricality will be applied by the condition in (14di), since the word ends in *-ous*, one of the specific suffixes mentioned in (14di) and accompanying note. *Heaviness* will also be triggered on the first and second heavy syllables.

(17)   mô.mén.tous (310)

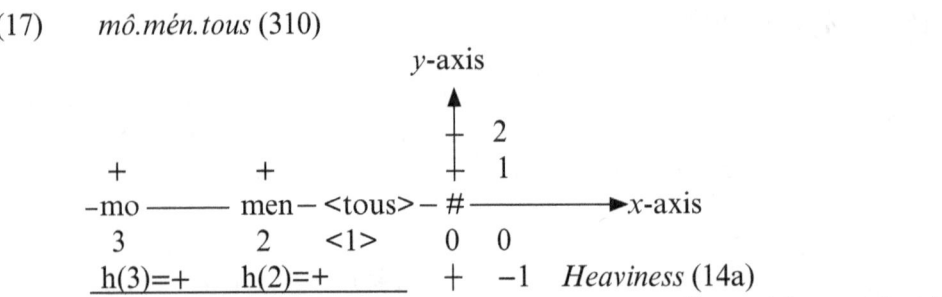

PFs activated in (17): [h(3)=+, h(2)=+]

However, for this type of word consisting of two successive heavy syllables to the left of the invisible extrametrical final syllable, we cannot determine the main stress solely by the Function *Heaviness* (14a), which at present is applied twice, on the first and second syllables. *Bounded Binarity* (14b) does not apply since the word is not composed of two successive light syllables. In order to account for the main stress, we need to enhance the stress by one on the second syllable. In *HV* (*HV*: 228) this is realised by 'Line 1 parameter settings [+HT, −BND, right]', which enhance *right* stress in such words. Similarly, therefore, in PFT we will assume a Positional Function *Rhythmic Adjustment* with an identical role. *Rhythmic Adjustment* is *obligatorily* triggered on the second syllable as (18) for main stress assignment.[28]

(18)   mô.mén.tous (310)

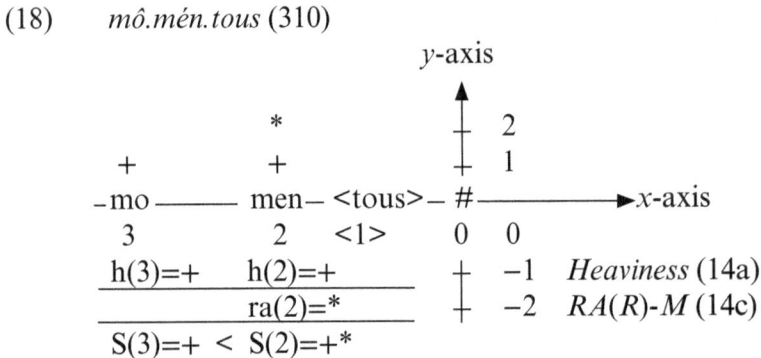

PFs activated in (18): [h(3)=+, h(2)=+, ra(2)=*]

Compared with the account of subsidiary stress assignment requiring 16 Positional Functions, it may seem too easy that we require only three Functions in addition to Extrametricality to account for main stress assignment in a significant number of words in English. Nevertheless, they can account for almost all word types, including nouns such as *a.gén.<da>*, *co.nún.<drum>*, *ma.rí.<na>*, *a.lú.mi.<num>*, *Cá.na.<da>*, adjectives such as *só.li.<d>*, *cér.tai.<n>*, *as.tó.ni.<sh>*, *su.pré.<me>*, *a.chíe.<ve>*, *i.ná.<ne>*, words with certain suffixes such as *pér.so.<nal>*, *à.nec.dó.<tal>*, *re.púg.<nant>*, *mô.mén.<tous>*, and words with final main stress such as *po.líce, brô.cáde, re.gíme*. As discussed in the first paragraph of section 2.2, these represent the core mechanism of stress placement in English words.

Notice also that we highlighted in Chapter 1 of this volume that a Latin stress rule is deeply embedded in the stress assignment mechanism of English words, namely 'stress is generally assigned to a heavy penult, while the antepenult receives stress if the penult is light' (Hayes 1982: 239) (see Chapter 4 of this volume). The Latin stress rule can be stated more simply as a principle in (19) if we take into account the observations and generalisations of the paragraph above and the statement at the beginning of this subsection with the help of Extrametricality.

(19) Extended Latin Stress
Given Extrametricality, stress is assigned to a heavy ultimate, while the penult receives stress if the ultimate is light.

It is this Extended Latin Stress that governs the main stress assignment of words in English, and this can be basically expressed by three Positional Functions and Extrametricality in (13) in PFT.

Note again that what we have done in section 2.2 is to replace the traditional system of rules for the main stress assignment of words with our treatment within the PFT framework. Although we may not be able to claim that this shows greater explanatory adequacy, it does show that what can be explained by traditional theories can also be accounted for by PFT. Further, as mentioned in section 2.1, we can use solely fundamental stress rules without auxiliary rules to explain subsidiary (secondary and tertiary) stress assignment, including word groups that could previously be explained only exceptionally.

3 Remaining issues in PFT

As outlined in previous sections, it would seem that Yamada's (2010, 2013a) system works well. However, this is not the case. Words such as those in (20), where main stress is assigned to the *left* of the subsidiary stress, remain unexplained in PFT.[29]

(20) a. *a.cé.ty.lène á.symp.tòte dé.sig.nàte* (verb) *ex[g.z]á.cer.bàte fôr.mál.de.hỳde ré.cog.nìze*
b. *ál.ka.lòid agg.lú.ti.nà.tive ân.tí.ci.pa.tòry con.fís.ca.tòry de.fá.ma.tòry dý.na.mìte in.hí.bi.tòry*

(Examples cited chiefly from *HV*: 234–55)

We will explore how these types of words are accounted for in PFT by taking up the typical examples *désignàte* from (20a) and *confiscatòry* from (20b) as representatives.

3.1 The *désignàte* word type in PFT

The newly developed account of PFT shows that, as outlined in Yamada (2013a), we require *three* Positional Functions to assign main stress correctly: *Heaviness, Bounded Binarity* and *Rhythmic Adjustment*. In the previous sections, we postulate these three PFs with the help of Extrametricality, following Hayes (1980, 1982, 1995), *HV* and others. With regard to *désignàte*, Extrametricality (14dii) applies to the final consonant /t/ since this is a verb, giving *de.sig.na<te>*. Because the remaining final two syllables are heavy, *Heaviness* is triggered on both, followed by *Rhythmic Adjustment* whose head parameter is set to *right*, as shown in (21).

(21)   *désignàte* (102)[30]

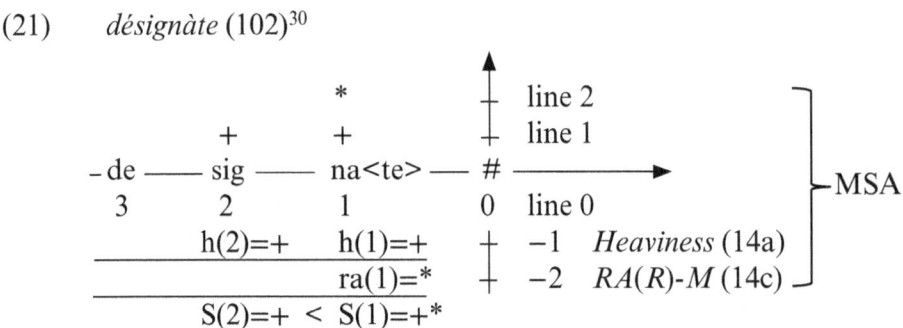

PFs activated in (21): [h(2)=+, h(1)=+, ra(1)=*]

Primary stress at this stage is placed on the final syllable.

Next, based on the placement of primary stress on the final syllable, *subsidiary* stress assignment (SSA) will be carried out by the combination of applicable PFs shown in section 2.1, following Yamada (2010), giving (22).[31]

(22)   *désignàte* (102)

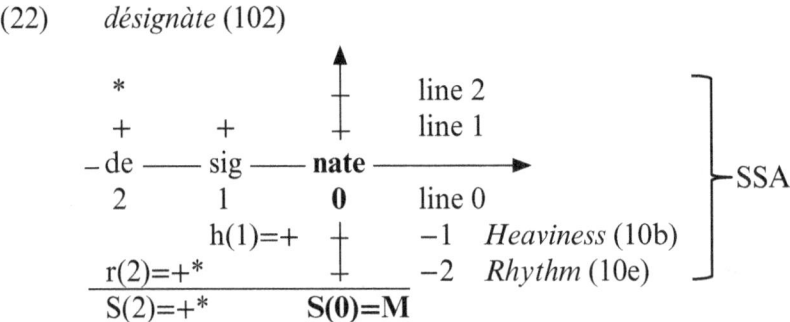

PFs activated in (22): [r(2)=+*, h(1)=+]

A Solution to Theoretical Shortcomings

Notice, however, that we have not achieved the required analysis and representation here; instead, we have an incorrect result with secondary stress on the first syllable and primary stress remaining on the final syllable: *dè.sig. náte (201).[32] The required stress pattern of the word is désignàte (102) with primary stress on the first syllable. Thus, we need to move the stress from the final syllable to the first syllable to give the correct output. Specifically, the positions of primary and secondary stress have to be reversed. Various methods have been proposed in previous studies to realise this stress movement. For instance, *SPE* (*SPE*: 96) employs an *Alternating Stress Rule*, and *HV* (*HV*: 235, 275, 276) applies a *Rhythm Rule* lexically. In our PFT version, we will postulate the Coordinate Axis Shift (CAS) lexically, in (23).[33]

(23) Coordinate Axis Shift (CAS) (lexical)
The origin (0, 0) of the Coordinate Axes involved in the subsidiary stress assignment is shifted to the next-highest stress position to the left as a new origin (0, 0); the stress value of the *original* next-highest stress position is copied back onto the 'old' origin in the reverse direction.

With the help of CAS in (23), we are able to obtain the following analysis and representation for this word, as in (24).[34]

(24) Analysis of *dé.sig.nàte* (102) with CAS[35]

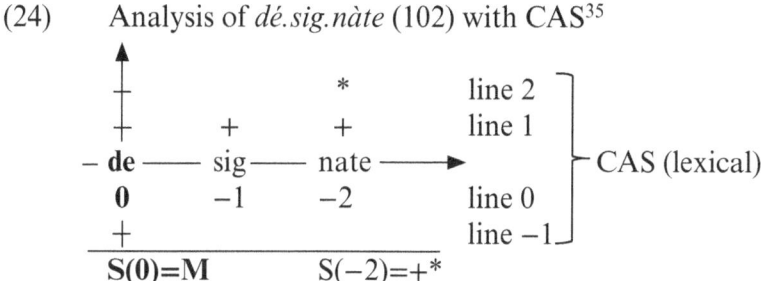

A new origin (0, 0) is set at the first syllable, numbered 0 (*de* in this case), and syllables are numbered rightward from that origin (as -1, -2 etc.). Subsidiary stress is assigned to the final syllable, numbered -2.

Now let us review all the processes of computation for *désignàte* in (21), (22) and (24). In (21), primary stress is assigned to the last syllable, numbered 1, by means of two *Heavinesses* (14a) triggered on syllables 2 and 1 with the help of the PF formulae $h(2) = +$ and $h(1) = +$, respectively. For main stress assignment, *Rhythmic Adjustment* (14c), whose parameter is set to the *right*, is triggered, giving the final stress as a *first* process of computation. In (22), *subsidiary* stress is assigned to the first syllable by the PFs *Heaviness* $h(1) = +$ and *Rhythm* $r(2) = +*$, yielding the subsidiary stress on the first syllable in this *second* process of computation. Finally, the positions of primary and secondary stress are reversed by Coordinate Axis Shift (CAS) in (24).

At first glance, this looks complicated, but the basics are simple: the positions of the primary and secondary stresses are reversed in certain lexically marked words employing a concept that has been used in classical generative phonology. In other words, CAS is lexically activated for these types of words in (20a). Although the activation is restricted to certain lexically specified words *with* final stress as a trigger, this is a kind of exceptional treatment in PFT.

3.2 The *con.fis.ca.tòry* word type in PFT

For a word such as *confiscatòry* in (20b), following the account in *HV* we also have to postulate that certain suffixes are treated lexically as 'suffixes that are stress domain', that is, they are treated as independent words regarding stress assignment. Thus, in the case of *confiscatòry*, for example, we will divide the word into two domains and calculate the stress assignment in each, as shown in (25).

(25)   Analysis of *con.fis.ca.tòry* (01020) in two stress domains

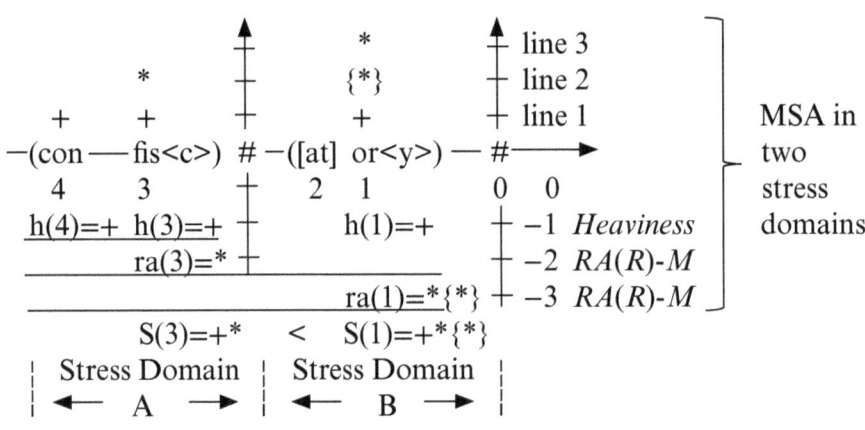

PFs activated in (25): [h(4)=+, h(3)=+, ra(3)=*, h(1)=+, ra(1)=*{*}]

Namely, by adopting the idea in *HV* (*HV*: 256), we postulate that this type of word is composed phonologically of two stress domains enclosed by parentheses.[36]

In (25), the constituent *confisc* is within Stress Domain A, while the suffix constituent *atory* is within Stress Domain B. For *confisc* in A, since it is *not* a noun, it is natural to treat it as non-nominal, that is, Extrametricality (14dii) is applied to the last consonant, yielding *con.fis.<c>*. Then, on line −1 *Heaviness* is activated on two heavy syllables, *con* and *fis*, by h(4) = + and h(3) = +, followed by *Rhythmic Adjustment* ra(3) = * on line −2 with the right head parameter (*RA(R)-M*) in Stress Domain A. The sum of the resulting stress values is mapped onto the stress representation plane, showing one stress value '+' on syllable 4 and two stress values '+, *' on syllable 3, for *con.fis.<c>* in Stress Domain A.

With regard to the suffix *atory* in Stress Domain B, Extrametricality (14dii) is again applied to the last *y* following the assumption that there is an underlying glide (*SPE*: 41), giving *a.tor<y>*.[37] Thus, *Heaviness h*(1) = + alone on line −1 is triggered in Stress Domain B. Then, the whole word *confis<c>* plus *ator<y>* is scanned to determine whether any other PFs are activated here, which triggers *Rhythmic Adjustment ra*(1) = * on line −3 (*RA(R)-M*).[38]

At this stage of computation, when we arrive at the stage of *confiscatory* as a single word constructed by two stress domains, we tentatively place the secondary stress at syllable number 3 and primary stress at syllable number 1 in (25). However, if we look at the phonetic facts, *con.fis.ca.tòry* (01020), main stress falls on syllable number 3 *fis<c>* and subsidiary stress on syllable number 1 *òr<y>*. In order to achieve this, we have to reverse the positions of primary and secondary stress. However, since there are already two coordinate *axes* in this case, we cannot use the method of moving the right coordinate axes from right to left. If we did so, we would be altering the existing syntactic constituent structure merely to explain the phonological phenomenon, which is theoretically inappropriate.[39] Therefore, in this case we will have to postulate again the following operation between the two stress domains, terming it *Stress Retraction*, as in (26).

(26)   Stress Retraction[40]
       Primary stress is retracted to the primary stressed position of the left domain when two stress domains are adjacent within a word.

With (26) applied, the primary stress on the final syllable is retracted to the primary stressed position of the left domain, giving *confiscatòry* with primary stress on the second syllable, as shown in (27).

(27)   Analysis of *con.fis.ca.tòry* (01020) by Stress Retraction in two stress domains

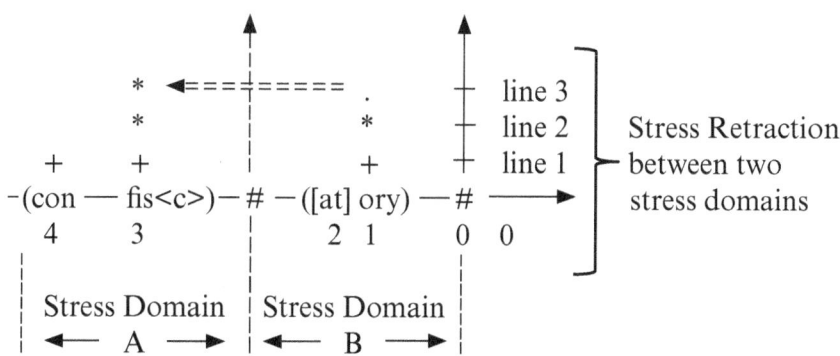

Notice here that Stress Retraction in (26) does not erase the distinction between the two stress domains.

To summarise the discussion here, first in (25) the two domains enclosed by parentheses are treated independently; then primary stress is placed on the final syllable *ory* in Stress Domain B when *confiscatory* is considered as a single word. In (27), the *final* primary stress is retracted to the highest stress position in Stress Domain A by Stress Retraction in (26).

3.3 Two types of primary–secondary stress patterns in PFT

Both Coordinate Axis Shift (23) in section 3.1 and Stress Retraction (26) in section 3.2 have the effect of moving the main stress to the left. Then, is there any motivation for treating the Coordinate Axis Shift and Stress Domain word types *differently*, as shown in (28)?

(28) a. Coordinate Axis Shift type (section 3.1)
 a.cé.ty.lène   á.symp.tòte   dé.sig.nàte (verb)   *ex[g.z]á.cer.bàte*
 fôr.mál.de.hỳde   ré.cog.nìze
 b. Stress Domain type (section 3.2)[41]
 (agg.lú.ti.n)([àt]i.ve)   (ál.ka.l)(òi.d)   (ân.tí.ci.p)([at]òr.y)
 (con.fís.c)([at]òr.y)   (de.fá.m)([at]òr.y)   (dý.na.m)(ì.te)
 (in.hí.bi.t)(òr.y)

In fact, there is. In the case of (28a), the Coordinate Axis Shift word type accompanied by syllable *weight* indication in (29), the main stress is shifted two syllables away from the stressed syllable at the end, *regardless of* the weight of the immediately preceding syllables.

(29) Coordinate Axis Shift type in PFT

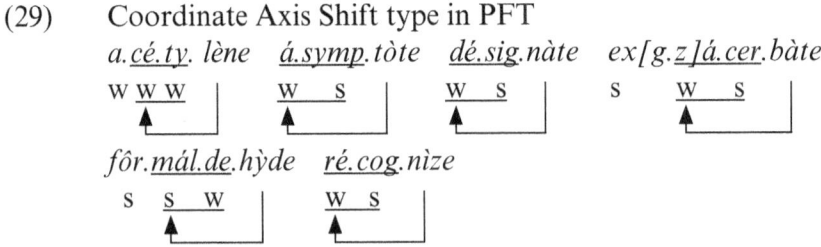

For example, *a.cé.ty.lène* has a light syllable, *ty*, described as *w* (for 'weak'), immediately before the final syllable *lène*, while *á.symp.tòte* has a heavy syllable, *symp*, described as *s* (for 'strong'), immediately before the final syllable *tòte*. Despite these differences, both words are assigned their actual main stress on the two preceding syllables, *a.cé.ty.lène* and *á.symp.tòte*, counted from the tentative last main stress in the middle stage of stress computation. Notice here that Coordinate Axis Shift in the PFT framework is almost the same operation as Hayes's (1980, 1982) *Strong Retraction* or *HV's Alternator*.

A Solution to Theoretical Shortcomings 307

In the case of (28b) on the other hand, the Stress Domain word type, as shown in (30) below with syllable *weight* indication, main stress assignment *respects* the syllable weight distinction.

(30)   Stress Domain type in PFT[42]
       a. (*agg.lú. ti.<n>*)([*àt*]*i<ve>*) (*ál.ka.<l>*)(*òi<d>*)
           s   w w   s w
           ↑   ↑

         (*ân.tí.ci.<p>*)([*at*]*òr<y>*)
           s w w
           ↑

         (*dý.na.<m>*)(*ì<te>*) (*in.hí.bi.<t>*)(*òr<y>*)
           s w   s w w
           ↑   ↑
      b. (*con.fis.<c>*)([*at*]*òr<y>*) (*de.fá.<m>*)([*at*]*òr<y>*)
           s s   s s
           ↑   ↑

For example, in *agglútinàtive, álkalòid, ântícipatòry, dýnamìte* and *inhíbitòry* in (30a), the weight of the syllable preceding the final syllable in each constituent in the left stress domain is *w* (underlined for emphasis in (30a)). On the other hand, in *confíscatòry* and *defámatòry* in (30b), it is *s* (underlined for emphasis in (30b)). Thus, if the syllable immediately preceding the final syllable in the left domain is *w*, primary stress falls on the *next* syllable to the left as in (30a).[43] When the syllable immediately preceding the final syllable is *s*, primary stress falls on the *s* syllable as in (30b). This generalisation is consistent with the generalisation regarding the stress assignment of words in English at the beginning of section 2.2: after applying Extrametricality to all types of words, if the last visible syllable is heavy, main stress is placed on the last visible syllable; otherwise, main stress is placed one syllable to the left. Since the word types in (30) consist of two stress domains, it seems quite natural that a constituent considered as one phonological word in its left domain in front of another would be in line with the generalisation concerning stress assignment as a single word. To summarise briefly, in 'primary–secondary' stress pattern words in (28), the Coordinate Axis Shift word type (28a) (section 3.1) does not respect syllable weight as in (29), while the Stress Domain word type (28b) (section 3.2) *does* as in (30a, b).

Then, why do we need distinct mechanisms for these two types of words when they show similar effects? The reason derives from the difference in the structure of the words as mentioned above. Those in (28a) fall within a single stress domain, while those in (28b) span two stress domains. Now, recall the discussions and generalisations at the end of section 2.2, where we summarise as (19) that stress assignment is governed by Extended Latin Stress. Extended Latin Stress covers all types of words with the help of Extrametricality, and also governs the stress assignment in the first stress domain in (28b). The fact that the first half of the word is considered a stress domain in (28b) means that it is treated as a phonological word. Extended Latin Stress governs a word, not part of a word. Though superficially similar, the structures of these two types of words are principally different. Through detailed analysis, we can reveal the hidden regularity in what seemed to be exceptions to the treatment in PFT; its solution cannot be found merely by looking at the surface.

Although the treatment of the types of words in section 3 is considered lexical, this does not always mean that it is ad hoc, meaning each word has to be described individually in the lexicon. In fact, those words that require a kind of exceptional treatment retain an internal regularity, as discussed in section 3.3. The Extended Latin Stress observed in the embedded structure is the same as that found in the larger constituent structure. This principle governs the phonological word as well. Thus, our lexical treatments are not entirely ad hoc, showing that the same kind of regularity can be found inside or outside the embedded structure as long as they are phonological words.

4 Advantages of PFT

4.1 Treatment of tertiary stress in PFT

A number of additional features of PFT are worth clarifying here. First is the treatment of tertiary stress. It is noteworthy that PFT can seamlessly account for tertiary stress within a single, unified system. Of course, tertiary stress, as in the antepenultimate syllable of *còndênsátion*, has been variously accounted for in the phonological tradition from *SPE* to *HV* and others. In those theories, however, words of the *informátion* type have always been problematic and could not be accounted for using the fundamental stress rules alone: they required certain supplementary patches. On the other hand, in Pater (1995, 2000), who attempted to account for subsidiary stress assignment in English within the framework of classic OT, tertiary stress seems to have posed a considerable challenge to the theory itself.

Further, in Wells (2008) the pronunciation of *condensation* is listed in two ways: *còn.dên.sá.tion* (2310) as a first-listed stress variant, and *còn.den.sá.tion* (2010) as a second-listed variant. It should be noted that the first and second syllables of the word have distinct stress values: the variant *còn.dên.sá.tion* (2310) shows secondary stress on *còn* and tertiary stress on *dên*, while *còn.den.sátion* (2010) shows secondary stress on *còn* and schwa on *den*. However, in the tableau (9ciii) where Pater (1995, 2000) attempts to account for the stress pattern, both the first and second syllables of the word show equal stress values as *còn.dèn.sá.tion* (2210). We can state that the apparent difference in stress between the first and second syllables is not explained by the mechanism in Pater (1995, 2000) or elsewhere in classic OT. Although it may be

A Solution to Theoretical Shortcomings 309

possible to explain it in a supplementary way using other, special devices, the difference in stress value between first and second syllables would still not be explained as a single mechanism within the framework of Pater (1995, 2000) and others. This contrasts with the treatment in PFT where tertiary stresses in words are systematically accounted for in a single mechanism.

4.2 Stress variants in PFT

Next, we will examine stress variants. We can account for stress variants by means of the following four PFs, which are considered to apply optionally in PFT: *Free Binarity*, *Rhythmic Adjustment*, *Stress Reduction* and *Sole Stress Resistance*. Further, *Farness* is also optional if and only if it is applied to a binary constituent. In addition, when stress variants are found in the lexical representation of a base form (for example *ségment* (Noun), *ségment* (Verb), *segmént* (Verb)), the PF *Category Selection* is activated, by which the appearance of two types of stress variants, for example *sègmentátion* (2010) and *sègmêntátion* (2310), can be accounted for. That is, the appearance of stress variants is explained using the optional application of the PF *Category Selection* in this case. Of course, other PFs are always obligatorily applied if their activation conditions are met; in other words, they are *not* optional. To take one more example, the word *adaptation* has two variants, *àdâptátion* (2310) and *àdaptátion* (2010); the occurrence of these variants is accounted for by assuming that the PF *Stress Reduction* is activated optionally on the antepenultimate syllable.[44] If it is not activated, it will result in the appearance of *àdâptátion* (2310); if it is activated, it will result in the appearance of *àdaptátion* (2010). For the sake of brevity, we list below only the PFs activated for each: *àdâptátion* (2310): [h(2)=+, f(2)=*, bna(2)=−, r(2)=+*, h(1)=+, t(1)=+]; *àdaptátion* (2010): [h(2)=+, f(2)=*, bna(2)=−, r(2)=+*, h(1)=+, t(1)=+, sr(1)=−]). The difference is the last PF, *Stress Reduction* (*SR*), that is, sr(1) = − in (10o), activated for *àdaptátion* (2010) but not *àdâptátion* (2310), creating two stress variants in this case.

Further, let us take two other stress variants, *explicatory* and *emanatory*.[45] The stress patterns of these words are given as *êxplícatôry* (31030), *éxplicatôry* (10030) and *émanatôry* (10030) in Wells (2008).[46] However, using an algorithm termed the data clarification method by Yamada (2010), the only stress pattern in American English (General American) that has to be treated for *explicatory* is 10020, with primary stress on the first syllable and secondary stress on the penultimate syllable. The first listed variant with a 31030 stress pattern in Wells (2008) therefore falls outside the scope of our consideration, focusing on the *primary* stress position. The stress data from the data clarification method for *emanatory* (10020) is identical to Wells's *emanatory* (10030) with regard to the placement of *primary* stress. Therefore, if we wish to account for the first-listed stress variant of *explicatory* (31030) in the word list of American English in Wells, we have to modify one of the

PF's parameter settings in the PFT framework. However, we would like to leave this point to future research. Thus, the data we need to account for now are *éxplicatòry* (10020) and *émanatòry* (10020). Our analysis can handle these two without a problem. Both words have two stress domains, (*expli<c>*) (*atory*) and (*ema<n>*)(*atory*), and additionally the last consonant of the first domain of each word is analysed as being extrametrical. As a result, the syllable weight pattern of *e[k.s]pli<c>* is *s–w*, that of *e.ma<n>* is *w–w*, and for both, Stress Retraction retracts the main stress to the first syllable, as in *éxplicàtory* (10020) and *émanatòry* (10020). In other words, if the last syllable of the first constituent in the first stress domain is light, as in *w*, the main stress is instead placed on the preceding syllable in the case of words with two stress domains.

4.3 Superimposition of PFs

What is the main difference between other theories and this one? This approach shows how to explain, in one basic mechanism, words types that have been consigned to the opposite ends of the two theories as exceptional. The PFs postulated here are always activated, and calculated simultaneously only once on the relevant syllables, provided that the conditions for their application are met. Further, there is no ordering relation in their application.[47] Nor is there any ranking relation among PFs. The absence of a ranking relation implies no such concept as violability in applying PFs.

However, certain dependency relations do exist. Certain results from other PFs may be used as conditions for the activation of another PF. PFs are mostly defined in relation to adjacent or neighbouring syllables and their prosodic attributes. However, note that even in these cases, there is no derivational relationship in the sense that words are derived from one category to another. Three PFs, *Rhythmic Adjustment*, *Stress Reduction* and *Sole Stress Resistance*, have a function to adjust the results from other PFs; however, they merely adjust the results of the computation made by other PFs.

To reiterate our point from a slightly different perspective: the stress *values* generated are the result of superimposing the values of the PFs activated on each syllable. In this sense, PFT can be considered a superimposition theory. Currently, three real numbers are assumed for American English drawn from PFs as values: 1, 2 and -1.[48] If each of the 16 Positional Functions postulated for subsidiary stress assignment and each of the three Positional Functions for main stress assignment for English satisfies its activation condition at each syllable position, then the PF whose activation is not optional is obligatorily activated at that syllable position. The results of the computation made by the activation are superimposed on each syllable to finally determine the overall stress pattern of the word. In the sense of superimposition on each syllable, the PFT is a new theory based on a completely different concept from the traditional prosodic theories or Optimality Theory.

Finally, this theory has been developed with programmability in mind. By programming these hypothetical and theoretical devices, the hypothesis can be easily tested and modified using an automatic machine-learning search of words through the relevant database after all PFs have been completely programmed, using the database as input and comparing the results of the computation with the actual input. Such an attempt and empirical testing are currently underway in Yamada et al. (2022), programming five basic and representative PFs out of the 16 proposed in PFT using the complete dataset of 52,447 words (lemmas) in the CELEX2 database.

5 Conclusions

This chapter has examined the two types of previous theories dealing with stress placement in English words, pointing out the problems in their exceptional treatment of words. We then outlined a third and new method that can successfully resolve those issues and others in a more regular framework.

In *SPE* and subsequent studies, one of the exceptional word types is illustrated by *information*, which has to be treated exceptionally by assuming a 'flat' internal structure. However, this causes problems both with cyclicity and 'plastered transparency'. In OT, on the other hand, the picture is reversed: the *condênsátion* word type is made the exception, while the *information* word type becomes the norm. OT solved the issue of the *information* word type but created another with the *condênsátion* word type, the cyclicity and opacity problems. For these problems or exceptions, lexical or exceptional treatments have to be employed in classic OT.

To solve these and other issues, we have presented a new, third approach, Positional Function Theory (PFT). With the new approach, using 16 Positional Functions we have accounted for *subsidiary* stress assignment in exceptional word types, such as *information* and *condênsátion*, in a principled way within a single fundamental system, without recourse to exceptional or lexical treatment. We have also shown how we can explain *main* stress assignment within the framework of PFT, postulating three Positional Functions that are practically the same as those used for subsidiary stress assignment, with the aid of Extrametricality. If we follow the method proposed by PFT, we can clarify most of the main and subsidiary stress assignments of words in American English without a problem. This problem did not seem to be easy to solve before PFT.

Further, we have demonstrated that the remaining issues of PFT can be solved by postulating two types of mechanisms in our system regarding words with a 'primary–secondary' stress pattern: that is, we have solved the *désignàte* (102) word type by Coordinate Axis Shift, and the *confíscatòry* (01020) word type by Stress Domain. By investigating these two types of words, we have found that one principle, namely Extended Latin Stress, governs the internal structure of the word, as well as the higher level of constituent structure, as seen in the embedded construction. This is what divides the two distinct types of stress assignment between words belonging to the Coordinate Axis Shift type and the Stress Domain type: the embedded construction can be seen in the latter. In the light of this theory, what appeared to be lexical exceptions turn out not to be so. It is successfully controllable. In other words, exceptional words have regularities that can be elucidated, and they can be dealt with within this new approach.

Appendix: Postulated Positional Functions and conditions for subsidiary stresses in English

Positional Functions

a. *Farness* (*F*) (Relative Positional Function)
  Subsidiary stress is placed as far left as possible from the position of primary stress, with the value '*' of the Function *Farness* by means of the formula $f(x) = y$, i.e. $f(x) = *$.
b. *Heaviness* (*H*) (Intrinsic Positional Function)
  Assign stress '+' to the heavy syllable by the formula $h(x) = y$ with the stress value '+', i.e. $h(x) = +$.
c. *Trace* (*T*) (Intrinsic Positional Function)
  Stress the position of trace with a value '+' using the expression $t(x) = +$, where a trace is defined as a position of stress given on an earlier cycle.
d. *Binarity* (*B*) (Intrinsic Positional Function)
  Add '+' under a syllable position where a Positional Function *Trace* is given, using the expression $b(x) = +$, if and only if the immediately following syllable is weak and unmarked for any other Function.
e. *Rhythm* (*R*) (Relative Positional Function)
  The Positional Function *Rhythm*, with the formula $r(x) = y$, is activated on the leftmost syllable if the syllable immediately preceding the primary stressed syllable bears stress. The stress value of $r(x) = y$ is '+*', i.e. $r(x) = +*$.
f. *Alveolar Consonant Sequence* (*ACS*) (Relative Positional Function)
  In an alveolar consonant concatenation across distinct syllables, the stress value of a heavy syllable ending in a nasal consonant immediately followed by the primary stressed syllable is augmented by one if the onset consonant of the primary stressed syllable is voiceless, or if the coda consonant immediately preceding the syllable in question is voiceless. The *ACS* is expressed by the formula $acs(x) = *$.
g. *Velar–Alveolar Sequence* (*VAS*) (Relative Positional Function)
  If a velar consonant of the coda of the syllable in question is immediately followed by an onset alveolar consonant of the primary stressed

syllable, and at the same time if a *Trace* is activated on the syllable in question, stress is assigned to the syllable ending with the velar consonant, by means of the formula $vas(x) = *$.

h. *Bare Nucleus Avoidance (BNA)* (Intrinsic Positional Function)
   Stress assignment is avoided on a non-branching bare nucleus at the leftmost edge of a word by the formula $bna(x) = -$, provided that no intrinsic Positional Function is applied to the bare nucleus.

i. *Edge Exemption I (EE-I)* (Relative Positional Function)
   i. If a binary constituent can be constructed by combining two successive light syllables which are immediately preceded by a bare nucleus at the left edge of the word, the bare nucleus is exempted from bearing stress.
   ii. As a result of *Edge Exemption*, a relative stress '*' is assigned to the left head of the binary constituent by means of the formula $eeI(x) = *$, along with a '+' given to the binary constituent by means of $b(x) = +$.

j. *Edge Exemption II (EE-II)* (Relative Positional Function)
   i. If a binary constituent can be constructed by combining two successive light syllables – the first of which has a *Trace* – that are immediately preceded by a *heavy syllable* at the left edge of the word, the *first syllable* is exempted from bearing *more* stress.
   ii. As a result of *Edge Exemption II*, a relative stress mark '*' is added to the left head of the binary constituent by means of the formula $eeII(x) = *$, along with '+' *vacuously* assigned to the binary constituent by means of the formula $b(x) = +$.

k. *Double Stop (DS)* (Relative Positional Function)
   For a successive segmental sequence across the first and second syllables immediately preceding the primary stressed syllable, if the first syllable ends in the alveolar nasal stop consonant /n/ immediately followed by the second syllable with a stop consonant as its onset, a stress mark '*' is placed under the second syllable by the formula $ds(x) = *$.

l. *Category Selection (CS)* (Relative Positional Function)
   For the primary stressed syllable in a category marked by *CSP* in the lexicon, a relative Positional Function termed *Category Selection (CS)* is activated, by means of the formula $cs(x) = *$, along with *Trace* due to the primary stress of the underlying form.

m. *Free Binarity (FB)* (Intrinsic Positional Function)
   In a successive sequence of light syllables before a primary stressed syllable, an intrinsic Positional Function *Free Binarity (FB)* is optionally triggered on the left head of each binary constituent created leftward from the primary stressed syllable, placing a stress for each binary constituent by the formula $fb(x) = +$.

n. *Rhythmic Adjustment (RA)* (Adjustment Function) (optional)
   When an even-stressed pattern appears, augment the leftmost of the relevant syllables by one, by means of the formula $ra(x) = *$.

o. *Stress Reduction (SR)* (Adjustment Function) (optional)
   Reduce weaker stress by one, by means of the formula
   $sr(x) = -$ (or $\neg *$).
p. *Sole Stress Resistance (SSR)* (Adjustment Function) (optional)
   Application of *Stress Reduction (SR)* is blocked by *Sole Stress Resistance (SSR)* by means of the formula $ssr(x) = @$ if the stress to be reduced is the sole stress before the primary stress.

Conditions or modifications

a. *Farness* is activated only when the same type of syllable appears successively on the same level.
b. Prohibition against double application
   Double application of the same type of Positional Function is not allowed on the same syllable.
c. Non-superimposition
   Relative Positional Functions may not be superimposed on the bound target, where the bound target is a target whose position of activation by Positional Function is specified precisely by definition.
d. *Farness* optionality
   The application of *Farness* to a binary constituent is optional.

Process in the lexicon

a. *Category Selection Process (CSP)*
   If identical category levels are assigned to a lexical item, a category must be appropriately selected in the lexicon before the lexical item is sent to morphology.

Postulated Positional Functions and conditions for Main Stress in English

a. *Heaviness (H)*
   Assign stress '+' to the heavy syllable by the formula $h(x) = y$ with the stress value '+', i.e. $h(x) = +$.
b. *Bounded Binarity* (obligatory) for main stress assignment (*BB(L)-M*)
   In a successive sequence of two light syllables metrically adjacent to the origin (0, 0), an intrinsic Positional Function *Bounded Binarity (BB)* is obligatorily triggered on the left head of the binary constituent, placing stress for the binary constituent by the formula $bb(x) = +$.
c. *Rhythmic Adjustment* (obligatory) for main stress assignment (*RA(R)-M*)
   When an even stressed pattern appears metrically adjacent to the origin (0, 0), augment the rightmost of the relevant syllables by one obligatorily, by means of the formula $ra(x) = *$.

d. Extrametricality (from Hayes 1980, 1982, 1995; *HV*)
   i. A final syllable with a short vowel is not counted in nouns and in certain suffixes.
   ii. A word-final consonant is not counted in non-nominals, i.e. verbs, adjectives, or others [partly adopted from a condition of the Accent Rule in *HV*].

Notes

This chapter is based on presentations given at the PAC 2015 International Conference: Advances in the Phonology and Phonetics of Contemporary English (held at Université Toulouse – Jean Jaurès, Toulouse, France, on 10 April 2015) and the 11th International Spring Forum 2018 (held at Hokkaido University, Hokkaido, Japan, on 12 May 2018). I would like to thank the conference organisers, the attendees, and all those who asked valuable questions and made comments. I would also like to thank an anonymous reviewer for valuable comments and suggestions, which have greatly helped me improve this chapter. Thanks also go to Stephen Howe for his helpful suggestions for improving the manuscript and style. Needless to say, all remaining deficiencies are my responsibility. This work was supported by JSPS Grants-in-Aid for Scientific Research Nos. 15K02622 and 19K00675.

1. There are numerous examples of this word type: *àffêctátion*, *èxpêctátion*, *incântàtion*, and so on. We use a circumflex instead of a grave accent to indicate a tertiary stressed vowel. This may be at variance with certain phonological conventions, but we prefer to always use the grave accent for secondary stressed vowels, regardless of whether a word has one or two subsidiary stress(es). Thereafter, parts under discussion are shown in boldface. Dots indicate syllable breaks.
2. The stress reduction here is based on *SPE*'s assumption that vowels without stress are eventually reduced to schwa or its equivalent.
3. In order to investigate a wide variety of stress data in English words and to determine the appropriate stress patterns (including stress variants) for Yamada's (2010) study, the following five major American dictionaries were examined: Kenyon and Knott (1953), Flexner (1987), Mish (1988), Wells (1990) (section on American English) and Soukhanov (1992). The results are consistent with Kenyon and Knott's (1953) descriptions for most of the words examined, and so the reader is referred primarily to Kenyon and Knott where necessary. If there are significant differences between Kenyon and Knott and the results yielded by the data clarification method, these are described accordingly. For further details, see Yamada (2010). In addition, closely related to the discussion in section 3, this method has revealed, for example, that words

with a primary–*secondary* (102) stress pattern, such as *désignàte* (102), are almost always described as primary–*tertiary* (103) in the American English descriptions in Wells (1990, 2008) (see Chapter 5 of this volume for the discussion on words in -*ate*). It would be interesting to know whether this difference is due to the editorial policy of the dictionary or to a difference in the linguistic facts. This may be a new research topic.

4. Ungrammatical examples or incorrect predictions are shown by an asterisk to the left of the examples.
5. We could call this problem the 'plastered opacity' problem, since by 'plastering over' the internal structure it becomes 'opaque'. However, let us save the term 'opacity' for true opacity (see Kiparsky 1971, 1973), which we will see in section 1.2, in words such as *còndênsátion* where it is difficult to explain why tertiary stress appears in the antepenultimate syllable of the word unless we consider the internal word structure and assume that the stress rules are applied cyclically from the innermost constituent. In any case, both the 'plastered transparency' problem and the 'opacity' problem are related to the ordering of rules.
6. Halle and Kenstowicz (1991) solved this problem with the noncyclic stratum's 'left to right' metrification but created another for the *còndênsátion* word type. For details, see Yamada (2010: 75–90). See also Halle and Keyser (1971); Ross (1972); Halle (1973a, 1973b); Kiparsky (1982a, 1982b); Mohanan (1982, 1985); Hammond (1984); Hayes (1984); Durand (1990); Idsardi (1992); Burzio (1994); Kenstowicz (1995); Collie (2007); Bermúdez-Otero (2012) and others, for this unsolved issue.
7. 'A unified fundamental rule system' means a set of rules that does not require any supplementary rules.
8. According to a reviewer of this chapter, the type of words in (6) could be treated by 'destressing' or 'vowel reduction'. However, those treatments are supplementary analyses applied *after* stress assignment. In this chapter, we will find a way to account for them by a one-time, unified stress rule.
9. These words are assumed to have lexical stresses as indicated on the boldface syllables, which are shown in the input on the tableau, where the selection of the optimal candidate is made with the help of the positional information of the lexical stress.
10. The ranking of constraints is shown in (9a), where ID-STRESS-S_1 is the highest.
11. The definitions, including their activation conditions, are given in the Appendix. See also Yamada (2010) for the motivation and implications for each. Further, as far as the universality of this theory is concerned, it is only a null hypothesis, which is assumed to be valid if no counterexamples are given. However, preliminary research by the author suggests that the PFT framework can explain quite accurately the pitch accent assignment mechanism in Tokyo Japanese, based on the analyses in Yamada (1990a, 1990b, 1992) in tandem with Haraguchi (1977, 1991).

12. After the name of the PF, such as *Farness* in (10a), its abbreviation is given in parentheses (for example *F*), followed by its formula with the stress value yielded by the formula. The formula for *Farness* is $f(x) = *$, meaning that the *Farness* Function gives one stress value '*' at position x counted leftward from the position of main stress. The distinction between '*' and '+' is shown in note 48 along with other symbols such as '@'. The symbol '¬*' in (10o) means 'non-*'; this option is used when there is only '*' (rather than '+') on the syllable that will undergo stress reduction (Yamada 2010: 292).
13. 'Lines −1, −2, −3, −4, −5 etc.' below line 0 are represented simply by negative numerals '−1, −2, −3, −4, −5 etc.' in this and the following analyses and representations; the names of PFs invoked for each line are shown.
14. PFs activated on each position for each word are shown under each analysis in vertical brackets. In this example and those that follow with vertical brackets, the space before and after the equals symbol '=' in the formula is not shown to save space.
15. The following is a very brief, simplified description of each Function: *Heaviness* = place stress '+' on the heavy syllable(s); *Farness* = place stress '*' on the farthest position from the main stress if the same type of syllable appears successively on the same level, that is, *con* and *den* with *Heaviness* triggered for each in this case; *Trace* = place stress '+' on the stem stressed position; *Alveolar Consonant Sequence (ACS)* = place stress '*' on the syllable with an alveolar coda consonant immediately followed by another alveolar onset of the main stressed syllable, highlighted by the underlined segments in (11); *Rhythm* = place two stress values '+, *' on the first syllable when stress is given immediately before the main stressed position. $S(2)$ = the sum of the stress value(s) on syllable position 2. $S(1)$ = the sum of the stress value(s) on syllable position 1. Here, *ACS* is shown in boldface for emphasis for the later discussion. For the full version, see the Appendix and Yamada (2010).
16. Here, the relevant coda consonant is highlighted by boldface with an underline.
17. This hypothesis applies to a relationship between the secondary and tertiary stresses, not between the primary and tertiary stresses.
18. For a comprehensive discussion including many types of words and for a comparison with earlier studies showing the various problems solved by PFT, see Yamada (2010).
19. When highlighting 'main' stress without considering the existence of subsidiary stress(es), we use the term '*main* stress' rather than 'primary stress'. The question of how to treat main stress assignment within the framework of PFT has been raised by Ohta (2013). This chapter is a further supplement to Yamada's (2013a) reply to that question.
20. These generalisations about the main stress positions are also discussed, in greater detail, in Chapter 8 of this volume. Now, in relation to the

generalisations made in Chapter 8, we would like to briefly discuss 'lexical' representations, which we believe require additional explanation here. Our fundamental standpoint is, in short, to elucidate the mechanism of children's language acquisition. A child at the stage of acquiring a language sets the parameters of that language based on the information they receive as input. What will they do when they encounter a word that does not match the parameters and phonological rules of their stage of construction? There is probably only one way: to 'mark' the 'word' as some 'exception' and store it in the mental lexicon, that is, to describe it in the underlying representation. This lexical entry may seem random, but it is possible to make regular groupings within it: one is a word group borrowed from or influenced by foreign languages, and the other is a word group that, for whatever reason, has an inherently lexical representation such as a 'long' or 'short' vowel (i.e. 'tense or 'lax' vowel) underlyingly. The former includes *sedán, occúlt* and *minarét* discussed in example (4) of Chapter 8, and *siésta* in example (5). For the latter, *violín, resúlt* in (4), *vermicélli, vanílla, spaghétti* and *proféssor* in (5), as well as *tomáto* (in this case the vowel *a* is 'long', i.e. 'tense' underlyingly) in example (20) of Chapter 8 can be mentioned. The words ending in -*y* in example (7) in Chapter 8 can be interpreted as a 'glide' in the underlying representation. Interestingly, evidence for this 'lexical marking' can be found in the geminate consonant spelling of examples such as *vermicélli, vanílla, spaghétti, proféssor* and others. This is partly related to this volume's discussions in Chapters 2, 4 and 5.

21. The motivation for the *Rhythmic Adjustment* Positional Function for main stress assignment will be discussed later in relation to examples (17) and (18).
22. The word boundary at the right end of the word is the origin (0, 0) of the coordinate plane on which the values yielded by PFs for main stress assignment in (13) are calculated and represented. The primary stressed position of the word is the origin of the coordinate axes for subsidiary stress assignment.
23. There are two types of values yielded by PFs, intrinsic and relative, but the distinction is not relevant to the current discussion.
24. As mentioned already, the specific suffixes include -*ant*, -*ous*, -*ent* etc. For this concept, we follow the treatment in *HV*.
25. The word boundary is shown by #.
26. The concept of 'foot' is implied in the definitions of *Binarity* (10d, Appendix d), *Free Binarity* (10m, Appendix m) and *Bounded Binarity* (14b, Appendix b for the Main Stress Rule), although the term itself is not explicitly stated. Likewise, in this theory, various traditional phonological concepts are reduced to PFs. See Zamma (2012) for criticism concerning the seemingly modest use of the concept of the foot in PFT.

27. *BB* is enclosed by ( ). Hereafter, unless otherwise necessary, the descriptions 'stress representation plane', 'stress computation plane' and 'line 0, 1, 2, 3, . . .' are omitted. The extrametrical element is enclosed by angled brackets < >.
28. The appearance of secondary stress on the first syllable on the stress representation plane is not a problem. The resulting tertiary stress on the first syllable *mô* is, in effect, a matter dealt with by subsidiary stress assignment.
29. This section answers Ohta's (2013) question on how to treat in PFT the stress patterns of words belonging to this group.
30. Hereafter, the terms '*y*-axis' and '*x*-axis' are also omitted to save space.
31. Hereafter, the main stressed position marked as M is highlighted in boldface.
32. We can disregard the quasi-tertiary stress on the second syllable *sig* in (22), since (22) is not the final stage of computation.
33. CAS is a lexical treatment applied to specific vocabulary: we have tried to explain as many words as possible without lexical treatment, but the attempt did not work well for these types of examples.
34. Extrametricality does not apply here, since it is to be applied at the beginning of the computation of main stress. (24) is involved in the computation of subsidiary stress as well as (22).
35. In Wells (2008), the word *designate* has a stress pattern (103), but in the analysis of the stress patterns of American English in Yamada (2010), it has the stress pattern (102). If the final syllable of this word indeed has tertiary stress, as described in Wells (2008), this needs to be accounted for; however, this is a subject for future research.
36. Notice here that if there is a discrepancy between the morphological information of a word and the phonological information of the constituents, we assume that language learners will not use the morphological information even if they happen to get access to that information first. In other words, in (25) for example, we assume that the morphological relationship between the adjective *confiscatòry* and the verb *cónfiscàte* will be lost when the two domains are perceived for this type of word. Therefore, the information for the main stress position of the verb *cónfiscàte* will not be used as the PF *Trace* in calculating the stress values of the adjective *confiscatòry*.
37. The final *y* becomes a vowel by a later rule, which is not our concern here.
38. {*} is automatically given by a convention on line 2 over the *x*-axis when Stress Domains A and B are scanned.
39. A stress domain is based on the syntactic constituent structure, on which the phonological structure is constructed.
40. This term relies, of course, on terms and concepts that have been variously analysed in the long tradition of phonology, including *SPE*, Liberman and Prince (1977), and so forth.

41. Certain types of words in (28b) as well as the certain types of words dealt with in this chapter may appear inadequately analysed from a morphological point of view. However, as mentioned in note 36, our current interest is in the first instance phonological, and from the viewpoint of language acquisition. We assume that the learner of the language under analysis acquires the grammar from the data based on the phonological structures they perceive, not from an etymological analysis of the linguistic material. Of course, morphology is also very important in linguistic analysis, and historical and morphological perspectives may explain many patterns that cannot usually be accounted for by phonological analysis alone. Allowing for this, we would nevertheless like to emphasise that the central issue of this chapter is how language learners construct their grammar in the face of stress patterns based on the constituent structure of words they perceive.
42. The syllable [at] in the examples in (30) is considered part of the affix for the purposes of stress assignment in *SPE* and others, which we follow.
43. The placement of the resulting main stress is marked by a vertical arrow.
44. In Kenyon and Knott (1953), *àdaptátion* (2010) is a first entry variant, while *àdâptátion* (2310) is a second entry variant. In Mish (1988) and Wells (2008), *àdâptátion* (2310) is a first entry variant, while *àdaptátion* (2010) is a second entry variant. In Flexner (1987), *àdaptátion* (2010) is the only entry word. In Soukhanov (1992), *àdâptátion* (2310) is also the only entry. Thus, according to the data clarification method of Yamada (2010), *àdâptátion* (2310) is the first candidate to deal with, and *àdaptátion* (2010) the second.
45. The question of how to deal with these examples was posed by an anonymous reviewer.
46. Technically, the words are in fact *explicatory* (31033, 10033) and *emanatory* (10033) in Wells (2008), but their resulting final tertiary stressed vowels will be dealt with as being 'tensed' by a post stress-assignment rule after cyclic stress assignment as in *explicatory* (10030), *emanatory* (10030). Thus, eventually the data to be accounted for are *explicatory* (31030, 10030) and *emanatory* (10030), as argued in this paragraph.
47. Note, however, that there is a clear ordering relationship in application between the main and subsidiary stress rules: the Main Stress Rule is applied first, then the subsidiary stress rule. They are never applied simultaneously.
48. We mention here that three real numbers are the results of the calculations of PFs. In fact, however, there are *four* kinds of stress values '+, *, −, @' yielded by PFs that correspond exactly to the real numbers. The values '+' and '*' correspond to the real number '1', the value '+*' to '2', '−' to '−1', and the value '@' prevents the application of *Sole Stress Resistance* (*SSR*), which is one of the PFs. The distinct representations between '*' and '+' are made by the calculation process: '*' is the result

of the calculation referring to the relative relationship between PFs, while '+' results from the analysis made by the intrinsic features of PFs involved. For details, see the discussion in Yamada (2010).

References

Baayen, R. H., R. Piepenbrock and L. Gulikers (1995), *CELEX2 LDC96L14*, Philadelphia: Linguistic Data Consortium.

Bermúdez-Otero, R. (2012), 'The architecture of grammar and the division of labour in exponence', in J. Trommer (ed.), *The Morphology and Phonology of Exponence*, Oxford: Oxford University Press, pp. 8–83.

Burzio, L. (1994), *Principles of English Stress*, Cambridge: Cambridge University Press.

Chomsky, N. and M. Halle (1968), *The Sound Pattern of English*, New York: Harper & Row.

Collie, S. (2007), 'English stress preservation and stratal optimality theory', PhD dissertation, University of Edinburgh.

Durand, J. (1990), *Generative and Non-Linear Phonology*, New York: Longman.

Flexner, S. G. (ed.) (1987), *The Random House Dictionary of the English Language*, 2nd edn, New York: Random House.

Halle, M. (1973a), 'Prolegomena to a theory of word formation', *Linguistic Inquiry* 4(1), 3–16.

Halle, M. (1973b), 'Stress rules in English: A new version', *Linguistic Inquiry* 4(4), 451–64.

Halle, M. and S. J. Keyser (1971), *English Stress: Its Form, Its Growth, and Its Role in Verse*, New York: Harper & Row.

Halle, M. and J.-R. Vergnaud (1987), *An Essay on Stress*, Cambridge, MA: MIT Press.

Halle, M. and M. Kenstowicz (1991), 'Free element condition and cyclic versus non-cyclic stress', *Linguistic Inquiry* 22(3), 457–501.

Hammond, M. (1984), 'Constraining metrical theory: A modular theory of rhythm and destressing', PhD dissertation, University of California.

Hammond, M. (1999), *The Phonology of English: A Prosodic Optimality-Theoretic Approach*, Oxford: Oxford University Press.

Haraguchi, S. (1977), *The Tone Pattern of Japanese: An Autosegmental Theory of Tonology*, Tokyo: Kaitakusha.

Haraguchi, S. (1991), *A Theory of Stress and Accent*, Dordrecht: Foris.

Hayes, B. (1980), 'A metrical theory of stress rules', PhD dissertation, MIT.

Hayes, B. (1982), 'Extrametricality and English stress', *Linguistic Inquiry* 13(2), 227–76.

Hayes, B. (1984), 'The phonology of rhythm in English', *Linguistic Inquiry* 15(1), 33–74.

Hayes, B. (1995), *Metrical Stress Theory: Principles and Case Studies*, Chicago: University of Chicago Press.

Idsardi, W. J. (1992), 'The computation of prosody', PhD dissertation, MIT.

Kenstowicz, M. (1995), 'Cyclic vs. non-cyclic constraint evaluation', *Phonology* 12(3), 397–436.

Kenyon, J. S. and T. A. Knott (1953), *A Pronouncing Dictionary of American English*, 4th edn, Springfield, MA: G. & C. Merriam.

Kiparsky, P. (1971), 'Historical linguistics', in W. O. Dingwall (ed.), *A Survey of Linguistic Science*, College Park, MD: University of Maryland Linguistics Program, pp. 576–642.

Kiparsky, P. (1973), 'Phonological representations', in O. Fujimura (ed.), *Three Dimensions of Linguistic Theory*, Tokyo: TEC, pp. 3–136.

Kiparsky, P. (1982a), 'From cyclic phonology to lexical phonology', in H. van der Hulst and N. Smith (eds), *The Structure of Phonological Representations*, Dordrecht: Foris, pp. 131–265.

Kiparsky, P. (1982b), 'Lexical morphology and phonology', in the Linguistic Society of Korea (ed.), *Linguistics in the Morning Calm*, Seoul: Hanshin, pp. 3–91.

Kiparsky, P. (2015), 'Stratal OT: A synopsis and FAQs', in Y. E. Hsiao and L.-H. Wee (eds), *Capturing Phonological Shades Within and Across Languages*, Newcastle upon Tyne: Cambridge Scholars Publishing, pp. 2–44.

Liberman, M. and A. Prince (1977), 'On stress and linguistic rhythm', *Linguistic Inquiry* 8(2), 249–336.

Liu, S. (2012), 'The role of the "basic variant" in subsidiary stress assignment for words', in *Proceedings of the 145th Meeting of the Linguistic Society of Japan*, pp. 40–5.

Liu, S. (2016), 'Subsidiary stress assignment of derived words in English', PhD dissertation, Fukuoka University.

McCarthy, J. J. and A. Prince (1993a), 'Prosodic morphology I: Constraint interaction and satisfaction', Manuscript, University of Massachusetts, Amherst and Rutgers University.

McCarthy, J. J. and A. Prince (1993b), 'Generalized alignment', in G. Booij and J. van Marle (eds), *Yearbook of Morphology 1993*, Dordrecht: Kluwer, pp. 79–153.

Mish, F. C. (ed.) (1988), *Webster's Ninth New Collegiate Dictionary*, Springfield, MA: Merriam-Webster.

Mohanan, K. P. (1982), 'Lexical phonology', PhD dissertation, MIT.

Mohanan, K. P. (1985), 'Syllable structure and lexical strata in English', *Phonology Yearbook* 2, 139–55.

Ohta, S. (2013), Review of *Subsidiary Stresses in English* by E. Yamada (2010), *English Linguistics* 30(1), 358–68.

Pater, J. (1995), 'On the nonuniformity of weight-to-stress and stress preservation effects in English', Manuscript, McGill University.

Pater, J. (2000), 'Non-uniformity in English secondary stress: The role of ranked and lexically specific constraints', *Phonology* 17(2), 237–74.

Pater, J. (2010), 'Morpheme-specific phonology: Constraint indexation and inconsistency resolution', in S. Parker (ed.), *Phonological Argumentation: Essays on Evidence and Motivation*, London: Equinox Publishing, pp. 123–54.

Prince, A. and P. Smolensky (1993), 'Optimality theory: Constraint interaction in generative grammar', Manuscript, Rutgers University and University of Colorado, Boulder. [(2004), *Optimality Theory: Constraint Interaction in Generative Grammar*, Oxford: Blackwell.]

Ross, J. R. (1972), 'A reanalysis of English word stress', in M. Brame (ed.), *Contributions to Generative Phonology*, Austin: University of Texas Press, pp. 229–323.

Soukhanov, A. H. (ed.) (1992), *The American Heritage Dictionary of the English Language*, 3rd edn, Boston: Houghton Mifflin.

Takeda, K. (2011), 'An analysis of subsidiary stress assignment of words in Californian English speakers based on Positional Function Theory', *Fukuoka Daigaku Eigogaku Eibei Bungaku Ronsyuu* 19, 38–56.

Tomioka, M. (2019), 'Non-ordering of application among positional functions in English words', *Fukuoka Daigaku Eigogaku Eibei Bungaku Ronsyuu* 27, 6–29.

Wells, J. C. (1990), *Longman Pronunciation Dictionary*, London: Longman.

Wells, J. C. (2008), *Longman Pronunciation Dictionary*, 3rd edn, Harlow: Pearson Education.

Yamada, E. (1990a), 'Stress assignment in Tokyo Japanese (1): Parameter settings and compound words', *Fukuoka Daigaku Jinbun Ronsoo* [*Fukuoka University Review of Literature & Humanities*] 21(4), 1575–604.

Yamada, E. (1990b), 'Stress assignment in Tokyo Japanese (2): Stress shift, and stress in suffixation', *Fukuoka Daigaku Jinbun Ronsoo* [*Fukuoka University Review of Literature and Humanities*] 22(1), 97–154.

Yamada. E. (1992), 'Parameter setting for abstract stress in Tokyo Japanese', in J. J. Ohala, T. M. Nearey, B. L. Derwing, M. M. Hodge and G. E. Wiebe (eds), *ICSLP 92 Proceedings: 1992 International Conference on Spoken Language Processing*, Alberta: University of Alberta, pp. 1267–70.

Yamada, E. (2010), *Subsidiary Stresses in English*, Tokyo: Kaitakusha.

Yamada, E. (2011a), 'Optionality in English subsidiary stress assignment', *Studies in English Literature (Regional Branches Combined Issue)* 3, 543–56.

Yamada, E. (2011b), 'A new account of subsidiary stresses in English words', *Phonological Studies* 14, 143–54.

Yamada, E. (2012), 'Stress assignment in English words: A preliminary analysis', Paper presented at the Tokyo Circle of Phonologists, held at the University of Tokyo, Komaba Campus, Tokyo, Japan, on 5 December 2012.

Yamada, E. (2013a), 'Main stress assignment in English words', *JELS* 30, 229–35.

Yamada, E. (2013b), 'A new account of stress assignment in English words: Positional Function Theory', Paper presented at the 2013 International Conference on English Linguistics, held at Korea University and Korea Military Academy, Seoul, Korea, on 5 July 2013.

Yamada, E. (2014), 'Treatment of Extrametricality in Positional Function Theory', Paper presented at the 5th International Conference on Phonology and Morphology, held at Chonnam National University, Gwangju, Korea, on 4 July 2014.

Yamada, E. (2015a), 'An overview of the approach to word stress in English in the generative tradition: from *SPE* to current optimality treatments', Paper presented at PAC 2015 International Conference: Advances in the Phonology and Phonetics of Contemporary English (Plenary Session), held at Université Toulouse – Jean Jaurès, Toulouse, France, on 10 April 2015.

Yamada, E. (2015b), 'Optimality theory and beyond: An analysis of English word stress using a new concept of "positional function"', Paper presented at PAC 2015 International Conference: Advances in the Phonology and Phonetics of Contemporary English (Workshop), held at Université Toulouse – Jean Jaurès, Toulouse, France, on 10 April 2015.

Yamada, E. (2016), 'Covert stress preservation of derived words in English', Paper presented at PAC 2016 International Conference: English Melodies, held at the Laboratoire Parole et Langage and Aix-Marseille University, Aix-en-Provence, France, on 1 October 2016.

Yamada, E. (2018), 'Theoretical shortcomings: Counterexamples to word stress treatments in English', Paper presented at the 11th International Spring Forum 2018, held at Hokkaido University, Hokkaido, Japan, on 12 May 2018.

Yamada, E., S. Hirokawa and C. Zeng (2022), 'Assessment of a subsidiary stress rule for English words based on a linguistic corpus', Paper presented at PAC 2021 International Conference: Spoken English Varieties, held at Université Toulouse – Jean Jaurès, Toulouse, France (online), on 3 September 2021.

Zamma, H. (2012), Review of *Subsidiary Stresses in English* by E. Yamada (2010), *Studies in English Literature* 53, 258–65.

Index

2NDARY, 277–8

Aboriginal English, 192–5, 201–3, 206, 213, 226, 241, 251
Aboriginal Englishes, 194, 203
Aboriginal languages, 69, 193, 195–200, 223, 234n
Aboriginal substratum stress pattern hypothesis, 195; *see also* initial stress hypothesis
Aboriginality, 195, 203, 213, 216
acrolect, 195
ALIGN(PW,R,MW,R), 271
ALIGNFTRT, 269
ALIGNPRWD[...], 270
Alternating Stress Rule, 155, 187, 303
American descriptivist, 8
American tradition, 6, 12, 16, 39
antepenultimate stress, 73, 133, 146n, 166, 173–4, 179, 186n, 187n, 267, 270–1
antepenultimate syllable, 28, 62, 125, 155, 216, 269, 289–90, 292, 295–6, 308–9, 316n
antepenultimate vowel, 17–18, 20
apheresis, 203
AusTalk, 201, 206–10, 213–16, 225, 229, 230, 233n, 234n
Australian Aboriginal English, 194–5
Australian English, 2, 68, 192–7, 199, 201–6, 233n, 285n
automatic machine-learning, 311

basilectal AbE, 202
basilectal Singlish, 241
basilectal variation, 202
basilectal varieties, 195, 241
borrowings, 54, 56, 65, 69, 76n, 118, 141, 143, 180, 285n

boundary, 9, 20, 26–7, 40, 42n, 43n, 62, 75n, 155–7, 178, 185n, 298, 318n
British tradition, 8, 10, 12, 39, 244
Brown corpus, 275

Cambridge English Pronouncing Dictionary, 69, 193, 197, 250
CAS, 303–4, 319n; *see also* Coordinate Axis Shift
checked vowel, 122–3, 126, 133, 136, 139, 145n, 146n
clash (concepts), 24, 26, 64, 165, 275, 277
CLASH (constraints), 35, 58, 277–8, 292
Class II, 27–8, 45n, 74n, 75n, 156, 185n
compound, 9, 12, 14–15, 28, 59, 63, 64, 67, 73, 75n, 76n, 160, 164–5, 168–71, 182, 186n, 198, 267
consonant cluster, 58–9, 63, 65, 67, 74n, 75n, 125–6, 135–40, 144n, 146n, 147n, 254–5, 258
constraint, 7, 35–7, 46n, 131, 166, 180, 255, 265, 269–72, 274–8, 284, 292
  morpheme-specific, 270
  ranking, 35, 278
  violable, 7, 33, 38, 40, 291
conversion, 89–96, 102–3, 107, 109–12, 161–2, 168, 183
coordinate axes, 295, 297–8, 303, 305, 318n
Coordinate Axis Shift, 288, 303, 306–7, 311–12
corpus data, 202, 242, 265, 281, 285n
corpus phonology, 193, 201, 211, 215
Correspondence Theory, 7
cyclic inheritance, 37, 41n, 290
cyclic or noncyclic application, 40
cyclic rule, 31, 40, 45n

cyclic stratum, 28, 40
cyclic stress inheritance, 290–1
cyclicity, 7, 28, 29, 41, 289, 290–1, 311

data clarification method, 289, 309, 315, 320n
diatone, 84, 109
diatonic stress, 84–5, 88, 105, 109–10, 111n; *see also* diatone
dictionary data, 57, 70–1, 119, 154, 160, 182, 192–3, 197, 201, 203, 215, 233, 255, 283
digraph, 74n, 123, 125–6, 136–7
distinctiveness, 13
disyllabic verbs, 69–70, 75n, 85, 91, 155–6, 177–9, 181–2, 193, 197–8, 201, 217, 234n, 255
diversity of English, 3

elision, 132, 147n, 203–4, 207, 209, 213–14
endonormative comparison, 194
endonormative stabilisation, 193
English stress pattern hypothesis, 196
ethnolectal varieties, 206
exceptions to stress rules, 69–70, 199, 201
exceptions to the theories, 288
Extended Latin Stress, 301, 307–8, 311
Extrametricality
  (concepts), 25, 29, 33–4, 40, 44n, 134
  (rules), 25, 30, 31, 45n, 46n, 175, 180, 297–302, 304–5, 307, 311, 315, 319n

FAITH, 36, 46n, 47n, 278, 284
flat internal structure, 311
'flat' structure, 290
foot, 25–6, 28, 32–4, 40, 41n, 42n, 43n, 44n, 45n, 46n, 202, 264, 268, 270, 299, 318n
  binary, 25–6, 34, 43n, 44n, 299
  construction, 25–6, 28, 40, 45n
foreign vowel, 128, 144n, 145n
free vowel, 122–3, 126, 128, 136–7, 144n, 145n
frequency, 70, 85–91, 93–6, 101, 103–8, 110, 111n, 112n, 146n, 161, 169, 186n, 233n, 280, 284, 293
FTBIN (FTBIN), 33–5, 40, 46n, 58, 264

GEN, 3, 36–7
generalized alignment, 270–1

generative phonology, 1, 6, 39–40, 55, 60, 304
Germanic Law, 156, 174, 177, 179–80
grid, 7, 23–4, 43n
Guierrian approach, 55–6, 60, 64, 68, 119, 126, 193, 195–202, 207
Guierrian School, 2, 56, 60, 71

Halle and Vergnaud (1987) *see* HV
Heavy Aboriginal English, 195
heavy syllable, 26, 42, 174, 256, 297–8, 306, 312–13, 314, 317n
HV, 29–34, 36, 39, 45n, 46n, 291, 293, 297–8, 300–4, 308, 315, 318n

iamb, 252–4
initial stress hypothesis, 196, 215
inner-circle, 240, 242, 244–6, 249–58, 261n
input optimization, 264–5, 274, 276, 277–9, 281–4
International Phonetic Association (IPA), 8
intervarietal stress stability, 196–201, 214, 216, 218–24
intraspeaker stress variation, 207, 209–11, 214–15, 228–31
intravarietal stress stability, 199, 201
IO-FAITH, 277

language contact, 192, 195, 201
Latin stress rule, 7, 17–18, 22, 30, 33–4, 40, 301
lax, 17–18, 20, 22, 41n, 145n, 147n, 175–6, 186n, 242–4, 253, 261n, 273, 318n
level, 9, 14, 16, 23–4, 28, 44n, 45n, 75n, 88, 120–1, 126–7, 129–30, 147n, 158, 185n, 199, 213, 226, 228, 244–5, 284
levels of stress, 11, 54, 295
Lexical Phonology, 1, 7, 8–9, 22, 27–9, 31–3, 37, 40, 45n, 75n, 120, 126
lexical subsystems, 66–8; *see also* subsystems
lexically marked set, 292
light Aboriginal English, 195, 212–15
light syllable, 274, 306
linear phonology, 7
loanwords from Aboriginal languages, 193, 195–7, 200, 223

Index 327

long vowels, 23, 43n, 58, 140, 175, 180, 202, 248, 265, 268, 270, 272–3
Longman Pronunciation Dictionary (LPD), 41n, 89, 193, 197–8, 200, 207, 215–19, 223–4
LxWd=PrWd, 269

Macquarie Dictionary (MD), 69, 160–1, 193, 196–7, 203–10, 215, 219–20, 230–2, 233n, 250
main stress assignment, 288, 296–8, 300–1, 303, 307, 310–11, 314, 317n, 318n
Main Stress Rule, 7, 17, 19–20, 22, 45n, 155, 289, 318n, 320n
mainstream, 3, 54, 194, 233n
markedness, 39, 243, 264, 275
Maxent, 284
mesolect, 243
Metrical Phonology, 1, 7–8, 22–33
Metrical Theory, 26, 29, 40, 45n
metrical tree, 23, 43n
monograph, 123
mora(s), 136, 175–6, 255, 273–4
morphological structure, 3, 10, 12, 15, 73, 158–9, 162, 164
morphology, 7, 9, 14–15, 27–9, 37, 47n, 57, 60, 67, 71, 73, 128, 134, 154–5, 160, 162, 165, 174, 177, 182, 246–7, 256, 267, 270, 284, 286, 314, 320n
MSR, 21, 27, 45n, 289, 291; *see also* Main Stress Rule

N–V pair, 105; *see also* noun–verb pair
non-linear approach, 7
non-rule-based theories, 2
noncyclic stratum, 28, 32, 40, 45n, 46n
NonFinality, 268
noun–verb pair, 83, 103

opacity, 7, 41n, 157, 292, 311, 316n
opaque prefixation, 71, 159, 166, 171, 174–6, 183
optimal candidate, 2, 33, 316n
Optimality Theory, 2, 7, 33, 40, 58, 186n, 264, 283, 288, 291, 310; *see also* OT pre, 1
ordering paradox, 28, 32, 45n
orthographic consonant geminates, 58, 118, 136, 138–9, 143
orthographic information, 2, 54, 71, 117, 121, 129, 136–7, 141–2, 193

OT, 7–8, 33, 36–40, 46n, 180, 264–5, 268, 271, 284, 291–3, 308, 311; *see also* pre-OT, Optimality Theory
outer-circle, 240, 261n
oxytone, 109
oxytonic stress, 89, 97, 100, 103

PAC, 1–2, 143n, 201, 206, 211–13, 216, 232, 233n, 240, 242–7, 249, 252, 257, 315n
  Australia, 201, 206, 211–13, 216, 232, 233n
parallel treatment, 291
parallelism, 2, 7, 33, 36, 38, 40
parameter, 30, 31, 64–5, 67, 73, 155, 169, 171, 298, 300, 302–4, 310
Parse-σ, 46n, 58, 264
Partially Ordered Grammar, 2, 7, 36
perception test, 213, 216, 245
PFT, 288, 293–4, 296–7, 300–4, 306, 308, 309–11, 316n, 317n, 318n, 319n; *see also* Positional Function Theory
phonological complexity, 264, 276, 281, 283
phonological representation, 22, 117, 131, 290
phonological word, 202, 307–8
plastered transparency, 290–1, 311, 316n
Plato's Problem, 8, 38–9
Positional Function Theory, 288, 293, 311; *see also* PFT
post-Bloomfieldian phonologists, 6
prefix, 9, 20, 32, 59–60, 64, 69, 74n, 83, 85, 89, 92–3, 112n, 146n, 154, 156, 159, 163, 165–6, 172, 177–8, 180–1, 184n, 185n, 197, 246, 248, 256
  etymological, 146n
  inseparable, 59, 60
  separable, 9, 59–60, 65, 74n, 83, 89
prefixed disyllabic words, 2, 181
prefixed multicategorials, 197–9, 201, 215, 218–20
prefixed words, 18, 60, 70, 111n, 157, 159, 163, 165, 179–82, 201
preservation of stress, 26; *see also* stress inheritance
primary–secondary stress pattern, 288, 306, 307, 311, 316n
programmability, 311

quantity sensitivity, 240–1, 252, 261n

r vowel, 123
r-sandhi, 134–5
Received Pronunciation, 8, 122, 241
recursion, 7, 41n, 290
recursiveness, 39, 47n
Rhythm Rule, 26, 31, 275, 303
RP, 8, 91, 241, 243–4, 252, 261n; *see also* Received Pronunciation
rule ordering, 41n, 291; *see also* ordering paradox
rule-based theories, 1

SBE, 68, 70, 76n, 197–8, 200–1, 209–11, 215, 217–20, 222–3, 229, 234n, 241–2, 244–6
schwa epenthesis, 202
secondary stress, 59, 64–6, 68, 75n, 138–40, 145n, 158, 180, 197, 199, 202, 207, 210, 275, 286n, 289, 295, 303, 305, 306–9, 311, 319n
Segmental Phonology, 1
semantic asymmetry, 98–9, 104, 107, 109
semantic differentiation, 97–8, 102, 105, 108, 110
semantic distinction, 101; *see also* semantic differentiation
semantic specialisation, 98–9, 109
semantic symmetry, 98, 109–10
serialism, 7, 37–8, 40
settler varieties, 193–4
Singaporean English, 3
Sound Pattern of English (SPE), 6, 8, 11, 53, 154, 288–9
spelling-to-sound correspondences, 2, 128, 145n
spoken data, 192–3, 201, 203, 205–6, 213, 215–16, 233n, 234n
SSA (Stray Syllable Adjunction), 25–6, 44n, 302; *see also* subsidiary stress assignment
Standard Aboriginal English, 192–5, 201–3, 206–7, 210, 212–16, 232, 241, 251
Standard American English, 68, 75n, 197
Standard Australian English, 68, 192–9, 200–3, 206, 209, 212–13, 214–24, 231; *see also* mainstream
Standard British English, 55, 68, 75n, 197, 241

strata, 28–9, 31–2, 37, 40, 46n, 54, 126
stratal OT, 2, 7, 36–8, 40
stress alternation, 83, 98, 108–10; *see also* diatone
stress change, 85, 88–91, 94, 100, 108
stress domain, 27, 270, 288, 304–7, 310–12, 319n
stress inheritance, 26, 289–92, 295
stress levels, 14–15; *see also* levels of stress; degrees of stress
stress reduction, 289, 294, 309–10, 314–15, 317n
Stress Retraction
 (concepts), 111n, 184n
 (rules), 23, 43n, 288, 305–6, 310
stress shift, 62–3, 75n, 85, 96, 167, 183, 203, 206–7, 209–10, 212–13, 215–16, 275
stress shift to initial syllable hypothesis, 203, 206–7, 212, 215–16
stress variant, 97, 112n, 308–9; *see also* stress variation
stress variation, 68–70, 76n, 83, 103, 193, 196–7, 199–201, 209, 215–16
stress-timed, 76n, 241
subsidiary stress assignment, 288–9, 293–4, 296–8, 300, 302–3, 308, 310–11, 318n, 319n
subsystems, 54–5, 66–8, 193
suffix, 25, 27–8, 35, 61–4, 75n, 92–3, 112n, 127, 132, 134, 145n, 156, 164–7, 172–3, 176, 179, 185n, 186n, 304–5
 Class I, 126–7, 166
 Class II, 127, 185n
 neutral, 60, 62, 67, 160, 284
 stress-preserving, 164–7, 171–2, 185n
 stress-shifting, 27, 160, 164–6, 185n, 187n
 strong, 60, 64, 126
superimposition theory, 310
syllabic consonant, 132–3
syllable weight, 3, 25, 31, 33, 40, 54, 64–5, 71, 154–5, 160, 174, 176, 177–8, 186n, 252–5, 265, 268, 306–7, 310
syllable-timed, 76n, 201, 207–8, 210, 241, 257
syntactic category, 108, 162, 169–70, 182
syntactic labels, 103; *see also* syntactic category

tense, 18–20, 22, 30, 40, 42n, 43n, 147n, 175–6, 186n, 243–4, 253, 257, 318
tertiary stress, 11, 15, 42n, 46n, 289–90, 295–6, 301, 308, 316n, 319n
transformational cycle, 7, 22, 39, 290
tree, 7, 23–5, 43n, 44n; *see also* metrical tree
Trisyllabic Shortening, 133, 145n
trochee, 75n, 252–4, 257, 268

UG, 38–9; *see also* universal grammar
universal grammar, 38, 55

variability, 141, 206, 266, 285n
Velar Softening, 129–30, 137–8

verbal noun, 98–9, 100, 102–3
violable constraints, 7, 33, 38, 40, 291
voicing, 184n, 272–4, 285n, 286n
vowel alternation, 119, 127, 130–1; *see also* Vowel Shift Rule
vowel reduction, 60, 71, 77, 135–6, 139–40, 144n, 145n, 146n, 157–8, 186n, 240, 246–7, 249, 257, 278, 316n
Vowel Shift Rule, 119–20, 144n

word-boundary, 9

Σ = [*μ́μ*], 268

EU representative:
Easy Access System Europe
Mustamäe tee 50, 10621 Tallinn, Estonia
Gpsr.requests@easproject.com

www.ingramcontent.com/pod-product-compliance
Lightning Source LLC
Chambersburg PA
CBHW081758300426
44116CB00014B/2158